Flutter Solutions for Web Development

Modern web development with Flutter, Dart, and AI integration

Zaid Kamil

www.bpbonline.com

First Edition 2025

ISBN: 978-93-65898-248

LIMITS OF LIABILITY AND DISCLAIMER OF WARRANTY

To View Complete
BPB Publications Catalogue
Scan the QR Code:

www.bpbonline.com

Dedicated to

My father ***S M Kamil*** *and my sister* ***Amna Ghazal***

About the Author

Zaid Kamil is a seasoned programmer, Google-certified Android developer, and an experienced coding trainer with expertise in Flutter, Kotlin, Java, Python, AI, and web technologies. With over a decade of experience in software development and training, he has mentored countless students and professionals, helping them excel in the tech industry.

He has authored a book on Android development and actively contributes to the developer community through open-source projects, workshops, and tech talks. Holding certifications from Google and IBM, he possesses deep knowledge in AI, cloud computing, and data science.

Apart from his professional endeavours, Zaid is passionate about learning and sharing his expertise. When not coding, he likes reading Brandon Sanderson books and playing video games. Through Flutter Solutions for web developers, he aims to provide a structured and hands-on learning experience for developers venturing into the world of mobile and web development.

About the Reviewers

- **Randal Schwartz** is a self-taught programmer, writer, trainer, and new media host with a passion for technology and creative pursuits. Throughout his career, Randal has honed his skills in various programming languages, including Perl, Dart, and Flutter, and has become a recognized expert in the field. Notably, he has authored several influential books on Perl programming.

  He is currently recognized as a Google Developer Expert in the areas of Dart and Flutter (one of 10 in the United States and 150 in the world). Randal's professional journey has taken him through diverse roles, from software developer and system administrator to consultant and technical writer. He has contributed his expertise to numerous organizations, including Stonehenge Consulting Services, Inc., O'Reilly & Associates, and TWiT.tv, where he hosted the popular show FLOSS Weekly.

  Beyond his technical prowess, Randal is also a gifted communicator and educator. He has lectured at conferences, provided technical training, and shared his insights through magazine articles and online platforms.

  Randal's unique blend of technical expertise, writing talent, and engaging personality has made him a sought-after speaker, author, and consultant in the tech industry.

- **Santosh Das** is a seasoned software developer and freelancer with extensive expertise in Flutter technology. With over six years of experience in software development, he has honed his skills in building high-performance mobile applications and contributing to the tech community.

  His keen eye for detail and deep understanding of Flutter's evolving ecosystem made him a valuable contributor to this book, ensuring technical accuracy, clarity, and relevance. This marks his second contribution as a technical reviewer, reflecting his commitment to maintaining high-quality standards in technical literature.

  Beyond technical reviewing, Santosh is passionate about exploring the latest advancements in Flutter, actively engaging with developers, and sharing his insights. His dedication to continuous learning and innovation makes him a trusted resource within the Flutter community.

Acknowledgement

Writing this book has been an enriching journey, and I am deeply grateful to the people who have supported me throughout. My father, S M Kamil, and my sister, Amna Ghazal have been my constant pillars of strength, offering their unwavering encouragement and belief in my dreams. A special mention to my mother, who is the most excited about this venture! Her enthusiasm is infectious, and her faith in me has been a guiding force.

I extend my gratitude to BPB Publications for their expertise, trust, and commitment to bringing this book to life. Their guidance and professionalism have been invaluable in shaping this work.

A huge thanks to the content editors and reviewers who have been instrumental in making this book better with their keen eye for detail, constructive feedback, and unwavering patience. Their contributions have refined every chapter, ensuring a smoother learning experience for the readers. A big shoutout to Bharvi Sharma, my go-to person for bouncing off ideas and seeking suggestions. Their insights have been invaluable in shaping this book.

Lastly, to my readers—thank you for choosing this book. Your curiosity and dedication to learning are what drive me to share knowledge. I hope this book helps you build remarkable web applications with Flutter and inspires you to explore new possibilities in the ever-evolving tech landscape.

Preface

The web is an integral part of our digital world, and developers are constantly looking for efficient ways to create beautiful, high-performance web applications. Flutter, originally designed for mobile development, has evolved into a powerful framework that allows developers to build cross-platform applications with a single codebase. Flutter Solutions for web developers is a practical guide that bridges the gap for web developers looking to leverage Flutter's capabilities for creating modern, interactive web applications.

This book covers everything from setting up Flutter for web development to mastering UI design, state management, and integrating APIs. Each chapter is structured to provide hands-on experience, helping developers transition smoothly from traditional web development to Flutter.

Flutter's ability to deliver stunning UIs, smooth animations, and seamless performance across different platforms makes it a game-changer for web developers. Whether you are a beginner in Flutter or an experienced developer seeking to expand your skills, this book aims to provide a solid foundation while keeping the learning process engaging. After all, what's better than writing less code and achieving more? (Aside from finally fixing a bug that's been haunting you for days!)

Beyond just syntax and concepts, this book encourages a problem-solving approach, helping developers think like Flutter engineers. As you navigate through the chapters, you'll discover how to optimize your workflow, tackle performance challenges, and deploy your applications with confidence.

Chapter 1: Mastering Dart Basics for Flutter- Begin your journey with Dart, the foundational language for Flutter development. This chapter introduces Dart's syntax, variables, data types, and control flow structures like loops and conditionals. By mastering these fundamentals, you will establish a strong base for Flutter development and understand how Dart's structure enables efficient coding.

Chapter 2: Advanced Dart Programming Techniques- Move beyond the basics into advanced Dart programming techniques. Explore object-oriented programming concepts such as classes, objects, inheritance, and polymorphism. Understand asynchronous programming with Future and Stream to manage concurrency effectively. Additionally, learn essential error-handling techniques to build more resilient Flutter applications.

Chapter 3: Designing Stunning UIs for the Web- Unlock the secrets to designing visually appealing and responsive user interfaces using Flutter's powerful widget system. This chapter covers the widget tree, layout models, state management techniques, and responsive design principles for web applications. Practical examples and best practices help you create intuitive and user-friendly UIs that adapt seamlessly to different screen sizes.

Chapter 4: Advanced UI Design and Animation- Take your UI skills to the next level with advanced layout techniques, interactive components, and animations that enhance user engagement. Learn how to create custom widgets, implement animations for smooth transitions, and design complex UI structures. This chapter also covers theming and styling to ensure a consistent and professional look for your applications.

Chapter 5: Incorporating Machine Learning and AI- Explore how to integrate machine learning and AI into Flutter web applications to add intelligent features. This chapter guides you through setting up AI frameworks, creating chatbots, implementing image recognition, and leveraging predictive analytics. By combining AI with Flutter, you can enhance user experiences and build smarter applications with real-world applications.

Chapter 6: Effective Debugging Techniques- Master debugging strategies to identify and resolve issues efficiently in Flutter applications. This chapter covers common debugging scenarios, the use of Flutter DevTools, handling exceptions, logging, and monitoring application performance. With practical insights and hands-on debugging exercises, you'll be able to maintain a smooth and error-free development process.

Chapter 7: Building Versatile Architectures and Integrating Firebase- Learn best practices for designing scalable and maintainable app architectures using Flutter. Explore different architectural patterns, including MVVM and clean architecture, to create well-structured applications. Additionally, understand how to integrate Firebase authentication and other Firebase services to add robust backend functionalities to your web apps.

Chapter 8: Performance Optimization Strategies- Optimize Flutter applications with performance profiling, memory management, and widget optimization techniques. This chapter dives into diagnosing performance bottlenecks, reducing load times, and improving resource efficiency. By applying these strategies, you will ensure a smooth, responsive, and high-performing web application that provides an excellent user experience.

By the end of this book, readers will have a solid understanding of Flutter for web development, enabling them to build feature-rich, responsive, and scalable applications efficiently. And hey, if nothing else, you'll at least be able to impress your developer friends with your newfound Flutter wizardry!

Code Bundle and Coloured Images

Please follow the link to download the
Code Bundle and the ***Coloured Images*** of the book:

https://rebrand.ly/5f32e0

The code bundle for the book is also hosted on GitHub at
https://github.com/bpbpublications/Flutter-Solutions-for-Web-Development.
In case there's an update to the code, it will be updated on the existing GitHub repository.

We have code bundles from our rich catalogue of books and videos available at **https://github.com/bpbpublications**. Check them out!

Errata

We take immense pride in our work at BPB Publications and follow best practices to ensure the accuracy of our content to provide with an indulging reading experience to our subscribers. Our readers are our mirrors, and we use their inputs to reflect and improve upon human errors, if any, that may have occurred during the publishing processes involved. To let us maintain the quality and help us reach out to any readers who might be having difficulties due to any unforeseen errors, please write to us at :

errata@bpbonline.com

Your support, suggestions and feedbacks are highly appreciated by the BPB Publications' Family.

Piracy

If you come across any illegal copies of our works in any form on the internet, we would be grateful if you would provide us with the location address or website name. Please contact us at **business@bpbonline.com** with a link to the material.

If you are interested in becoming an author

If there is a topic that you have expertise in, and you are interested in either writing or contributing to a book, please visit **www.bpbonline.com**. We have worked with thousands of developers and tech professionals, just like you, to help them share their insights with the global tech community. You can make a general application, apply for a specific hot topic that we are recruiting an author for, or submit your own idea.

Reviews

Please leave a review. Once you have read and used this book, why not leave a review on the site that you purchased it from? Potential readers can then see and use your unbiased opinion to make purchase decisions. We at BPB can understand what you think about our products, and our authors can see your feedback on their book. Thank you!

For more information about BPB, please visit **www.bpbonline.com**.

Join our book's Discord space

Join the book's Discord Workspace for Latest updates, Offers, Tech happenings around the world, New Release and Sessions with the Authors:

https://discord.bpbonline.com

Table of Contents

CHAPTER 1

Mastering Dart Basics for Flutter

Introduction

In the first chapter, we will cover the dynamic language designed for crafting fast and efficient applications across diverse platforms. Dart stands at the forefront of modern software development, offering a robust technical envelope tailored for client-side environments. From its foundational role in Flutter, to its support for essential developer tasks, Dart promises a seamless experience in building responsive applications for web, mobile, and desktop platforms.

Structure

The chapter covers the following topics:

- Introduction to Dart
- Installing Dart
- Installing Flutter
- Creating a Dart project
- Basic concepts of Dart
- Variables and data types
- Control flow

- Function and scope
- Mini project: food ordering program

Objectives

At the end of this chapter, you will have a strong understanding of Dart's foundational elements, including its history, installation process, syntax and core programming concepts. You will be proficient in setting up both Dart and Flutter environments and will be able to write basic dart programs utilizing variables, data types, control flow statements and functions.

Introduction to Dart

Dart is a versatile and powerful programming language developed by *Google*. It is designed for building high-performance applications across various platforms, including mobile, web, and desktop. Dart's syntax is clean and easy to understand, making it an excellent choice for both beginners and experienced developers. With its robust set of features and strong support for asynchronous programming, Dart enables developers to create responsive and efficient applications. This segment provides a comprehensive overview of the Dart programming language.

Benefits of learning a new language

In today's interconnected world, reaching users across multiple platforms while maintaining quality is essential for keeping them engaged and satisfied. Flutter revolutionizes cross-platform development by enabling you to deploy applications for Android, iOS, and the web from a single codebase. At the heart of Flutter's versatility lies Dart, a programming language uniquely suited for this task.

Dart accelerates Flutter app development with its emphasis on speed and efficiency. One of Flutter's most beloved features, hot reload, epitomizes this efficiency by injecting updated Dart source code into your running app and instantly rebuilding the UI in under a second. This seamless integration allows developers to see their changes in real-time, drastically reducing compile and debug cycles typical in mobile development.

In today's competitive landscape, delivering high-quality experiences is non-negotiable. Traditionally, achieving this meant managing separate teams for each platform. Dart simplifies this process by empowering a single team to build high-fidelity Flutter apps for Android, iOS, and the web. Its production-grade compilers translate Dart code into optimized ARM and x64 machine code for mobile devices, ensuring swift app startup and fluid animations. For web applications, Dart can compile to JavaScript, allowing it to run in any modern web browser. Additionally, Dart is capable of compiling to WebAssembly, a binary instruction format for a stack-based virtual machine, which provides desktop-like performance for web applications.

Beyond its technical prowess, Dart's intuitive syntax makes it accessible to developers familiar with languages, like Java, Swift, and JavaScript. Its ease of adoption facilitates a smooth transition into building robust applications with Flutter.

Together, Dart and Flutter redefine multi-platform development, empowering developers to create exceptional user experiences seamlessly across Android, iOS, and the web.

Dart development history

Dart was introduced by Google in October 2011, developed by *Lars Bak* and *Kasper Lund*, with the ambitious goal of providing a structured and efficient alternative to JavaScript for web development. This new language was designed to address the limitations faced by web developers and to offer a more organized approach to building web applications. To demonstrate Dart's capabilities, Google released *Dartium* around 2012, a specialized version of the *Chromium* browser that could run Dart applications natively using the Dart **virtual machine** (**VM**). This early implementation showcased Dart's potential to improve client-side web development. The following figure provides a visual representation of dart development timeline over the years:

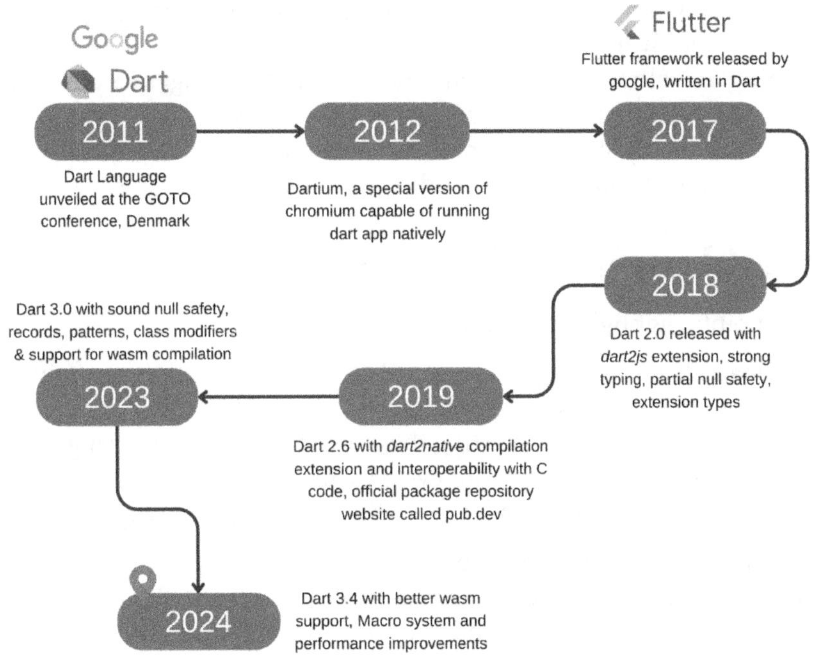

Figure 1.1: *Dart timeline*

Despite its promise, Dart faced significant challenges in gaining traction within the web development community. The dominance of JavaScript and the reluctance of developers to adopt a new language and runtime posed substantial barriers to Dart's widespread adoption.

In 2017, the turning point for Dart came when it was adopted as the language for Flutter, Google's UI toolkit designed for building natively compiled applications for mobile, desktop, and web from a single codebase. This shift marked Dart's expansion beyond its original web focus, opening new opportunities and audiences. Dart's integration with Flutter transformed its trajectory.

In 2018, Dart version 2.0 was released with a shift in focus from Dart VM in Chrome to compiling Dart code to JavaScript. In 2019, Dart 2.6 arrived that introduced dart2native extension which allowed native compilation to *Linux*, *macOS* and *Windows* Desktop platforms. Developers could now create self-contained executables without needing to install Dart SDK.

In 2023, Dart 3.0 was released. It introduced features, like sound null safety, records, patterns and class modifiers. Additionally, it enabled compilation to WebAssembly.

At the time of writing, Dart version 3.4 has been released.

Dart features

Dart is a type-safe, object-oriented, class-based programming language designed to be efficient and versatile. It incorporates garbage collection, which automatically manages memory, helping developers avoid common memory management issues. Dart uses C-style syntax, making it familiar and accessible to those who have experience in C, C++, Java, or JavaScript. This syntax style emphasizes readability and simplicity. Let us look at some advance features the language provides.

Advanced language features

The following points highlight the features of Dart language:

- **Hot reload**: The most popular feature of Dart, particularly prominent in Flutter development. It enables developers to swiftly update code changes in a running Dart application without restarting the entire application or losing its current state. This accelerates the development cycle by instantly reflecting code modifications, facilitating rapid prototyping and real-time debugging of applications.

- **Optional typing with type inference**: Dart features type inference, which means the compiler can automatically deduce the types of variables and expression based on the context. This reduces the need for explicit type annotations, making the code more concise and readable while still maintaining strong type safety.

- **Null safety**: Another pivotal feature of Dart was introduced to enhance the reliability and robustness of code. It ensures that variables cannot have null values unless explicitly allowed, thereby significantly reducing the occurrence of null reference errors during runtime.

- **Mixins and interfaces**: Dart supports mixins, a way to reuse a class's code in multiple class hierarchies. Mixins enable code reuse without the complexities of multiple inheritance, making it easier to manage shared functionality across different classes. It also supports interfaces, defining a contract that classes can implement.
- **Reified generics**: In programing languages, such as Java, generics are implemented using type erasure, meaning that generic type information is erased at runtime and compiler ensures type safety only at compile time. At runtime, generics are treated as raw types. However, in Dart, generics are reified, meaning that generic type information is retained at runtime. This allows dart to perform type checks and enforce type safety even after the code is compiled.
- **Asynchronous programming**: Supports asynchronous operations through async-await syntax, facilitating efficient handling of background tasks.

The following figure summarizes all the main dart language features:

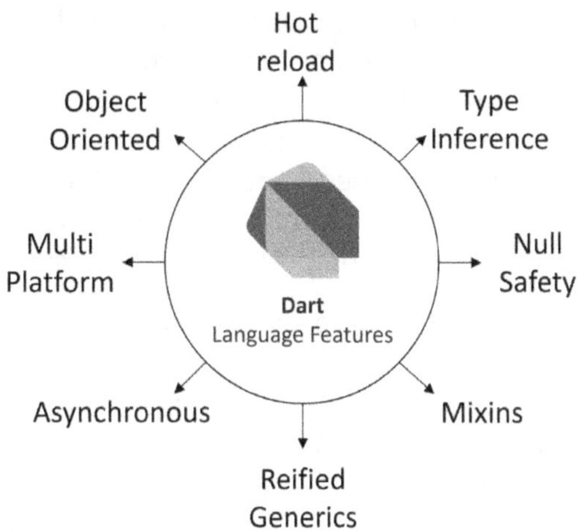

Figure 1.2: *Dart language features*

Dart compiler

Dart's compiler technology provides versatile ways to execute code across different platforms:

Native platform

For mobile and desktop applications, Dart offers two compilation options:

- **Dart VM with Just-in-Time (JIT) compilation**: During development, this compiler supports fast iteration cycles with features like hot reload for quick updates and live metrics collection for performance insights via DevTools.

- **Ahead-of-Time (AOT) compiler**: When preparing apps for production deployment, Dart's AOT compiler translates Dart code into native ARM or x64 machine code. This results in consistent and fast startup times for your application.

Web platform

For web applications, Dart's compilers adapt to various needs, such as:

- **Development mode**: Dart can compile to JavaScript or WebAssembly, enabling efficient testing and development.
- **Production mode**: Dart optimizes code for deployment, ensuring high performance and compatibility across web browsers.

Dart native

During development, the Dart VM's JIT compiler facilitates rapid iteration cycles crucial for debugging and refining applications. The VM supports live debugging features and incremental recompilation, enhancing developer productivity. When transitioning to production environments, Dart's AOT compiler generates optimized machine code, ensuring your application launches swiftly and maintains consistent performance. Dart's AOT-compiled apps run on a streamlined Dart runtime that enforces strong type safety and manages memory efficiently. This runtime employs fast object allocation and a generational garbage collector, optimizing performance and stability.

The following figure shows how dart targets various platforms:

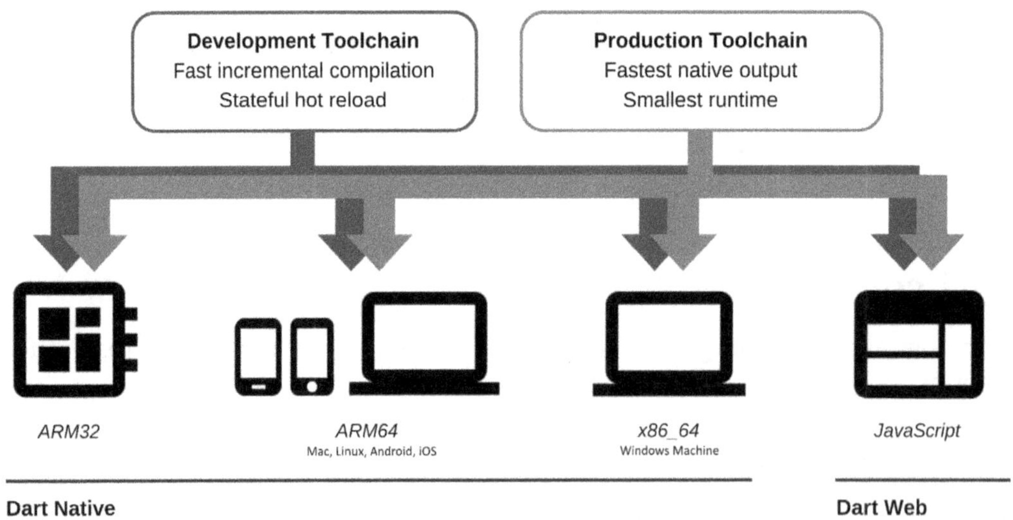

Figure 1.3: Dart supported targets

Installing Dart

While you do not strictly need to install Dart separately before installing Flutter, it can be beneficial to do so. Flutter comes with its own bundled Dart SDK, ensuring that the necessary version of Dart is included. However, understanding how to install Dart independently can be useful for standalone Dart projects or if you want to use the Dart SDK outside of Flutter. The following sections contain detailed instructions for installing Dart on Windows, Linux, and macOS, followed by installing Flutter. The following figure describes which package manager is required on which platform:

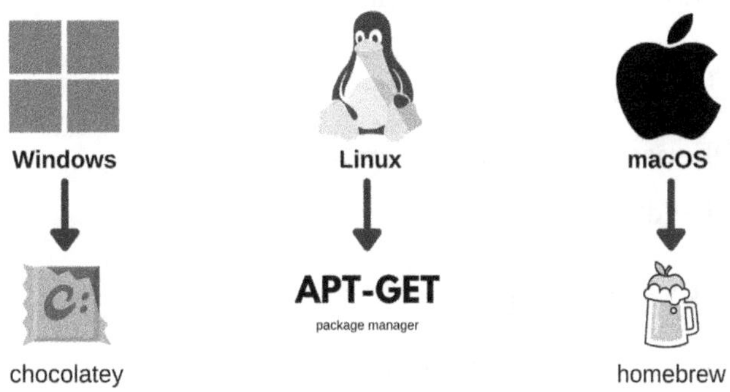

Figure 1.4: *Platforms and package manager for installing Dart*

Installing Dart on Windows

This segment provided detailed instruction for installing dart on windows platform. The following are the prerequisites for installing Dart on Windows:

- Administrative privileges
- **Recommended**: Chocolatey package manager

Installing chocolatey

Chocolatey is a powerful package manager for Windows that simplifies the process of installing, updating, and managing software. It uses the command line to automate software management, making it easy to install applications and tools without manual downloads and installations.

Visit the website **https://chocolatey.org/install#individual** to install chocolatey.

Installing Dart SDK

To install Dart open *PowerShell* or **command prompt** (**cmd**) with administrator privileges. Then, run the following command:

```
choco install dart-sdk
```

This command will download the **dart-sdk** and then execute a script to set the environment variables need for windows to remember the installation path of Dart.

Verifying installation

To verify if Dart is installed on the system, you can run the following command in PowerShell or cmd:

```
dart -version
```

This command will show the installed version of **dart-sdk**.

Upgrading Dart SDK

To upgrade Dart SDK, use the following command:

```
choco upgrade dark-sdk
```

Uninstalling Dart SDK

To uninstall the Dart SDK, run the following command:

```
choco uninstall dart-sdk
```

To remove the Dart configuration files from system, run the following command:

```
Remove-Item-Recurse-Force^-Path$env:LOCALAPPDATA\.dartServer,$env:APPDATA\.
dart,$env:APPDATA\.dart-tool
```

Installing Dart on Linux

If you are going to work on Linux based system, the following steps will guide you on how to setup and install dart. The only prerequisite for installing Dart on Linux is Root or Sudo access.

Installing Dart via Apt Repository on Debian/Ubuntu systems

Open the terminal and run the following commands, one command at a time. A slash (\) at the end of a line indicates that the command continues on the next line:

```
sudo apt-get update && sudo apt-get install apt-transport-https

wget -qO- https://dl-ssl.google.com/linux/linux_signing_key.pub \
  | sudo gpg  --dearmor -o /usr/share/keyrings/dart.gpg

echo  'deb  [signed-by=/usr/share/keyrings/dart.gpg  arch=amd64]  \  https://
```

```
storage.googleapis.com/download.dartlang.org/linux/debian stable main' \
  | sudo tee /etc/apt/sources.list.d/dart_stable.list

sudo apt-get update && sudo apt-get install dart
```

Installing Dart as Debian package

To install the Dart SDK as a Debian package, first download the Dart SDK Debian package from **https://storage.googleapis.com/dart-archive/channels/stable/release/latest/linux_packages/dart_3.4.4-1_amd64.deb** and then run the following command:

```
sudo dpkg -i dart_3.4.0-1_amd64.deb
```

The filename depends on the version number of dart-sdk, so you will have to update filename accordingly at the time of installation.

Verifying Dart installation

To verify your installation, open the terminal, and run the following command:

```
dart -version
```

You should see the installed version of Dart.

Upgrading the Dart SDK

To upgrade Dart using the **apt-get**, run the following command:

```
sudo apt-get update && sudo apt-get install dart
```

Uninstalling the Dart SDK

To uninstall Dart from your Linux system, run the following commands:

```
sudo apt-get remove -y dart
rm -rf  ~/.dart*
```

If you install the Dart SDK using **dpkg** command, run the following commands to remove it:

```
sudo dpkg --purge dart
dpkg -l | grep dart
```

Installing Dart on macOS

If you are going to use macOS, the following segment highlights all the steps required to install Dart.

Prerequisites

The following are the prerequisites to install Dart on macOS:

- Administrative privileges
- Homebrew package manager

Installing Homebrew

Homebrew is a popular package manager for macOS (and Linux) that simplifies the installation, updating, and management of software. It operates through the command line, allowing users to easily install a wide range of applications, tools, and utilities with simple commands.

Visit this webpage **https://brew.sh/** and follow the instruction to install Homebrew on macOS.

Installing Dart SDK

To install Dart, run the following commands after opening the terminal:

```
brew tap dart-lang/dart
brew install dart
brew info dart
```

The last command will show you which version(s) of dart you have installed.

Verifying Dart installation

To verify your installation, open the terminal, and run the following command:

```
dart -version
```

You should see the installed version of Dart.

Uninstalling Dart

To uninstall Dart SDK, run the following commands:

```
brew uninstall dart
rm -rf ~/.dart*
```

Installing Flutter

Flutter is a UI toolkit from Google that helps you create natively compiled applications for mobile, web, and desktop from a single codebase. This book will focus on the Flutter part of web app development. Here is a how to install Flutter on your device either it is a Windows, macOS, or Linux system.

Hardware and software requirements for Flutter

To install and run Flutter, your environment must meet the following hardware and software requirements. Here is a table outlining the minimum requirements for different platforms:

Hardware	Minimum	Recommended
CPU	4 cores	8 cores
Memory (RAM)	8 GB	16 GB
Screen resolution	1366 x 768	1920 x 1080
Free disk space	10 GB	10 GB (for ide and additional tools)

Table 1.1: *Hardware requirements*

The following table shows software requirement for Flutter:

Software	Requirements	Website
Tools	Git for version control	**https://git-scm.com/downloads**
IDE	IntelliJ IDEA	**https://www.jetbrains.com/idea/download**
Browser	Chrome/Edge/Safari	

Table 1.2: *Software requirements*

Installing Flutter on Windows

Flutter supports the 64-bit version of Microsoft Windows 10 or later. Ensure your Windows version includes Windows PowerShell 5 or later.

To install Flutter, you need to download the Flutter SDK bundle, move it to your desired location, and then extract the SDK. The following detailed steps will help you set up Flutter on your Windows system:

1. **Download the Flutter SDK**: First, download the Flutter SDK bundle from its official website at **docs.flutter.dev/get-started/install**. This bundle contains the latest stable release of the Flutter SDK. If you need other release channels or older builds, you can also find them in the SDK archive.

   The Flutter SDK should download to the default Windows download directory: **`%USERPROFILE%\Downloads`**. If you have changed the location of your **`Downloads`** directory, replace this path with your current **`Downloads`** directory path. For now, we can use **`C:/users/<MyUsername>/downloads`**

2. **Create an installation folder**: Create a folder where you can install Flutter. Consider creating a directory at `%USERPROFILE% (C:\users\{username}\) or %LOCALAPPDATA% (C:\users\{username}\AppData\Local)`

Note: Do not install Flutter in a directory that contains special characters or spaces or requires elevated privileges. For example, C:\Program Files fails both conditions.

3. **Extract the SDK**: Extract the Flutter SDK file into the directory you created. Extract it manually through windows explorer or use the following PowerShell command to expand the archive:

```
Expand-Archive `
      -Path $env:USERPROFILE\Downloads\flutter_windows_3.22.2-stable.
zip `
      -Destination $env:USERPROFILE\dev\
```

After extraction, the Flutter SDK should be located in the `C:\Users\{username}\dev\flutter` directory.

Note: Always choose the latest stable version released by flutter team.

a. **Update your Windows PATH variable**: To run Flutter commands in PowerShell or cmd, add Flutter to the PATH environment variable. This section presumes that you installed the Flutter SDK in `%USERPROFILE%\dev\flutter`. You can follow the given steps:

   i. Press the windows button and search for `system environment variables`.

   ii. Select the first option that pops with the name, **Edit the system environment variables**. A small window will open.

b. Select the button at the bottom named **Environment Variables**. The environment variables window will show up.

c. Inside the top section called **user variables**, scroll to find the variable called `Path` and click on the **Edit** button. Another window will open called **Edit environment variables**.

d. Click on the new button on top right, this creates a new editable row to add the path.

e. Type `%USERPROFILE%\dev\flutter\bin` and press *Enter* to confirm.

f. Close all the windows by pressing **OK** (on all three small windows).

g. Close all the opened PowerShell or cmd windows and all the **Integrated Development Environment** (IDE).

h. Open PowerShell or cmd again and type **`flutter --version`** command and it should show up the version of flutter and dart.

4. **Check your development setup**: After installing Flutter, it is crucial to validate that all components of your development environment are correctly set up. The **`flutter doctor`** command performs this validation, ensuring that all necessary tools and dependencies are properly installed. Perform the given steps:

   a. Open PowerShell

   b. Run command **`flutter doctor`**

   This command checks your system for all the components needed to develop Flutter apps and reports their status. If you have followed the installation process correctly, the output should resemble the following figure:

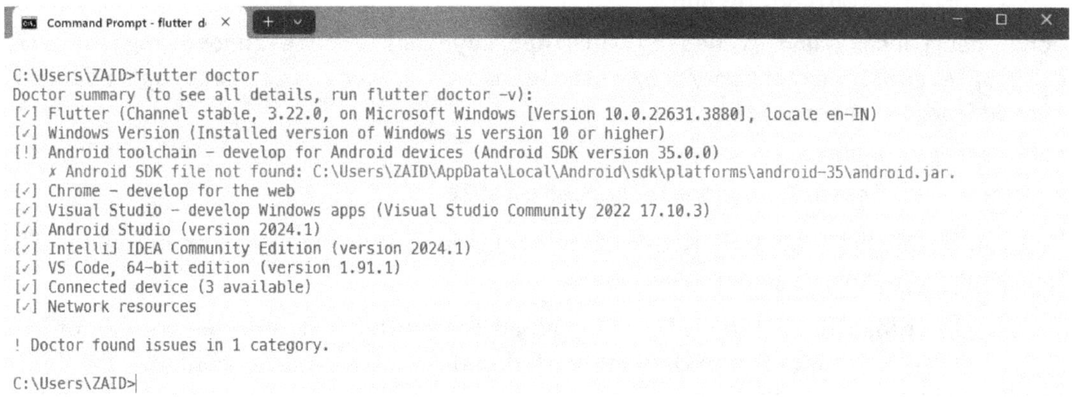

***Figure 1.5:** Sample flutter doctor output*

With these steps completed, you have successfully installed Flutter on your Windows machine and configured the environment to run Flutter commands.

Installing Flutter on Linux

To write and compile Flutter code for web on Linux, you must have a supported version of Linux and the necessary software packages. Flutter supports Debian Linux 11 or later and Ubuntu Linux 20.04 LTS or later. Also to develop Flutter on Linux, ensure you have the tools installed, like **`bash`**, **`file`**, **`mkdir`**, **`rm`**. Check for the tools using the command:

```
which bash file mkdir rm
```

The output should resemble the following content:

```
/bin/bash
/usr/bin/file
/bin/mkdir
/bin/rm
```

Installing required packages and Google Chrome

Install the necessary packages with the following commands in the terminal:

```
sudo apt-get update -y && sudo apt-get upgrade -y
sudo apt-get install -y curl git unzip xz-utils zip libglu1-mesa
```

To debug JavaScript code for web apps, install Google Chrome by running the following commands:

```
wget https://dl-ssl.google.com/linux/linux_signing_key.pub -O /tmp/google.pub
gpg --no-default-keyring \
    --keyring /etc/apt/keyrings/google-chrome.gpg \
    --import /tmp/google.pub
echo 'deb [arch=amd64 signed-by=/etc/apt/keyrings/google-chrome.gpg] http://dl.google.com/linux/chrome/deb/ stable main' | sudo tee /etc/apt/sources.list.d/google-chrome.list
sudo apt-get update -y
sudo apt-get install -y google-chrome-stable
```

You can install the Flutter SDK using the VS Code Flutter extension or manually. The following steps cover manual installation:

1. **Download the Flutter SDK**: Download the Flutter SDK bundle from its official website at **docs.flutter.dev/get-started/install**. This bundle contains the latest stable release of the Flutter SDK.

   The Flutter SDK should download to the default Linux download directory: `~/Downloads/`

2. **Create an installation folder**: Create a directory where you want to store Flutter SDK. For example, `/usr/bin`, then run the following command:

   ```
   sudo mkdir -p /usr/bin/
   ```

3. **Extract the SDK**: Extract the SDK file into the created directory by running the following tar command:

   ```
   tar -xf ~/Downloads/flutter_linux_3.22.2-stable.tar.xz -C /usr/bin/
   ```

   After extraction, the Flutter SDK should be in the `/usr/bin/flutter` directory.

4. **Adding Flutter to the PATH**: To run Flutter commands in a shell, add Flutter to the `PATH` environment variable. Check which shell starts when you open a new terminal window:

   ```
   echo $SHELL
   ```

To add Flutter to your PATH, use the following command for **bash** shell:

```
echo 'export PATH="/usr/bin/flutter/bin:$PATH"' >> ~/.bash_profile
source ~/.bash_profile
```

For **zsh** shell

```
echo 'export PATH="/usr/bin/flutter/bin:$PATH"' >> ~/.zshrc
source ~/.zshrc
```

5. **Check your Flutter setup**: The Flutter doctor command validates that all components of a complete Flutter development environment are installed. Open the terminal and run the following command:

```
flutter doctor
```

The output should resemble the following:

```
Running flutter doctor...
Doctor summary (to see all details, run flutter doctor -v):
[✓] Flutter (Channel stable, 3.22.1, on Ubuntu 20.04 (LTS), locale en)
[!] Android toolchain - develop for Android devices
[✓] Chrome - develop for the web
[!] Android Studio (not installed)
[!] Linux toolchain - develop for Linux desktop
[✓] VS Code (version 1.89)
[✓] Connected device (1 available)
[✓] Network resources

! Doctor found issues in 3 categories.
```

You can now start developing Flutter apps on your Linux machine.

Installing Flutter on macOS

Operating system requirements: Flutter supports macOS 10.15 (Catalina) or later. This guide presumes your Mac runs **zsh** as the default shell. If you are using a Mac with Apple silicon, you need to install **Rosetta 2** to run some Flutter components:

```
sudo softwareupdate --install-rosetta --agree-to-license
```

You need the following tools to develop Flutter on macOS:

- **Google Chrome**: Download it from the **google.com/chrome**
- **Git** (version 2.27 or later): Install it by running **brew install git**
- **IntelliJ** (IDEA community edition): Get it from **Jetbrains.com/idea/download**

To develop Flutter apps for the web on macOS, follow the given steps to ensure you have the necessary operating system, development tools, and software packages:

1. **Download the Flutter SDK**: Download the Flutter SDK bundle from its official website at **docs.flutter.dev/get-started/install**. Depending on your macOS laptop microchip, you will download either a bundle for *Intel* or *Apple Silicon* from the website. This bundle contains the latest stable release of the Flutter SDK. The Flutter SDK should download to the macOS default download directory: **`~/Downloads/`**.

2. **Create an installation folder**: Create a directory where you want to store Flutter. Open terminal and enter folder name for example:

   ```
   mkdir ~/development
   ```

3. **Extract the SDK**: Extract the SDK file into the created directory by running the following command in terminal window:

   ```
   unzip ~/Downloads/flutter_macos_arm64_3.22.2-stable.zip -d ~/development/
   ```

   After extraction, the Flutter SDK should be in the **`~/development/flutter`** directory.

4. **Add Flutter to the PATH**: To run Flutter commands in the Terminal, add Flutter to the PATH environment variable. This book presumes your Mac runs the latest default shell, **`zsh`**. **`Zsh`** uses the **`.zshenv`** file for environment variables. To add flutter to the path, follow the given steps:

   a. Launch your preferred text editor.

   b. If it exists, open the **`Zsh`** environmental variable file **`~/.zshenv`** in your text editor. If it does not, create **`~/.zshenv`** file.

   c. Copy the following line and paste it at the end of your **`~/.zshenv`** file:

      ```
      export PATH=$HOME/development/flutter/bin:$PATH
      ```

   d. Save your **`~/.zshenv`** file.

   e. To apply this change, restart all open terminal sessions.

5. **Check your installation**: The **`flutter doctor`** command validates that all components of a complete Flutter development environment are installed. To check open your terminal and run:

   ```
   flutter doctor
   ```

   As you chose to develop for the web, you do not need all components. If you followed this guide, the result of your command should resemble:

   ```
   Running flutter doctor...
   Doctor summary (to see all details, run flutter doctor -v):
   ```

```
[✓] Flutter (Channel stable, 3.22.1, on macOS 14.4.0 23E214 darwin-
arm64, locale en)
[!] Android toolchain - develop for Android devices
[✓] Chrome - develop for the web
[!] Xcode - develop for iOS and macOS (Xcode not installed)
[!] Android Studio (not installed)
[✓] VS Code (version 1.89)
[✓] Connected device (1 available)
[✓] Network resources

! Doctor found issues in 3 categories.
```

You are now ready to start developing Flutter apps on your macOS system.

Configuring the IntelliJ IDEA IDE

Flutter applications can be developed on various editors, like Visual Studio Code, Android Studio and IntelliJ IDEA. For this book, we are going to use and focus on IntelliJ IDEA, as the IDE of choice for developing apps.

IntelliJ IDEA, developed by *JetBrains*, is a robust IDE renowned for its extensive feature set tailored for *Java, Kotlin, Dart,* and other JVM-based languages. It excels in providing advanced coding assistance, refactoring, and code analysis tools that enhance developer productivity. Key features include intelligent code completion, which suggests context-aware code snippets and predicts the next relevant coding steps.

Its deep integration with version control systems like Git allows seamless collaboration and version management. IntelliJ IDEA's robust debugging capabilities enable developers to efficiently debug their applications with advanced breakpoints, watches, and inline variable values. Additionally, it supports a wide array of plugins and extensions, facilitating customization and support for various frameworks and technologies. Its intuitive user interface, combined with powerful refactoring tools and built-in support for testing frameworks, makes IntelliJ IDEA a preferred choice for developers seeking a comprehensive and efficient development environment.

IntelliJ IDEA is available in various editions for download and installation from the official JetBrains website (**https://www.jetbrains.com/idea/download**). You can choose from the following editions:

- **Community edition**: Free and open source (recommended)
- **IntelliJ IDEA Ultimate**: Commercial version

Configuring IntelliJ IDEA Community Edition for Flutter development involves installing both the Flutter and Android (optional) plugins. These plugins provide the tools and features to develop Flutter apps, such as code completion, syntax highlighting, widget editing assists, debugging, and more. Install the flutter plugin by following the given steps:

1. Open IntelliJ IDEA.
2. On the welcome screen, select **Plugins**.
3. Search for the Flutter Plugin:
    a. In the Plugins area, click on the **Marketplace** tab.
    b. Type **`Flutter`** into the search bar.
4. Install the Flutter Plugin:
    a. Locate the Flutter plugin in the search results.
    b. Click the **Install** button.
    c. IntelliJ IDEA may prompt you to install the Dart plugin as well. If prompted, confirm to install the Dart plugin.
    d. After the installation is complete, restart IntelliJ IDEA.

The following figure guides you about the IntelliJ IDEA plugin selection:

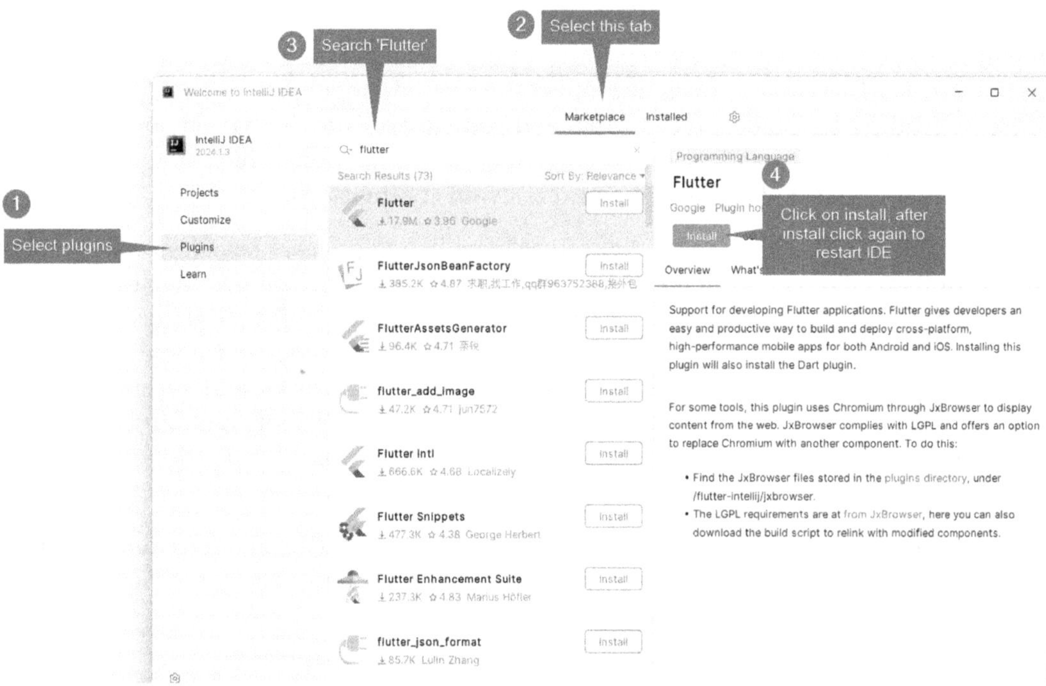

Figure 1.6: *Flutter plugin inside the plugin settings window of IntelliJ IDEA*

5. Create a demo flutter project to test:
   a. To create a new project, Navigate to **File** | **New** | **Project**.
   b. Select Flutter option from the sidebar list.
   c. Provide the Flutter SDK path by browsing its location and click **Next**.
   d. Enter project name.
   e. From the list of platforms, deselect everything except **Web**.
   f. Click **Create** button to create the project. For better understanding look at the following figure:

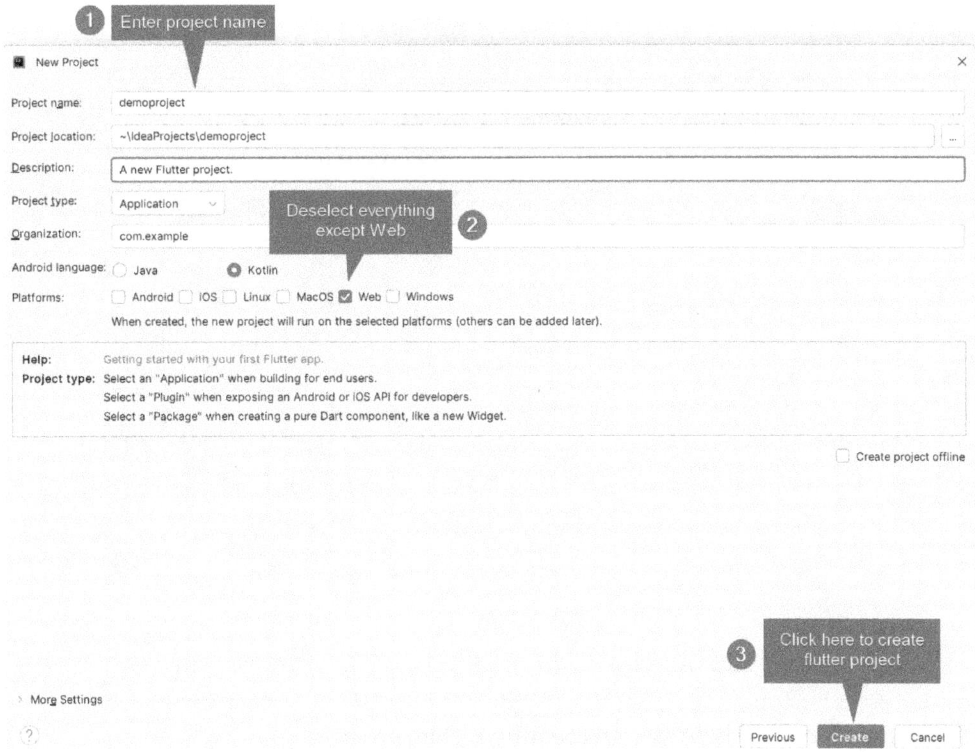

***Figure 1.7:** New project configuration window for flutter project*

6. Run your flutter app in the browser:
   a. In the Project view, navigate to the **`lib`** directory and open the **`main.dart`** file if not already opened.
   b. If no target device is selected, choose a target device, in our case select web browser from the dropdown on the toolbar at the top.
   c. Click the **Run** button (a green play icon) in the toolbar, or right-click on the **`main.dart`** file and select **`Run 'main.dart'`** option.

If every step is done correctly, then have now configured IntelliJ IDEA Community Edition for Flutter development with the necessary plugins. You can start developing, running, and debugging Flutter applications within IntelliJ IDEA.

Creating a Dart project

The best way to learn a language is by writing programs and that is what we are going to do. Launch IntelliJ IDEA community edition, close any already opened project from the file menu. Then, install the Dart plugin if not already installed, as shown in the following figure:

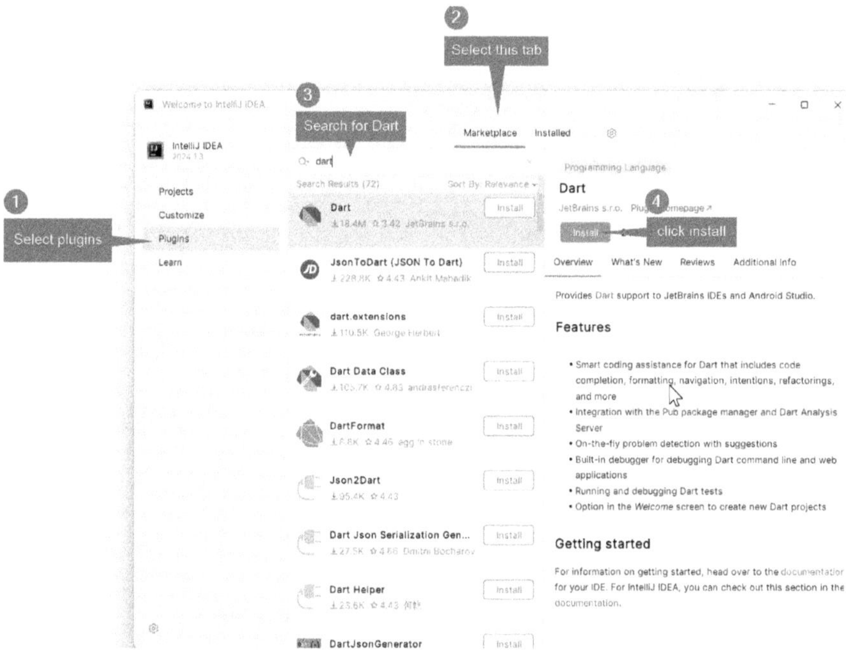

Figure 1.8: Dart plugin installation from IntelliJ IDEA welcome screen

The following steps will help you in creating a Dart project:

1. On the welcome screen of IntelliJ IDEA, click on **New Project**, as shown in the following figure:

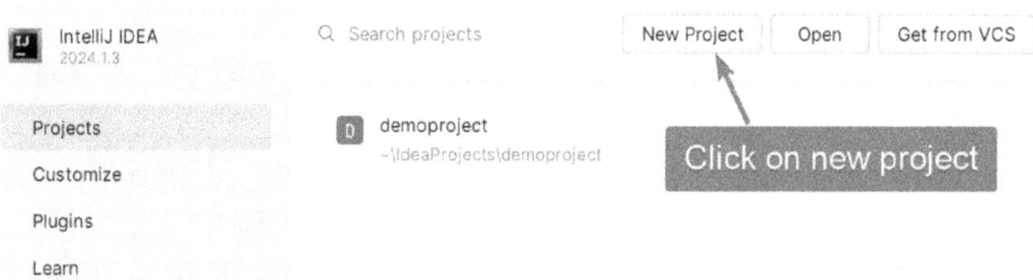

Figure 1.9: IntelliJ IDEA project launch window

2. Select Dart from the sidebar, browse and locate the Dart SDK, that you have installed earlier on your machine. Then, uncheck the generate sample content option and press **Next** as shown in the following figure:

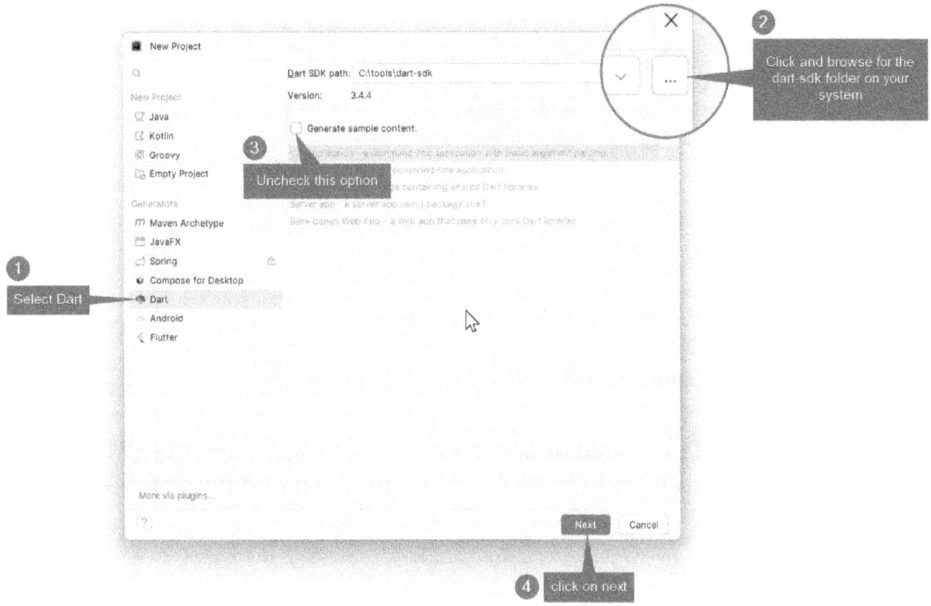

Figure 1.10: New project window in IntelliJ IDEA

3. On the new project window, just write the name of project as **`dart-basics`**. No other change is required. Finally, click the **Create** button to launch the project as shown in the following figure:

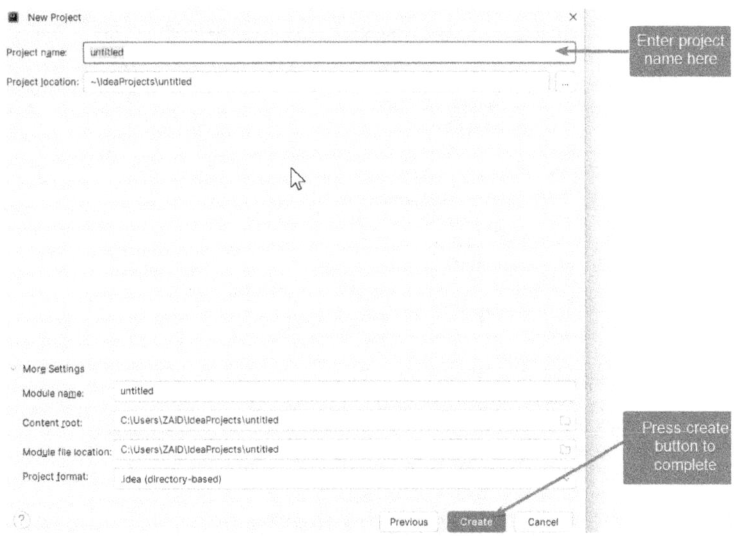

Figure 1.11: Project configuration window in IntelliJ IDEA

A new IntelliJ IDEA project window will open, as shown in the following figure:

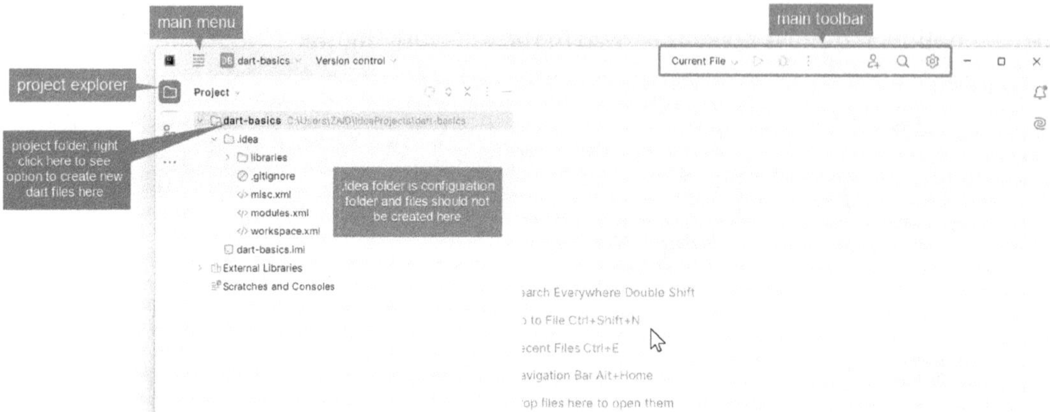

***Figure 1.12:** IntelliJ IDEA user interface components*

4. Create a new Dart file called **`hello`**, by right clicking on the project folder and then selecting the Dart option in the new submenu as shown in the following figure:

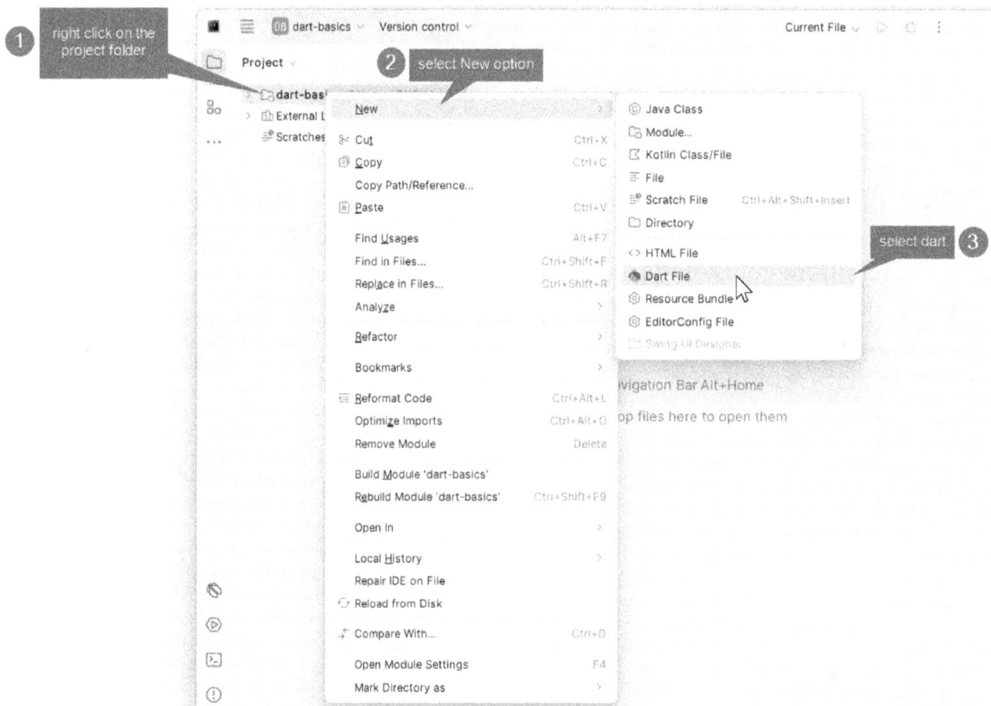

***Figure 1.13:** Creating a new dart file*

5. Enter the filename with or without the **`.dart`** extension in the small popup in the center of IDE, as shown in the following figure:

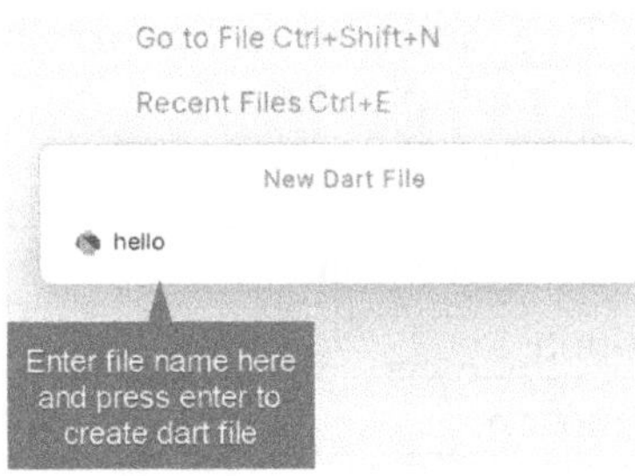

Figure 1.14: *Popup for writing the filename in IntelliJ IDEA*

A **hello.dart** file with open, where you can start writing code.

Basic concepts of Dart

This section will give you information about the basic concepts in Dart language.

main() function

Every Dart application begins with the top-level **main()** function, the starting point of execution. In Dart, functions that do not explicitly return a value are assigned the **void** return type. To display text on the console, you can use the top-level **print()** function. Let us start with a classic code and write in the **hello.dart** file:

```
void main(){
  print("Hello, New world");
}
```

Click on the run(play icon) on the top which prints **Hello, New World** to the console, marking your entry into Dart programming.

In the preceding example, the **main()** function does not take any arguments and simply prints a string to the console. This is the most basic form of a Dart program, and it demonstrates the essential structure of a Dart application.

The **main()** function can also take a **List<String>** parameter, which allows it to accept command-line arguments. This is particularly useful for command-line applications that need to process user input from the command line.

Operators

Operators in programming are special symbols or keywords that are used to perform operations on variables and values. Dart supports a variety of operators, which can be categorized into different types, based on their functionality:

- **Arithmetic operators**: They are used to perform basic mathematical operations like addition, subtraction, multiplication, division, and modulus (remainder). The following table lists the arithmetic operator:

Operator	Description	Example
+	Addition	`a + b`
-	Subtraction	`a - b`
*	Multiplication	`a * b`
/	Division	`a / b`
~/	Integer Division	`a ~/ b`
%	Modulus (Remainder)	`a % b`

***Table 1.3:** Arithmetic operator in Dart*

- **Assignment operators**: These are used to assign values to variables, combined with arithmetic operations if needed. The following table shows the operator, example and its equivalent expression:

Operator	Example	Equivalent to
=	`a = b`	$a = b$
+=	`a += b`	$a = a + b$
-=	`a -= b`	$a = a - b$
*=	`a *= b`	$a = a * b$
/=	`a /= b`	$a = a / b$
~/=	`a ~/= b`	$a = a \sim/ b$
%=	`a %= b`	$a = a \% b$

***Table 1.4:** Assignment operators in Dart*

- **Comparison operators**: They are used to compare two values and return a Boolean result (true or false) as show in the following table:

Operator	Description	Example	Result
==	Equal to	`a == b`	True if a is equal to b, otherwise false
!=	Not equal to	`a != b`	True if a is not equal to b, otherwise false
>	Greater than	`a > b`	True if a is greater than b, otherwise false
<	Less than	`a < b`	True if a is less than b, otherwise false
>=	Greater than or equal to	`a >= b`	True if a is greater than or equal to b, otherwise false
<=	Less than or equal to	`a <= b`	True if a is less than or equal to b, otherwise false

***Table 1.5:** Comparison operators in Dart*

- **Logical operators:** They are used to combine multiple conditions and return a Boolean result. There are three logical operators as shown in the following table:

<table>
<tr><th>Operator</th><th>Description</th><th>Example</th><th>Result</th></tr>
<tr><td>&&</td><td>Logical AND</td><td>a && b</td><td>true if both a and b are true, otherwise false</td></tr>
<tr><td>||</td><td>Logical OR</td><td>a || b</td><td>true if either a or b is true, or both are true, otherwise false</td></tr>
<tr><td>!</td><td>Logical NOT</td><td>!a</td><td>true if a is false, and false if a is true</td></tr>
</table>

Table 1.6: *Logical operators in Dart*

- **Type test operators**: They are used to check the type of an object at runtime, as shown in the following table:

Operator	Description	Example	Result
is	Type test	obj is String	True if obj is of type String, otherwise false
is!	Negated type test	obj is! String	True if obj is not of type String, otherwise false

Table 1.7: *Type test operators in Dart*

- **Bitwise operators:** They perform operations on bits and are used in low-level programming and specific algorithms, as shown in the following table:

<table>
<tr><th>Operator</th><th>Description</th><th>Example</th><th>Result</th></tr>
<tr><td>&</td><td>Bitwise AND</td><td>a & b</td><td>Bitwise AND of a and b</td></tr>
<tr><td>|</td><td>Bitwise OR</td><td>a | b</td><td>Bitwise OR of a and b</td></tr>
<tr><td>^</td><td>Bitwise XOR</td><td>a ^ b</td><td>Bitwise XOR of a and b</td></tr>
<tr><td>~</td><td>Bitwise NOT (Unary)</td><td>~a</td><td>Bitwise NOT of a (inverts bits)</td></tr>
<tr><td><<</td><td>Left Shift</td><td>a << b</td><td>Shifts bits of a left by b positions</td></tr>
<tr><td>>></td><td>Right Shift</td><td>a >> b</td><td>Shifts bits of a right by b positions</td></tr>
</table>

Table 1.8: *Bitwise operators in Dart*

- **Conditional operators:** They provide a compact way to evaluate expressions based on conditions as listed in the following table:

Operator	Description	Example	Result
expr1 ?? expr2	Null-aware coalescing operator	a ?? b	Evaluates to a if a is not null, otherwise evaluates to b
expr1 ? expr2 : expr3	Conditional (ternary) operator	a ? b : c	Evaluates to b if a is true, otherwise evaluates to c

Table 1.9: *Conditional operators in Dart*

These operators cover a wide range of functionalities, from basic arithmetic and comparison to more advanced bitwise operations and conditional checks, providing developers with powerful tools to manipulate data and control program flow in Dart.

Comments

Comments in programming are used to explain and document code. They are ignored by the compiler and are solely for the benefit of developers. Dart supports the following three types of comments:

- **Single-line comments**: Start with // and are used for brief explanations.
- **Multi-line comments**: Start with /* and end with */, useful for longer explanations or commenting out code blocks.
- **Documentation comments**: Start with /// or /** and */, used to generate API documentation and can include special tags for more structured information.

Keywords

Keywords in programming are reserved identifiers that have special meanings and purposes in the Dart programming language. These keywords cannot be used as identifiers (such as variable names, function names, class names, etc.) because they are already predefined and used by the language itself. Here is a list of keywords in Dart:

- **Control flow statements**:

  ```
  if, else, switch, case, default, for, while, do, break, continue,
  return
  ```

- **Data types and variable declaration**:

  ```
  var, final, const, late, dynamic, void, typedef
  ```

- **Classes and inheritance**:

  ```
  class, extends, with, implements, super, abstract
  ```

- **Functions and methods**:

  ```
  function, sync, async, await
  ```

- **Error handling**:

  ```
  try, catch, on, throw, finally
  ```

- **Namespace management and libraries**:

  ```
  import, export, library, part, part of
  ```

- **Operators and literals**:

  ```
  is, as, in, assert, operator, this, new, true, false, null
  ```

- **Miscellaneous:**

  `get, set, cascade (..), extension, required, late`

These keywords serve various purposes, such as defining control flow, declaring variables, defining classes and functions, handling exceptions, importing/exporting libraries, and managing operators and literals.

Note: Using these keywords as identifiers in your Dart code will result in a compilation error, as they are reserved for specific language constructs and functionalities.

Displaying output

The print function in Dart is straightforward and is used to display information on the console. It can be used to print strings, numbers, and other objects by converting them to a string representation. Create a new file called **`display.dart`** in the IDE and type the following code:

```
void main() {
  print('Hello, World!');
  print(123);
  print(3.14);
  print(true);

  var name = 'Dart';
  print('Welcome to $name!');
}
```

Do not worry about the variable declaration and datatype, it will be discussed in the next section. Run the code by clicking the play icon near the **`main()`** function as shown in the following figure:

***Figure 1.15:** Running the current file in IDE*

Libraries

In Dart, a library is a collection of code that can include variables, functions, classes, and other definitions. It serves as a unit of encapsulation and code organization. Every Dart app starts with the `main()` function, and Dart programs can consist of one or more libraries.

To use functions, classes, or variables defined in a library within another Dart file, you need to import the library. Imports allow Dart programs to use code defined in external libraries or other Dart files. Dart supports several types of imports, such as:

- **Importing core libraries:** You can import Dart's core libraries using the **`dart:`** scheme. These libraries provide fundamental functionality for Dart programming.
- **Importing files:** You can import Dart files directly using relative or absolute paths. This is useful for organizing code across different files within the same project.
- **Importing packages:** Dart uses the **`package:`** scheme to import code from external packages published on **pub.dev**. These packages extend Dart's functionality and are managed using the pub package manager.
- **Importing multiple items:** You can import multiple libraries or items from the same library using the **`show`** and **`hide`** keywords.

Here is an example of various types importing in dart:

```
import 'dart:math';  // import core libraries
import 'package:http/http.dart'; // import libraries from external packages
import 'path/to/my_other_file.dart'; // import a file from the same package
import 'dart:async' show Future, Stream; // import only part of a library
import 'dart:math' hide max; // import all except one part of a library
```

Taking input

The **`stdin`** object in the **dart:io** library is used to read input from the console. This is commonly used for command-line applications. To take a simple input from the user and print it, you can use the following code:

```
// user_input.dart
// Reading input from the user
import 'dart:io';

void main() {
  print('Enter your name:');
```

```
  String? name = stdin.readLineSync(); // Reading input from the user
  print('Hello, $name!');
}
```

To take numerical input, you will often need to parse the input from a string to the desired type, such as an integer or a double. Try the following example:

```
// parsing_input.dart
// Taking numeric input from the user
import 'dart:io';

void main() {
  print('Enter your age:');
  String? input = stdin.readLineSync();
  if (input != null) {
    int age = int.parse(input); // Parsing the input to an integer
    print('You are $age years old.');
  }
}
```

You can take multiple inputs from the user and process them accordingly. When taking input, it is essential to handle potential errors, such as parsing failures.

Note: When writing a new program, try to assign static values to variables and test your logic. After the program logic is achieved, you can remove the static values and replace them with user inputs. This will result in better programs and faster code test cycles.

Pubspec.yaml file

The **`pubspec.yaml`** file is a crucial configuration file for Dart and Flutter projects. It serves multiple purposes, including managing project dependencies, specifying metadata about the project, and configuring various aspects of the project, such as assets and package versions. It is required whenever you want to add a third-party library (dependency) to your project. You do not need it in the current project, but it is an important part of dart and flutter ecosystem.

Importance of pubspec.yaml

The following reasons is why **`pubspec.yaml`** is important:

- **Dependency management**: The **`pubspec.yaml`** file is central to managing your project's dependencies. When you specify a package in the dependencies section and run **`dart pub get`** or **`flutter pub get`**, Dart's package manager fetches the specified versions of the packages and installs them in your project.

- **Project configuration**: The pubspec.yaml file also configures various aspects of your project, including the SDK version, assets, and fonts, ensuring that your project is correctly set up to run and build.
- **Collaboration**: By specifying all dependencies and configurations in pubspec.yaml, it becomes easier for other developers to set up the project on their machines. They only need to run pub get to install all necessary dependencies, ensuring a smooth and consistent development environment.

Components of pubspec.yaml

The following are the components of **`pubspec.yaml`**:

- **Project metadata:** This section contains basic information about the project, such as its name, version, and description.
- **Environment:** This section specifies the Dart SDK version required for the project. It ensures that the project uses a compatible version of the Dart SDK.
- **Dependencies**: This section lists the packages that your project depends on. These can include both regular dependencies and development dependencies.
- **Dependency overrides**: This section allows you to override specific versions of dependencies. This is useful for testing new versions of a package or for working around version conflicts.
- **Assets**: In Flutter projects, this section is used to specify assets, like images, fonts, and other resources.
- **Fonts**: Also specific to Flutter, this section allows you to specify custom fonts.
- **Executors and builders (optional)**: For more advanced use cases, you might need to specify executors and builders if you are using code generation or other build tools.

Example of pubspec.yaml file

Here is a complete example of a **`pubspec.yaml`** file for a sample Flutter project:

```
name: my_flutter_app
description: A new Flutter application
version: 1.0.0

environment:
  sdk: ">=2.12.0 <3.0.0"

dependencies:
  flutter:
```

```
      sdk: flutter
    http: ^0.13.3
    provider: ^5.0.0

  dev_dependencies:
    flutter_test:
      sdk: flutter

  flutter:
    assets:
      - assets/images/
      - assets/sounds/

    fonts:
      - family: Raleway
        fonts:
          - asset: fonts/Raleway-Regular.ttf
          - asset: fonts/Raleway-Bold.ttf
            weight: 700
```

Variables and data types

The following sections gives you a detailed breakdown of variables and datatypes in Dart.

Variables

In programming, variables are used to store data that can be referenced and manipulated in a program. Dart is a statically typed language, which means that the type of a variable is known at compile time. However, Dart also supports type inference, allowing you to declare variables without explicitly specifying their type.

Declaring variables using the var keyword

When you declare a variable with **var**, Dart infers the type based on the initial value. Create a new file called **inferred_variables.dart** in the IDE and write the following code:

```
void main() {
  var name = 'Alice'; // Inferred as String
  var age = 30; // Inferred as int
  var height = 5.9; // Inferred as double
```

```
    var isStudent = true; // Inferred as bool

    print(name); // Outputs: Alice
    print(age); // Outputs: 30
    print(height); // Outputs: 5.9
    print(isStudent); // Outputs: true
}
```

Explicit type declaration in variables

You can also explicitly specify the type of a variable. Create a new file called **explicit_variables.dart** and test the code in it, it will gave you the same output as before, showing darts flexibility:

```
void main() {
    String name = 'Alice';
    int age = 30;
    double height = 5.9;
    bool isStudent = true;

    print(name); // Outputs: Alice
    print(age); // Outputs: 30
    print(height); // Outputs: 5.9
    print(isStudent); // Outputs: true
}
```

If you want a variable to hold values of different types, you can use the **dynamic** keyword. However, using dynamic is generally discouraged unless necessary, as it bypasses Dart's type checking.

```
dynamic variable = 'Alice';
print(variable); // Outputs: Alice

variable = 30;
print(variable); // Outputs: 30
```

Defining variable using final and const keyword

Dart provides **final** and **const** keywords for declaring variables that will not change. A **final** variable can be set only once, and its value is determined at runtime. A **const** variable is a compile-time constant. Its value must be known at compile time, and it cannot be changed. The benefit of using **final** is that you can assign a value to a variable only once. The benefit of using **const** is that the value of the variable is declared before compiling. Create a new file, call it **fixed_variables.dart** and test the following code:

```
void main(){
  final name = 'Zaid Kamil';
  final age = 33;
  const pi = 3.1415;
  const gravity = 9.8;

  print(name);    // Outputs: Zaid Kamil
  print(age);     // Outputs: 33
  print(pi);      // Outputs: 3.1415
  print(gravity); // Outputs: 9.8
}
```

Null safety

Dart enforces sound null safety, a feature designed to prevent null dereference errors. A null dereference error occurs when you access a property or call a method on an expression that evaluates to null. Null safety allows the Dart compiler to detect these potential errors at compile time, transforming possible runtime errors into compile-time errors. Null safety introduces the following three key concepts:

- **Nullable and non-nullable types**:
  - Nullable types can hold null values and are declared by appending a ? to the type.
  - Non-nullable types cannot hold null values and must be initialized before use.

  You can refer to the following code as an example:

```
String? name;  // Nullable type. Can be null or a string.
String name;  // non-
nullable type. Must be a string and can't be null.
```

- **Variable initialization**:
  - Nullable variables default to null.
  - Non-nullable variables must be initialized before use.
  - Dart ensures that non-nullable variables are initialized before they are accessed.
- **Sound null safety**:
  - The Dart compiler flags errors related to null values at edit time.
  - This includes variables that are not initialized with non-null values or are assigned null values.

Default values

Uninitialized variables of nullable types have a default value of null. This applies to all types, including numeric types, as numbers are objects in Dart. This is shown in the following command:

```
int? counter;
assert(counter == null); // counter is null by default.
```

Late variables

The **late** keyword in Dart is used to declare variables that are non-nullable but will be initialized after their declaration. This is useful in scenarios where a variable cannot be initialized at the point of declaration but is guaranteed to be assigned a value before it is used.

The following ate the use cases for late variables:

- **Deferred initialization**: Sometimes, the value of a variable cannot be determined at the time of declaration. In such cases, you can use it late to tell the Dart compiler that the variable will be initialized later.
- **Lazy initialization**: Lazy initialization refers to delaying the initialization of a variable until it is first accessed. This can be beneficial when the initialization process is expensive, and the variable might not always be needed.

String interpolation

String interpolation in Dart allows you to embed expressions within string literals. This feature makes it easy to create strings dynamically by inserting variable values or expressions directly into the string content.

Syntax: To perform string interpolation in Dart, you use **${expression}** within a string literal to embed the result of evaluating **expression**, as shown in the following code example:

```
void main() {
  String name = 'Jinwoo';
  int age = 19;

  // Using string interpolation
  print('My name is $name and I am $age years old.');

  // String interpolation with expressions
  print('Next year, I will be ${age + 1} years old.');
}
```

Data types

Dart is a statically typed language, which means you must explicitly define the type of every variable, or Dart infers the type based on the assigned value. The following table summarizes Dart datatypes along with their descriptions and use cases:

Datatype	Description	Use case
`int`	Represents whole numbers.	Counting items, indexing, mathematical operations.
`Double`	Represents fractional numbers.	Calculations requiring decimal precision.
`String`	Represents a sequence of characters.	Storing text, outputting messages, formatting data.
`Bool`	Represents true or false values.	Conditional statements, Boolean logic.
`List`	Represents an ordered collection of objects.	Storing and manipulating sequences of items.
`Map`	Represents a collection of key-value pairs.	Associating values with keys for quick lookup.
`Set`	Represents an unordered collection of unique items.	Ensuring all items are unique, set operations.
`Runes`	Represents UTF-32 string characters.	Handling Unicode characters and emojis.
`Symbol`	Represents an operator or identifier in a Dart program.	Reflection, identifying methods and fields dynamically.
`Null`	Represents an absence of a value.	Nullable types, indicating that a variable can be null.

***Table 1.10:** Datatypes in Dart*

Create a file called **`datatypes.dart`** in the IDE and test the following code:

```
void main(){
  int age = 25;
  int year = 2024;
  double height = 1.75;
  double pi = 3.14159;
  String name = 'Zaid Kamil';
  String message = "Dart is Love";
  bool isAuthor = true;
  bool isEmployee = true;
  List<int> numbers = [1, 2, 3, 4, 5];
  List<String> names = ['Dalinar', 'Kaladin', 'Shallan', 'Jasnah'];
```

```
  Map<String, int> ratings = {'Dart': 5, 'Flutter': 5, 'Java': 3, 'Kotlin': 4};
  Map<int, String> products = {1: 'Laptop', 2: 'Smartphone', 3: 'Tablet'};
  Set<int> uniqueNumbers = {1, 2, 3, 4, 5};
  Set<String> uniqueOrders = {'Windrunner', 'Skybreaker', 'Edgedancer', 'Truthwatcher'};
  Runes input = Runes('\u2665 \u{1f600}'); // Unicode characters
  String emojis = String.fromCharCodes(input); // "♥ 😀"
  Symbol libraryName = #exampleLibrary;
  print("Data Types in Dart");
  print("number: age = $age & year = $year");
  print("double: height = $height & pi = $pi");
  print("String: name = $name & message = $message");
  print("bool: isAuthor = $isAuthor & isEmployee = $isEmployee");
  print("List<int>: numbers = $numbers");
  print("List<String>: names = $names");
  print("Map<String, int>: ratings = $ratings");
  print("Map<int, String>: products = $products");
  print("Set<int>: uniqueNumbers = $uniqueNumbers");
  print("Set<String>: uniqueOrders = $uniqueOrders");
  print("Runes: input = $input & emojis = $emojis");
  print("Symbol: libraryName = $libraryName");
}
```

Each datatype comes with their own properties and method, which you will learn as you progress further.

Control flow

Control flow in programming refers to the order in which individual statements, instructions, or function calls are executed or evaluated within a program. It dictates the path that the program takes during its execution, determining which operations are performed based on certain conditions and criteria. Proper understanding and use of control flow are essential for writing efficient and logical programs. Let us start with a conditional statement first.

Conditions

Create a new Dart file for each of the following code example and try to run the same program but with different values. To make these codes better you can later implement user input in your programs.

If statement

The **if** statement in Dart is used to execute a block of code if a specified condition evaluates to true. The following code demonstrates this:

```
// condition_1.dart
// Checking if a character is a hero
void main() {
  String character = 'Goku';

  if (character == 'Goku') {
    print('Goku is a powerful hero!');
  }
}
```

If-else statement

The **if-else** statement allows you to execute one block of code if the condition is true and another block if it is false. Try the following code in your IDE:

```
// condition_2.dart
// Determining a character's alignment
void main() {
  String character = 'Vegeta';

  if (character == 'Goku') {
    print('Goku is a powerful hero!');
  } else {
    print('Vegeta is a fierce rival but sometimes an ally.');
  }
}
```

If-else if ladder

The if-else if ladder allows you to check multiple conditions sequentially. Try the following simple program:

```
// condition_3.dart
// Checking power levels
void main() {
  String character = 'Naruto';
  int powerLevel = 9000;

  if (character == 'Goku') {
    print('Goku is a powerful hero!');
  } else if (character == 'Naruto') {
    print('Naruto has a power level of $powerLevel!');
  } else if (character == 'Saitama') {
    print('Saitama is the most powerful hero!');
  }
  else {
    print('Other characters in the anime.');
  }
}
```

if-case statement

While the three preceding conditional statements are common in almost all languages, the if-case statement needs a deeper look. The if-case statement in Dart is a way to match a value against a pattern and execute code if the pattern matches. This feature, available in Dart 3.0 and later, allows for concise pattern matching and de-structuring. If the value matches the pattern, the associated branch is executed with any variables defined in the pattern being in scope. Try the following code:

```
// condition_4.dart
// Checking coordinates
void main() {
  var pair1 = [4, 5];
  var pair2 = [4, 5, 6];
  if (pair1 case [int x, int y]) {
    print('Pair1 is a 2D coordinate.');
  } else {
    print('Pair1 is not a 2D coordinate.');
  }
  if (pair2 case [int x, int y]) {
    print('Pair2 is a 2D coordinate.');
  } else {
```

```
      print('Pair2 is not a 2D coordinate.');
    }
  }
```

In the preceding code, we have two pairs of coordinates, **pair1** and **pair2**. We want to check if each pair is a 2D coordinate. We use the case keyword to match the structure of the pair with the pattern **[int x, int y]**. If the pair matches the pattern, we print that it is a 2D coordinate; otherwise, we print that it is not a 2D coordinate.

Let us say we have a simple example involving characters from the popular *Brandon Sanderson's Mistborn*. We will check if a character is a Mistborn and print their abilities, as shown in the following code:

```
// condition_5.dart
// checking if character is a Mistborn or Misting
void main() {
  var character = ['Vin', 'Mistborn'];

  if (character case [String name, 'Mistborn']) {
    print('$name is a Mistborn with all Allomantic powers!');
  } else if (character case [String name, 'Misting']) {
    print('$name is a Misting with a single Allomantic power.');
  } else {
    print('Unknown character.');
  }
}
```

In the preceding example, if a character is a Mistborn, the message Vin is a Mistborn with all Allomantic powers! will be printed. If character was a Misting, the respective message would be printed. If the character does not match either pattern, it prints **Unknown character**.

As shown in the preceding examples, the if-case statement in Dart provides a powerful way to match and de-structure values concisely.

Switch statement

The switch statement allows you to execute one block of code from multiple options based on the value of an expression. Try the following code:

```
// condition_6.dart
// Power level classifications
void main() {
  int powerLevel = 8000;
```

```

  switch (powerLevel) {
    case 9000:
      print('Over 9000! It\'s Goku\'s power level!');
      break;
    case 8000:
      print('It\'s over 8000! Strong, but not quite Goku.');
      break;
    default:
      print('Power level is unknown.');
  }
}
```

Guard clause

A guard clause is a conditional statement placed at the beginning of a function to handle special cases, often to prevent the main body of the function from executing. The following code example demonstrates this:

```
// condition_7.dart
// Handling transformations
void main() {
  String form = 'Super Saiyan';

  if (form != 'Super Saiyan') {
    print('Transforming into $form!');
  } else {
    print('Already in $form.');
  }
}
```

Guard clauses are a way to handle special cases or conditions at the beginning of a function, allowing you to exit the function early if a certain condition is met. This helps in keeping the code clean and avoiding nested conditions. Try the following example:

```
// condition_8.dart
// Checking Access to the Restricted Section
void main() {
  String character = 'Hermione';
  bool hasPermission = false;

  if (!hasPermission) {
```

```
        print('$character is not allowed to enter restricted section.');
        return;
      }
      print('$character is allowed to enter restricted section.');
    }
```

In this example, the guard clause **`if (!hasPermission)`** checks if the character does not have permission. If the condition is true, it prints a message and exits the function early using **`return`**. This way, the rest of the code is only executed if the character has permission.

Note: Using guard clauses is a good practice in Dart and other programming languages to keep your code clean, readable, and maintainable.

Loops

Loops are a fundamental concept in programming that allows you to execute a block of code multiple times. Loops are useful when you need to repeat a task multiple time. They help reduce code duplication and make your programs more concise and easier to read. For example, if you want to print a message five times, using a loop is much more efficient than writing the print statement five times.

Dart provides several types of loops to help you accomplish repetitive tasks efficiently. Let us explore each type of loop.

For loop

The for loop in Dart is commonly used when you know in advance how many times you want to execute a statement or a block of statements. Dart provides two styles of for loops: the traditional **`for`** loop and the **`for-in`** loop:

- **Traditional for loop**: The traditional for loop consists of three parts: initialization, condition, and increment/decrement. Its syntax is similar to Java, C. Try the following example:

```
// for_loop_1.dart
// Using for loop in Dart
void main() {
  // example 1
  for (int i = 1; i <= 5; i++) {
    print(‘🍕 Pizza slice $i›);
  }
  // example 2 - even numbers
  print('Even numbers between 1 and 10:');
```

```
  for (int i = 2; i <= 10; i += 2) {
    print("🏳 $i»);
  }
  // sum of all odd numbers between 1 and 10
  int sum = 0;
  for (int i = 1; i <= 10; i += 2) {
    sum += i;
  }
  print('Sum of all odd numbers between 1 and 10: $sum');
}
```

Note: Adding emojis in code is not necessary, but it make the output engaging. For inserting emojis, press Win + . (Windows key + period) on Windows, press Ctrl + Cmd + Space on macOS system. On Linux it can vary depending on the distribution and desktop environment.

- **for-in loop**: The for-in loop is used to iterate over a collection of items, such as a list or a set. Try the following code:

```
// for_loop_2.dart
// Using for loop to iterate over a list in Dart
void main() {
  List<String> fruits = ['🍎 Apple›, '🍌 Banana›, '🍇 Grape›, '🍉 Watermelon›];

  // Print each fruit in the list
  for (String fruit in fruits) {
    print(fruit);
  }
}
```

While loop

The while loop executes a block of code as long as a specified condition is true. Try the following example:

```
// while_loop.dart
// Using while loop in Dart
void main() {
  var count = 1;
  while (count <= 5) {
    print('🍩 Donut $count');
```

```
    count++;
  }

  // sum of all digits
  var num = 12345;
  var sum = 0;
  while (num > 0) {
    sum += num % 10;
    num ~/= 10;
  }
  print('Sum of all digits: $sum›);
}
```

Do while loop

The do-while loop is similar, but it guarantees that the block of code will execute at least once. The following code demonstrates it:

```
// do_while_loop.dart
// Using do-while loop in Dart
void main() {

  var count = 1;
  do {
    print('🍦 Ice cream cone $count');
    count++;
  } while (count <= 5);

  // loop when apples are greater than 5
  var apples = 1;
  do {
    print('You have 🍎 Apple $apples›);
    apples--;
  } while (apples > 5);
}
```

Break and continue

The **break** statement is used to exit a loop prematurely, while the **continue** statement skips the rest of the current iteration and proceeds to the next iteration.

The following code is an example of **break** in loop:

```
// loop_break.dart
// Using break statement in a loop in Dart
void main() {
  for (int i = 1; i <= 10; i++) {
    if (i == 6) {
      print('Breaking at $i 🚫');
      break;
    }
    print('Number: $i');
  }
}
```

The following code is an example of **continue** in a loop:

```
// loop_continue.dart
// Using continue statement in a loop in Dart
void main() {
  for (int i = 1; i <= 10; i++) {
    if (i % 2 == 0) {
      continue; // Skip even numbers
    }
    print('🎈 Balloon $i›);
  }
}
```

These can also be used along with **while** and **do-while** loops.

Function and scope

Functions are fundamental building blocks in Dart, as in any programming language. They encapsulate a piece of logic that can be reused, making code more modular, readable, and maintainable. You are going to explore various aspects of Dart functions, including return values, named parameters, optional positional parameters, shorthand functions, and more. Functions help in:

- **Reusability**: Write once, use multiple times.
- **Modularity**: Break down complex problems into smaller, manageable tasks.
- **Maintainability**: Easier to update and fix bugs.
- **Readability**: Make code easier to understand.

The syntax of a function in Dart is composed of several components, including the return type, the function name, parameters, and the function body as shown in the following code:

```
returnType functionName(parameters) {
  // Function body
  // Code to be executed
}
```

The basic structure is broken into the following parts:

- **returnType**: Specifies the type of value that the function returns. If the function does not return a value, use **`void`**.
- **functionName**: The name of the function, used to call it.
- **parameters**: A comma-separated list of inputs for the function, enclosed in parentheses.
- **Function body**: Contains the statements that define what the function does, enclosed in curly braces **`{}`**.

Dart is a **true object-oriented language**, which means that even functions are objects and have a type, **`Function`**. This allows functions to be assigned to variables, passed as arguments to other functions, and even allows instances of Dart classes to be called as if they were functions. Create a new file and write some functions as shown in the following code:

```
// func_1.dart
// Simple function usage in Dart
void shout(String message) {
  print("😃${message.toUpperCase()}!");
}

void whisper(String message) {
  print("🥱${message.toLowerCase()}...");
}

void main() {
  // calling the functions directly
  shout("Plus Ultra!");
  whisper("Plus Ultra!");
  /*
  Demo of first-class functions concept in Dart
  By storing the functions in a variable
```

```
  Here talk is a variable that stores the shout function
  */
  Function talk = shout;
  talk('I am here!');
  // updating the talk variable to store the whisper function
  talk = whisper;
  talk('I am here!');
}
```

Return values

Functions can return values. The return type is specified before the function name. Return value can be of any datatype. Look at the following lengthy code example, but write one function at a time and then call it in **`main()`** function:

```
// func_2.dart
// Function with return type in Dart
import 'dart:math';

// function with int return type
int diceRoll() {
  return Random().nextInt(6) + 1;
}

// function with double return type
double areaOfCircle(double radius) {
  return 3.14 * radius * radius;
}

// function with String return type
String emojiMessage() {
  var num = Random().nextInt(300);
  if (num <= 100) {
    return '🎉 Party time!';
  } else if (num <= 200) {
    return '🎈 Balloon 🎈';
  } else {
    return '🎲 Roll the dice!';
  }
```

```
}
// function with List return type
List<int> generateRandomNumbers() {
  List<int> randomNumbers = [];
  for (int i = 0; i < 5; i++) {
    randomNumbers.add(Random().nextInt(100));
  }
  return randomNumbers;
}

void main() {
  // calling function inside print()
  print('🎲 Dice rolled: ${diceRoll()}');
  print('🎲 Dice rolled: ${diceRoll()}');
  print('🎲 Dice rolled: ${diceRoll()}');
  // calling function and storing result
  double radius = 10;
  double area = areaOfCircle(radius);
  print('Area of circle with radius $radius: $area');
  // calling function inside print()
  print('Area of circle with radius 5: ${areaOfCircle(5)}');

  print(emojiMessage());
  print(emojiMessage());

  List<int> result = generateRandomNumbers();
  print('Random numbers: $result');
}
```

Parameters

Functions can have various types of parameters (arguments), including required positional parameters, named parameters, and optional positional parameters

Required positional parameters

A function can have any number of required positional parameters. These parameters must be passed in the correct order when the function is called, as shown in the following code:

```
// func_3.dart
// Required positional parameters in Dart functions
int cubeVolume(int side) {
  return side * side * side;
}

void printHero(String name, String quirk) {
  print('$name has the quirk $quirk.');
}

void main() {
  // parameter is required
  print(cubeVolume(3));
  // both parameters are required
  printHero('Tanjiro', 'Water Breathing');
  printHero('Zenitsu', 'Thunder Breathing');
  printHero('Inosuke', 'Beast Breathing');
}
```

Optional positional parameters

Optional positional parameters are enclosed in square brackets `[]` and are optional. They can have default values, as shown in the following code example:

```
// func_4.dart
// Function with optional positional parameters in Dart
int power(int base, [int exponent = 2]) {
  int result = 1;
  for (int i = 0; i < exponent; i++) {
    result *= base;
  }
  return result;
}

void main() {
  print('2^2: ${power(2)}');
  print('2^3: ${power(2, 3)}');
  print('2^4: ${power(2, 4)}');
  var ans = power(10, 4);
```

```
    print('ans is $ans');
}
```

Named parameters

Named parameters are optional by default and can be made required using the required keyword. They are enclosed in curly braces **{}**, as shown in the following code:

```
// func_5.dart
// Named parameters in Dart functions
void printCharacter({required String name, String? heroName}) {
  // Datatype? makes the parameter optional
  if (heroName != null) {
    print('$name also known as $heroName.');
  } else {
    print('$name is not a hero.');
  }
}

void main() {
  printCharacter(name: 'Tony Stark', heroName: 'Ironman');
  // order can be changed
  printCharacter(heroName: 'Captain America', name: 'Steve Rogers');
  printCharacter(name: 'Odin');
  printCharacter(name: 'Loki', heroName: 'God of Mischief');
  printCharacter(name: 'Nick Fury');
}
```

Shorthand functions

For functions with a single statement, Dart provides shorthand syntax using the **=>** (fat arrow) operator. You can define a function with a function (nested function) in dart as shown in following code:

```
// func_6.dart
// Shorthand syntax for defining functions in Dart

void main() {
  /*
  Defining a function using the shorthand syntax
  use the fat arrow (=>) to define the function body
```

```
    no need to use the curly braces and return keyword
    */
    void shout(String message) => print("${message.toUpperCase()}!");
    void whisper(String message) => print("${message.toLowerCase()}");
    int power(int base, [int exponent = 2]) => base * exponent;

    // calling the functions directly
    shout("Plus Ultra!");
    whisper("Plus Ultra!");
    print('2^3: ${power(2, 3)}');
    print('2^4: ${power(2, 4)}');
}
```

Anonymous functions

Dart supports anonymous functions, often used in callbacks or where a function is required temporarily. These are functions without a name, also known as **lambda functions** or **closures**.

They are used when you need a function for a short period of time. They are defined using the fat arrow (=>) syntax. The syntax is as follows:

```
var functionName = (parameters) {
  // function body
};
```

Anonymous functions are useful when you need to pass a function as an argument to another function (callback function). Take a look at the functions in the following code:

```
// func_7.dart
// Anonymous functions in Dart

void main() {
  // Anonymous function with no parameters
  var add = (int a, int b) {
    return a + b;
  };
  print(add(2, 3));

  // Anonymous function with parameters
  var multiply = (int a, int b) => a * b;
  print(multiply(2, 3));
```

```

  // Anonymous function with no return type
  var greet = () {
    print('Hello, World!');
  };
  greet();
}
```

Lexical scope

Lexical scope refers to the region in the source code where a variable is defined and accessible. In Dart, variables are accessible within the block or function in which they are defined, and in any nested blocks or functions. This means that inner functions have access to variables declared in their outer functions, as shown in the following code:

```
// lexical_scope.dart
// Lexical scope in Dart
void main() {
  var outerVar = 'I am an outer variable';

  void innerFunction() {
    var innerVar = 'I am an inner variable';
    print(outerVar); // Accessing outer variable
    print(innerVar); // Accessing inner variable
  }

  innerFunction();
  // print(innerVar); // Error: innerVar is not accessible here
}
```

In the preceding example:

- **outerVar** is accessible inside **innerFunction** because of lexical scoping.
- **innerVar** is not accessible outside **innerFunction**.

Lexical closures

A closure is a function object that has access to variables in its lexical scope, even when the function is used outside of its original scope. Closures capture and remember the variables from their lexical context, as shown in the following code:

```
// lexical_closure.dart
// Closure in Dart
Function createAdder(int addend) {
  return (int value) => value + addend;
}

void main() {
  var add5 = createAdder(5);
  var add10 = createAdder(10);

  print(add5(2)); // 7
  print(add10(2)); // 12
}
```

In the preceding example:

- **createAdder** returns a function that adds a given number (**addend**) to its argument (**value**).
- The returned function is a closure that captures the addend variable from its lexical scope.
- When **add5** and **add10** are called, they retain the value of addend that was in scope when they were created

Tear-offs

A tear-off refers to passing a function as a value without calling it. In Dart, you can pass a reference to a function directly to other functions or store it in variables. This is useful for callbacks or event handlers, as shown in the following figure:

```
// tear_offs.dart

// Tear off example in Dart
void shout(String message) {
  print(message.toUpperCase());
}

void main() {
  var heroes = ['Katara', 'Aang', 'Sokka', 'Toph', 'Zuko'];
  /*
  Using a tear-off, no parentheses are needed
  the forEach method expects a function that
```

```
    takes a single argument as String
      */
    heroes.forEach(shout);
  }
```

In this example, **`shout`** is passed as a function reference to **`forEach`** without invoking it. **`forEach`** calls shout for each element in the heroes list.

Let us combine these concepts with the following comprehensive example:

```
// final_func.dart
// A comprehensive example of closures in Dart
Function createGreeter(String greeting) {
  return (String name) {
    var fullGreeting = '$greeting, $name!';
    print(fullGreeting);
  };
}

void main() {
// greetHero and greetVillain are closures
  var greetHero = createGreeter('👋 Hello›);
  greetHero('Dalinar');
  greetHero("Kaladin");
  greetHero("Adolin");
  var greetVillain = createGreeter('🥊Get lost');
  greetVillain('Sadeas');
  greetVillain('Moash');
}
```

With this your introduction to functions is complete, but writing more practice will help you get proficient in functions.

Mini project: food ordering program

In this mini project we want users to select food items and quantity. Then, the program will calculate the total cost, and displays the order summary. The code will be modular and is broken down into following functions:

- **displayMenu function**: Displays the food menu with prices and a confirmation option.
- **getUserChoice function**: Prompts the user to enter their menu choice (a number between one and five).

- **getQuantity function**: Prompts the user to enter the quantity of the chosen item.
- **calculateCost function**: Calculates the total cost of the selected item based on the choice and quantity.
- **displayOrderSummary function**: Displays the order summary, including item names, quantities, individual costs, and total cost.
- **The main function**: The main function orchestrates the overall flow of the program:
    - Displays the menu.
    - Gets user choices and quantities.
    - Calculates the costs and adds them to the order lists.
    - Displays the order summary and a thank you message upon order confirmation.

Create a new Dart file in the IDE and name it as **`food_ordering.dart`** and then write the following code:

```
import 'dart:io';

// Function to display the menu
void displayMenu() {
  print("Welcome to the Food Ordering System!");
  print("Here is our menu:");
  print("1. Paneer Butter Masala - ₹250");
  print("2. Chicken Biryani - ₹200");
  print("3. Veg Pulao - ₹150");
  print("4. Masala Dosa - ₹100");
  print("5. Confirm Order");
}

// Function to get the user's choice
int getUserChoice() {
  print("Enter your choice (1-5):");
  int choice = int.parse(stdin.readLineSync()!);
  return choice;
}

// Function to get the quantity of the chosen item
int getQuantity() {
  print("Enter the quantity:");
  int quantity = int.parse(stdin.readLineSync()!);
```

```
    return quantity;
  }

  // Function to calculate the cost of the selected item
  int calculateCost(int choice, int quantity) {
    int cost = 0;
    switch (choice) {
      case 1:
        cost = 250 * quantity;
        break;
      case 2:
        cost = 200 * quantity;
        break;
      case 3:
        cost = 150 * quantity;
        break;
      case 4:
        cost = 100 * quantity;
        break;
      default:
        print("Invalid choice.");
    }
    return cost;
  }

  // Function to display the order summary
  void displayOrderSummary(List<String> items, List<int> quanti-
  ties, List<int> costs) {
    print("\nOrder Summary:");
    int totalCost = 0;
    for (int i = 0; i < items.length; i++) {
      print("${quantities[i]} x ${items[i]} = ₹${costs[i]}");
      totalCost += costs[i];
    }
    print("Total Cost: ₹$totalCost");
  }

  // Main function
```

```
void main() {
  List<String> orderedItems = [];
  List<int> orderedQuantities = [];
  List<int> orderedCosts = [];

  while (true) {
    displayMenu();
    int choice = getUserChoice();
    if (choice == 5) {
      break;
    }

    int quantity = getQuantity();
    int cost = calculateCost(choice, quantity);

    if (cost > 0) {
      String itemName;
      switch (choice) {
        case 1:
          itemName = "Paneer Butter Masala";
          break;
        case 2:
          itemName = "Chicken Biryani";
          break;
        case 3:
          itemName = "Veg Pulao";
          break;
        case 4:
          itemName = "Masala Dosa";
          break;
        default:
          itemName = "Unknown Item";
      }

      orderedItems.add(itemName);
      orderedQuantities.add(quantity);
      orderedCosts.add(cost);

```

```
        print("Added $quantity x $itemName to your order. Cost: ₹$cost\n");
      }
    }

    print("Order Placed Successfully!");
    displayOrderSummary(orderedItems, orderedQuantities, orderedCosts);
    print("Thank you for your order!");
  }
```

After writing the program, run is with the Shift+F10, and the result should be displayed in the console(terminal), a menu should display all food items, and you have to enter a number to select the item. Try all options to understand the working of code.

Conclusion

In this chapter, we have explored several core concepts in Dart, which is a powerful and flexible language designed for modern app development. We started with the basics of Dart syntax, understanding how to write and run simple programs. We covered essential elements like the main() function, variables, control flow statements, and functions, illustrating how each component works with practical examples. The chapter also provided a detailed explanation of functions, including return values, named parameters, optional positional parameters, shorthand functions, and more advanced concepts like lexical scope, closures, and tear-offs. Through these topics, we learned how Dart treats functions as first-class objects, allowing for a high degree of flexibility and functionality in programming.

The next chapter deals with concepts like object-oriented principals, asynchronous and synchronous code in dart, which is necessary to understand before you starting making projects in dart and flutter.

Points to remember

- Dart is an object-oriented language designed for modern app development.
- The main() function is the entry point of Dart programs, where execution begins.
- Null safety in Dart prevents runtime errors by enforcing non-nullable types.
- Functions in Dart are first-class objects, allowing them to be assigned to variables and passed as arguments.
- Dart supports various types of parameters: required positional, named, and optional positional.
- Lexical scope in Dart determines the visibility and accessibility of variables.

- Lexical closures enable functions to access variables from their enclosing scope even after the enclosing function has finished execution.
- Dart's string interpolation simplifies combining variables and strings within text.
- Loops like for, while, and do-while provide efficient ways to iterate over data.
- Dart's modular approach with imports and libraries enhances code organization and reusability.

Multiple choice questions

1. **Entry point of every Dart application**:
   a. start()
   b. launch()
   c. main()
   d. execute()

2. **Which keyword is used to declare a nullable type in Dart's null safety**:
   a. nullable
   b. nonNull
   c. ?
   d. !

3. **How are Dart functions treated in terms of their type?**
   a. They are instances of the function type.
   b. They have no specific type.
   c. They are treated as dynamic types.
   d. They are instances of the void type.

4. **What does Dart use for string interpolation?**
   a. { }
   b. [ ]
   c. ( )
   d. < >

5. **Which Dart feature ensures variables are initialized before use and prevents null dereference errors at compile time?**
    a. String interpolation
    b. Type inference
    c. Lexical closures
    d. Null safety

Answer

1	c
2	c
3	a
4	d
5	d

Questions

1. Write a Dart function calculateBMI that takes two parameters: weight (in kilograms) and height (in meters). Calculate the BMI using the formula: BMI = weight / (height * height).
2. Create a Dart function printEvenNumbers that takes an integer parameter n. Print all even numbers from 1 to n (inclusive). Use a for loop to iterate through the numbers.
3. Create a Dart function countVowels that takes a String parameter str and returns the number of vowels (a, e, i, o, u) in the string. Ignore case sensitivity.
4. Convert all the functions that have static value for variable and change it into user input based using stdin.readLineSync() function.

Key terms

- **Dart**: A modern, object-oriented programming language developed by Google.
- **Variables**: Named storage locations used to store data values in Dart.
- **Functions**: Blocks of code that perform a specific task and can be reused.
- **Control Flow**: Techniques for altering the flow of program execution, such as if, else, for, while, do-while, and switch.
- **Null Safety**: Dart's feature that prevents null reference errors at runtime.

- **Lexical Scope**: The scope of variables determined by their location in the source code.
- **Closures**: Functions that can capture variables from their lexical scope.
- **String Interpolation**: Embedding expressions inside string literals to produce dynamic strings.
- **Named Parameters**: Parameters passed to a function by name, enhancing clarity and flexibility.
- **Optional Parameters**: Parameters that can be omitted when calling a function, either positional or named.

CHAPTER 2
Advanced Dart Programming Techniques

Introduction

As you advance in your journey with Dart, mastering the language's more sophisticated features becomes essential for developing robust and scalable Flutter applications. In this chapter, we explore advanced Dart programming techniques that are essential for developing robust Flutter applications. You will explore **object-oriented programming (OOP)** principles such as classes, objects, inheritance, and polymorphism, which are crucial for maintaining clean and scalable code. The chapter also covers asynchronous programming with Futures and Streams, highlighting the importance of handling asynchronous tasks efficiently. Error handling and exceptions are also discussed to ensure your applications remain reliable.

Structure

This chapter covers the following topics:

- Object-oriented programming in Dart
- Classes and objects
- Inheritance and polymorphism
- Asynchronous programming

- Comparing synchronous and asynchronous code in Dart
- Error handling and exceptions
- Mini project: Fortune Cookie Oracle

Objectives

By the end of *Chapter 2, Advanced Dart Programming Techniques*, you will have a comprehensive understanding of advanced Dart programming techniques, including object-oriented programming principles, the implementation of classes, objects, inheritance, and polymorphism. You will also gain proficiency in asynchronous programming using Future and Stream, understand the differences between synchronous and asynchronous code, and be adept at handling errors and exceptions. Additionally, you'll apply these concepts in a practical mini-project.

Object-oriented programming in Dart

Dart, like many modern programming languages, supports OOP as one of its core paradigms. OOP is a powerful way to structure and manage your code, especially as projects grow in complexity. By organizing your code around objects—entities that combine data and behavior—OOP allows you to create more modular, reusable, and scalable applications. In this section, we will explore the key concepts of OOP in Dart and understand how these principles can be applied to build robust and maintainable code.

Need for object-oriented programming

While Dart supports first-class functions, making it highly flexible for functional programming paradigms, OOP remains crucial for several reasons, such as:

- **Modularity**: OOP allows for breaking down complex problems into smaller, more manageable objects, each encapsulating its own data and behavior. This modularity makes code easier to understand, maintain, and debug.
- **Reusability**: Through inheritance and polymorphism, OOP promotes the reuse of existing code. By creating a base class with common functionality, you can extend and customize behavior in derived classes without rewriting code.
- **Abstraction**: OOP helps in managing complexity by allowing you to abstract and encapsulate details. You can expose only necessary parts of an object's interface, hiding the internal workings, which simplifies interactions and reduces the risk of errors.
- **Design patterns**: Many design patterns, which provide solutions to common software design problems, are based on OOP principles. Utilizing these patterns can lead to more robust and maintainable code.

- **Scalability**: OOP is particularly useful in large codebases and team environments, where different team members can work on separate objects or components independently, facilitating collaboration and parallel development.
- **Community and ecosystem**: Most frameworks, libraries, and tools in Dart and Flutter are designed with OOP in mind. Understanding OOP principles is essential to effectively use and integrate these resources.

The following figure summarizes the benefits of OOP:

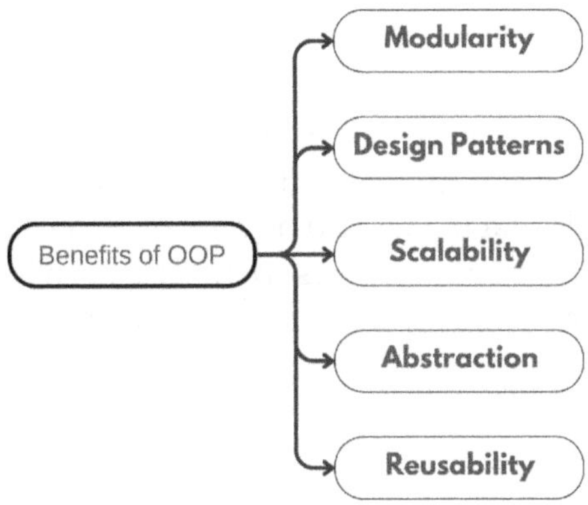

Figure 2.1: *Benefits of OOP*

While first-class functions and functional programming offer powerful ways to write concise and expressive code, combining these with OOP principles allows developers to leverage the strengths of both paradigms, resulting in more versatile and maintainable applications. In the next section you will learn about the principles of OOP.

Understanding the principles of OOP

OOP is like organizing a game world where each character (object) has its own unique abilities (methods) and characteristics (properties). In Dart, OOP helps you manage your code by breaking down complex problems into smaller, more manageable parts using **classes** and **objects**. Let us explore the key principles of OOP.

The following are the principles of OOP:

- Encapsulation
- Inheritance
- Polymorphism
- Abstraction

Encapsulation

Encapsulation is like having a magical creature, say a dragon, that keeps its treasure (data) hidden in a cave (class). Only the dragon knows how to guard and use its treasure. In programming, this means an object's data is kept safe inside a class, and only specific functions (methods) can access or modify it. This ensures that the inner workings of an object are hidden from the outside world, just like a dragon's treasure is hidden from the villagers.

Inheritance

Inheritance is like a wizard passing down his magical powers to his apprentice. The apprentice learns all the spells (methods) and characteristics (properties) from the wizard but can also learn new spells that the wizard never knew. In Dart, a class (child) can inherit the properties and methods of another class (parent). This allows for the creation of new classes that reuse and extend existing code, just like an apprentice wizard building on the knowledge of their master.

Polymorphism

Polymorphism is like a shape-shifting sorcerer who can take on multiple forms. Imagine a creature that can be a dragon in one moment and a phoenix in the next. In programming, polymorphism allows objects to be treated as instances of their parent class, even though they may have different forms (derived classes). This means a single function can work with different types of objects, just like a spell that works on both dragons and phoenixes.

Abstraction

Abstraction is like a magical map that shows only the important landmarks without detailing every tree and rock. It helps you focus on the big picture without getting lost in the details. In programming, abstraction means creating simple, easy-to-understand interfaces for more complex code. This is done by defining abstract classes and methods that outline what needs to be done, without specifying how. It is like a map guiding you to the treasure without revealing every step of the journey.

By understanding these principles—encapsulation, inheritance, polymorphism, and abstraction—you can master OOP in Dart, creating code that is more organized, reusable, and easier to maintain. To use these principles, you must first know how to create classes and objects in Dart.

Classes and objects

In Dart, classes and objects are the building blocks of OOP. Open IntelliJ IDEA and create a new project. Click on the hamburger icon on top left and then select **New** | **Project** and press Enter. Select Dart project and name it **dart-advanced**, and hit create. A popup might ask you to where to open the new project, select either **This window** or **New Window** to launch the project. When the project is ready, you are ready to dive into classes and objects concept.

Classes

A class is like a blueprint for creating objects. It defines a type of object by encapsulating data for the object (fields) and methods to manipulate that data. Think of a class as a character template in a *story*. For example, we can create a class called Ninja to represent ninjas. Create a new Dart file in the IDE, and add the following code:

```
// class_ex1.dart
class Ninja {
  // Fields - properties of the class
  String name;
  String village;
  int level;

  // Constructor - helps to initialize the fields
  Ninja(this.name, this.village, this.level);

  // Method - helps to show the details of the ninja
  void showDetails() {
    print('Ninja: $name, Village: $village, Level: $level');
  }
}

void main() {
  // Creating an object of the class
  Ninja naruto = Ninja('Naruto Uzumaki', 'Leaf', 7);
  Ninja sasuke = Ninja('Sasuke Uchiha', 'Leaf', 10);
  naruto.showDetails();
  Sasuke.showDetails();
}
```

The preceding class has a lot of parts, let us break them down.

Fields

Fields are variables that belong to a class. They hold the data or state of an object. In our Ninja class, **`name`**, **`village`**, and **`level`** are fields. It can be of two types:

- **Instance fields**: These fields belong to a specific instance(object) of a class. Each object has its own copy of instance fields.
- **Static fields**: These fields belong to the class itself rather than any specific instance. They are shared among all instances of the class.

Create a new file to test the following code:

```
// fields.dart

class Ninja {
  // Instance fields
  String name;
  String village;

  // Static field
  static int ninjaCount = 0;

  Ninja(this.name, this.village) {
    ninjaCount++; // Increment ninja count whenever a new ninja is created
  }
}

void main() {
  Ninja naruto = Ninja(‘Naruto Uzumaki’, ‘Leaf’);
  Ninja sasuke = Ninja(‘Sasuke Uchiha’, ‘Leaf’);
  Ninja kakashi = Ninja(‘Kakashi Hatake’, ‘Leaf’);

  print('Ninja Count: ${Ninja.ninjaCount}'); // Output: Ninja Count: 3
}
```

In the preceding example, we have a class **`Ninja`** with two instance fields **`name`** and **`village`**, and a static field **`ninjaCount`**. The **`ninjaCount`** field is incremented whenever a new ninja object is created. We access the static field using the class name **`Ninja.ninjaCount`**.

Note: In Dart, the underscore (_) is used to indicate that a field or method is private to its library. This means that the field or method is not accessible from outside the library in which it is declared.

Constructors

Constructors are special methods used to create and initialize objects. They have the same name as the class and are called automatically when an object is created. Constructors set the initial values for the fields of an object. In our first example above, **`Ninja(this.name, this.village, this.level)`** is a constructor.

Methods

Methods are functions defined within a class that describe the behaviors or actions of the objects. In games, books or anime, methods are like the abilities or moves of a character, such as casting a spell or performing a special attack.

Objects

Objects are instances of classes. They are the concrete realizations of the blueprints defined by classes. In books and shows, objects are like individual characters created from character templates. Each object can have its own unique state and behavior based on the class it is instantiated from.

The following are the types of objects in Dart:

- Instance objects
- Singleton objects
- Anonymous objects

Instance objects

These are the most common type of objects. Each instance object is created using the new keyword (optional in Dart) and represents a unique instance of a class. Each object has its own set of fields and methods. Test the following code:

```
// instance_object.dart

class Hero {
  String name;
  String ability;

  Hero(this.name, this.ability);

  void showAbility() {
    print('$name uses $ability.');
  }
```

```
}

void main() {
  // Creating instance objects
  Hero goku = Hero('Goku', 'Kamehameha');
  Hero luffy = Hero('Luffy', 'Gum-Gum Pistol');

  goku.showAbility(); // Output: Goku uses Kamehameha.
  luffy.showAbility(); // Output: Luffy uses Gum-Gum Pistol.
}
```

In the preceding code snippet, we have created a class **Hero** with fields **name** and **ability**. We have also defined a constructor to initialize the fields and a method **showAbility()** to display the hero's ability. Finally, we have created two instances(objects) inside the **main()** function with the help of **Hero** class.

Singleton objects

A Singleton object is a design pattern that restricts the instantiation of a class to a single instance. This is useful when exactly one object is needed to coordinate actions across the system. It is used for advanced use cases.

The Singleton pattern is commonly employed in scenarios where a single, consistent instance is essential for the entire application. Here are a few typical use cases:

- **Configuration manager**: To manage application settings and ensure consistent access to configurations across the application.
- **Database connection**: To manage a single connection to the database, avoiding the overhead of multiple connections.
- **Logging service**: To handle logging throughout the application with a single point of access.
- **Cache manager**: To manage a cache of frequently accessed data with a single instance.

Try the following example in IDE:

```
// singleton.dart
class SettingsManager {
  // Private constructor
  SettingsManager._privateConstructor();

  // Static field to hold the single instance
```

```
  static final SettingsManager _instance = SettingsManager._privateConstructor();

  // Factory constructor to return the single instance
  factory SettingsManager() {
    return _instance;
  }

  // A map to hold settings as key-value pairs
  final Map<String, String> _settings = {};

  // Method to update a setting
  void setSetting(String key, String value) {
    _settings[key] = value;
  }

  // Method to retrieve a setting
  String? getSetting(String key) {
    return _settings[key];
  }
}

void main() {
  // Fetching the Singleton instance
  SettingsManager manager1 = SettingsManager();

  // Setting a value using the first reference
  manager1.setSetting('theme', 'dark');

  // Fetching the Singleton instance again (same instance)
  SettingsManager manager2 = SettingsManager();

  // Retrieving the value using the second reference
  print(manager2.getSetting('theme')); // Output: dark

  // Verifying both references point to the same instance
  print(manager1 == manager2); // Output: true
}
```

In the preceding code, demonstrates the Singleton design pattern in Dart using a **SettingsManager** class to manage application settings. A private constructor ensures that only one instance of the class can exist, and a static field holds this single instance. The factory constructor always returns the same instance, maintaining the Singleton property. The class includes a private map **_settings** to store key-value pairs for settings, along with methods **setSetting()** and **getSetting()** to update and retrieve settings, respectively. In the main function, two references to **SettingsManager** (**manager1** and **manager2**) are created, both pointing to the same instance. This is demonstrated by updating a setting using one reference and fetching it using the other, as well as confirming that both references are equal, showcasing the utility and consistency of the Singleton pattern.

Object lifecycle

In Dart, objects of a class follow three-stage life:

- **Creation**: Objects are created using constructors defined in their class.
- **Usage**: Objects are used to call methods and access fields defined in their class.
- **Destruction**: In Dart, objects are automatically garbage collected when they are no longer in use.

Access modifiers

In Dart, access modifiers control the visibility and accessibility of class members (fields and methods). By default, class members are **public**, meaning they can be accessed from anywhere, both inside and outside their defining library. For example, in a **Car** class, a public field **brand** can be set to **Toyota** and a public method **start()** can be called to initiate the car's engine, showcasing unrestricted access across the application.

Dart also supports private members, which are denoted by prefixing an **underscore (_)** before the member's identifier. Private members can only be accessed within the same Dart library where they are defined. For instance, a private field **_engineType** in a **Car** class can store sensitive engine details, and a private method **_startEngine()** can be used internally to start the engine using **_engineType**. These private members ensure that implementation details are hidden from outside code, enhancing encapsulation and reducing accidental misuse.

Note: Unlike some other programming languages, Dart does not have a protected access modifier.

Types of constructors and constructor overloading

Different programming problems may require different solutions; thus, Dart provides us four different types of constructors.

Default constructor

A default constructor has no parameters and is implicitly provided if no other constructors are defined, as shown in the following code:

```
class DefaultExample {
  DefaultExample() {
    print('Default constructor called');
  }
}
```

Parameterized constructor

A parameterized constructor takes arguments to initialize fields, as shown in the following code:

```
class ParameterizedExample {
  String name;
  int age;

  ParameterizedExample(this.name, this.age);

  void showDetails() {
    print('Name: $name, Age: $age');
  }
}
```

Named constructor

Named constructors allow you to create multiple constructors with different names, as shown in the following code:

```
class NamedExample {
  String name;
  int age = 0; // Default value

  NamedExample(this.name, this.age);

  // Named constructor
  NamedExample.withoutAge(this.name);

  void showDetails() {
```

```
      print('Name: $name, Age: $age');
    }
  }
```

Let us combine the preceding example into one code example:

```
// constructors.dart
// default, parameterized, and named constructors
class DefaultExample {
  DefaultExample() {
    print('Default constructor called');
  }
}

class ParameterizedExample {
  String name;
  int age;

  ParameterizedExample(this.name, this.age);

  void showDetails() {
    print('Name: $name, Age: $age');
  }
}

class NamedExample {
  String name;
  int age = 0; // Default value

  NamedExample(this.name, this.age);

  // Named constructor
  NamedExample.withoutAge(this.name);

  void showDetails() {
    print('Name: $name, Age: $age');
  }
}

```

```
void main() {
  // Creating objects of the classes
  DefaultExample example1 = DefaultExample();

  ParameterizedExample example2 = ParameterizedExample('Alice', 25);
  example2.showDetails();

  NamedExample example3 = NamedExample('Bob', 30);
  NamedExample example4 = NamedExample.withoutAge('Charlie');

  example3.showDetails();
  example4.showDetails();
}
```

Factory constructor

A factory constructor is a special type of constructor that can return an instance of the class, potentially from a cache, or create a new instance as needed. You can test the following code:

```
// factory_constructor.dart
// a class Circle with factory constructor
class Circle {
  double radius;

  // Private constructor
  Circle(this.radius);

  // Factory constructor to return an instance of Circle
  factory Circle.fromDiameter(double diameter) {
    return Circle(diameter / 2);
  }

  // Getter to calculate the area of the circle
  double get area => 3.14 * radius * radius;
}

void main() {
  Circle circle1 = Circle(5);
```

```
    // Using factory constructor to create a circle from diameter
    Circle circle2 = Circle.fromDiameter(10);

    print('Area of circle1: ${circle1.area}');
    print('Area of circle2: ${circle2.area}');
  }
```

In the preceding code, we have a class **Circle** with a private constructor **Circle(this.radius)** and a factory constructor **Circle.fromDiameter(double diameter)**. The factory constructor returns an instance of Circle based on the diameter provided. We create two instances **circle1** and **circle2** using the regular constructor and the factory constructor, respectively. Both instances have the same area, as the factory constructor calculates the radius based on the diameter provided. The output of the areas of **circle1** and **circle2** is 78.5, confirming that the factory constructor is working as expected.

Constructor overloading

In many programming languages, constructor overloading allows a class to have multiple constructors with different parameter lists. However, Dart does not support traditional constructor overloading directly. Instead, Dart uses named constructors and optional parameters to achieve similar functionality. This approach allows you to define multiple constructors with different parameter lists and initializations, similar to traditional constructor overloading in other programming languages. Use the following code to test:

```
// overloading.dart
// positional parameters and named parameters for overloading
class PositionalEx {
  String name;
  int age;

  PositionalEx(this.name, [this.age = 10]);

  void showDetails() {
    print('Name: $name, Age: $age');
  }
}

class NamedParamEx {
  String name;
  int age;

```

```
  // required keyword is used to make the parameter mandatory
  NamedParamEx({required this.name, this.age = 10});

  void showDetails() {
    print('Name: $name, Age: $age');
  }
}

void main() {
  PositionalEx example1 = PositionalEx('Kakashi', 30);
  PositionalEx example2 = PositionalEx('Naruto');
  example1.showDetails();
  example2.showDetails();

  NamedParamEx example3 = NamedParamEx(name: 'Sasuke', age: 12);
  NamedParamEx example4 = NamedParamEx(name: 'Sakura');

  example3.showDetails();
  example4.showDetails();
}
```

Types of methods

In Dart, class methods are categorized based on their usage and characteristics. The primary types are discussed in the next sections.

Instance methods

Instance methods operate on instances of a class. They can access instance variables and other instance methods. Try the following example:

```
// instance_methods.dart
// A class Book with instance methods
class Book {
  String title;
  String author;

  Book(this.title, this.author);

  // Instance method to display book details
```

```
    void displayBookDetails() {
      print('Title: $title');
      print('Author: $author');
    }
  }

  void main() {
    Book bookA = Book('The Way of Kings', 'Brandon Sanderson');
    bookA.displayBookDetails();
  }
```

Static methods

Static methods are called on the class itself rather than on instances of the class. They cannot access instance variables or instance methods directly but can access static variables and static methods. The following example shows the use of static method:

```
// static_methods.dart
// A class Alchemist with a static method
class Alchemist {
  String name;
  String specialty;

  Alchemist(this.name, this.specialty);

  // Instance method
  void transmute() {
    print('$name performs $specialty transmutation.');
  }

  // Static method
  static void study() {
    print('Studying alchemy principles...');
  }
}

void main() {
  Alchemist.study(); // called without creating an instance
  Alchemist edward = Alchemist('Edward Elric', 'Metal');
```

```
    edward.transmute();
  }
```

Getter methods

Getter methods are used to access the value of private variables. They allow controlled access to instance variables. Test the following example:

```
// getters.dart
class Circle {
  // Private property cant be accessed directly
  double _radius;

  Circle(this._radius);

  // Getter for _radius
  double get radius => _radius;
}

void main() {
  Circle circle = Circle(5.0);
  print(circle.radius); // Output: 5.0
}
```

Setter methods

Setter methods are used to modify the value of private variables. They allow controlled modification of instance variables, often with validation. Create the following example which is extension of previous example:

```
// setters.dart
// A class Circle with a setter for the radius property
class Circle {
  double _radius;

  Circle(this._radius);

  // Getter for _radius
  double get radius => _radius;

  // validates and sets the new radius
  set radius(double newRadius) {
```

```
    if (newRadius > 0) {
      _radius = newRadius;
    } else {
      print('Radius must be positive.');
    }
  }
}

void main() {
  Circle circle = Circle(5.0);
  circle.radius = 10.0; // Set the new radius
  print(circle.radius);
  circle.radius = -5.0; // Attempt to set an invalid radius
}
```

Class modifiers

Class modifiers in Dart are keywords that alter the behavior and accessibility of classes. They define how the class and its members are used within the code. Here are the primary class modifiers in Dart:

- **No modifier**: Allows unrestricted permission to construct or subtype from any library. It is the default.
- **Abstract**: Defines a class that does not require a full, concrete implementation of its entire interface. It is used when you want a class to be subclassed but not instantiated. Try the following code example:

```
// modifier_abstract.dart
abstract class Food {
  void prepare(); // Abstract method
}

class Pizza extends Food {
  @override
  void prepare() {
    print("Preparing pizza dough and adding toppings");
  }
}

class Salad implements Food {
```

```
    @override
    void prepare() {
      print("Chopping vegetables and adding dressing");
    }
  }
```

Note: Abstract classes cab be subclassed using extend or implement keyword

- **base**: Enforces inheritance of a class or mixins implementation. Used when you want to ensure certain guarantees about a class's implementation. A base class disallows implementation outside of its own library. Mixins will be discussed in the next section. The implementation of base class is given as follows:

```
// modifier_base.dart

// Base class ensuring certain methods are always inherited
base class Food {
  void eat() {
    print("Eating food");
  }
}

// Subclass implementing the base class
base class Pasta extends Food {
  void prepare() {
    print("Boiling pasta and adding sauce");
  }
}

void main() {
  var pasta = Pasta();
  pasta.prepare();
  pasta.eat();
}
```

Note: You must mark any class which implements or extends a base class as base, final, or sealed. This prevents outside libraries from breaking the base class guarantees.

- **interface**: Defines an interface that can be implemented but not extended outside its defining library. It is used when you want to provide a common interface without allowing inheritance. Try the following code for implementing an interface:

```dart
// modifier_interface.dart
interface class Food {
  void prepare() {}
}

class Burger implements Food {
  @override
  void prepare() {
    print("Grilling patty and adding toppings");
  }
}
```

- **final**: Prevents subtyping from a class outside of the current library. Used when you want to close the type hierarchy and prevent any subclasses, as demonstrated in the following example:

```dart
// modifier_final.dart

final class JunkFood {
  void prepare() {
    print("Opening packet and eating junk food");
  }
}

// can't extend final class outside the library
final class Chips extends JunkFood {
  @override
  void prepare() {
    print("Opening packet and eating chips");
  }
}
```

Note: Final classes can be extended or implemented within the same library. The final modifier encompasses the effects of base, and therefore any subclasses must also be marked base, final, or sealed.

- **sealed**: Creates a known and enumerable set of subtypes, allowing exhaustive checks in switch statements and mappings as well. It is used when you want to define a closed set of subclasses. The following code example demonstrates this:

```
// modifier_sealed.dart

sealed class SeaFood {
  void prepare() {
    print("Cleaning and cooking seafood");
  }
}

class Fish extends SeaFood {
  @override
  void prepare() {
    print("Cleaning fish 🐟");
    print("Cooking fish 🐟");
    print("Serving fish 🍽️");
  }
}

void main() {
  // error can't instantiate directly
  // var seafood = SeaFood();
  var fish = Fish();
  fish.prepare();
}
```

Note: Sealed classes are implicitly abstract.

enums

enumerated types, often called **enumerations** or **enums**, are a special kind of class used to represent a fixed number of constant values. enums in Dart are automatically extended from the enum class and are sealed, meaning they cannot be subclassed, implemented, mixed in, or explicitly instantiated.

To declare a simple enumerated type, use the **enum** keyword followed by the list of values to be enumerated, shown as follows:

```
// enum_simple.dart
enum Screen{
  home,
  profile,
  settings
```

```
}

void main() {
  // Accessing enum values
  print(Screen.home);
  // Accessing enum name
  print(Screen.profile.name);
  // Accessing enum index
  print(Screen.settings.index);
  // Accessing all enum values
  print(Screen.values);
}
```

Dart allows for enhanced enum declarations where enums can have fields, methods, and constant constructors limited to a fixed number of known constant instances. The syntax is similar to normal classes but with additional requirements, mentioned as follows:

- Instance variables must be final.
- All generative constructors must be constant.
- Factory constructors can only return one of the fixed, known enum instances.
- No other class can be extended as enum is automatically extended.
- Overrides for **`index`**, **`hashCode`**, or the equality operator `==` are not allowed.
- A member named **`values`** cannot be declared in an enum.
- All instances of the enum must be declared at the beginning of the declaration, with at least one instance declared.

Try the following example:

```
// enum_advanced.dart
// Advanced enum example
enum Meal implements Comparable<Meal> {
  // enum values
  simple(burger: 199, fries: 50, drink: 100),
  premium(burger: 299, fries: 100, drink: 150),
  deluxe(burger: 399, fries: 150, drink: 200);

  // final fields
  final int burger;
  final int fries;
  final int drink;
```

```

  // Constructor
  const Meal({required this.burger, required this.fries, required this.drink});

  // Total cost of the order
  int get total => burger + fries + drink;

  // Compare orders based on total cost
  @override
  int compareTo(Meal other) => total.compareTo(other.total);
}

void main() {
  final orders = [Meal.simple, Meal.premium, Meal.deluxe];
  orders.sort();
  for (final order in orders) {
    print('$order, Total: \$${order.total}');
  }
}
```

In the preceding example, an advanced **`enum Meal`** is declared to represent different types of meal orders with varying costs. The enum has three instances: **`simple`**, **`premium`**, and **`deluxe`**, each initialized with specific costs for a burger, fries, and a drink. The **`Meal`** enum implements the **`Comparable`** interface, allowing instances to be compared based on the total cost of the meal, calculated as the sum of the burger, fries, and drink prices. The total cost is accessed through a getter method **`total()`**. The **`main`** function creates a list of meal orders and sorts them in ascending order of their total cost and displays them using loops.

To conclude, enums provide a powerful way to represent a fixed set of related values in Dart, making your code more readable and less error-prone.

Inheritance and polymorphism

Inheritance and polymorphism are key principles of OOP that enable code reusability and flexibility. In this section, we will explore these concepts in detail and illustrate them with examples.

Inheritance

Inheritance allows a class to inherit properties and methods from another class. The class that inherits is called the **subclass** (or derived class), and the class being inherited from is called the **superclass** (or base class). Consider a fantasy world with magical creatures, where we have a base class **`Creature`** and subclasses like **`Elf`**, **`Orc`** and **`Dragon`**. We will create a **`Creature`** class and then create **`Elf`**, **`Orc`** and **`Dragon`** classes which will inherit from **`Creature`** class. All subclasses will inherit the properties and methods of the superclass. However, they can also have their own properties and methods. This allows us to reuse the code and also add new functionality to the subclasses. Create a new file and write the following code:

```
// Inheritance.dart
// Program to demonstrate inheritance in Dart
class Creature {
  String name;
  int health;

  Creature(this.name, this.health);

  void attack() {
    print('🤜 $name attacks!›);
  }
}
// <subclass> extends <superclass>
class Elf extends Creature {
  String weapon;

  Elf(String name, int health, this.weapon) : super(name, health);

  void useMagic() {
    print('$name uses magic with $weapon.');
  }
}

class Orc extends Creature {
  String strength;

  Orc(String name, int health, this.strength) : super(name, health);

```

```
  void smash() {
    print('$name smashes with strength of $strength.');
  }
}
class Dragon extends Creature {
  String fire;

  Dragon(String name, int health, this.fire) : super(name, health);

  void breatheFire() {
    print('$name breathes fire with $fire.');
  }
}

void main() {
  Elf legolas = Elf('Legolas', 100, '🏹 Bow and Arrow ‹);
  Orc azog = Orc('Azog', 120, '💪 Brute Force›);
  // var is used to declare a variable without specifying its type
  var smaug = Dragon('Smaug', 500, '🔥 Fire›);
  legolas.attack();
  legolas.useMagic();

  azog.attack();
  azog.smash();

  smaug.attack();
  smaug.breatheFire();
}
```

super keyword in Dart

The **super** keyword in Dart is used to refer to the superclass of a class. It allows a subclass to access and call properties and methods, including constructors, defined in its superclass. This is particularly useful for method overriding and constructor chaining.

When a method in a subclass overrides a method in its superclass, the subclass can still call the superclass's version of the method using the **super** keyword.

Types of inheritance

The following are the types of inheritance:

- **Single inheritance**: Single inheritance is when a class inherits from one and only one superclass. This is the most common form of inheritance.
- **Multilevel inheritance**: Multilevel inheritance occurs when a class is derived from another derived class, forming a chain of inheritance.
- **Hierarchical inheritance**: Hierarchical inheritance is when multiple classes inherit from a single superclass. This creates a tree-like structure.
- **Multiple inheritance (using mixins)**: Dart, like many modern programming languages, avoids direct multiple inheritance to prevent complexities such as the diamond problem. The diamond problem occurs when a class inherits from two parent classes that share a common base class, leading to ambiguity about which version of an inherited method or property to use. To address this limitation effectively, Dart offers mixins—a powerful feature that provides a way for classes to inherit functionality from multiple sources without the challenges of traditional multiple inheritance. Mixins allow developers to reuse properties and methods across different classes in a controlled and predictable manner, ensuring clarity and safety in the codebase. This approach combines the flexibility of multiple inheritance with the simplicity of single inheritance, making it a robust solution for creating reusable and maintainable code.

Mixins

Mixins are a way of reusing a class's code in multiple class hierarchies. A mixin is a class that contains methods and properties for other classes to use. Unlike regular inheritance, mixins are used to add functionality to classes without being a direct parent class. This is particularly useful for sharing behavior among classes that do not share a common ancestor. Unlike normal inheritance, a mixin does not imply an **is-a** relationship but more of a **has-a** or **can-do** relationship. In *Brandon Sanderson's Mistborn* book series, characters can gain various powers from ingesting different metals. Let us use this idea to demonstrate mixins in Dart.

Defining mixins

Let us see how to create mixin in Dart. In the Mistborn book series, different metals grant different powers. We will create mixins for a few of these abilities, then create a base class and sub class with mixins, shown as follows:

```
// mixins.dart
// Mixins example in Dart
mixin Pewter {
```

```
  void enhanceStrength() {
    print('Strength enhanced with Pewter.');
  }
}

mixin Tin {
  void enhanceSenses() {
    print('Senses enhanced with Tin.');
  }
}

mixin Steel {
  void pushMetals() {
    print('Pushes metals with Steel.');
  }
}

mixin Iron {
  void pullMetals() {
    print('Pulls metals with Iron.');
  }
}

// Base class
class Allomancer {
  String name;

  Allomancer(this.name);

  void introduce() {
    print('I am $name, an Allomancer.');
  }
}

// `with` keyword is used to add mixins to a class
class Mistborn extends Allomancer with Pewter, Tin, Steel, Iron {
  Mistborn(String name) : super(name);
```

```

  @override
  void introduce() {
    print('I am $name, a Mistborn.');
  }
}

void main() {
  var vin = Mistborn('Vin');
  vin.introduce(); // Output: I am Vin, a Mistborn.
  vin.enhanceStrength(); // Output: Strength enhanced with Pewter.
  vin.enhanceSenses(); // Output: Senses enhanced with Tin.
  vin.pushMetals(); // Output: Pushes metals with Steel.
  vin.pullMetals(); // Output: Pulls metals with Iron.
}
```

Polymorphism

Polymorphism is a fundamental concept in OOP that allows objects to be treated as instances of their parent class rather than their actual class. It enables a single interface to represent different underlying data types. Polymorphism is crucial for designing flexible and scalable software systems.

Polymorphism in Dart can be broadly categorized into two types:

- **Compile-time polymorphism (static polymorphism)**: This type of polymorphism is achieved through method overloading. Dart does not support traditional method overloading directly, but it supports named constructors, which can be seen as a form of overloading.
- **Run-time polymorphism (dynamic polymorphism)**: This type of polymorphism is achieved through method overriding. It allows a subclass to provide a specific implementation of a method that is already defined in its superclass.

Compile-time polymorphism

Dart does not support method overloading, but you can achieve similar behavior using named constructors, as shown in the following example:

```
// ct_polymorphism.dart
// Compile-time polymorphism example in Dart
class Spell {
  String name;
```

```

  // Default constructor
  Spell(this.name);

  // 2 Named constructor
  Spell.fireball() : name = '🔥Fireball🔥';

  Spell.iceBlast() : name = '❄️  Ice Blast❄️  ';

  void cast() {
    print('Casting $name.');
  }
}

void main() {
  Spell fireSpell = Spell.fireball();
  Spell iceSpell = Spell.iceBlast();

  fireSpell.cast();
  iceSpell.cast();
}
```

Here, we have a class **`Spell`** with a default constructor and two named constructors, **`fireball`** and **`iceBlast`**. The **`cast()`** method prints the name of the spell being cast. it is called **compile-time polymorphism** because the method cast is resolved at compile time based on the object type.

Run-time polymorphism

Run-time polymorphism is achieved through method overriding. This allows a subclass to provide a specific implementation for a method that is already defined in its superclass. Let us use the world of Harry Potter to illustrate run-time polymorphism. Consider a base class **`MagicalCreature`** with a method speak. Subclasses like **`Phoenix`**, **`HouseElf`**, and **`Centaur`** will override the speak method:

```
// rt_polymorphism.dart
// Run-time polymorphism example in Dart

class MagicalCreature {
  String name;

```

```
  MagicalCreature(this.name);

  void speak() {
    print('$name makes a magical sound.');
  }
}

// Subclass 1
class Phoenix extends MagicalCreature {
  Phoenix(String name) : super(name);

  void speak() {
    print('$name sings a beautiful, haunting melody.');
  }
}

// Subclass 2
class HouseElf extends MagicalCreature {
  HouseElf(String name) : super(name);

  void speak() {
    print('$name says, "Master has given $name a sock!"');
  }
}

// Subclass 3
class Centaur extends MagicalCreature {
  Centaur(String name) : super(name);

  void speak() {
    print('$name says, "Mars is bright tonight."');
  }
}

void main() {
  // List of MagicalCreature objects
  List<MagicalCreature> creatures = [
```

```
      Phoenix('Fawkes'),
      HouseElf('Dobby'),
      Centaur('Firenze')
    ];

    for (var creature in creatures) {
      creature.speak();
    }
  }
```

Note: The @override annotation in Dart is used to indicate that a method in a subclass is intended to override a method in its superclass. This annotation serves several purposes that help improve code readability, maintainability, and error detection.

Interfaces

In Dart, interfaces are abstract classes that define a contract for classes to implement. They specify a set of methods and properties that implementing classes must provide. Interfaces in Dart enable code abstraction, polymorphism, and support for multiple inheritances through mixins.

Declaring interfaces

Interfaces in Dart are declared using **abstract classes**. An abstract class can have abstract methods (methods without implementation) that must be overridden by any class that implements the interface, shown as follows:

```
// Interface declaration
abstract class CanFly {
  void fly();
}

abstract class CanSwim {
  void swim();
}

abstract class CanWalk {
  void walk();
}
```

Abstract classes

Abstract classes in Dart are classes that cannot be instantiated directly. They are designed to serve as blueprints for other classes to inherit from and provide a way to define a common interface that multiple derived classes must implement. Abstract classes may contain both abstract methods (methods without implementation) and concrete methods (methods with implementation). Here is how an abstract class is defined in Dart:

Implementing interfaces

A class in Dart can implement one or more interfaces by providing implementations for all the methods declared in those interfaces. Interfaces allow objects of different classes to be treated uniformly through their common interface type, enabling polymorphic behavior. Interfaces can extend other interfaces, inheriting their method declarations. This allows for building more specific contracts based on existing ones. Let us demonstrate interfaces with an example inspired by animal behaviors:

```
// interface.dart
// A simple example of an interface in Dart

// Interface
abstract class CanMakeSound {
  void makeSound();
}

// Class implementing the interface
class Dog implements CanMakeSound {
  @override
  void makeSound() {
    print('Dog barks.');
  }
}

// Class implementing another interface
class Bird implements CanMakeSound {
  @override
  void makeSound() {
    print('Bird chirps.');
  }
}

```

```
void main() {
  Dog dog = Dog();
  Bird bird = Bird();

  dog.makeSound(); // Output: Dog barks.
  bird.makeSound(); // Output: Bird chirps.
}
```

Subtyping

Subtyping is a concept in programming languages, particularly in OOP, that defines a relationship between types where a value of one type can be substituted for a value of another related type. In Dart, subtyping plays a crucial role in type hierarchies, inheritance, and polymorphism.

In Dart, subtyping can be understood through the relationship between classes, interfaces, and their instances.

Types of subtyping in Dart

In Dart, subtyping manifests in several forms:

- **Class subtyping**: A subclass is a subtype of its superclass, inheriting its properties and methods.
- **Interface subtyping**: A class that implements an interface is a subtype of that interface, providing its own implementation of interface methods.
- **Subtype polymorphism**: Objects of subclasses and classes that implement interfaces can be used interchangeably with their supertypes, supporting polymorphic behavior.

Extension methods in Dart

Extension methods allow you to extend existing types in Dart, providing additional functionality without altering the original class. This feature is particularly useful when you cannot modify the source code of classes, such as those from third-party libraries or built-in types. To create an extension, you use the **`extension`** keyword followed by a name for the extension and the type you want to extend. The syntax for creating extension is given below:

```
extension ExtensionName on Type {
  // New methods or getters/setters
}
```

Within the extension body, you can define new methods, getters, and setters. Let us understand this with two examples.

Example: adding a custom method to a String class

Let us say you have a **String** class, and you want to add a method that checks if the string contains the word "**anime**". You can extend the **String** class using an extension as shown in the example below:

```
// extension_1.dart
extension AnimeString on String {
  bool containsAnime() {
    return this.contains('anime');
  }
}

void main() {
  String description1 = "I love watching One piece anime";
  String description2 = "I love watching ben10 cartoon";

  if (description1.containsAnime()) {
    print("This string talks about anime!");
  } else {
    print("No anime here.");
  }

  if (description2.containsAnime()) {
    print("This string talks about anime!");
  } else {
    print("No anime here.");
  }
}
```

In the above example, the extension **AnimeString** extends the **String** class, adding the **containsAnime()** method. Inside the **containsAnime()** method, we use **this.contains('anime')** to check if the word "**anime**" is present in the string. In the **main** method, we use the new **containsAnime()** method to check whether the string contains the word "anime" and print appropriate messages.

Example: adding a custom method to a List

Let us extend the **List** class to create a method that finds all anime characters whose names contain a specific substring, shown in the code below:

```
// extension_2.dart
extension AnimeCharacterList on List<String> {

  // Method to find anime characters based on a search query
  List<String> findAnimeCharacters(String searchQuery) {
    // this refers to the List<String> being extended
    return this.where((character) =>
        character.toLowerCase().contains(searchQuery.toLowerCase())).toList();
  }
}

void main() {
  List<String> animeCharacters = [
    "Naruto Uzumaki",
    "Sakura Haruno",
    "Luffy Monkey",
    "Ichigo Kurosaki",
    "Edward Elric"
  ];
  // Using the extension method to find anime characters
  List<String> result = animeCharacters.findAnimeCharacters("Sak");
  print(result);  // Output: [Sakura Haruno]
}
```

In the above program, the extension **AnimeCharacterList** extends the **List<String>** type, adding the **findAnimeCharacters()** method. The **findAnimeCharacters()** method uses the **where()** function to filter the list, returning only the names that contain the search query, ignoring case. In the main method, we call **findAnimeCharacters("Sak")** on a list of anime character names and print the result.

As you can see from the above examples, extensions make Dart more flexible and expressive, letting developers augment standard and third-party types to better fit specific needs without cluttering the original classes.

Asynchronous programming

Asynchronous programming in Dart introduces powerful techniques for handling tasks that do not need to be completed immediately, enabling applications to remain responsive and efficient. Asynchronous programming has a very steep learning curve but is essential for writing fast, responsive, reactive programs.

Introduction to asynchronous programming

Dart leverages two primary constructs for asynchronous operations: `Future` and `Stream`. Futures represent the result of asynchronous operations, allowing code to continue executing while waiting for the operation to be completed. On the other hand, Streams provide a sequence of asynchronous events over time, enabling reactive programming paradigms where applications respond to data as it becomes available. Understanding these concepts is essential for developing Dart applications that are capable of handling concurrent tasks and responding to changing data dynamically. It provides several key benefits:

- **Improved responsiveness**: By allowing tasks to run concurrently without blocking the main thread, asynchronous operations ensure that user interfaces remain smooth and responsive. This responsiveness is crucial for providing seamless user experience, especially in applications that handle complex computations or network operations.
- **Efficient resource management**: Asynchronous programming helps optimize resource usage by allowing tasks to be executed independently and efficiently. This capability reduces idle time and maximizes the utilization of system resources, leading to better overall performance.
- **Scalability**: Applications can scale more effectively with asynchronous programming, as they can handle multiple tasks concurrently. This scalability is particularly important for server-side applications handling numerous client requests or performing extensive data processing.
- **Simplified code structure**: Futures and Streams provide a structured approach to managing asynchronous operations, promoting clearer and more maintainable code. The use of async and await keywords in Dart simplifies asynchronous code, making it easier to write and understand compared to traditional callback-based approaches.
- **Support for reactive programming**: Streams enable reactive programming patterns where applications react to data as it arrives. This capability is essential for real-time applications, event-driven systems, and user interfaces that need to update dynamically based on changing data or user interactions.

- **Error handling**: Futures and Streams in Dart come with robust error handling mechanisms, allowing developers to efficiently manage and propagate errors that occur during asynchronous operations. This ensures applications remain stable and can gracefully recover from unexpected conditions.

Working with Future and async/await

In Dart, a Future represents a computation that will eventually complete to produce a value or an error. It allows non-blocking execution of tasks, enabling efficient handling of asynchronous operations. Test the following example:

```
// future_1.dart
// Example 1: Simulating a delayed operation using Future
Future<void> fetchUserData() async {
  print("Fetching user data...");
  await Future.delayed(Duration(seconds: 2)); // Simulate network delay
  print("User data fetched successfully!");
}

void main() {
  fetchUserData(); // Initiating asynchronous operation
  print("Program continues to execute other tasks...");
}
```

fetchUserData() simulates fetching user data asynchronously using **Future.delayed**. The **await** keyword ensures that the program waits for the Future to complete before continuing, demonstrating how Dart manages asynchronous operations without blocking the main thread.

The **async** and **await** keywords in Dart simplify asynchronous code by allowing sequential execution of asynchronous operations, making code more readable and maintainable. The following example demonstrates how you can perform sequential asynchronous tasks using **async**/**await**, ensuring each task completes before the next one begins:

```
// future_2.dart
// Example 2: Sequential execution using async/await
Future<void> performTasks() async {
  print("Task 1 started...");
  await Future.delayed(Duration(seconds: 2)); // Simulate task delay
  print("Task 1 completed.");

  print("Task 2 started...");
  await Future.delayed(Duration(seconds: 1)); // Simulate task delay
```

```
    print("Task 2 completed.");
  }

  void main() {
    performTasks(); // Initiating sequential asynchronous tasks
    print("Main function continues...");
  }

  // Output:
  // Task 1 started...
  // Main function continues...
  // Task 1 completed.
  // Task 2 started...
  // Task 2 completed.
```

In the preceding example, **`performTasks()`** demonstrates sequential execution of asynchronous tasks using **`async`** and **`await`**. Each task (simulated with **`Future.delayed`**) executes sequentially, allowing clear and intuitive control flow even in asynchronous scenarios.

Implementing Streams for reactive programming

Streams in Dart provide a powerful way to handle sequences of asynchronous events or data flows. They are particularly useful for implementing reactive programming patterns, where components react to changes or events in real-time. Let us explore how Streams work in Dart, along with practical examples.

A **Stream** in Dart represents a sequence of asynchronous events. It emits data over time, allowing consumers to react to each event as it occurs. Streams are useful for scenarios like real-time data processing, event-driven architectures, and handling continuous data flows.

Lifecycle of Streams in Dart

Using Streams effectively in Dart requires understanding their lifecycle, managing subscriptions, and handling errors appropriately. They empower developers to build responsive, event-driven applications that can handle complex asynchronous workflows seamlessly. Here is a detailed overview of the key stages in the lifecycle of a Stream:

- **Creation:** Streams in Dart are created using **`StreamController`** or factory methods like **`Stream.fromIterable`** or **`Stream.periodic`**. The creation phase initializes the stream and prepares it to emit events.

- **Subscription:** Once a Stream is created, consumers subscribe to it using the **`listen`** method. This establishes a connection to the Stream and specifies how to handle incoming events, errors, and stream closure.
- **Event emission:** During its lifecycle, a Stream emits events asynchronously. Events can represent data values, errors, or notifications about stream closure (**`done`** event).
- **Handling events:** Listeners attached to a Stream handle incoming events (**`data`**) as they occur. This phase allows consumers to react to changes or data updates in real-time, facilitating reactive programming patterns.
- **Stream closure:** When all data has been emitted and the stream no longer has events to process, it is closed using the **`close()`** method. This step is crucial to release resources associated with the stream and prevent memory leaks.

Creating a Stream

In Dart, you can create a custom Stream by extending **`StreamController`** or using factory methods like **`Stream.fromIterable`** or **`Stream.periodic`**. Here is an example using **`StreamController`** to emit a sequence of numbers:

```
// future_stream.dart
// Example: Creating a stream controller in Dart
import 'dart:async';

void main() {
  // Creating a stream controller with integer data type
  var controller = StreamController<int>();

  // Adding data to the stream
  for (int i = 1; i <= 5; i++) {
    controller.sink.add(i);
  }

  // Closing the stream (important to prevent memory leaks)
  controller.close();

  // Listening to the stream
  controller.stream.listen(
    (data) => print('Received: $data'),
    onDone: () => print('Stream closed'),
    onError: (error) => print('Error: $error'),
```

```
  );
}
```

We create a **StreamController<int>** to manage our stream of integers. Numbers 1 through 5 are added to the stream using **controller.sink.add(i)**. The stream is closed using **controller.close()** once all data has been added.

We listen to the stream using **controller.stream.listen**, where each emitted event (data) is processed, and we handle stream closure (**onDone**) and errors (**onError**).

Use cases of Streams

Streams are invaluable for scenarios such as:

- **Real-time data processing**: Handling continuous Streams of data from sensors, databases, or user interactions.
- **Event-driven architectures**: Reacting to user input, network events, or system notifications in real-time.
- **Asynchronous operations**: Coordinating multiple asynchronous tasks and responding to their completion or errors.

Isolates in Dart

In Dart, **isolates** are used to achieve concurrency and parallelism. An isolate is a separate thread of execution that does not share memory with other isolates. This is different from traditional threads in languages like Java or C++, where threads share memory space. Instead, isolates communicate with each other by passing messages. This makes isolates a safer and more efficient way to perform tasks concurrently without the risk of memory corruption or race conditions. Imagine you are building a group chat app where each user can comment in a group. To simulate efficient handling of multiple comments without blocking the UI, we can use isolates. Take a look at the example below:

```
import 'dart:isolate';

void processComment(String comment) {
  // Simulate a long processing task
  print('Processing comment: $comment');
}

void main() {
  List<String> comments = [
    'I love this post!',
    'Great discussion here!',
```

```
      'Cant wait for the next update!›,
      'Thanks for sharing this info.'
      'I m learning a lot from this post.›,
      'This is a great resource.',
      'I m glad I found this post.›,
    ];

    //  new isolate for each comment to simulate concurrent processing
    for (var comment in comments) {
      Isolate.spawn(processComment, comment);
    }
  }
```

In the above program, the **`processComment()`** function simulates the task of processing a comment (e.g., storing it in a database or performing analysis). In the **`main()`** function, **`Isolate.spawn()`** is used to spawn a new isolate for each comment. Each isolate runs in its own memory space and processes the comments concurrently. This approach allows the app to handle multiple comments at the same time, without blocking the main UI thread, ensuring a smooth user experience.

Benefit of using isolate

The following are the benefits of using isolate:

- **Concurrency**: Isolates allow you to run multiple tasks at the same time, improving the performance of your Dart applications.
- **No shared memory**: Since each isolate has its own memory, there are no concerns about race conditions or shared memory corruption.
- **Efficiency**: By offloading heavy tasks to isolates, you can keep the main thread free to handle user interactions and other essential tasks.

Comparing synchronous and asynchronous code in Dart

In Dart, understanding the difference between synchronous and asynchronous code is crucial for writing efficient and responsive applications. Synchronous code executes in a linear fashion, where each operation must be completed before the next one starts. This can lead to delays and unresponsive behavior if tasks are time-consuming. In contrast, asynchronous code allows tasks to run concurrently, enabling the application to perform other operations while waiting for tasks to be finished. This is particularly useful for handling multiple I/O operations or parallel tasks without blocking the main execution thread.

Understanding synchronous execution

In Dart, synchronous code executes line by line in a sequential manner. Each operation must be completed before the next one begins, blocking the execution until the current task finishes. Synchronous operations are straightforward but may lead to delays when tasks are time-consuming or involve waiting for external resources. For example, try the following code:

```
// synchronous.dart
// Example: Synchronous execution in Dart
void main() {
  print('Task 1 started...');
  performTask1(); // Synchronous task
  print('Task 1 completed.');

  print('Task 2 started...');
  performTask2(); // Synchronous task
  print('Task 2 completed.');
}

void performTask1() {
  // Simulate time-consuming task
  for (int i = 0; i < 10000000000; i++) {}
}

void performTask2() {
  // Simulate another task
  print('Performing task 2...');
}
```

Difference between synchronous and asynchronous code

Synchronous execution in Dart can lead to delays and a frozen user interface when tasks are time-consuming. On the other hand, asynchronous code allows tasks to run concurrently, ensuring that the application remains responsive by continuing with other tasks while waiting for I/O operations or computations to finish. This approach is beneficial for handling multiple I/O requests or parallel computations effectively.

Aspect	Synchronous	Asynchronous
Execution model	Execute tasks sequentially, blocking execution	Allows tasks to run concurrently without blocking
Handling delays	Delays occur, freezes UI during time-consuming tasks	Prevents freezing, continues other tasks while waiting
Concurrency	Executes one task at a time	Manages multiple tasks simultaneously

Table 2.1: *Comparing synchronous and asynchronous code*

Handling concurrency and performance considerations

Concurrency and performance considerations are crucial aspects when designing applications, especially in Dart where asynchronous programming plays a significant role. Here is a detailed explanation of how Dart handles these aspects.

Concurrency management

Concurrency in Dart refers to the ability to execute multiple tasks simultaneously. This is particularly important in scenarios where applications need to handle multiple operations concurrently without blocking the main thread. Dart achieves concurrency primarily through asynchronous programming using Future, async/await, and Stream. Dart employs various techniques to handle concurrency effectively, such as:

- **Asynchronous operations**: Dart's Future and async/await keywords allow developers to execute tasks asynchronously. This means that while one task is waiting for an I/O operation or a time-consuming computation, other tasks can continue to run independently. For example, when fetching data from a remote server, Dart can initiate multiple requests concurrently and handle responses as they arrive.
- **Isolates**: Dart supports isolates, which are separate memory heaps that run concurrently with the main application thread. Isolates enable true parallelism by allowing multiple tasks to execute simultaneously across different CPU cores. This is particularly useful for computationally intensive tasks like image processing or complex calculations.

Performance optimization

Optimizing performance in Dart involves several strategies to ensure efficient resource utilization and responsiveness:

- **Non-blocking I/O**: Asynchronous operations prevent the main thread from waiting idly for I/O operations to be completed. This frees up resources and allows the application to remain responsive, enhancing overall user experience.
- **Event-driven architecture**: Dart's support for Streams facilitates event-driven programming, where components react to events or data updates in real-time. This pattern reduces latency and improves application responsiveness by handling data as soon as it becomes available.
- **Memory management**: Effective memory management is crucial for performance. Dart's garbage collector automatically manages memory allocation and deallocation, ensuring efficient use of system resources and preventing memory leaks.

Best practices

To effectively handle concurrency and optimize performance in Dart applications, consider the following best practices:

- **Use asynchronous APIs**: Prefer asynchronous APIs (Future, Stream) for I/O-bound operations to avoid blocking the main thread.
- **Avoid locking operations**: Minimize long-running, synchronous operations that could freeze the application's UI or degrade performance.
- **Profile and monitor**: Regularly profile your Dart code to identify performance bottlenecks and optimize critical paths. Tools like Dart Observatory and Dart DevTools can help monitor memory usage, CPU performance, and application responsiveness.

Error handling and exceptions

Dart provides several mechanisms to manage errors effectively, including the use of try, catch, on, and finally blocks, as well as the creation of custom exceptions and error propagation strategies. Understanding and implementing these techniques is essential for building resilient software that can manage and recover from errors efficiently.

Handling errors and exceptions in Dart

Error handling and exceptions play a crucial role in maintaining robustness and reliability in Dart applications. Understanding how to effectively handle errors using `try`, `catch`, `on`, and `finally` blocks, as well as implementing custom exceptions, is essential for building resilient software. Let us explore these concepts in detail:

try, catch, on and finally blocks

In Dart, error handling is managed using try, catch, on, and finally blocks, which allow developers to gracefully handle exceptions and recover from errors.

Let us understand about them briefly:

- **try and catch blocks**: Used together to catch and handle exceptions that occur within a try block. The catch block specifies the type of exception to catch and provides code to handle the exception. Test the following example:

```
// try_catch.dart
void main() {
  try {
    // Risky operation that may throw an exception
    int result = 10 ~/ 0;
    // Above line will throw an IntegerDivisionByZeroException
  } catch (e) {
    // Handling the exception
    print('Exception caught: $e');
  }
}
```

- **on block**: Specifies a specific type of exception to catch. This is useful when different exceptions need different handling strategies, as shown as follows:

```
// try_on.dart
// Exception handling using try-on block
import 'dart:io';

void main() {
  try {
    print("Enter a number: ");
    // throws FormatException if input is not a number
    var num = int.parse(stdin.readLineSync() ?? '');
    print("You entered: $num");
  } on FormatException {
    print("Invalid number");
  }
}
```

- **finally block**: Executes code regardless of whether an exception was thrown or not. It is typically used for cleanup actions such as closing files or releasing resources, shown as follows:

```
// try_finally.dart
// Exception handling using try-finally block
import 'dart:io';
void addNumbers(int a, int b) {
  print("Sum: ${a + b}");
}

void main() {
  try {
    print("Enter first number: ");
    var num1 = int.parse(stdin.readLineSync() ?? '');
    print("Enter second number: ");
    var num2 = int.parse(stdin.readLineSync() ?? '');
    addNumbers(num1, num2);
  } on FormatException {
    print("Invalid number");
  }
  finally {
    print("Program completed!");
  }
}
```

Custom exceptions and error propagation

Dart allows developers to define custom exceptions by extending the built-in **Exception** class or any other existing exception class. Custom exceptions help in distinguishing different error conditions within an application. Test the following code:

```
// custom_exception.dart
// Custom exception example in Dart
class NetworkException implements Exception {
  final String message;

  NetworkException(this.message);

  @override
  String toString() => 'NetworkException: $message';
}

```

```
void fetchData() {
  try {
    // Simulating network operation
    throw NetworkException('Failed to fetch data from server.');
  } catch (e) {
    print('Error occurred: $e');
  }
}

void main() {
  fetchData();
}
```

Error propagation

Error propagation involves passing exceptions up the call stack to higher levels of the application for centralized handling or logging. This allows developers to manage errors at appropriate levels, ensuring consistent error reporting and recovery strategies. Test the following example:

```
// error_propagation.dart

class NetworkException implements Exception {
  final String message;

  NetworkException(this.message);

  @override
  String toString() => 'NetworkException: $message';
}

void fetchData() {
  try {
    // Simulating network operation
    throw NetworkException('Failed to fetch data from server.');
  } catch (e) {
    print('Error occurred: $e');
    // Propagate the error further if needed
    rethrow; // Re-throws the current exception
```

```
  }
}

void main() {
  try {
    fetchData();
  } catch (e) {
    print('Error in main function');
    // Propagate the error further if needed
  }
}
```

By mastering error handling techniques, you can build resilient applications that gracefully handle unexpected errors and maintain reliability.

Mini project: Fortune Cookie Oracle

Implementing a mini project in Dart is a fun way to practice classes, asynchronous programming with Future, error handling, and enhancing user experience. The Fortune Cookie Oracle will randomly display fortunes to users, simulating the experience of cracking open a fortune cookie and receiving a message. Here is a breakdown of task required:

- **Importing necessary libraries**:
  - **`dart:async`** Provides support for asynchronous programming, including **`Future`** and **`Stream`** classes.
  - **`dart:math`** Provides mathematical functions and constants, including the **`Random`** class for generating random numbers.
- **FortuneCookie class**: Representing a fortune cookie with methods to fetch random fortunes asynchronously. It encapsulates the functionality of the Fortune Cookie Oracle.
  - **_fortunes**: A private list of fortune messages, each with an emoji to enhance the user experience.
  - **getFortune() method**: An asynchronous method that simulates a delay (like the time taken to crack open a fortune cookie) and then randomly selects and returns a fortune from the list.
- **Asynchronous programming**: Using Future and async/await to simulate delays and fetch fortunes.
- **Error handling**: Handling errors gracefully, especially when fetching fortunes or in case of unexpected issues.

- **User interaction**: Displaying fortunes with emojis for a better user experience.

Let us explore a practical example. The following is a code snippet for a simple yet engaging Fortune Cookie Oracle. This program simulates receiving a fortune from a virtual fortune cookie. It demonstrates how to use asynchronous programming with Future, manage delays, and handle random number generation. Here is how the **FortuneCookie** class is set up to provide random fortunes, and how the main function orchestrates the process of delivering a fortune to the user.

```
// fortune_cookie_oracle.dart
import 'dart:async';
import 'dart:math';

class FortuneCookie {
  // List of fortunes with emojis
  static const List<String> _fortunes = [
    "🔮 Your future is bright!»,
    "🍀 Good things are coming your way.»,
    "🌟 Success is in your future.»,
    "💖 Love and happiness await you.»,
    "⏳ Patience is a virtue; good things take time.",
    "🌈 A rainbow of opportunities is coming your way.»,
  ];

  // Method to fetch a random fortune
  Future<String> getFortune() async {
    // Simulate delay
    await Future.delayed(Duration(seconds: 2));
    // Randomly select a fortune
    int index = Random().nextInt(10);
    return _fortunes[index];
  }
}

void main() async {
  var oracle = FortuneCookie();
  print("🔮   🔮🔮🧙‍♂️🥠🥠🥠");
  print("Welcome to the Fortune Cookie Oracle!");
  try {
    print("Cracking open your virtual fortune cookie...");
```

```
      String fortune = await oracle.getFortune();
      print("🥠 Your fortune: $fortune»);
    } catch (e) {
      print("Your fortune could not be revealed. Try again later.");
    }
  }
```

Run your Dart program to see it simulate the experience of receiving a fortune from a fortune cookie. The message displayed will vary randomly each time the program runs.

Conclusion

In this chapter, we explored the essential skills for enhancing your Dart programming proficiency, crucial for building robust Flutter applications. Beginning with a comprehensive exploration of OOP principles, we covered the fundamentals of classes, objects, inheritance, and polymorphism. We then, transitioned into asynchronous programming using Futures and Streams, contrasting synchronous and asynchronous code execution to handle concurrency effectively. Error handling mechanisms like try, catch, and finally were detailed to ensure application reliability.

In the next chapter, we will shift our focus to Designing Stunning UIs for the Web. This section will immerse you in the world of Flutter, where you will learn how to craft visually appealing and interactive web interfaces. From setting up new projects to mastering Flutter widgets and state management, you will explore various techniques to create responsive and engaging user experiences.

Points to remember

- Use default, parameterized, and named constructors for flexibility.
- an underscore (_) prefix to mark fields as private.
- Use the async keyword for asynchronous functions.
- Use the await keyword to wait for a Future to complete.
- Use try, catch, on, and finally blocks to handle errors.
- Apply the extends keyword on subclass to inherit from a superclass.
- Apply the with keyword to apply mixins for code reuse.
- Use the @override annotation to indicate method overrides.
- Declare abstract classes using the abstract keyword.
- Use the implements keyword to implement an interface.

Multiple choice questions

1. **In Dart, which keyword is used to create a class that cannot be instantiated and is intended to be subclassed?**
   a. final
   b. abstract
   c. const
   d. static
2. **What is the purpose of the Future class in Dart?**
   a. To represent a sequence of asynchronous events.
   b. To create and initialize objects.
   c. To represent a value that will be available in the future.
   d. To handle errors and exceptions.
3. **Which of the following is true about the @override annotation in Dart?**
   a. It is used to prevent a method from being overridden.
   b. It indicates that a method is intended to override a method in a superclass.
   c. It allows a class to inherit properties and methods from another class.
   d. It is used to define a common interface for subclasses.
4. **In the context of Dart, what is a mixin?**
   a. A class that can be instantiated multiple times.
   b. A way to reuse a class's code in multiple class hierarchies.
   c. A method used to override a superclass method.
   d. An asynchronous function that uses Future and await.
5. **What is the use of on block in exception handling?**
   a. To specify a type of exception to catch.
   b. To log error messages to the console.
   c. To execute code regardless of whether an exception is thrown.
   d. To rethrow the caught exception for further handling.

Answer

1	b
2	c
3	b
4	b
5	a

Questions

1. Implement a Singleton pattern in Dart. Ensure that your class cannot be instantiated more than once and provide a global point of access to the instance.
2. Write an asynchronous function that simulates fetching data from a server. The function should use Future.delayed to introduce a delay and then return a string message. Handle any potential errors using try, catch, and finally blocks.
3. Define an abstract class Shape with an abstract method area(). Then, create two subclasses, Circle and Rectangle, that implement the area method. Write a program to calculate and print the area of a circle and a rectangle.
4. Create a Dart program that uses Streams to print a sequence of numbers from 1 to 10, with a 1-second interval between each number. Ensure that the program handles any potential errors that may occur during the stream processing.

Key terms

1. **OOP**: OOP in Dart involves using classes, objects, inheritance, and polymorphism to create reusable and modular code.
2. **Classes and objects**: Classes are blueprints for creating objects. They contain fields (variables) and methods (functions) that define the behavior of the objects.
3. **Fields**: Fields are variables defined within a class that represent the state or properties of the class.
4. **Constructors**: Constructors are special methods used to create and initialize objects of a class. Dart supports default constructors, parameterized constructors, and named constructors.
5. **Methods**: Methods are functions defined within a class that operate on the class's fields and provide behavior for the objects.
6. **Asynchronous** Programming: Asynchronous programming in Dart uses Future, async, and await to handle operations that take time to complete without blocking the main thread.

7. **Future and async/await**: Future represents a value that will be available in the future. async and await are used to write asynchronous code in a synchronous style.
8. **Streams**: Streams are used for handling a sequence of asynchronous events. They are useful for scenarios where multiple values are expected over time.
9. **Error handling**: Error handling in Dart is done using try, catch, on, and finally blocks to manage exceptions and ensure the application remains robust.
10. **Custom exceptions**: Custom exceptions can be created by extending the Exception class to handle specific error conditions in an application.
11. **Inheritance**: Inheritance allows one class to inherit the properties and methods of another class, promoting code reuse and hierarchy.
12. **Polymorphism**: Polymorphism enables a single interface to represent different underlying forms (data types). It allows methods to be used interchangeably even if they are part of different classes.
13. **Mixins**: Mixins provide a way to reuse a class's code in multiple class hierarchies. They are useful for adding functionality to classes without using inheritance.
14. **super keyword**: The super keyword is used to refer to the superclass and call its methods or constructors.
15. **@override annotation**: The @override annotation is used to indicate that a method is intended to override a method in a superclass.
16. **Abstract classes**: Abstract classes cannot be instantiated and are used to define a common interface for subclasses. They can contain abstract methods that must be implemented by subclasses.
17. **Interfaces**: Dart uses classes as interfaces, meaning any class can be used as an interface. Classes can implement multiple interfaces.
18. **Singleton pattern**: The Singleton pattern ensures a class has only one instance and provides a global point of access to it. This is useful for managing shared resources or configurations.

Additional resources

1. **https://dart.dev/language/classes**
2. **https://dart.dev/libraries/async/async-await**
3. **https://dart.dev/language/error-handling**

CHAPTER 3
Designing Stunning UIs for the Web

Introduction

In this chapter, we will explore Flutter and understand how to create beautiful, interactive responsive UI for web applications. Whether you are new to Flutter or looking to deepen your understanding, this chapter will guide you through the essentials of setting up a new project, understanding Flutter widgets, and building intuitive and visually appealing UIs. We will also touch on state management techniques and design patterns to enhance your app's usability. By the end of this chapter, you will have a solid foundation to create standout web interfaces using Flutter's powerful widget system.

Structure

In this chapter, we will cover the following topics:

- Setting up a new Flutter project
- Creating and running a web app
- Introduction to Flutter widgets
- Understanding the widget tree
- Layout models in Flutter
- State management techniques

- Designing responsive UIs for web
- Design patterns
- Navigating and routing
- Project: Dart byte

Objectives

The objective of this chapter is to equip you with the knowledge and skills needed to design compelling and responsive user interfaces for web applications using Flutter. You will learn how to set up and run a new Flutter project, understand the basics of Flutter widgets, and build complex layouts. Through practical examples and a hands-on project, DartByte, you will gain the confidence to create stunning UIs that provide an exceptional user experience.

Setting up a new Flutter project

For this chapter, your first step will be to set up a new Flutter project. Launch IntelliJ IDEA and create a new Flutter project (refer to *Chapter 1, Mastering Dart Basics for Flutter*) for detailed instructions). If you have the previous Dart-advanced project open, do the following:

1. **Start a new project:** On the main menu bar, next to the hamburger icon, you will see the name of the current project. Click on it and then choose **New Project**, as shown in the following figure:

***Figure 3.1:** Creating a new project*

2. **New project window:** A new project window will pop up. Select "**Flutter**" from the sidebar and press the "**Next**" button, as displayed in the following figure:

Figure 3.2: Creating new flutter project

3. **Project configuration:** Select a project name using lowercase letters and underscores only (snake case). You can also update the project description (optional).
4. **Project type:** Select application for this project
5. **Platform selection:** In the platform section, uncheck everything except "**Web**" since we are targeting the web platform right now. Other platforms can be enabled later or in new projects. Take a look at the following figure for better idea:

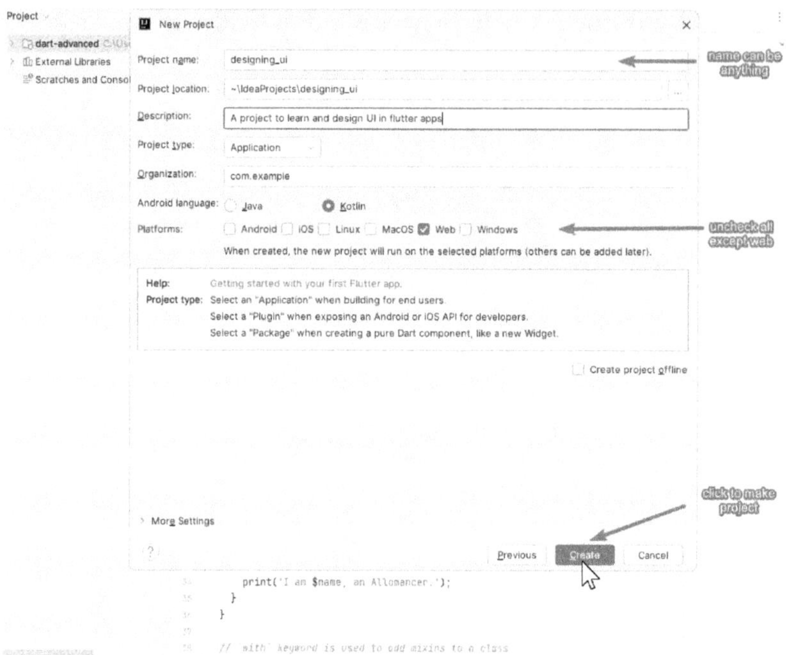

Figure 3.3: Configuring the project

6. **Create project:** Do not change anything else and hit "**Create**" to complete the project creation process. Wait for IntelliJ IDEA to create and generate all files for the project and the window should look like the following figure:

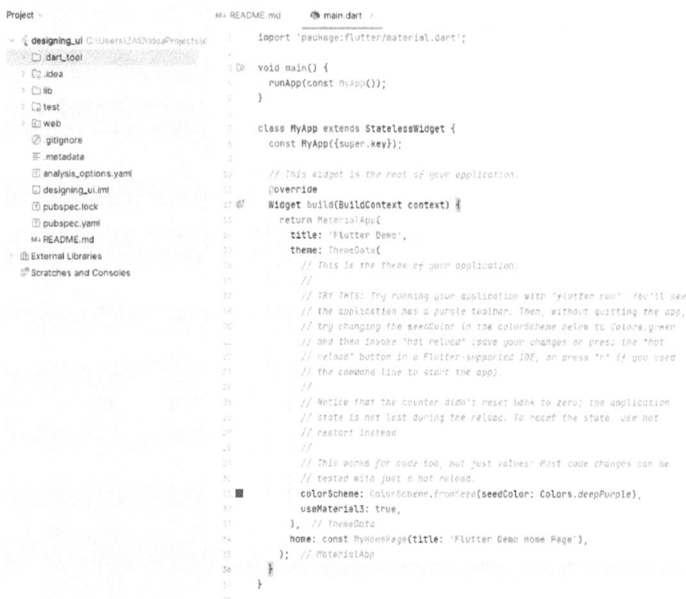

Figure 3.4: The new flutter project in IntelliJ IDEA

Note: For practice projects, the organization can be *com.example*, but for real projects, the organization must typically be the domain name of your organization.

Project structure

At the core of every Flutter project is the project root directory that organizes various aspects of the application. As shown in the following figure, the project panel of IntelliJ IDEA, you will find the following folders and files as show in the *Figure 3.5*:

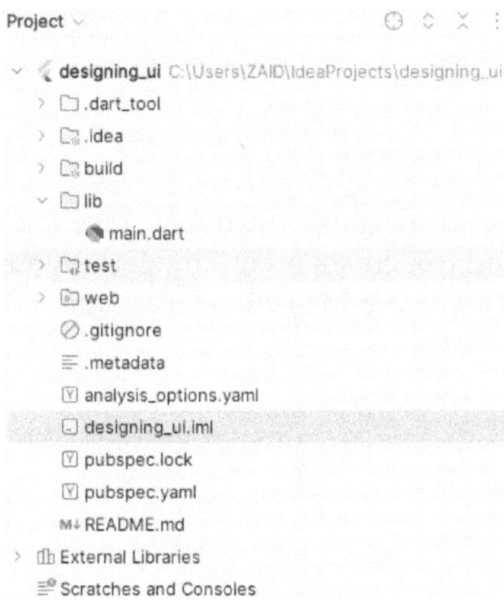

Figure 3.5: *Flutter project structure (web only)*

The following table is breakdown of each folder and files in a basic flutter project:

Folder/file	Description
`.dart_tool/`	A folder that contains support code and is not to be touched.
`.idea/`	Contains project-specific settings for IntelliJ IDEA, not for modification.
`android/`	Hosts Android-related file, that is used to generate the android application. Its where you can integrate native android code.
`ios/`	Similar to the android/directory, but for iOS specific files. You can integrate native iOS code here.
`lib/`	This is the folder where you are going to do most of your work. All your dart files will be created in this folder.
`test/`	This folder contains Dart test, which are required for testing the project.
`web/`	Contains files that are required for futter to run inside web browser.
`.gitignore`	A version control file that dictates what files and folder to ignore.

`.metadata`	Stores metadata about the project.
`analysis_options.yaml`	A file that contains linting rules, and can be modified.
`designing_ui.iml`	IntelliJ IDEA module file.
`pubspec.lock`	Manages the versions of dependencies locked for the project.
`pubspec.yaml`	A project critical file that has information on project dependencies, assets, fonts, flutter version, etc.
`README.md`	A markdown file that can be used for documenting the project.

Table 3.1: *Flutter files and folder description*

lib/ directory

The **`lib/`** directory is where you are going to do most of the work. By default, only the **`main.dart`** file is available, but you can create other directories yourself as need arises. Look at the following figure, which show the **`lib/`** directory content for a simple ecommerce app:

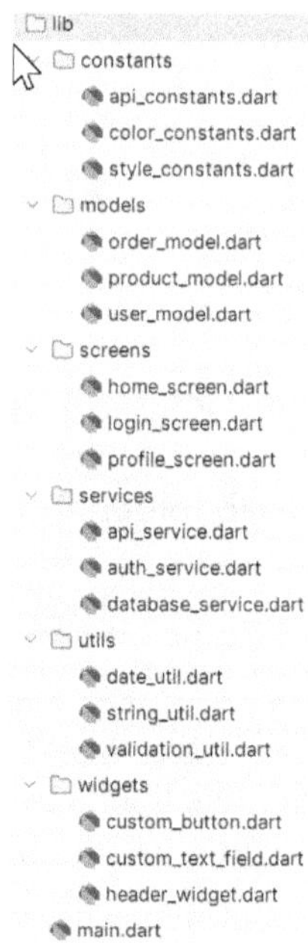

Figure 3.6: *A simple ecommerce app folder and file structure in lib directory*

Managing assets and localization

Managing assets and localization is a key part of creating a robust Flutter application. You can create these folders directly inside your project root, outside **`lib/`** directory, as shown in the following:

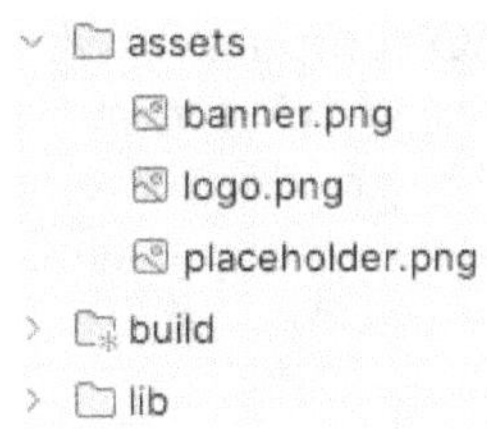

Figure 3.7: A sample assets/ directory in flutter

assets/: The **assets/** directory is designated for storing static resources such as images, videos, fonts, and other multimedia files used in your application. To use these assets in your Flutter project, you need to declare them in the **pubspec.yaml** file, which helps Flutter bundle these resources into your app during the build process.

Need for Flutter for the web

Originally launched for mobile development, Flutter now supports web applications. Here are a few reasons that makes Flutter for the web remarkable:

- **Single codebase:** Write once, deploy on iOS, Android, Desktop and the web.
- **Fast development:** Hot reload lets you quickly see changes, speeding up development.
- **Expressive and flexible UI:** Rich pre-designed widgets simplify creating complex UIs.
- **Performance:** Flutter's architecture ensures fast, efficient web applications for a smooth user experience.

The following figure summarizes the need of flutter for the web:

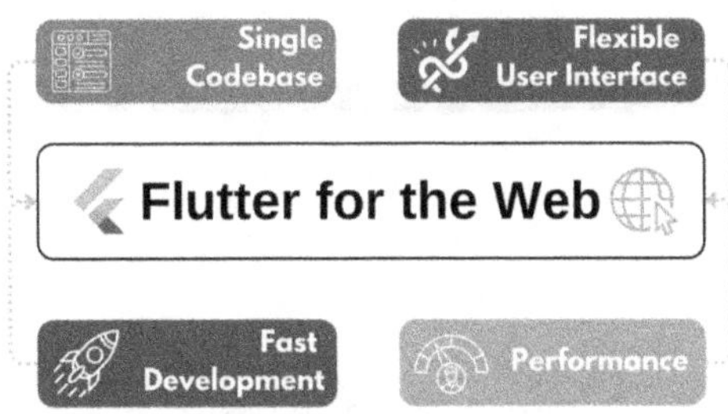

Figure 3.8: Benefits of using flutter for the web

Operating Flutter in a web environment

The Flutter engine, originally designed in C++, uses standard browser APIs for web apps to run with high performance and graphical fidelity. Flutter supports two web renderers: the HTML renderer, which uses HTML, CSS, and JavaScript for lightweight apps with decreased load times and better SEO compatibility but limited graphics capabilities; and the CanvasKit renderer, which uses WebAssembly and Skia for superior performance and consistent rendering of complex graphics, though it results in larger file sizes and longer load times. By default, Flutter web apps use CanvasKit on desktop browsers and the HTML renderer on mobile browsers.

Understanding main.dart

In Flutter, **main.dart** serves as the entry point for your application and is typically located in the **lib** folder. You can remove the default sample counter app code below the **main()** function. Here is a basic setup for **main.dart**:

```
void main() {
  runApp(
    MaterialApp(
      title: "The Todo List",
      home: Text("Hello, My World!"),
    ),
  );
}
```

In the **main()** function, **runApp()** is called with a **MaterialApp** widget, which is the root of the Flutter application. **MaterialApp** is configured with a title (**"The Todo List"**) and a home widget, set to a **Text** widget displaying **"Hello, World!"**.

Creating and running a web app

To make the shown interface in *Figure 3.9*, you need to create a new Flutter widget, **MyFirstApp** that displays a message in the center of screen:

***Figure 3.9:** Creating you first web app in Flutter*

Widgets are the core building blocks of a Flutter application's user interface; they are discussed in detail in the next section. In your code, replace the **`main()`** function code and add **`MyFirstApp`** class, shown as follows:

```
void main() {
  runApp(MyFirstApp());
}

class MyFirstApp extends StatelessWidget {
  @override
  Widget build(BuildContext context) {
    return MaterialApp(
      title: "The Todo List»,
      theme: ThemeData(
        primarySwatch: Colors.brown,
      ),
      home: Scaffold(
        body: Center(
          child: Text(
            'Welcome to the Todo List! 📝',
            style: TextStyle(fontSize: 24),
          ),
        ),
      ),
    );
  }
}
```

Here is a detailed breakdown of the code:

```
class MyFirtApp extends StatelessWidget {
  // ...
}
```

You defined a new class called **`MyFirstApp`**. It extends **`StatelessWidget`**, which means it is an immutable widget that describes part of the user interface, shown as follows:

```
@override
Widget build(BuildContext context) {
  // ...
}
```

build() method is called when the widget is inserted into the widget tree. It describes the part of the user interface represented by this widget, shown as follows:

```
return MaterialApp(
  // ...
);
```

MaterialApp is the root widget of the app. It provides many basic app features like theme, navigation, and title. It uses material design principles for its layout and styling, shown as follows:

```
title: "The Todo List",
```

Above line sets the title of the app, which is used by the browser to identify the app, shown as follows:

```
theme: ThemeData(
  primarySwatch: Colors.brown,
),
```

This line defines the app's theme. Here, it sets the primary color scheme to brown:

```
home: Scaffold(
  // ...
),
```

Scaffold is a basic layout structure that implements the material design visual layout:

```
body: Center(
  child: Text(
    'Welcome to the Todo List! 📝',
    style: TextStyle(fontSize: 24),
  ),
),
```

The main screen displays a centered text saying **"Welcome to The Todo List! 📝"** in a large font. Center widget centers its child. Text widget displays the welcome message. The text style is set to have a font size of 24.

This is a very basic starting point for a todo list app.

Running the app

Running a Flutter project in IntelliJ IDEA is straightforward and user-friendly, making it easy for developers to quickly start building and testing their applications. With just a couple of clicks, you can have your Flutter app up and running on a device or web browser. You can follow the given steps:

1. Select a target device or browser:
    a. Open **`main.dart`** in your editor.
    b. Use the dropdown menu in the top toolbar to select a target device or browser (e.g., Chrome, Edge, or connected emulators).
2. Run the app:
    a. Click the play icon (▶) next to the dropdown menu or in the left margin of the **`main.dart`** editor.
    b. Your Flutter app will run on the selected device or browser, allowing you to see your code in action and begin development and debugging.

The following figure highlights the UI for the running the app:

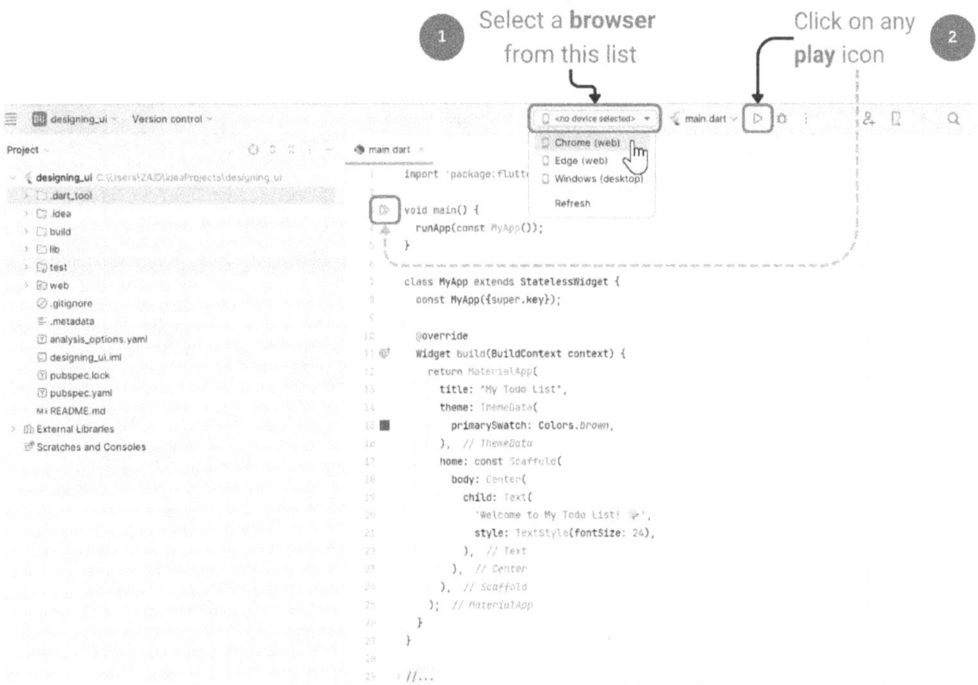

Figure 3.10: Steps to run the flutter app

Note: To run the project from the terminal, press Alt+F12 (option+F12 for macOS) to open it and then type flutter run and then select the device you want to run the project on.

If your app is not running, it may have errors. IntelliJ IDEA provides hints to help identify and correct them. For instance, typing the **S** in StatelessWidget in lowercase is an error due to Dart's case sensitivity. Here is how to find and fix errors:

- **Folders hinting code errors:** In the project explorer, folders with a red squiggly underline indicate errors in some files.
- **File inspection:** Lines with errors have a red squiggly underline, helping you spot issues quickly.
- **Error stripe:** On the right side of the editor, the error stripe shows errors and warnings in your file. Hover over red bars for details.
- **Error icons:** An icon at the top right shows the number of errors and warnings. Clicking it opens a detailed list of issues.
- **Error trace in the run panel:** If the application fails to compile, the Run panel displays detailed error messages, including the file name, line number, and specific error, as shown in the following figure:

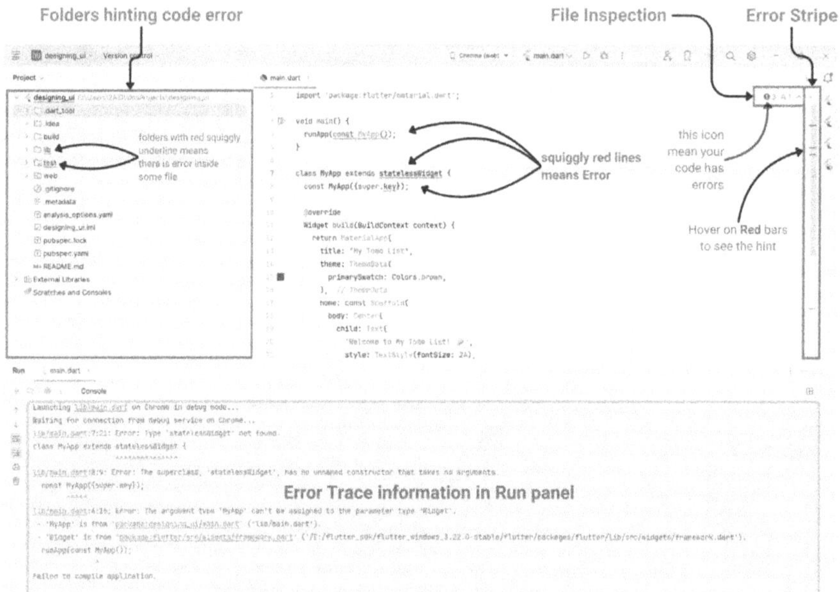

Figure 3.11: How to look for coding errors

The common mistakes include:

- **Typos and syntax errors:** Misspelling class or method names and incorrect syntax. Always double-check for typos.
- **Incorrect imports:** Forgetting or importing wrong packages. Ensure all required packages are correctly imported.
- **Incorrect widget usage:** Using the wrong widget or missing required parent widgets, like using a `Text` widget without a Scaffold or MaterialApp.
- **Constructor errors:** Not providing required parameters or using incorrect names. Ensure all necessary arguments are correctly passed.

- **Mismatched data types:** Assigning wrong data types to variables or methods. Verify correct data types are used.

After you successfully run your app, the selected browser will open, and display the result, similar to the following *Figure 3.12*:

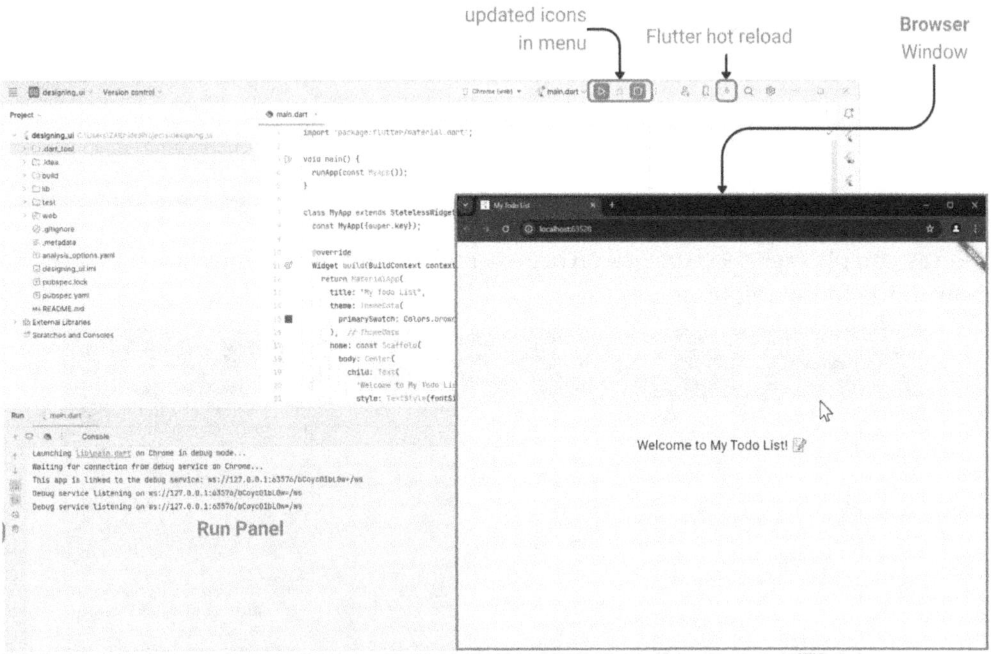

***Figure 3.12:** A running Flutter app in browser*

You do not need to run the app again thanks to the feature that made Flutter so popular: **hot reload**. Hot reload allows you to make changes in your code, such as changing text, and see the updates instantly without restarting the app. If the changes are not reflected automatically, you can press the save (*Ctrl* + *S*) to trigger hot reload manually. Make the following changes in code, to change the color scheme of app and font size of **`Text`** widget:

```
class MyFirstApp extends StatelessWidget {
    ...
    return MaterialApp(
      title: "The Todo List",
      theme: ThemeData(
        colorScheme: ColorScheme.fromSwatch(
          primarySwatch: Colors.teal,
        ),
      ),
      home: const Scaffold(
```

```
          body: Center(
            child: Text(
              'Welcome to the Todo List! 📝',
              style: TextStyle(fontSize: 50),
            ),
          ),
        ),
      );
    }
  }
```

As soon as you press *Ctrl* + *S* or click on browser window, the user interface will be updated as show in the following figure:

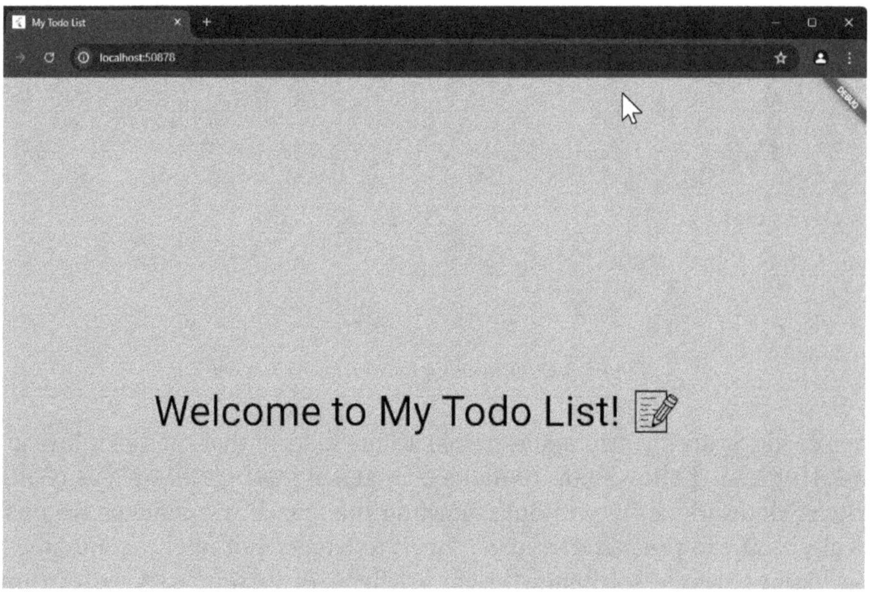

Figure 3.13: *Hot reload feature demonstration in flutter app*

Note: The const keyword is used in the beginning of a widget to mark it as a compile-time constant, which can improve performance by reducing the need for unnecessary rebuilds and ensuring that the widget remains immutable.

Flutter inspector

The Flutter inspector is a powerful tool for examining and debugging your Flutter application's widget tree. It allows you to visualize the layout and state of your widgets in real-time. The following figure shows the Flutter inspector in action:

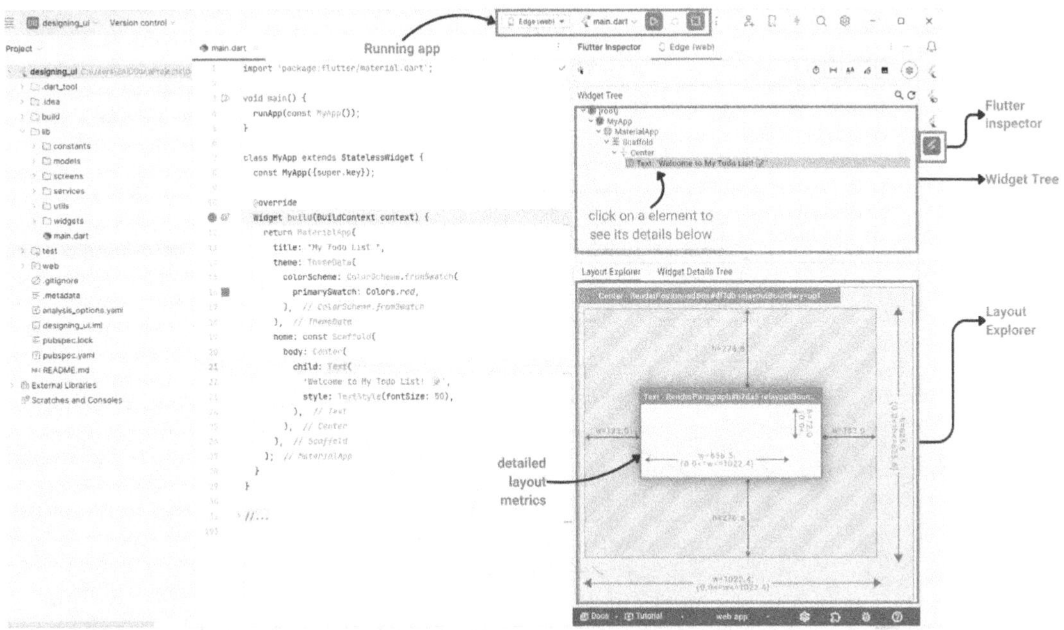

***Figure 3.14:** Flutter inspector panel*

Introduction to Flutter widgets

In Flutter, every component is a widget. Widgets serve as the fundamental elements of a Flutter app's user interface, encompassing all screen elements such as layout structures, text, images, icons, and more. The widget system in Flutter is extremely versatile, enabling the creation of intricate UIs effortless.

Types of widgets

Widgets can be categorized into two types, such as:

- **Stateless widgets**: These are immutable widgets that do not change their state once they are built. They are ideal for UI elements that do not need to react to user interactions or other dynamic changes.
- **Stateful widgets**: These widgets manage a mutable state that can update over time. They are used for UI components that need to update dynamically in response to user actions, data changes, or other events.

Widgets in Flutter are organized in a hierarchical structure called **the widget tree**. The root of the tree is usually the **`MaterialApp`** or **`CupertinoApp`** widget, and branches represent various UI components. This tree structure helps Flutter to efficiently manage and render the UI. For example, look at the following figure:

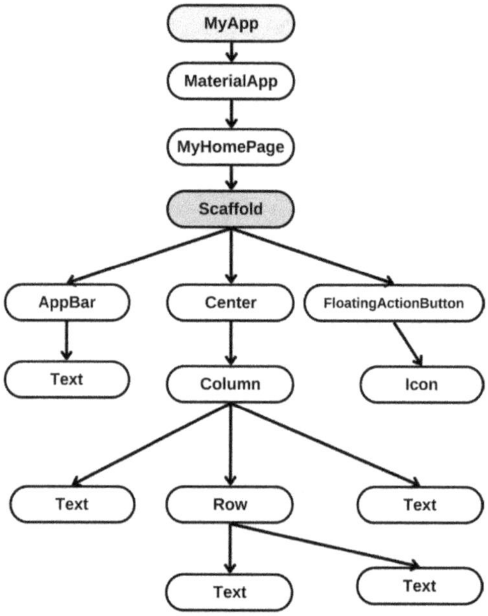

Figure 3.15: The Flutter widget tree example

Commonly used widgets

Everything in Flutter is a widget, but learning all of them in one go is not a good idea. The correct way is you start from the most common to slowly moving to advanced widgets. In this section, you will learn about the most used widgets available.

Text

The **`Text`** widget is used to display a string of text in a single style. It allows you to control the appearance of text in your app, including font size, weight, color and more. The data property is required which is the text to be displayed. Look at the following example:

```
Text(
  'Welcome, Knight!',
  style: TextStyle(fontSize: 25, color: Colors.blue),
  textAlign: TextAlign.center,
  maxLines: 2,
);
```

Icon

The **`Icon`** widget is used to display graphical icons. You can use built-in icons provided by flutter. Here is how the **`Icon`** widget is written:

```
Icon(
        Icons.person,
        color: Colors.yellow,
        size: 46,
);
```

Buttons

Buttons allow users to interact with your app. All button widgets require the following two properties:

- **onPressed**: The callback that is called when the button is tapped.
- **child**: The widget below this widget in the tree.

Flutter provides several types of buttons to handle different use cases, such as:

- **ElevatedButton**: A button with a shadow, which gives a 3D effect. Take a look at the following example:

```
ElevatedButton(
  onPressed: () {
    print('Elevated Button Pressed');
  },
  child: const Text('Elevated Button'),
);
```

- **TextButton**: A flat button without a shadow as shown in the following code:

```
TextButton(
  onPressed: () {
    print('Temperature Decreased by 1');
  },
  child: const Text('Decrease Temperature'),
);
```

- **OutlinedButton**: A button with a border. A simple snippet is given as follows:

```
OutlinedButton(
  onPressed: () {
    print('Outlined Button Pressed');
  },
  child: const Text('Outlined Button'),
);
```

- **IconButton**: A button with an icon instead of text. The following snippet is example implementation of **`IconButton`**:

```
IconButton(
  onPressed: () {
    print('Icon Button Pressed');
  },
  icon: const Icon(Icons.star),
);
```

SizedBox

The **`SizedBox`** widget is used to create a box with a specified size. It is often used for adding space between widgets. Look at the following code:

```
SizedBox(
  width: 50,
  height: 50,
);
```

GestureDetector

The **`GestureDetector`** widget detects gestures. It can be used to wrap any widget and provide it with gesture detection capabilities. It can recognize a lot of gestures, such as:

- **onTap**: Called when the user taps on the widget.
- **onDoubleTap**: Called when the user double-taps on the widget.
- **onLongPress**: Called when the user long-presses on the widget.

Check the following code:

```
GestureDetector(
  onTap: () {
    // Handle your gesture here
  },
  child: Icon(
    Icons.favorite,
    color: Colors.blue,
    size: 50,
  ),
);
```

Appbar

The **AppBar** widget is a material design app bar that can be placed at the top of a Scaffold. It typically contains a title and actions list and leading icon. The following code is a snippet with **AppBar**:

```
AppBar(
  title: const Text('Secret Shopping List›),
  actions: [
    IconButton(
      icon: const Icon(Icons.person),
      onPressed: () {
        // Handle account action
      },
    ),
    IconButton(
      icon: const Icon(Icons.more_vert),
      onPressed: () {
        // Handle more action
      },
    ),
  ],
);
```

Scaffold

The **Scaffold** widget provides a high-level structure for a material design app. It can include **AppBar**, **Drawer**, **BottomNavigationBar**, **FloatingActionButton**, etc. Your main content goes inside the **body** argument. Here is a sample snippet with **Scaffold** widget:

```
Scaffold(
  body: const Center(
    child: Text(
      'Add Items to Shop! ⍰',
      style: TextStyle(fontSize: 50),
    ),
  ),
  appBar: AppBar(
    title: const Text('Secret Shopping List'),
  ),
```

```
    floatingActionButton: FloatingActionButton(
      onPressed: () {
        // Add your onPressed code here!
      },
      child: const Icon(Icons.add),
    )
  );
```

Padding

The **Padding** widget in Flutter adds empty space (padding) around its child widget. This is useful for creating breathing room between UI elements and ensuring that content is not cramped. The padding widget requires padding and child property. Here is an example for padding:

```
Padding(
  padding: const EdgeInsets.all(14.0),
  child: Text('Ahoy, Captain!'),
)
```

Card

The **Card** widget is used to create a material design card. Cards are surfaces that display content and actions on a single topic. The following is a sample code for **Card** widget:

```
Card(
  elevation: 6,
  child: Padding(
    padding: const EdgeInsets.all(14.0),
    child: Text('This is cool card.'),
  ),
);
```

Here, **EdgeInsets** is a class in Flutter that represents the amount of space to be added around a widget. It is commonly used for padding and margins. **EdgeInsets** can be specified in different ways to suit various layout needs. The elevation property is the z-coordinate at which to place the card, it will add a shadow behind the card depending on the elevation value.

Using images in Flutter project

Flutter supports adding both raster (bitmap) and vector images to your app.

Adding images to your Flutter app

Start by adding the image(s) to your project, as discussed in the *Managing assets and localization* section.

You can update the **pubspec.yaml** file, as shown in the following code:

```
flutter:
  assets:
    - assets/images/my_image.png
```

Or, you can just add the folder path to access all images, shown as follows:

```
flutter:
  assets:
    - assets/images/
```

In IntelliJ IDEA, you will need to click on the "**pub get**" command on the strip (on top of file) showing Flutter commands, to allow Flutter to update the assets list. Now, you can use the **Image.asset** widget to display the image added inside the project, as shown in the following snippet:

```
Image.asset(
  "assets/images/goku.png",
  width: 200,
  height: 200,
),
```

You can also add images that are on the internet, using **Image.network** widget. Here is quick snippet showing it in action:

```
Image.network(
  'https://picsum.photos/512?image=1',
  width: 200,
  height: 200,
),
```

Vector images like **Scalable Vector Graphics (SVG)** can be displayed using the **flutter_svg** package. The version of the package is subject to change as be easily checked using, Flutter "**pub outdated**" command in terminal. To add the package, open the **pubspec.yaml** file and update the **dependencies** shown as follows:

```
dependencies:
  flutter_svg: ^2.0.10+1
```

Now, add a SVG image to the **assets/images** folder and then write the following code:

```
import 'package:flutter/material.dart';
import 'package:flutter_svg/flutter_svg.dart';

class SvgExample extends StatelessWidget {
  @override
  Widget build(BuildContext context) {
    return Scaffold(
      body: Center(
        child: SvgPicture.asset(
          'images/icon.svg',
          semanticsLabel: 'Knight',
          width: 200,
          height: 200,
        ),
      ),
    );
  }
}

void main() {
  runApp(
    MaterialApp(
      home: SvgExample(),
    ),
  );
}
```

Building custom widgets

In Flutter, building custom widgets is a powerful way to create reusable components that can simplify your UI development process. This allows you to create consistent and maintainable code. Imagine we are building a simple card widget that displays a character from an anime series.

Creating a reusable widget

We will start by creating a custom widget for the card. First create a package inside **lib/** folder and name is widget. Then create a new Dart file inside this folder, name its **anime_card_widget.dart**. Then, add the following code:

```
import 'package:flutter/material.dart';

class AnimeCard extends StatelessWidget {
  final String name;
  final String imagePath;
  final String description;

  const AnimeCard({
    super.key,
    required this.name,
    required this.imagePath,
    required this.description,
  });

  @override
  Widget build(BuildContext context) {
    return Padding(
      padding: const EdgeInsets.all(8.0),
      child: Card(
        elevation: 4.0,
        shape:
            RoundedRectangleBorder(borderRadius: BorderRadius.circular(10.0)),
        child: Padding(
          padding: const EdgeInsets.all(8.0),
          child: Column(
            crossAxisAlignment: CrossAxisAlignment.center,
            children: [
              Image.asset(imagePath, height: 350, fit: BoxFit.cover),
              const SizedBox(height: 16.0),
              Text(
                name,
                style: const TextStyle(
                  fontSize: 20,
                  fontWeight: FontWeight.bold,
                ),
              ),
              const SizedBox(height: 5.0),
```

```
                    Text(
                      description,
                      textAlign: TextAlign.center,
                    ),
                    const SizedBox(height: 8.0),
                  ],
                ),
              ),
            ),
          );
        }
      }
```

In the preceding code, we created a custom widget called **`AnimeCard`**. This widget takes three parameters: **`name`**, **`imagePath`**, and **`description`**. It builds a card with the character's image, name, and a brief description. Before writing the next part of code, please add three or more images, to **`assets/images`** folder.

Passing data to custom widgets

Now, update the **`main.dart`** file with following code:

```
import 'package:flutter/material.dart';
import 'widgets/anime_card_widget.dart';

void main() {
  runApp(const MyAnimeApp());
}

class MyAnimeApp extends StatelessWidget {
  const MyAnimeApp({super.key});

  @override
  Widget build(BuildContext context) {
    return MaterialApp(
      title: 'Anime Characters',
      theme: ThemeData(
        primarySwatch: Colors.green,
      ),
      home: const MyHomeScreen(),
```

```
    );
  }
}

class MyHomeScreen extends StatelessWidget {
  const MyHomeScreen({super.key});

  @override
  Widget build(BuildContext context) {
    return Scaffold(
      appBar: AppBar(title: const Text('Favorite Anime Charac-
ters')),
      body: SizedBox(
        width: 400,
        child: ListView(
          padding: const EdgeInsets.all(15.0),
          children: const [
            AnimeCard(
              name: 'Naruto Uzumaki',
              imagePath: 'assets/images/naruto.jpg',
              description:
                  'A ninja from the Hidden Leaf Vil-
lage with a dream of becoming Hokage.',
            ),
            AnimeCard(
              name: 'Goku',
              imagePath: 'assets/images/goku.jpg',
              description:
                  'A Saiyan from Earth who strives to be the stron-
gest fighter in the universe.',
            ),
            AnimeCard(
              name: 'Monkey D. Luffy',
              imagePath: 'assets/images/luffy.jpg',
              description:
                  'A pirate with the goal of find-
ing the One Piece and becoming the Pirate King.',
            ),
```

```
              ],
            ),
          ),
        );
      }
    }
```

In this example, we created a **MyHomeScreen** widget that uses our **AnimeCard** custom widget to display a list of anime characters. We pass the character's name, image path, and description to each **AnimeCard** instance, without actually creating the whole 50 lines of cards every time, saving time and resources. The output should be something like shown in the following figure:

***Figure 3.16:** Custom widget and its implementation in Flutter*

Thus, building custom widgets in Flutter allows you to create reusable and consistent components for your app. By passing data to these widgets, you can make them flexible and adaptable to different contexts.

Understanding the widget tree

When you are working with Flutter, you are dealing with a widget tree, a crucial concept for building and rendering your app. Let us break down the basics and understand how it all works.

Widget tree basics

Each widget is a building block of your app's user interface. Just like in a real tree, where there is a parent (root and trunk, from which everything grows), and the children (branches and leaves of the tree). Similarly, in Flutter, a widget can have other widgets nested inside it, forming a hierarchical structure.

Parent-child relationships

In a tree, every branch (widget) has a parent, and it can also have children (sub-branches or leaves). For example, a `Scaffold` widget might have an **`AppBar`** and a **`Body`**, which are its children. The parent-child relationship defines how widgets are structured and laid out, as shown in the following figure:

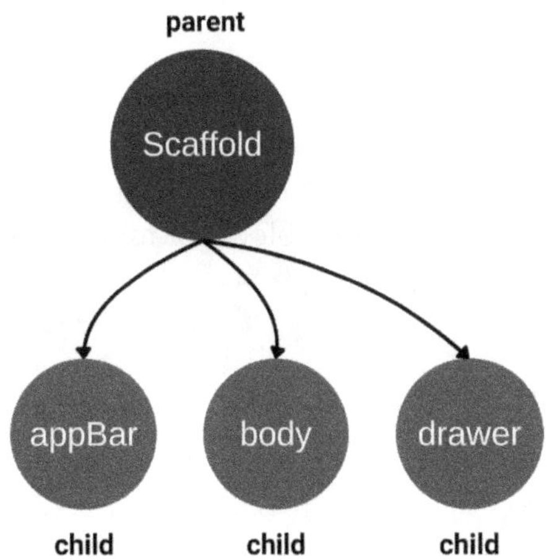

Figure 3.17: *Parent child relationship in Flutter*

You start with a root widget (like `MaterialApp`) and build outwards. Each widget you add can have its own set of child widgets, forming branches and leaves of the tree. Take a look at the following figure:

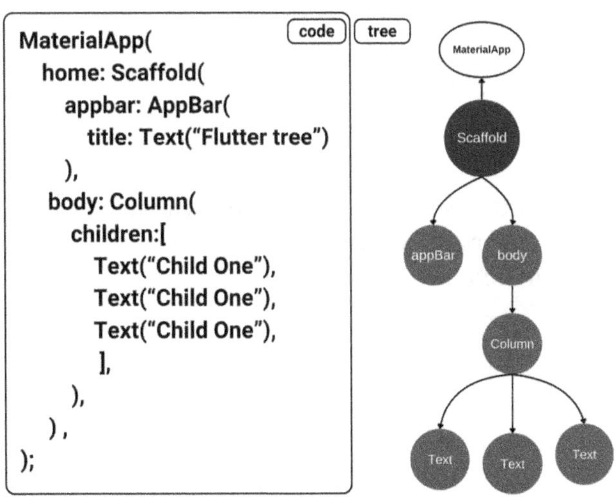

Figure 3.18: *Flutter code represented in a tree diagram*

Layout models in Flutter

In Flutter, layout models help you design and arrange widgets in your app. These models can be broadly categorized into single-child layouts, multi-child layouts, and complex layouts. Understanding these will help you create flexible and responsive designs.

Single-child layouts

Single-child layouts are containers that hold only one child widget. Let us explore some of the common single-child layouts.

Container

The **Container** widget is like a box that you can style, position, and size. It can hold a single child and is often used as a building block for more complex layouts. Take a look at given snippet:

```
Container(
  color: Colors.orange,
  width: 120,
  height: 120,
  child: Text('Kaladin'),
)
```

Center

The **Center** widget centers its child within itself:

```
Center(
  child: Text('Sylphrena'),
);
```

Expanded

The **Expanded** widget in Flutter is used to take up the available space within a **Row**, **Column**, or **Flex** widget, distributing space according to its flex factor. The following code snippet shows **Expanded** widget in action:

```
Row(
  children: [
    Expanded(
      child: Container(color: Colors.blue, height: 120),
    ),
    Expanded(
```

```
      child: Container(color: Colors.red, height: 120),
    ),
  ],
);
```

Multi-child layouts

Multi-child layouts can hold more than one child. These are essential for creating complex UIs.

Column

The **Column** widget arranges its children in vertical layout. As shown in the following code, we are putting three text widgets inside a column:

```
Column(
  children: const <Widget>[
    Text('Dalinar'),
    Text('Jasnah'),
    Text('Shallan'),
  ],
);
```

Row

The **Row** widget arranges its children in horizontal layout. Look at the following code snippet:

```
Row(
  children: const <Widget>[
    Text('Renarin'),
    Text('Szeth'),
    Text('Lift'),
  ],
);
```

Stack

The **Stack** widget allows children to be layered on top of each other. For example, putting three containers on top of each other as shown in the following snippet:

```
Stack(
  children: <Widget>[
    Container(
      color: Colors.blue,
      width: 100,
      height: 100,
    ),
    Container(
      color: Colors.red,
      width: 75,
      height: 75,
    ),
    Container(
      color: Colors.green,
      width: 35,
      height: 35,
    ),
  ],
);
```

ListView

The **ListView** widget displays its children as a scrollable list. Here is a small code snippet:

```
ListView(
  children: const [
    Text('Hoid'),
    Text('Dalinar'),
    Text('Shallan'),
  ],
);
```

GridView

The **GridView** widget arranges its children in a grid. You are put data inside rows and columns using this widget as shown in the following snippet:

```
GridView.count(
  crossAxisCount: 3,
  children: const [
    Text('Apples'),
```

```
        Text('Bananas'),
        Text('Cherries'),
        Text('Dates),
      ],
    );
```

Complex layouts

Complex layouts in Flutter combine multiple layout widgets and often include nested structures, custom positioning, and advanced alignment techniques. They are used for building intricate and dynamic user interfaces.

Nested layouts

Nested layouts involve embedding one layout widget within another to achieve a sophisticated structure. For example, a **Row** inside a **Column** or vice versa. The code snippet below show an example of this:

```
Column(
  children: [
    Row(
      mainAxisAlignment: MainAxisAlignment.spaceBetween,
      children: [
        Text('Kaladin'),
        Text('Sylphrena'),
      ],
    ),
    Container(
      color: Colors.orange,
      padding: const EdgeInsets.all(8.0),
      child: Text('Dalinar'),
    ),
  ],
);
```

Custom positioned layouts

Using the **Positioned** widget inside a **Stack**, you can precisely place widgets anywhere within a parent container. The code snippet below demonstrates this custom layout:

```
Stack(
  children: [
    Container(
      color: Colors.grey,
      height: 200,
      width: 200,
    ),
    Positioned(
      top: 50,
      left: 50,
      child: Container(
        color: Colors.blue,
        height: 50,
        width: 50,
      ),
    ),
  ],
);
```

Grid-based complex layouts

Advanced grid layouts can be achieved using **`GridView.builder`** or **`CustomScrollView`** for dynamic and optimized content display. Given below is a sample code snippet for this layout:

```
GridView.builder(
  gridDelegate: const SliverGridDelegateWithFixedCrossAxisCount(
    crossAxisCount: 3,
    crossAxisSpacing: 10,
    mainAxisSpacing: 10,
  ),
  itemBuilder: (context, index) {
    return Container(
      // Loops through the colors in the Colors.primaries list
      color: Colors.primaries[index % Colors.primaries.length],
    );
  },
  itemCount: 18,
);
```

Slivers for advanced scrolling

Flutter's **`CustomScrollView`** and slivers allow you to create highly dynamic and scrollable layouts. For instance, combining a **`SliverAppBar`** with other sliver widgets creates a scrolling UI with app bar effects. The following code snippet shows its implementation:

```
CustomScrollView(
  slivers: [
    const SliverAppBar(
      expandedHeight: 150.0,
      floating: false,
      pinned: true,
      flexibleSpace: FlexibleSpaceBar(
        title: Text('SliverAppBar Example›),
      ),
    ),
    SliverList(
      delegate: SliverChildBuilderDelegate(
        (BuildContext context, int index) {
          return ListTile(
            title: Text('Item $index'),
          );
        },
        childCount: 50,
      ),
    ),
  ],
);
```

By integrating these complex layouts, you can craft highly functional and visually appealing interfaces tailored to diverse user needs.

State management techniques

State management is a fundamental concept in Flutter development that deals with how the state of an application is handled and maintained over time.

Understanding state

State represents the dynamic aspects of your app, such as user inputs, animations, fetched data, etc. In Flutter, the state determines how widgets render and behave. Flutter offers various ways to manage state, ranging from simple to advanced techniques. One of the simplest methods involves using **setState** and **InheritedWidget**.

setState

setState is a method provided by the **StatefulWidget** class. It is used to update the state of a widget and trigger a rebuild of the widget tree. This method is suitable for small applications with straightforward state requirements.

For example: Imagine you have a Stormlight Archive app that displays the number of books read. You want to increment the count each time the user reads a book, then you can update your **main.dart** file and update the code, shown as follows:

```
import 'package:flutter/material.dart';

void main() {
  runApp(BookCounter());
}

class BookCounter extends StatefulWidget {
  @override
  _BookCounterState createState() => _BookCounterState();
}

class _BookCounterState extends State<BookCounter> {
  int _booksRead = 0;

  void _increaseCount() {
    setState(() {
      _booksRead++;
    });
  }

  @override
  Widget build(BuildContext context) {
    return MaterialApp(
      home: Scaffold(
        appBar: AppBar(
          title: const Text("Stormlight Archive Tracker"),
          centerTitle: true,
```

```
          leading: const Icon(Icons.list),
        ),
        body: Center(
          child: Column(
            mainAxisAlignment: MainAxisAlignment.center,
            children: <Widget>[
              Text(
                'Books read:',
                style: Theme.of(context).textTheme.headlineMedium,
              ),
              Text(
                '$_booksRead',
                style: TextStyle(
                    fontSize: 100,
                    fontWeight: FontWeight.bold,
                    color: Colors.red[300]),
              ),
              ElevatedButton(
                onPressed: _increaseCount,
                child: Text("Read Another Book"),
              ),
            ],
          ),
        ),
      ),
    );
  }
}
```

In this example, the **setState()** method updates the **_booksRead** variable, and the UI is rebuilt to reflect the new count. The result should look something like the following figure:

Figure 3.19: *A simple book counter app using stateful widget and setState()*

InheritedWidget

`InheritedWidget` is a more advanced and efficient way to manage state across multiple widgets. It allows you to make state changes down the widget tree without explicitly passing the state through constructor parameters.

Advanced state management

As applications grow in complexity, managing state efficiently becomes more challenging. Advanced state management solutions offer more robust and scalable ways to handle state, making it easier to build and maintain large applications. Some popular advanced state management techniques in Flutter include Provider, Riverpod, and Bloc.

Provider

Provider is a wrapper around InheritedWidget, making it easier to manage state and dependencies. It offers a simple and clean way to inject dependencies and manage state across your app.

Riverpod

Riverpod is a modern and robust state management solution for Flutter. It is a complete rewrite of Provider and aims to provide better performance and improved API.

Bloc

Business Logic Component (Bloc) is a popular state management library that uses the Bloc pattern to separate business logic from UI. It leverages Streams for state management, making it suitable for complex and large-scale applications.

Designing responsive UIs for web

Creating websites with responsiveness involves ensuring that they can adapt well to various screen sizes and orientations, providing an optimal viewing experience across different devices. Responsive design is essential for delivering a positive user experience, accommodating mobile phones, tablets, and desktop computers alike. An example of a responsive user interface is demonstrated as follows:

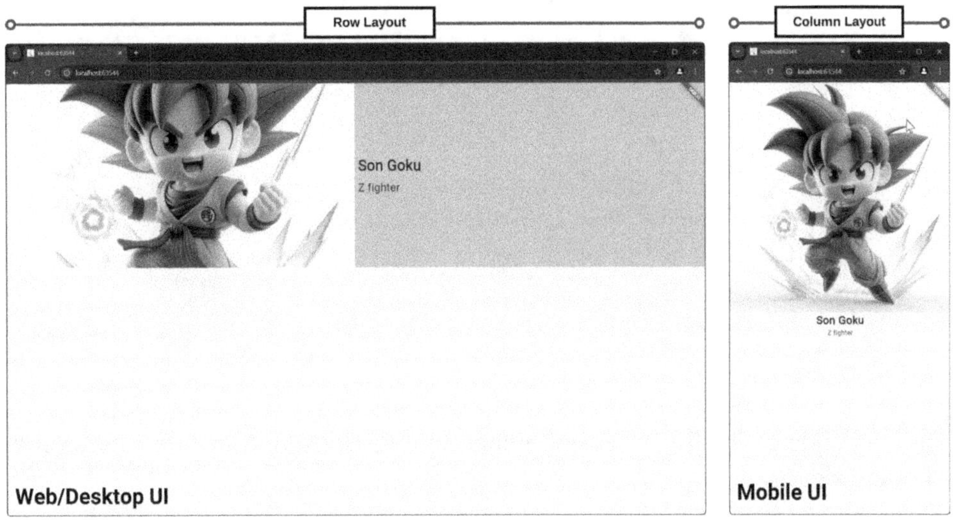

Figure 3.20: Example of a responsive UI in Flutter

Media queries and layout builders

In Flutter, media queries and layout builders are crucial elements for developing responsive designs. MediaQuery offers details about the current screen size and orientation, enabling informed decisions about utilizing screen space effectively. An example demonstrating these concepts is provided in the following example:

```
import 'package:flutter/material.dart';

void main() {
  runApp(MyResponsiveWidget());
}

class MyResponsiveWidget extends StatelessWidget {
  @override
  Widget build(BuildContext context) {
    var screenSize = MediaQuery.of(context).size;
```

```

    return MaterialApp(
      home: Scaffold(
        body: Container(
          color: screenSize.width < 600 ? Colors.yellow : Colors.green,
          child: Center(
            child: screenSize.width < 600
                ? const Text('Small Screen', style: TextStyle(fontSize: 48))
                : const Text('Large Screen', style: TextStyle(fontSize: 48)),
          ),
        ),
      ),
    );
  }
}
```

Running this code in IntelliJ IDEA will generate a responsive user interface as shown in the following figure:

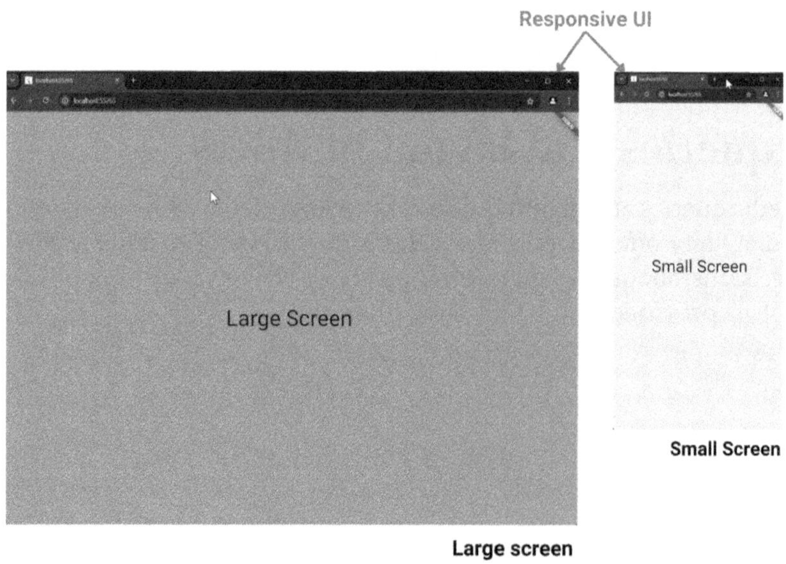

***Figure 3.21**: A responsive interface using MediaQuery in Flutter*

Resizing the window will change the background and text of the app, depending on the width of screen.

LayoutBuilder and OrientationBuilder

For more control over the layout based on constraints and orientation, you can use **`LayoutBuilder`** and **`OrientationBuilder`**. The **`LayoutBuilder`** widget in Flutter is used to construct a widget tree that adheres to the constraints imposed by the parent widget. It allows for responsive designs by dynamically adjusting layouts to different screen sizes and orientations. **`OrientationBuilder`**, as the name suggest allows you to control the layout structure depending on the orientation of screen.

ResponsiveBuilder package

Responsive widgets adjust their layout and behavior based on screen size and orientation. The **`responsive_builder`** package simplifies building responsive widgets. Open the **`pubspec.yaml`** file and add inside dependencies section (**`responsive_builder: ^0.7.1`**). Then, next, run pub get to download and integrate the package into the project. The following code snippet shows its implementation:

```
ResponsiveBuilder(
  builder: (context, sizingInformation) {
    if (sizingInformation.deviceScreenType == DeviceScreenType.mobile) {
      return Text('Mobile Screen');
    } else {
      return Text('Desktop Screen');
    }
  },
);
```

Responsive widgets dynamically adapt to the screen size and orientation. Combining **`MediaQuery`**, **`LayoutBuilder`**, and **`OrientationBuilder`** with responsive design principles ensures a smooth user experience across all devices.

Design patterns

Design patterns are standardized solutions to common software design problems. The following are the key patterns:

- **BLoC**: Disconnects business logic from the UI using Streams to manage state and events, enhancing scalability and maintainability.
- **Provider**: A lightweight state management solution that simplifies data sharing across widgets using **`ChangeNotifier`** for notifications and Provider for wrapping the widget tree.

- **Singleton**: Ensures a single instance of a class throughout the app's lifecycle, useful for global state or services, implemented with a private constructor and static instance.
- **Repository**: Abstracts data access with a repository interface, providing a clean API for data operations.
- **Model-View-ViewModel (MVVM)**: Separates data, UI, and logic into Model (data and business logic), View (UI), and ViewModel (bridge and logic handling).

Navigating and routing

Navigation and routing are crucial aspects of any mobile application. They define how users move between different screens and how data is passed around. In Flutter, the Navigator and Routes are essential tools for handling navigation and routing efficiently.

Basic navigation

The **`Navigator`** widget manages a stack of **`Route`** objects and provides methods to manipulate the stack, such as pushing and popping routes.

- **Pushing routes**: This involves adding a new route to the stack, which typically results in displaying a new screen.
- **Popping routes**: This involves removing the topmost route from the stack, which typically results in going back to the previous screen.

To understand, create a new file called **`navigation_ex.dart`** inside the lib folder and then write the following code:

```
import 'package:flutter/cupertino.dart';
import 'package:flutter/material.dart';

void main() {
  runApp(MaterialApp(
    home: MyHomeScreen(),
    debugShowCheckedModeBanner: false,
  ));
}

class MyHomeScreen extends StatelessWidget {
  @override
  Widget build(BuildContext context) {
    return Scaffold(
      appBar: AppBar(
```

```
        title: Text('Home Screen'),
        centerTitle: true,
        actions: [
          TextButton(
            onPressed: () {
              Navigator.push(
                context,
                CupertinoPageRoute(builder: (context) => MySecondScreen()),
              );
            },
            child: Text("Second Screen"),
          ),
          SizedBox(width: 25),
        ],
      ),
      body: Container(
        color: Colors.blue[100],
        child: Center(
          child: ElevatedButton(
            onPressed: () {
              Navigator.push(
                context,
                MaterialPageRoute(builder: (context) => MySecondScreen()),
              );
            },
            child: Text('Go to the Second Screen'),
          ),
        ),
      ),
    );
  }
}

class MySecondScreen extends StatelessWidget {
  @override
  Widget build(BuildContext context) {
```

```
      return Scaffold(
        appBar: AppBar(
          title: Text('The Second Screen'),
          centerTitle: true,
        ),
        body: Container(
          color: Colors.yellow[200],
          child: Center(
            child: ElevatedButton(
              onPressed: () {
                Navigator.pop(context);
              },
              child: Text('Click to go back'),
            ),
          ),
        ),
      );
    }
  }
```

In this example, the **MyHomeScreen** navigates to the **MySecondScreen** using **CupertinoPageRoute** for iOS-style transitions and **MaterialPageRoute** for standard transitions. The **MySecondScreen** allows returning to the **MyHomeScreen** with **Navigator.pop(context)**. Running the app will look like the following figure:

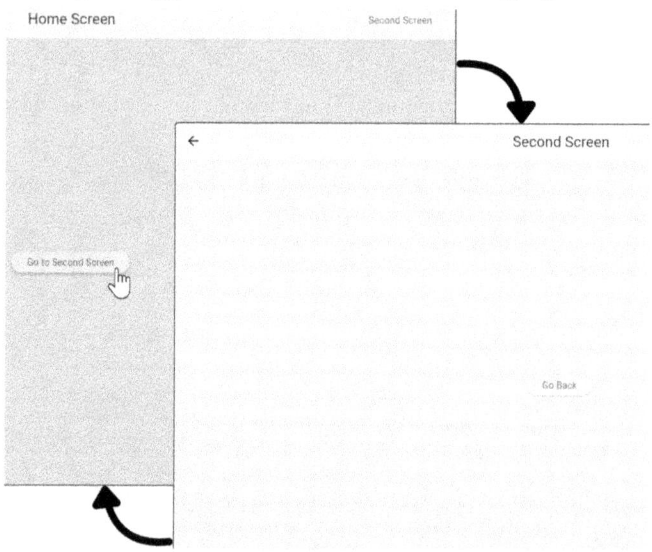

***Figure 3.22:** Simple navigation in Flutter*

Named routes

Named routes simplify navigation in Flutter by using route names instead of directly managing route objects. Here is a quick example with **navigation_ex2.dart**:

```
import 'package:flutter/material.dart';

void main() {
  runApp(MaterialApp(
    initialRoute: '/',
    routes: {
      '/': (context) => MyHomeScreen(),
      '/second': (context) => MySecondScreen(),
      '/third': (context) => MyThirdScreen(),
    },
  ));
}

class MyHomeScreen extends StatelessWidget {
  @override
  Widget build(BuildContext context) {
    return Scaffold(
      appBar: AppBar(title: const Text('The Home Screen')),
      body: Center(
        child: Row(
          mainAxisAlignment: MainAxisAlignment.center,
          children: [
            ElevatedButton(
              onPressed: () {
                Navigator.pushNamed(context, '/second');
              },
              child: const Text('Go to Second Screen'),
            ),
            SizedBox(width: 24),
            ElevatedButton(
              onPressed: () {
                Navigator.pushNamed(context, '/third');
              },
              child: const Text('Go to Third Screen'),
```

```
            ),
          ],
        ),
      ),
    );
  }
}

class MySecondScreen extends StatelessWidget {
  @override
  Widget build(BuildContext context) {
    return Scaffold(
      appBar: AppBar(title: Text('The Second Screen')),
      body: Center(
        child: ElevatedButton(
          onPressed: () {
            Navigator.pop(context);
          },
          child: Text('Go to home'),
        ),
      ),
    );
  }
}

class MyThirdScreen extends StatelessWidget {
  @override
  Widget build(BuildContext context) {
    return Scaffold(
      appBar: AppBar(title: Text('The Third Screen')),
      body: Center(
        child: ElevatedButton(
          onPressed: () {
            Navigator.pop(context);
          },
          child: Text('Go to home'),
        ),
```

```
          ),
      );
    }
}
```

In this example, **MaterialApp** defines three named routes: '/' for **MyHomeScreen**, **'/second'** for **MySecondScreen**, and **'/third'** for **MyThirdScreen**. Buttons on **MyHomeScreen** navigate to the other screens using **Navigator.pushNamed**, while the other screens have buttons to return using **Navigator.pop**.

Project: DartByte

Creating apps is the best way to learn Flutter (or any framework). The project DartByte will be a simple project, that will help you understand how to make an application with multiple widgets, to make a good look UI. You will be making something like the following figure:

Figure 3.23: The DartByte user interface

Setting up the project

In IntelliJ IDEA, click open the project names on the top left and select new project options. The select the Flutter option and press **Next**. Configure the project as shown in the following figure:

Figure 3.24: *DartByte project configuration*

main.dart file

The DartByte project is divided into several classes, each handling a specific part of the UI. It demonstrates Flutter's widget structure, responsive design, and how to build a web-friendly layout. All the code will be written inside **`main.dart`** file for this project. Let us break it down widget by widget.

Main class - DartByteApp

The project starts with the **`DartByteApp`** class, which extends StatelessWidget. This class defines the overall app structure, starting with the **`MaterialApp`** widget inside the **`build()`** method. It sets the title of the app to 'Dart byte' and customizes the scroll behavior to allow drag gestures from different pointer devices, essential for web applications. The debug banner is disabled, and the home is set to the **`ByteBoardPage`**. Write the following code:

```dart
import 'dart:math';
import 'dart:ui';

import 'package:flutter/material.dart';

void main() {
  // run the DartByteApp widget
  runApp(const DartByteApp());
}

class DartByteApp extends StatelessWidget {
  const DartByteApp({super.key});

  @override
  Widget build(BuildContext context) {
    return MaterialApp(
      title: 'Dart byte',
      scrollBehavior: const MaterialScrollBehavior().copyWith(
        // for web we need to add mouse and unknown as a drag devices
        dragDevices: {
          PointerDeviceKind.unknown,
          PointerDeviceKind.touch,
          PointerDeviceKind.mouse,
        },
      ),
      // remove debug banner
      debugShowCheckedModeBanner: false,
      // set the home page
      home: const ByteBoardPage(),
    );
  }
}
```

ByteBoardPage

This class is responsible for rendering the main body of the app. It is also a **StatelessWidget** and contains a **Scaffold** widget with an **AppBar** that features a search icon. The body of the page uses a **LayoutBuilder** to create a responsive layout. If the screen width is greater than 1200 pixels, the content is displayed in a **Row** that centers the child widgets horizontally. Otherwise, it displays a **Placeholder** for smaller screens. The **Row** contains a **SingleChildScrollView** to allow scrolling for the main content, which consists of three widgets: **TopSlider**, **RecommendedNews**, and **AllArticleRow**. Add **ByteBoardPage** widget class in **main.dart** file as shown in the following code:

```
class ByteBoardPage extends StatelessWidget {
  const ByteBoardPage({super.key});

  @override
  Widget build(BuildContext context) {
    return Scaffold(
        appBar: AppBar(
          title: const Text('DartByte'),
          // add actions to the right corner of app bar
          actions: [
            IconButton(
              icon: const Icon(Icons.search),
              onPressed: () {},
            ),
          ],
        ),
        body: LayoutBuilder(
            builder: (BuildContext context, BoxConstraints constraints) {
          // check if the width is greater than 1200
          if (constraints.maxWidth > 1200) {
            return const Row(
                // mainAxisSize set to max to take full width
                mainAxisSize: MainAxisSize.max,
                mainAxisAlignment: MainAxisAlignment.center,
                crossAxisAlignment: CrossAxisAlignment.center,
                children: [
                  // create a fixed width container in the center
                  SizedBox(
                      width: 1200,
                      child: SingleChildScrollView(
                          child: Column(
                              // the 3 sections of the page
                              children: [
```

```
                        TopSlider(),
                        RecommendedNews(),
                        AllArticleRow(),
                      ])))
              ]);
          } else {
            // if the width is less than 1200, return a placeholder
            return const Placeholder();
          }
        }));
    }
  }
```

TopSlider

The **TopSlider** class is a horizontally scrolling list of news cards. Inside the **SizedBox** widget, it uses a **Scrollbar** and **ListView** with **scrollDirection** set to **Axis.horizontal** to allow horizontal scrolling. The list contains instances of **ByteNewsCard**, each displaying a news article. The cards are hardcoded with different news items, and the widget sets a height of **400 pixels** to accommodate the slider. Add a **TopSlider** widget to your file by running the following code:

```
class TopSlider extends StatelessWidget {
  @override
  Widget build(BuildContext context) {
    return SizedBox(
        // sets the height of the slider
        height: 400,
        width: double.infinity,
        child: Expanded(
            child: Scrollbar(
                // horizontal scroll view
                child: ListView(
                    scrollDirection: Axis.horizontal,
                    // ByteNewsCard widget is used to display the news
                    children: const [
              ByteNewsCard("Dart collections", "Noor ul Aman", 1),
              ByteNewsCard("Web is Amazing", "Zaid Kamil", 2),
              ByteNewsCard("Responsive Design", "Amna Ghazal", 3),
              // todo add more cards
```

```
            ]))));
    }
  }
```

ByteNewsCard

The **ByteNewsCard** class defines the individual cards in the **TopSlider**. Each card has a title, author, and image (represented by an ID). The **Card** widget is styled with rounded corners, shadows (via **elevation**), and padding. The image for the card is fetched from a random image service using the **Image.network** widget, and the fit: **BoxFit.cover** property ensures the image covers the available space. In the following figure the title and author are displayed with some basic styling like font size and weight. Create a **ByteNewsCard** widgets as shown:

```
class ByteNewsCard extends StatelessWidget {
  final String title;
  final String author;
  final int imgId;

  const ByteNewsCard(this.title, this.author, this.imgId, {super.key});

  @override
  Widget build(BuildContext context) {
    return Card(
        // this is used to clip the card shape
        clipBehavior: Clip.antiAliasWithSaveLayer,
        shape:
            RoundedRectangleBorder(borderRadius: BorderRadius.circular(10.0)),
        elevation: 5,
        margin: const EdgeInsets.all(10),
        child: Column(children: [
          // Image.network is used to load the image from the network
          Image.network(
            "https://picsum.photos/id/$imgId/500/300",
            // fits the image to cover the whole area
            fit: BoxFit.cover,
          ),
          Padding(
```

```
          padding: const EdgeInsets.all(8.0),
          child: Column(children: [
            Text(title,
                style: const TextStyle(
                  fontSize: 20,
                  fontWeight: FontWeight.bold,
                )),
            const SizedBox(height: 8),
            Text('by $author'),
          ]))
      ]));
  }
}
```

RecommendedNews

This class generates a row of four recommendation cards. Each card shows a random image and a random number of views (between 0 and 1000) for that article. It uses **`List.generate()`** to create four cards, each wrapped in an **`Expanded`** widget to ensure equal width distribution across the screen. The cards are styled similarly to **`ByteNewsCard`**, with an image at the top and text below, and are contained within a **`Row`**. Now, add **`RecommendedNews`** widget like the following code:

```
class RecommendedNews extends StatelessWidget {
  @override
  Widget build(BuildContext context) {
    return Padding(
        padding: const EdgeInsets.all(8.0),
        child: Row(
          // generate 4 cards in a row
          children: List.generate(4, (index) {
            // generate random views for each card between 0 and 1000
            var views = (index + 1) * Random().nextInt(1000);
            return Expanded(
                // each card is wrapped in an expanded widget to take equal space
                child: Card(
                    clipBehavior: Clip.antiAliasWithSaveLayer,
                    shape: RoundedRectangleBorder(
```

```
                          borderRadius: BorderRadius.circular(10.0)),
                      elevation: 5,
                      margin: const EdgeInsets.all(10),
                      child: Column(children: [
                        // Load the image from the network
                        Image.network(
                          "https://picsum.photos/id/${index+10}/500/500",
                          fit: BoxFit.fill,
                        ),
                        Padding(
                            // add padding to the text
                            padding: const EdgeInsets.all(8.0),
                            child: Column(children: [
                              // cocatenate the index with the text
                              Text(
                                'Dartbyte #${index + 1}',
                                style: const TextStyle(
                                  fontSize: 20,
                                  fontWeight: FontWeight.bold,
                                ),
                              ),
                              const SizedBox(height: 8),
                              Text('Views: $views'),
                            ]))
                      ]));
            }),
          ));
    }
  }
```

AllArticleRow

AllArticleRow displays a grid of articles, structured into two columns, each containing a different number of articles (6 in the first, 5 in the second). The **Row** ensures the articles are aligned next to each other, and each column is an **Expanded** widget. Inside the columns, **List.generate()** is used to create a series of **NewsArticleItem** widgets. Create the **AllArticlesRow** widget as shown:

```
class AllArticleRow extends StatelessWidget {
  @override
  Widget build(BuildContext context) {
    return Padding(
      padding: const EdgeInsets.all(8.0),
      child: Row(
          // align the items to the start
          crossAxisAlignment: CrossAxisAlignment.start,
          // 2 columns in a row
          children: [
            Expanded(
              child: Column(
                // generate 6 news article items
                children: List.generate(6, (index) {
                  return NewsArticleItem();
                }),
              ),
            ),
            Expanded(
                child: Column(
                    // generate 5 news article items
                    children: List.generate(5, (index) {
              return NewsArticleItem();
            })))
          ]),
    );
  }
}
```

NewsArticleItem

This widget creates a simple container with a **CircleAvatar** and a text label. The container has padding and a border to create a card-like appearance. The **CircleAvatar** represents a placeholder for a potential image, and the text label shows the article title. The **Expanded** widget ensures that the text takes up the remaining space in the row layout. This widget is repeated in both columns of the **AllArticleRow**. Finally add the **NewsArticleItem** widget to complete the code:

```
class NewsArticleItem extends StatelessWidget {
  @override
  Widget build(BuildContext context) {
    // return a container with margin, padding, border and border radius
    return Container(
        margin: const EdgeInsets.all(8),
        padding: const EdgeInsets.all(8),
        decoration: BoxDecoration(
            border: Border.all(color: Colors.grey),
            borderRadius: BorderRadius.circular(8)),
        child: Row(children: [
          // create a circle avatar
          CircleAvatar(backgroundColor: Colors.green[300], radius: 20),
          const SizedBox(width: 8),
          // let the text take the remaining space in the row
          const Expanded(
            child: Text('News article title'),
          )
        ]));
  }
}
```

Each section of the app contributes to building a web-compatible, responsive, and visually appealing news board. The design is modular, with distinct classes handling different parts of the UI, making it easy to modify or extend individual components.

Conclusion

As we have explored in this chapter, designing stunning and responsive UIs for the web using Flutter's powerful widget system opens up a world of creative possibilities. By understanding the importance of responsiveness, we can create interfaces that seamlessly adapt to various screen sizes and orientations, ensuring a consistent user experience across all devices. We have explored practical techniques such as using MediaQuery, LayoutBuilder, and responsive packages like ResponsiveBuilder, which provide the tools needed to handle the dynamic nature of web interfaces effectively.

In the next chapter, you will learn about advanced user interface design, responsive layouts and adding animation in Flutter.

Points to remember

- **Understand responsiveness**: Create interfaces that adapt seamlessly to different screen sizes and orientations.
- **Leverage LayoutBuilder**: Employ LayoutBuilder to dynamically adapt the layout based on the available space.
- **Responsive widgets**: Integrate responsive packages like ResponsiveBuilder to simplify the creation of adaptable UIs.
- **Experiment and innovate**: Continuously explore new techniques and push creative boundaries to craft engaging web interfaces.

Multiple choice questions

1. **What is the command to apply dependencies in Flutter project from the terminal?**
   a. flutter pub upgrade
   b. flutter pub get
   c. flutter help
   d. flutter load pub
2. **In Flutter, how does the widget tree concept help in managing the UI components of an application?**
   a. It allows widgets to manage their state independently.
   b. It simplifies network requests and data handling.
   c. It organizes widgets hierarchically, enabling efficient updates and rendering.
   a. It provides built-in navigation functionalities.

Answers

1.	b
2.	c

Questions

1. Create a new flutter app called Movie-Rating. Implement a ListView Builder and ListTile to display 25 movies and their ratings in vertical scroll.

Additional resources

1. **https://docs.flutter.dev/ui/layout# standard-widgets**
2. **https://docs.flutter.dev/ui/navigation**
3. **https://docs.flutter.dev/ui/assets/assets-and-images**
4. **https://docs.flutter.dev/ui/widgets**

CHAPTER 4
Advanced UI Design and Animation

Introduction

In this chapter, you will understand the art of crafting visually stunning and highly interactive user interfaces using Flutter. We will explore advanced concepts like custom widgets, sophisticated animations, and performance optimization, guiding you through practical implementations that elevate your web applications. By the end, you will be equipped to design seamless, responsive, and dynamic UIs that offer an exceptional user experience.

Structure

The chapter covers the following topics:

- Custom widgets and components
- Working with animations
- Optimizing animation for performance
- Advanced layout techniques for web
- Theming and styling
- Practical: Staggered menu implementation
- Practical: Hero animation implementation
- Practical: Adding theme and style to DartByte

Objectives

The objective of this chapter is to equip you with the skills and knowledge to design and implement advanced user interfaces in Flutter that are not only visually appealing but also highly functional and responsive. You will learn how to create custom widgets and components, work with complex animations, optimize performance, and apply advanced layout techniques tailored for the web. Through hands-on examples and practical applications, such as implementing staggered menus and hero animations, you will gain the ability to enhance user interactions, ensure validation, and apply consistent theming and styling to your projects, ultimately elevating the overall user experience.

Custom widgets and components

In this section, we will explore the power of custom widgets in Flutter and how they enable you to create flexible, reusable, and modular UI components that enhance the maintainability and scalability of your applications. Building on the concepts covered in *Chapter 3, Designing Stunning UIs for the Web*, where we discussed custom components and data passing logic, we will now focus on making custom widgets in our upcoming Flutter projects.

Understanding custom widgets

Custom widgets are the building blocks of a well-structured Flutter application. By creating custom widgets, you encapsulate complex UI elements into reusable components, making your codebase more organized and easier to maintain. The benefits of Custom Widgets are shown in the following figure:

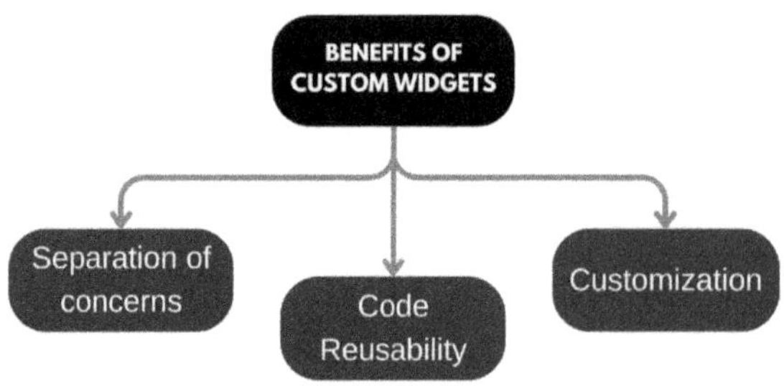

Figure 4.1: *Benefits of creating custom widgets in flutter*

The following are the key benefits of creating custom widgets:

- **Code reusability**: Custom widgets allow you to reuse complex UI elements across different parts of your application, reducing redundancy.
- **Separation of concerns**: By breaking down your UI into smaller, self-contained widgets, you maintain a clear separation of concerns, improving readability and testability.

- **Customization**: Custom widgets enable you to tailor UI components to meet specific design requirements, providing a unique and consistent user experience.

Types of custom widgets

There are two main types of custom widgets:

- **Stateless widgets**: These are used when the UI component does not need to manage any mutable state. While they do not change based on internal state changes, their appearance can still change if the data or properties passed to them are updated. These widgets are ideal for static elements that do not require real-time updates based on user interaction.
- **Stateful widgets**: These are used when the UI component needs to update dynamically, based on user interactions or other events. Stateful widgets can maintain and manage their own internal state, making them suitable for elements that require real-time changes or updates in response to various conditions.

Create a custom container

Let us create a custom container widget in Flutter that displays an image with a darkened overlay and centered text. This type of component is versatile and can be used for headers, banners, or any part of your UI where you want to combine text and imagery in a visually appealing way. The **`MyCustomContainer`** widget will be the custom component that allows you to create a container with a background image, a title text, and optional parameters for height and width. Additionally, it includes a **`ColorFilter`** to apply a darkening effect to the image, ensuring the text remains readable. For this, open a Flutter project in IntelliJ IDEA, the inside the **`lib/`** directory create **`components`** directory. Inside it create a dart file, name it **`my_custom_container.dart`**. The following is the implementation of our custom container:

```
// components/my_custom_container.dart
import 'package:flutter/material.dart';

class MyCustomContainer extends StatelessWidget {
  final String title;
  final String imageUrl;
  final double height;
  final double width;

  // constructor
  const MyCustomContainer({
    super.key,
    required this.title,
```

```
    required this.imageUrl,
    this.height = 500,
    this.width = double.infinity,
  });

  @override
  Widget build(BuildContext context) {
    return Container(
      height: height,
      width: width,
      // decoration to add image and text
      decoration: BoxDecoration(
        // image decoration adds image to the container
        image: DecorationImage(
          image: NetworkImage(imageUrl),
          fit: BoxFit.cover,
          // color filter to darken the image
          colorFilter: ColorFilter.mode(
            Colors.black.withValues(alpha: 0.5),
            BlendMode.darken,
          ),
        ),
      ),
      // alignment to center the text
      child: Align(
        child: Text(
          title,
          // text styling
          style: const TextStyle(
            color: Colors.white,
            fontSize: 50,
            fontWeight: FontWeight.bold,
          ),
          textAlign: TextAlign.center,
        ),
      ),
    );
  }
}
```

Note: Adding comments is a good habit, as they explain the purpose and functionality of various sections, making the code more understandable and maintainable for others or your future self. So, remember to add comments to your code.

To use the **`MyCustomContainer`** in your application, simply import the widget and include it in your layout:

```
// main.dart
import 'package:flutter/material.dart';
import 'components/my_custom_container.dart';

void main() {
  runApp(const MyCustomApp());
}

class MyCustomApp extends StatelessWidget {
  const MyCustomApp ({super.key});

  @override
  Widget build(BuildContext context) {
    return MaterialApp(
      title: 'Custom Banner,
      // setting basic theme
      theme: ThemeData(
        primarySwatch: Colors.blue,
      ),
      home: const MyLandingPage(),
    );
  }
}

class MyLandingPage extends StatelessWidget {
  const MyLandingPage({super.key});

  @override
  Widget build(BuildContext context) {
    return const Scaffold(
      body: Column(children: [
        // custom container inside the column
```

```
        MyCustomContainer(
          title: 'Flutter Custom Container',
          imageUrl: 'https://picsum.photos/1000?image=15',
        ),
      ]),
    );
  }
}
```

The output should look like the following figure:

Figure 4.2: A banner implemented using custom widget

In this example, the **`MyLandingPage`** widget utilizes the **`MyCustomContainer`** to display a full-width container with a **`height`** of 500 pixels. The background image is sourced from a URL, and a title text is centered within the container. The darkened overlay ensures that the title remains clearly visible against the image background. By creating this custom widget, you will be able to customize the container with:

- **Dynamic images**: You can easily switch out the image by changing the **`imageUrl`** parameter, making this widget highly versatile for different sections of your application.
- **Responsive dimensions**: By adjusting the **`height`** and **`width`** parameters, you can adapt this container to various screen sizes, ensuring it looks great on both mobile and web platforms.

With a solid understanding of custom widgets and components, you have now equipped yourself with the tools to create visually appealing and reusable UI elements. However, static UI elements can only take you so far. To truly captivate users and bring your interfaces to life, it is essential to incorporate animations that enhance user interaction and create a more engaging experience.

Working with animations

Animations in Flutter are a powerful way to add motion and fluidity to your applications. They can range from simple transitions to complex sequences that respond to user input, providing visual feedback and guiding the user through different states of your app. Flutter's animation framework is both flexible and easy to use, allowing developers to implement both implicit and explicit animations with minimal code.

Fundamental animation concepts in Flutter

At the heart of Flutter's animation system are a few core concepts that form the foundation for creating dynamic user interfaces. Some of the are:

- **Animations**: Animations in Flutter are defined by an Animation object, which represents the changing value of a property over time. This can be a simple fade-in/fade-out, a complex path-based animation, or anything in between.
- **Curves**: Curves define the rate of change of an animation over time. Flutter provides a range of pre-defined curves, such as linear, easeln, easeOut, and more, which you can use to fine-tune the feel and timing of your animations.
- **Controllers**: Animation controllers are responsible for managing the playback of an animation. They control the start, stop, and speed of an animation, allowing you to create complex, interactive animations.
- **Listeners and notifications**: Animation objects in Flutter can emit notifications when their value changes, allowing you to synchronize your UI with the animation's progress or trigger additional actions.

Types of animations in Flutter

Flutter offers two primary types of animations: Implicit Animations and Explicit Animations as shown in the following figure:

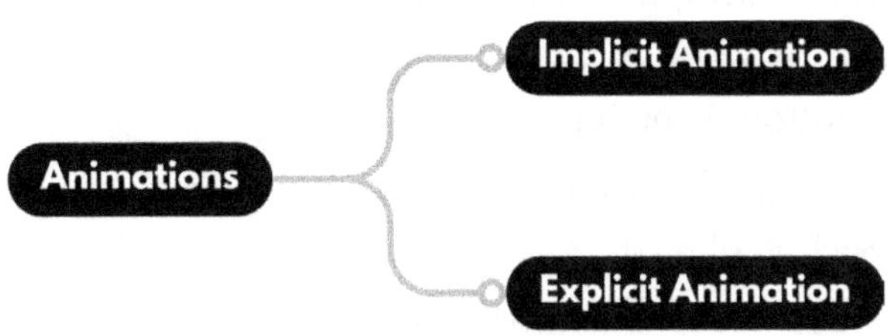

Figure 4.3: Two types of animation in Flutter

Let us discuss these briefly:

- **Implicit animations** are the easier of the two to implement. They automatically handle the animation's lifecycle for you. These animations are great for simple effects where you want the framework to manage the details. Examples include animations like fading, resizing, or changing colors.

- **Explicit animations**, on the other hand, give you more control over the animation's behavior. You will need to manage the animation's lifecycle, using controllers to start, stop, and reverse animations. This type is ideal for more complex scenarios where you need precise control over the animation sequence.

Implementing implicit animations

Implicit animations are an excellent starting point for adding simple animations to your Flutter applications without needing to manage the complexities of animation controllers and state changes manually. Implicit animations in Flutter are built into the framework, allowing you to animate properties of widgets without manually managing animation states. These animations automatically handle the transition between the widget's old and new states, making them ideal for straightforward animations like color changes, size adjustments, and opacity changes.

For almost every property change you want to animate, Flutter offers an **`AnimatedFoo`** widget. The *Foo* represents various widget properties like size, alignment, color, or even decoration. This powerful design allows you to explore animations tailored to specific widget properties without manual animation controllers. It is highly encouraged to experiment with different animated widgets to learn their behavior and potential use cases. Here is a list of a few key widgets for implicit animations:

- **AnimatedContainer**: Animates changes in its properties, such as size, color, and padding.
- **AnimatedOpacity**: Smoothly transitions the opacity of a widget.
- **AnimatedAlign**: Animates the alignment of a child widget within its parent.
- **AnimatedPositioned**: Animates the position of a widget within a stack.

Some practical use cases for implicit animations will be:

- **User feedback**: Providing visual feedback on user interactions, such as changing the color of a button when it is pressed.
- **State changes**: Animating widgets when their state changes, like expanding or collapsing a section of a UI.
- **Simple transitions**: Implementing simple transitions between different states of a widget, such as fading in and out or resizing.

Let us implement it using the following figure, where tapping on dragon image will make it grow and shrink in animated style:

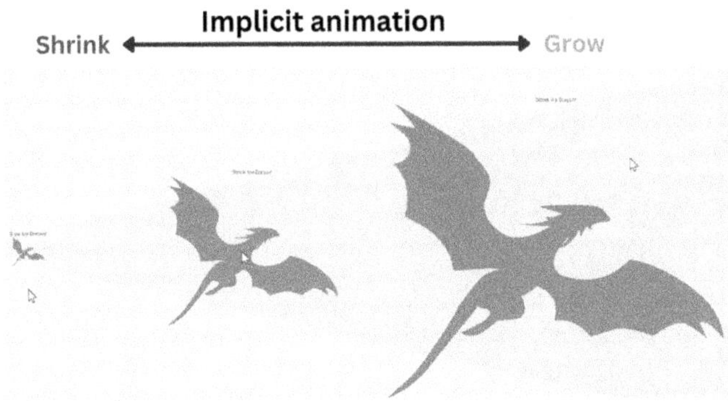

Figure 4.4: *Implicit animation showing grow and shrink on an image*

Write the following code in your IDE, in a new Dart file:

```
// implicit_animation.dart
import 'package:flutter/material.dart';

void main() {
  runApp(MaterialApp(
    // set home to AnimatedImage
    home: AnimatedImage(),
  ));
}

// AnimatedImage is a StatefulWidget
class AnimatedImage extends StatefulWidget {
  @override
  _AnimatedImageState createState() => _AnimatedImageState();
}

// _AnimatedImageState is a State of AnimatedImage
class _AnimatedImageState extends State<AnimatedImage> {
  // _isPressed is a boolean variable
  bool _isPressed = false;

  @override
  Widget build(BuildContext context) {
    return Scaffold(
      body: Center(
        child: Column(
```

```
          mainAxisAlignment: MainAxisAlignment.center,
          children: [
            Text(_isPressed ? 'Shrink the Dragon!' : 'Grow the Dragon!'),
            // add GestureDetector to the AnimatedContainer
            GestureDetector(
              onTap: () {
                // set _isPressed to the opposite of its current value
                setState(() {
                  _isPressed = !_isPressed;
                });
              },
              child: AnimatedContainer(
                // set duration to 1 second
                duration: const Duration(seconds: 1),
                // set width to 1000.0 if _isPressed is true, otherwise set it to 100.0
                width: _isPressed ? 1000.0 : 100.0,
                child: ColorFiltered(
                  // apply a color filter to the image
                  colorFilter: const ColorFilter.mode(
                    Colors.blue,
                    BlendMode.srcIn,
                  ),
                  // add any image here
                  child: Image.asset("images/dragon.png"),
                )
              )
            )
          ]
        )
      )
    );
  }
}
```

In the preceding Flutter app, the user interface is built using a **Scaffold** widget, which provides a basic app structure. Inside it, there is a centered column containing two main elements: a text widget and the animated container. The text at the top changes based on the current state, either prompting the user to grow or shrink the dragon. Following this is the main interactive element - the dragon image wrapped in a **`GestureDetector`**. This detector allows the app to respond to user taps.

When the user taps the image, a state change triggers the animation. The dragon image, placed inside an **`AnimatedContainer`**, smoothly transitions between two widths over one second, creating the illusion of growth or shrinkage. The image is loaded from the app's assets and passes through a **`ColorFiltered`** widget, which applies a blue tint to it.

Implementing explicit animations

Unlike implicit animations, explicit animations give you full control over the animation's behavior, allowing for more complex and customizable effects. Explicit animations require a bit more setup compared to implicit animations but offer greater flexibility. With explicit animations, you manually control the animation's duration, curves, and playback, enabling you to create sophisticated animations tailored to your specific needs. The following are the key concepts:

- **AnimationController**: Manages the animation's lifecycle, including start, stop, and reverse.
- **Tween**: Defines the range of values the animation will interpolate between.
- **Animation**: Represents the current state of the animation, providing value updates over time.
- **AnimationBuilder**: A widget that builds animations based on the animation's current value.

Explicit animations are ideal for scenarios where you need fine-grained control over the animation's behavior. Here are some practical use cases:

- **Custom UI components**: Creating unique animations for custom widgets that require specific timing, curves, or sequences.
- **Complex transitions**: Implementing intricate transitions between different states or views in your application.
- **Interactive animations**: Animations that respond to user interactions, such as dragging or tapping, requiring precise control over timing and effects.

Let us create a simple explicit animation that animates a widget's position:

```
// explicit_animation.dart
import 'package:flutter/material.dart';

void main() {
  runApp(MaterialApp(
    // set home to the MovingBox widget
```

```
      home: MovingBox(),
    ));
}

class MovingBox extends StatefulWidget {
  @override
  _MovingBoxState createState() => _MovingBoxState();
}

// SingleTickerProviderStateMixin allows the animation controller to work
class _MovingBoxState extends State<MovingBox>
    with SingleTickerProviderStateMixin {
  // _controller controls the animation
  late AnimationController _controller;
  // _animation will animate the position of the box using an Offset
  late Animation<Offset> _animation;

  @override
  void initState() {
    super.initState();
    // creates an AnimationController that repeats the animation
    _controller = AnimationController(
      // set the duration to 2 seconds
      duration: const Duration(seconds: 2),
      // vsync is set to this to use the SingleTickerProviderStateMixin
      vsync: this,
    )..repeat(reverse: true);

    // _animation animates the position of the box
    _animation = Tween<Offset>(
      // set the start position to (0.0, 0.0)
      begin: Offset.zero,
      // set the end position to (5.0, 5.0)
      end: const Offset(5.0, 5.0),
    ).animate(
      // use a CurvedAnimation to apply a curve to the animation
```

```
      CurvedAnimation(
        parent: _controller,
        curve: Curves.easeInOut,
      ),
    );
  }

  @override
  Widget build(BuildContext context) {
    return Scaffold(
      // set the body to a SlideTransition widget
      body: SlideTransition(
        // sets position of the box using the _animation
        position: _animation,
        child: Container(
          width: 150,
          height: 150,
          decoration: BoxDecoration(
            color: Colors.blue.shade200,
            borderRadius: BorderRadius.circular(10),
          ),
        ),
      ),
    );
  }

  @override
  void dispose() {
    // dispose the controller when the widget is removed from the tree
    _controller.dispose();
    super.dispose();
  }
}
```

In the above code, the main function starts the app by displaying the **MovingBox** widget. Inside this widget, we use a **StatefulWidget** to manage the animation. An **AnimationController** is used to control the timing of the animation, set to last two seconds and repeat in reverse, making the box move back and forth. The movement is defined by a **Tween**, which interpolates the box's position from the top-left corner (0, 0) to a point (5, 5), creating a smooth diagonal motion. The actual movement happens in the **SlideTransition** widget, which applies the animated position to the box. The box itself is a 150x150 pixel container with a blue color and rounded corners. Finally, when the widget is no longer needed, the dispose method ensures that the animation controller is properly cleaned up to avoid memory leaks.

Creating custom animations with AnimationBuilder

AnimationBuilder is a versatile widget that provides a way to build animations based on an **Animation** object. It allows you to customize how the animation's value affects your widget tree. Let us code an example that uses **AnimationBuilder**:

```
// custom_animation.dart
import 'dart:math';
import 'package:flutter/material.dart';
void main() {
  runApp(const MaterialApp(
    // Set the home to the RotatingScalingWidget
    home: RotatingScalingWidget(),
  ));
}
class RotatingScalingWidget extends StatefulWidget {
  const RotatingScalingWidget({super.key});

  @override
  createState() => _RotatingScalingWidgetState();
}

class _
RotatingScalingWidgetState extends State<RotatingScalingWidget>
    with SingleTickerProviderStateMixin {
  // AnimationController to control the animations
  late AnimationController _controller;
  // Animations for scaling & rotating the widget
  late Animation<double> _scaleAnimation;
  late Animation<double> _rotateAnimation;

  @override
  void initState() {
```

```
    super.initState();
    // Initialize the AnimationController with a duration of 2 seconds
    _controller = AnimationController(
      duration: const Duration(seconds: 2),
      vsync: this,
    )..repeat(reverse: true); // Repeat the animation in reverse

    // Define the scale animation from 0.5 to 5
    _scaleAnimation = Tween<double>(begin: 0.5, end: 5).animate(
      // bounceIn curve for a bouncing effect
      CurvedAnimation(parent: _controller, curve: Curves.bounceIn),
    );

    // Define the rotate animation 360 degrees
    _rotateAnimation = Tween<double>(begin: 0.0, end: 2 * pi).animate(
      // fastOutSlowIn curve for smooth rotation - try different curves
      CurvedAnimation(parent: _controller, curve: Curves.fastOutSlowIn),
    );
  }

  @override
  Widget build(BuildContext context) {
    return Scaffold(
      body: Center(
        child: AnimatedBuilder(
          animation: _controller,
          builder: (context, child) {
            // Apply scaling and rotation transformations
            return Transform.scale(
              scale: _scaleAnimation.value, // sets the scale value
              child: Transform.rotate(
                angle: _rotateAnimation.value, // sets angle value
                child: Container(
                  color: Colors.green,
                  width: 100, // Set the container width
```

```
                  height: 100, // Set the container height
                ),
              ),
            );
          },
        ),
      ),
    );
  }

  @override
  void dispose() {
    // Dispose the controller when the widget is removed from the tree
    _controller.dispose();
    super.dispose();
  }
}
```

This Flutter app creates an animated widget that simultaneously scales, and rotates over time. The app starts by running a MaterialApp that displays the **RotatingScalingWidget** widget. This widget is a StatefulWidget, meaning it can maintain state and update its appearance over time. The main state logic is handled within the **_RotatingScalingWidgetState** class. Upon initialization (**initState**), an **AnimationController** is created to manage the timing of the animations. The controller is set to run for two seconds and repeat in reverse, creating a continuous back-and-forth animation.

Three animations are defined using the **Tween** class:

- **_scaleAnimation**: This scales the widget's size from half its original size (0.5) to five times its original size (5), also using the **Curves.easeInOut** curve.
- **_rotateAnimation**: This rotates the widget from 0 radians (no rotation) to 2π radians (a full 360-degree rotation), again following the **Curves.easeInOut** curve.

The build method constructs the widget tree. Inside it, an **AnimatedBuilder** widget listens to the **AnimationController** and rebuilds its child whenever the animation values change. Inside it, **Transform.scale** scales the child widget, and **Transform.rotate** applies the rotation. The animated child itself is a simple green container with a fixed size of 100x100 pixels. Finally, the dispose method ensures the **AnimationController** is properly disposed of when the widget is removed from the tree, preventing memory leaks.

Optimizing animation for performance

While implicit animations are convenient, they do come with some performance considerations. It is important to ensure that the animations do not cause unnecessary re-rendering of the widget tree, which can affect the performance of your application. The best practices for implicit animation would be:

- **Avoid frequent rebuilds**: Use widgets that are stable and do not change frequently to avoid excessive rebuilding.
- **Minimize overdraw**: Ensure that your animations do not cause widgets to be drawn multiple times unnecessarily.
- **Child parameter**: Using the child parameter in implicit animations can improve performance by ensuring that static parts of your widget tree are not rebuilt on every frame.

On the other hand, Explicit animations offer a high degree of customization, but they also require careful management to ensure optimal performance. The best practices for explicit animation would be:

- **Minimize rebuilds**: Use **`AnimatedBuilder`** to avoid unnecessary widget rebuilds and improve performance.
- **Manage resources**: Dispose of **`AnimationController`** properly to free up resources when no longer needed.

Finally, advanced animations can impact performance, especially with complex scenes or high frame rates. To ensure smooth animations, consider the following practices:

- **Minimize overdraw**: Avoid unnecessary painting by using widgets that do not overlap.
- **Use repaint boundary**: Isolate parts of the widget tree to reduce repainting overhead.
- **Optimize animation frequency**: Adjust the frame rate to balance visual smoothness and performance.

Advanced layout techniques for web

In this section, we will guide you through setting up a responsive Flutter project that adjusts seamlessly to different screen sizes—whether mobile, tablet, or desktop.

Default project structure

To implement a responsive design, the following project structure should be followed as shown in the following figure:

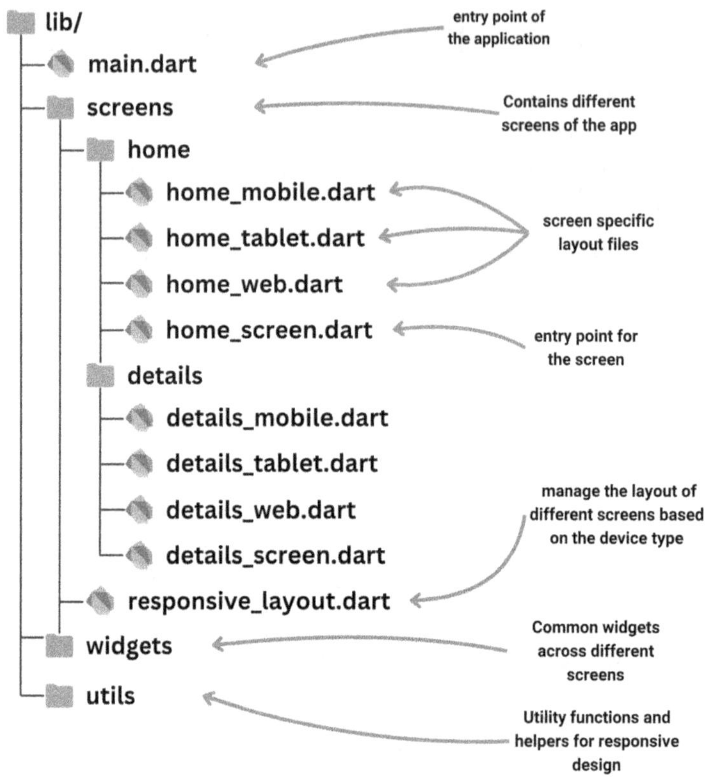

Figure 4.5: *The project structure for creating responsive user interface*

This new project structure has the following parts:

- **main.dart**: Entry point of the application.
- **screens/**: Contains different screens of the app.
- **home/ and details/**: Sample screens (page) for the application with separate files for mobile, tablet, and desktop layouts.
- **responsive_layout.dart**: Manages responsive layout logic.
- **widgets/**: Common widgets used across different screens.
- **utils/**: Utility functions and helpers for responsive design.

ResponsiveLayout widget

Inside the screens folder, we have the **`responsive_layout.dart`** file, which contains a **`ResponsiveLayout`** widget. This widget adapts its layout based on the screen size. This ensures that your app looks good and functions well on different devices, such as mobile phones, tablets, and desktops. You will write the code shown as follows:

```
// responsive_layout.dart
import 'package:flutter/material.dart';

class ResponsiveLayout extends StatelessWidget {
  // 3 Widgets for Mobile, Tablet and Web/Desktop
  final Widget mobileLayout;
  final Widget tabletLayout;
  final Widget webLayout;

  const ResponsiveLayout({
    super.key,
    required this.mobileLayout,
    required this.tabletLayout,
    required this.webLayout,
  });

  @override
  Widget build(BuildContext context) {
    // LayoutBuilder to get the constraints
    return LayoutBuilder(builder: (context, constraints) {
      // Check the maxWidth of the constraints
      if (constraints.maxWidth < 500) {
        // if less than 500, return mobileLayout
        return mobileLayout;
      } else if (constraints.maxWidth < 1100) {
        // if less than 1100, return tabletLayout
        return tabletLayout;
      } else {
        // if more than 1100, return webLayout
        return webLayout;
      }
    });
  }
}
```

This widget is particularly useful for creating responsive designs that work well on different devices, such as mobile phones, tablets, and web browsers. The core functionality of the **ResponsiveLayout** widget is defined in its build method, which uses the **LayoutBuilder** widget. **LayoutBuilder** provides the constraints parameter, which contains information about the available space for the widget. By checking the **constraints.maxWidth**, the widget determines which layout to render. If the width is below 500 pixels, it returns the **mobileLayout**. If the width falls between 500 and 1100 pixels, it displays the **tabletLayout**. For widths above 1100 pixels, it returns the **webLayout**. This approach ensures that the layout adapts dynamically to the screen size, making the application look good on various devices and screen resolutions.

Recently the amazing Flutter team has released **flutter_adaptive_scaffold** package that offers a responsive and adaptive scaffold for Flutter apps, automatically adjusting the layout to accommodate different screen sizes and orientations. It includes support for navigation destinations and a flexible body area. Ideal for building apps that seamlessly adapt to both mobile and desktop platforms. Visit **https://pub.dev/packages/flutter_adaptive_scaffold** for details.

> **Note: Responsive Breakpoints for Mobile devices can be less than or equal to 600px. For tablet devices it can be between 600px and 1200px. For web/desktop devices it can be greater than 1200px. These breakpoints are not set in stone and can be adjusted to your preference.**

Using the ResponsiveLayout class

To effectively use the **ResponsiveLayout** widget in your Flutter project, you should define separate layout widgets for mobile, tablet, and desktop devices. For instance, you can create **HomeMobile**, **HomeTablet**, and **HomeDesktop** widgets for the home screen, and then use the **ResponsiveLayout** widget in your **home_screen.dart** to switch between these layouts based on the device's screen width.

First, create a file **home_mobile.dart** inside the **screens/home/** folder:

```
// screens/home/home_mobile.dart
import 'package:flutter/material.dart';

class HomeMobile extends StatelessWidget {
  const HomeMobile({super.key});

  @override
  Widget build(BuildContext context) {
    return const Scaffold(
      body: Center(
        child: Text('HOME: Mobile Layout'),
      ),
    );
```

```
  }
}
```

Similarly, create **home_tablet.dart** for tablet layout:

```
// screens/home/home_tablet.dart
import 'package:flutter/material.dart';

class HomeTablet extends StatelessWidget {
  const HomeTablet({super.key});

  @override
  Widget build(BuildContext context) {
    return const Scaffold(
      body: Center(
        child: Text('HOME: Tablet Layout'),
      ),
    );
  }
}
```

Then, create **home_web.dart** for the web layout:

```
// screens/home/home_web.dart
import 'package:flutter/material.dart';

class HomeWeb extends StatelessWidget {
  const HomeWeb({Key? key});

  @override
  Widget build(BuildContext context) {
    return const Scaffold(
      body: Center(
        child: Text('HOME: Web Layout'),
      ),
    );
  }
}
```

Finally, create the **home_screen.dart**, where the **ResponsiveLayout** widget will be called:

```dart
// screens/home/home_screen.dart
import 'package:flutter/material.dart';

import '../responsive_layout.dart';
import 'home_mobile.dart';
import 'home_tablet.dart';
import 'home_web.dart';

class HomeScreen extends StatelessWidget {
  const HomeScreen({super.key});

  @override
  Widget build(BuildContext context) {
    return const ResponsiveLayout(
      mobileLayout: HomeMobile(),
      tabletLayout: HomeTablet(),
      webLayout: HomeWeb(),
    );
  }
}
```

In the **main.dart** file, call the **HomeScreen** widget to load your home screen:

```dart
// main.dart
import 'package:flutter/material.dart';
import 'screens/home/home_screen.dart';

void main() {
  runApp(const MyApp());
}

class MyApp extends StatelessWidget {
  const MyApp({super.key});

  @override
  Widget build(BuildContext context) {
    return MaterialApp(
      title: "Responsive Flutter App",
      home: const HomeScreen(),
```

```
      scrollBehavior: const MaterialScrollBehavior().copyWith(
        dragDevices: {
          PointerDeviceKind.touch,
          PointerDeviceKind.mouse,
          PointerDeviceKind.unknown,
        },
      ),
    );
  }
}
```

The **`scrollBehavior`** property is used to customize how scrolling behaves in your application, allowing you to tailor it for different input devices and scenarios. It ensures a consistent scrolling experience on both web/desktop and mobile platforms.

Run your app, then in the browser open browser **devtools** and toggle device toolbar icon to check the responsive behavior (or just resize your browser window). It will show different layouts as shown in the following figure:

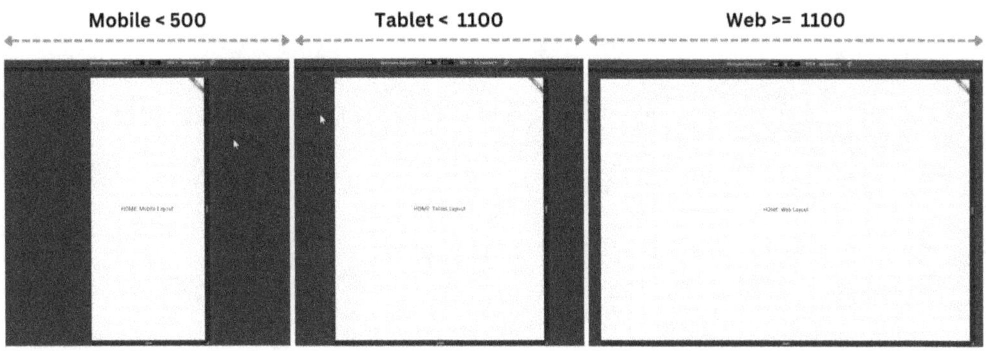

Figure 4.6: *Responsive layout demonstration for mobile, tablet and web screens*

This approach, can be complex for beginners but ensures that your app's UI is adaptive and provides an optimal user experience across different devices, maintaining a clean and organized project structure. If you have multiple screens, you can set up routing to navigate between them, follow the steps provided in *Chapter 3, Designing Stunning UIs for the Web*. This method not only enhances the user experience but also makes your codebase more maintainable and scalable.

Note: For simplicity, this book will focus on the web layout, while the mobile and tablet layouts will contain placeholder widgets. The mobile and tablet layouts can be used for practicing your skills in building user interfaces.

Theming and styling

Theming and styling are crucial for creating a consistent and visually appealing user interface in Flutter applications. This section covers how to effectively use themes and styling to enhance the look and feel of your Flutter app. It explores the use of theme data, custom themes, and styling widgets to ensure a cohesive design across various platforms and screen sizes.

Understanding themes in Flutter

Themes in Flutter provide a way to consistently apply visual properties across an app. A theme defines the colors, font styles, and other visual properties for various UI components, ensuring a unified look throughout the application. The **MaterialApp** widget has a **theme** property that allows you to define a default theme for the entire app. This theme is then inherited by all widgets within the **MaterialApp**. Try the following code for **main.dart**:

```
// main.dart
import 'package:flutter/material.dart';
import 'screens/home/home_screen.dart';

void main() {
  // set MyThemedApp as the entry point
  runApp(const MyThemedApp());
}

class MyThemedApp extends StatelessWidget {
  const MyThemedApp({super.key});

  @override
  Widget build(BuildContext context) {
    return MaterialApp(
      // set the theme for the app
      theme: ThemeData(
          // set the primary color to blue
          primarySwatch: Colors.blue,
          // set the text theme for the app
          textTheme: const TextTheme(
            displayLarge:
                TextStyle(fontSize: 57.0, fontWeight: FontWeight.bold),
            headlineMedium:
                TextStyle(fontSize: 28.0, fontStyle: FontStyle.italic),
```

```
            bodyMedium: TextStyle(fontSize: 14.0),
          )),
      home: const MyHomePage(),
    );
  }
}
```

In the preceding code, **ThemeData** defines the primary and accent colors, as well as custom text styles. To implement this, update the **home_web.dart** as shown in the following snippet:

```
// screens/home/home_web.dart
import 'package:flutter/material.dart';

// web layout
class HomeWeb extends StatelessWidget {
  const HomeWeb({super.key});

  @override
  Widget build(BuildContext context) {
    return Scaffold(
        appBar: AppBar(
          title: const Text('Themes and Text Styles'),
        ),
        body: Center(
            child: Column(
                mainAxisAlignment: MainAxisAlignment.center,
                // Theme.of(context) returns the current theme
                children: [
              // styles are applied based on the current theme
              Text("Heading One",
                  style: Theme.of(context).textTheme.displayLarge),
              Text("Heading Two",
                  style: Theme.of(context).textTheme.headlineMedium),
              Text("Sample Body Text",
                  style: Theme.of(context).textTheme.bodyMedium),
            ])));
  }
}
```

To utilize your theme in specific widgets, use the **`Theme.of(context)`** method to access the theme data. This method retrieves the nearest **`Theme`** widget in the widget tree, applying the app-wide theme if no standalone theme is found. If you do not provide a theme in the **`MaterialApp`** constructor, Flutter will automatically use a default theme for your application. The output for the web layout will be as shown in the following figure:

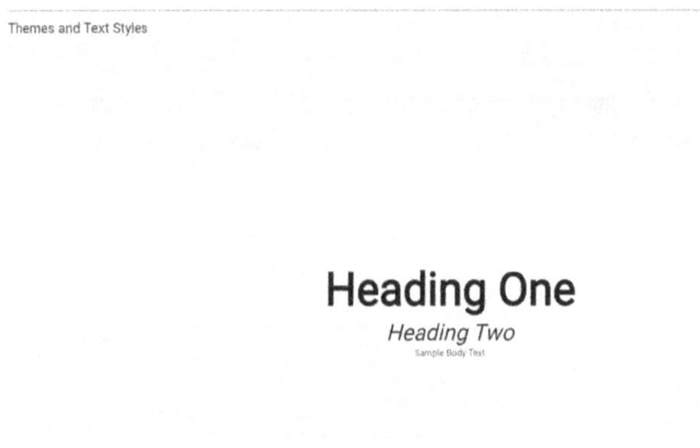

Figure 4.7: *Theme customization in Flutter*

`ThemeData` is the central class for configuring themes. It includes properties for colors, typography, and component-specific styles. You can customize various aspects, such as:

- **Color scheme**: Define primary, secondary, and background colors.
- **Text theme**: Set global text styles, including font size, weight, and family.
- **Button theme**: Customize button appearances like color, shape, and elevation.

Note: As of Flutter version 3.16, the default theme is Material 3.

Styling widgets

In addition to using themes, you can style individual widgets to customize their appearance. Let us take a look at a few examples of styling widgets in Flutter:

- **Text styles**: Style text using the **`TextStyle`** class. You can set properties such as font size, color, weight, and family. Here is a small example:

```
Text(
  'Styled Text',
  style: TextStyle(
    fontSize: 20.0,
    color: Colors.blue,
    fontWeight: FontWeight.bold,
  ),
);
```

- **Container decoration**: Use the **`BoxDecoration`** class to style containers with properties like color, border, radius, and box shadows. For example:

```
Container(
  padding: EdgeInsets.all(16.0),
  // decoration is used to customize container
  decoration: BoxDecoration(
    color: Colors.teal,
    borderRadius: BorderRadius.circular(8.0),
    boxShadow: [BoxShadow(color: Colors.black26, blurRadius: 4.0)],
  ),
  child: Text('Styled Container'),
);
```

- **Buttons**: Customize button styles using **`ElevatedButton`**, **`TextButton`**, and **`OutlinedButton`** properties. You can modify color, shape, and elevation. To style a button, try this code:

```
ElevatedButton(
  onPressed: () {},
  style: ElevatedButton.styleFrom(
    primary: Colors.teal,
    shape: RoundedRectangleBorder(
      borderRadius: BorderRadius.circular(8.0),
    ),
    elevation: 5.0,
  ),
  child: Text('Styled Button'),
);
```

Practical: Staggered menu implementation

Based on the concepts you learnt in this chapter; you are now going to create a new Flutter project and make a responsive menu with a pinch of animation for an application landing page. You will be using a Flutter library **`flutter_staggered_grid_view`** for this project. The final output of the project on web/desktop layout will look like the following figure:

***Figure 4.8:** Staggered menu screen final output*

To start, create a new project based on the responsive project structure discussed in the *Advanced Layout Techniques for web* section. Create the following folders and files as shown in the following table:

#	File path	Description
1	**`lib/screens/responsive_layout.dart`**	Contains **`LayoutBuilder`** to handle which layout should be displayed based on screen width.
2	**`lib/screens/main_menu/menu_screen.dart`**	Starting point of **`MainMenuScreen`**.
3	**`lib/screens/main_menu/menu_mobile.dart`**	The mobile layout file for the app.
4	**`lib/screens/main_menu/menu_tablet.dart`**	The tablet layout file for the app.
5	**`lib/screens/menu_menu/menu_web.dart`**	The web/desktop layout for the app.
6	**`lib/widgets/menu_tile.dart`**	Contains **`MenuTile`** widget for a single item in the menu grid.
7	**`lib/main.dart`**	The starting point of the app.

***Table 4.1:** Required files for the staggered menu app*

Once you have created the files and folders, follow the given steps:

1. **Add required dependency**: The first step will be to add the **`staggered_grid_view`** package in **`pubspec.yaml`**. It is required to make the **`StaggeredGrid`**,

StaggeredGridTile widgets available. Open the terminal inside IntelliJ IDEA and run the following command (internet required):

```
flutter pub add staggered_grid_view
```

2. **Create the ResponsiveLayout widget**: Define a **ResponsiveLayout** widget that dynamically selects and displays different layouts based on the screen width. The code for **ResponsiveLayout** is given in the *Advanced Layout Technique for Web* section.

3. **Create the MainMenuScreen widget**: The **MainMenuScreen** widget serves as the entry point for the main menu of the application. It uses the **ResponsiveLayout** widget to determine and display the appropriate layout—**MenuMobile**, **MenuTablet**, or **MenuWeb**—based on the screen width. Depending on whether the screen is classified as mobile, tablet, or web, the respective layout component is rendered. Write the code as given here:

```
// screens/main_menu/menu_screen.dart
import 'package:flutter/material.dart';

import '../responsive_layout.dart';
import 'menu_mobile.dart';
import 'menu_tablet.dart';
import 'menu_web.dart';

// entry point for the main menu screen
class MainMenuScreen extends StatelessWidget {
  const MainMenuScreen({super.key});

  @override
  Widget build(BuildContext context) {
    // return the responsive layout widget based on the screen width
    return const ResponsiveLayout(
      mobileLayout: MenuMobile(),
      tabletLayout: MenuTablet(),
      webLayout: MenuWeb(),
    );
  }
}
```

All three layouts are not yet declared so you will get errors when passing them inside **ResponsiveLayout** widget. So, open the **menu_mobile.dart** file and write the code given:

```
// screens/main_menu/menu_screen.dart
import 'package:flutter/material.dart';

// the mobile layout for the menu screen
class MenuMobile extends StatelessWidget {
  const MenuMobile({super.key});

  @override
  Widget build(BuildContext context) {
    // a placeholder scaffold with a centered text widget
    return const Scaffold(
        // todo make the menu for mobile
        body: Center(
            child: Text(
      'Menu : Mobile Layout ',
      style: TextStyle(fontSize: 20),
    )));
  }
}
```

Now, add the **menu_tablet.dart** file and write the following code:

```
// screens/main_menu/menu_tablet.dart
import 'package:flutter/material.dart';

// the tablet layout for the menu screen
class MenuTablet extends StatelessWidget {
  const MenuTablet({super.key});

  @override
  Widget build(BuildContext context) {
    // a placeholder scaffold with a centered text widget
    return const Scaffold(
        // todo make the menu for tablet
        body: Center(
            child: Text(
      'Menu : Tablet Layout',
      style: TextStyle(fontSize: 20),
    )));
```

```
    }
}
```

The project focuses on the web layout, so the mobile and tablet layout are just for placeholders. They can be updated later, as they will be good for practice.

4. **Create the web layout**: The **MenuWeb** widget creates a responsive web layout for a main menu screen. It uses a Scaffold to structure the layout, with padding applied around the content. Inside the Scaffold, a **ListView** is used to handle scrolling, while a **StaggeredGrid** is employed to display the menu tiles in a flexible grid. Each tile has custom dimensions, defined using **StaggeredGridTile.count**. The **MenuTile** widget inside each tile shows relevant menu options, including titles, images, and icons, with proper spacing to maintain a clean, organized design, as shown in code below:

```
// screens/main_menu/menu_web.dart
import 'package:flutter/material.dart';
import 'package:flutter_staggered_grid_view/flutter_staggered_grid_view.dart';
import 'package:staggered_menu/widgets/menu_tile.dart';

// the web layout for the menu screen
class MenuWeb extends StatelessWidget {
  const MenuWeb({super.key});

  // list of menu items
  static const List<Map<String, dynamic>> menuItems = [
    {"title":"Home","imgId":"11",
     "icon":Icons.home,"crossAxis":2, "mainAxis": 2},
    {"title": "Dashboard", "imgId": "12",
     "icon": Icons.dashboard, "crossAxis": 1, "mainAxis": 1},
    {"title": "Settings", "imgId": "13",
     "icon": Icons.settings, "crossAxis": 1, "mainAxis": 1},
    {"title": "Messages", "imgId": "14",
     «icon»: Icons.message, «crossAxis»: 1, «mainAxis»: 1},
    {"title": "Notifications", "imgId": "15",
     «icon»: Icons.notifications, «crossAxis»: 1, «mainAxis»: 1},
    {"title": "Photos", "imgId": "16",
     «icon»: Icons.photo, «crossAxis»: 2, «mainAxis»: 1},
    // TODO : add more items - experiment with crossaxis and mainaxis values
```

```
  ];

  @override
  Widget build(BuildContext context) {
    return Scaffold(
      // add padding to the body
      body: Padding(
          padding: const EdgeInsets.all(15.0),
          // the Listview containing the staggered grid view
          child: ListView(children: [
            // the staggered grid view
            StaggeredGrid.count(
                crossAxisCount: 6, // no of columns
                mainAxisSpacing: 15, // spacing between the rows
                crossAxisSpacing: 15, // spacing between the columns
                // a list of staggered grid tiles
                children: menuItems.map((item) {
                  return StaggeredGridTile.count(
                    crossAxisCellCount: item["crossAxis"],
                    mainAxisCellCount: item["mainAxis"],
                    // the menu tile widget with title, image id and icon
                    child: MenuTile(
                      title: item["title"],
                      imgId: item["imgId"],
                      icon: item["icon"],
                    ),
                  );
                }).toList())
          ])),
    );
  }
}
```

Until you create the **MenuTile** and its widget, your code will show error.

5. **Create MenuTile widget**: The **MenuTile** widget is a stateful widget used for displaying interactive menu items with an **image**, **title**, and **icon**. It consists

of two parts: **MenuTileImage**, which shows an image based on the **imgId** and a **MenuTileContent**, which presents the title and icon with adjustable font size. Write the **MenuTile** widget as shown:

```
// lib/widgets/menu_tile.dart
import 'package:flutter/material.dart';

import ‘menu_tile_content.dart’;
import ‘menu_tile_image.dart’;

class MenuTile extends StatefulWidget {
  final String title;
  final String imgId;
  final IconData icon;

  const MenuTile({
    super.key,
    required this.title,
    required this.imgId,
    required this.icon,
  });

  @override
  State<MenuTile> createState() => _MenuTileState();
}

class _MenuTileState extends State<MenuTile> {
  double fontSize = 30.0;
  double imageScale = 2.0;

  @override
  Widget build(BuildContext context) {
    var imgUrl = "https://picsum.photos/500/500?image=${widget.imgId}";

    return Stack(alignment: Alignment.center, children: [
      MenuTileImage(imgUrl: imgUrl),
      MenuTileContent(
        title: widget.title,
```

```
          icon: widget.icon,
          fontSize: fontSize,
        ),
      ]);
    }
  }
```

6. **Create MenuTileImage widget**: The **`MenuTileImage`** widget is a stateless widget responsible for displaying an image as the background of a menu tile. It uses a **`ClipRRect`** to apply rounded corners to the image and ensures the image fits perfectly within its boundaries using a **`SizedBox`**. The image is fetched from the provided URL (**`imgUrl`**) using **`Image.network`** and displayed with a **`BoxFit.cover`** to maintain visual appeal, making it a responsive and polished background for the menu tile. Write the given code to make the widget:

```
// lib/widgets/menu_tile_image.dart
import 'package:flutter/material.dart';

class MenuTileImage extends StatelessWidget {
  final String imgUrl;

  const MenuTileImage({super.key, required this.imgUrl});

  @override
  Widget build(BuildContext context) {
    return ClipRRect(
      borderRadius: BorderRadius.circular(10),
      child: SizedBox(
        width: double.infinity,
        height: double.infinity,
        child: Image.network(
          imgUrl,
          fit: BoxFit.cover,
        ),
      ),
    );
  }
}
```

7. **Create MenuTileContent widget**: The **`MenuTileContent`** widget is a simple, stateless component designed to display a menu item's icon and title. It uses a

Column to center-align its contents, with the icon displayed above the text. Create the widget using the code given below:

```
// lib/widgets/menu_tile_content.dart
import 'package:flutter/material.dart';

class MenuTileContent extends StatelessWidget {
  final String title;
  final IconData icon;
  final double fontSize;

  const MenuTileContent({
    super.key,
    required this.title,
    required this.icon,
    required this.fontSize,
  });

  @override
  Widget build(BuildContext context) {
    return Column(
      mainAxisAlignment: MainAxisAlignment.center,
      children: [
        Icon(icon, size: 50, color: Colors.white),
        Text(title, style: TextStyle(
           fontSize: fontSize,
           color: Colors.white),
        ),
      ],
    );
  }
}
```

8. **Integrate into main.dart**: The final step, **main.dart** defines the main entry point for the "Staggered Menu App." The **StaggeredMenuApp** class is a **StatelessWidget**. The **MainMenuScreen** is set as the home screen, and the debug banner is removed. Additionally, the app's scroll behavior is customized to support drag gestures from various input devices, such as touch, mouse, and unknown devices.

9. Run the app to test your code.

Practical: Hero animation implementation

The next Flutter project showcases hero animation implementation in a web layout. Hero animation creates a smooth transition animation from one screen to another screen, and help to visually connect the two pages, making the **user experience** (**UX**) intuitive and engaging. The output should look like the following figure:

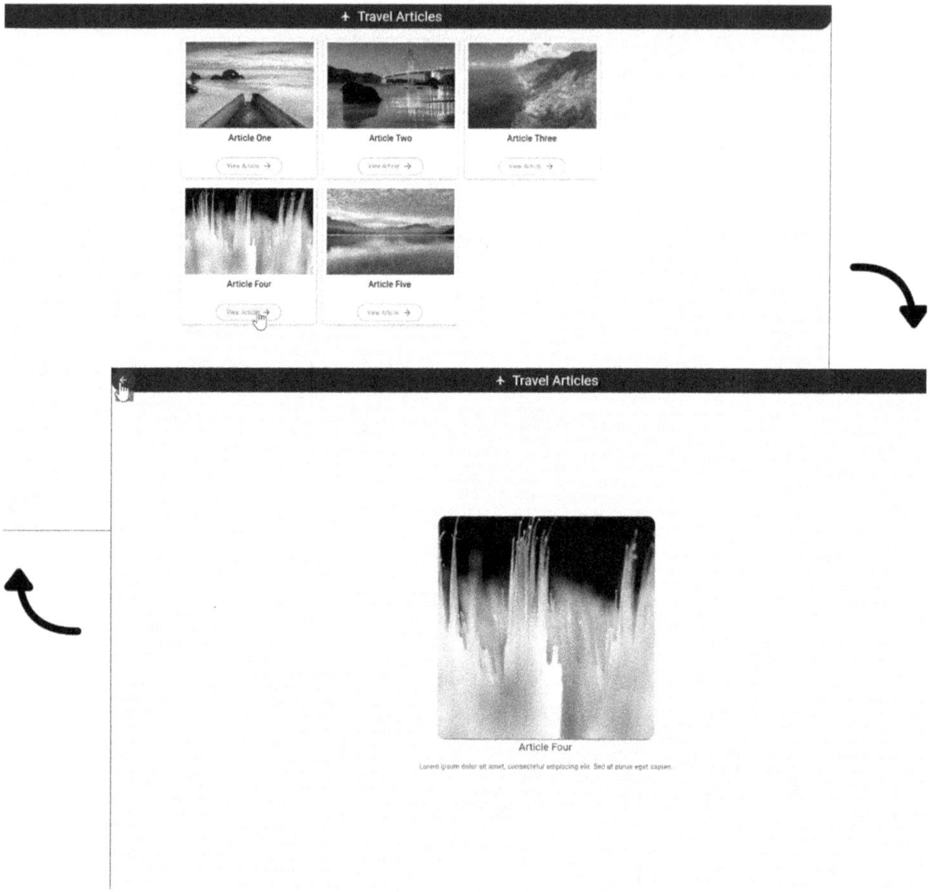

Figure 4.9: *The final output of Hero animation app*

Create a new Flutter project and set up the following files and folder as shown in the following table:

#	File path	Description
1	**lib/models/Article.dart**	Defines the Article model, representing data related to an article.
2	**lib/screens/detail/detail_screen.dart**	Contains the `DetailScreen` class, for displaying details of a selected item or article in a mobile layout.
3	**lib/screens/detail/detail_web.dart**	Contains the `DetailWeb` class, responsible for details of an item or article in a web layout.
4	**lib/screens/home/home_screen.dart**	Defines the `HomeScreen` class, represents the main screen or list view for articles in a mobile layout.
5	**lib/screens/home/home_web.dart**	Defines the `HomeWeb` class, representing the main screen for articles in a web layout.
6	**lib/screens/home/responsive_layout.dart**	Implements the responsive layout logic, switching between mobile, tablet, and web layouts depending on screen size.
7	**lib/widgets/article_item.dart**	Contains a custom widget to display an individual article item in a list.
8	**lib/widgets/hero_app_bar.dart**	Contains the `HeroAppBar` widget, a custom app bar.
9	**lib/main.dart**	Entry point of the app.

Table 4.2: *Files required for the project-Hero Animation*

After completion of file and folder creation, you can follow the given steps:

1. **Setup assets**: Create a folder in your Flutter app called **assets**, inside it creates a subfolder called **images** and put your images here. Then uncomment the assets segment the **pubspec.yaml** file and add the following line:

```
assets:
    - assets/images/
```

2. **Create the model and data list**: Define an **Article** model class with three fields: title, image, and description, all required through its constructor. It also includes a static method **fetchAll()** that returns a list of predefined **Article** objects, each containing a title, image path, and description. Write the following code:

```
// models/Article.dart
class Article {
  final String title;
  final String image;
  final String description;
```

```
  // constructor
  Article({
    required this.title,
    required this.image,
    required this.description,
  });
  // Add a static method to fetch all articles
  static List<Article> fetchAll() {
    // return a list of articles
    return [
      Article(
        title: 'Article One',
        image: ‘assets/images/image1.jpg’,
        description:
            'Lorem ipsum dolor sit amet, consectetur adipiscing elit. Sed ut purus eget sapien.',
      ),
      Article(
        title: 'Article Two',
        image: ‘assets/images/image2.jpg’,
        description:
            'Lorem ipsum dolor sit amet, consectetur adipiscing elit. Sed ut purus eget sapien.',
      ),
      // todo add more articles
    ];
  }
}
```

3. **Create article widget**: Define a widget called **`ArticleItem`** that displays an article with an image and title. It uses the **`Hero`** widget to create a smooth transition animation for the article image when navigating to a detail screen. The widget is styled with a white background, rounded corners, and a shadow for a card-like appearance. It includes an **`OutlinedButton`** that, when pressed, navigates to a detail page, passing the article as an argument. The layout is structured with the image taking up most of the space, and the title and button arranged below it. Write the code as shown:

```
// widgets/article_item.dart
import 'package:flutter/material.dart';
import 'package:hero_animation/models/Article.dart';

class ArticleItem extends StatelessWidget {
  final Article article;
  const ArticleItem({super.key, required this.article});

  @override
  Widget build(BuildContext context) {
    return Container(
        margin: const EdgeInsets.all(8),
        padding: const EdgeInsets.all(8),
        decoration: BoxDecoration(
            color: Colors.white,
            borderRadius: BorderRadius.circular(8),
            boxShadow: const [
              BoxShadow(
                color: Colors.grey,
                offset: Offset(0, 2),
                blurRadius: 4,
              )
            ]),
        child: Column(children: [
          Expanded(
              flex: 3, // take a lot of space
              // Hero widget is used to animate
              // the image when navigating to the detail screen
              child: Hero(
                  // The tag must be unique for each image
                  tag: article.image,
                  child: Image.asset(
                    article.image,
                    width: double.infinity,
                    fit: BoxFit.cover,
                  ))),
          const SizedBox(height: 8),
```

```
          Expanded(
            flex: 1,
            child: Column(
              children: [
                Text(article.title,
                    style: const TextStyle(
                      fontSize: 20,
                      fontWeight: FontWeight.bold,
                    )),
                OutlinedButton(
                    onPressed: () {
                      Navigator.of(context).pushNamed(
                        '/detail',
                        arguments: article,
                      );
                    },
                    child: const Row(
                      mainAxisSize: MainAxisSize.min,
                      children: [
                        Text('View Article'),
                        const SizedBox(width: 8),
                        Icon(Icons.arrow_forward_rounded),
                      ],
                    )),
              ],
            )),
        ]));
    }
  }
```

4. **Create custom AppBar**: Define a custom **HeroAppBar** widget that implements **PreferredSizeWidget** to specify its size. This widget creates an **AppBar** with a rounded bottom edge and a title consisting of an icon and text, styled with a white font on a dark grey background. The title is centered, and the **AppBar** has a preferred height of 56 pixels. The build method configures the visual appearance, including the title style and background color. The following code will make the AppBar:

```dart
// widgets/hero_app_bar.dart
import 'package:flutter/material.dart';

// PreferredSizeWidget is a mixin that
// can be used to specify the size of the widget
class HeroAppBar extends StatelessWidget implements PreferredSizeWidget {
  const HeroAppBar({super.key});

  @override
  Widget build(BuildContext context) {
    return AppBar(
      shape: const RoundedRectangleBorder(
        // vertical radius of 30 for the bottom of app bar
        borderRadius: BorderRadius.vertical(
          bottom: Radius.circular(30),
        ),
      ),
      title: const Row(
        mainAxisSize: MainAxisSize.min,
        children: [
          Icon(Icons.flight),
          SizedBox(width: 16),
          Text('Travel Articles'),
        ],
      ),
      titleTextStyle: const TextStyle(color: Colors.white, fontSize: 32),
      centerTitle: true,
      backgroundColor: Colors.grey.shade900,
      foregroundColor: Colors.white,
    );
  }

  @override
  Size get preferredSize => const Size.fromHeight(56);
}
```

5. **Create HomeScreen and HomeWeb widgets**: Before creating **HomeScreen** Widget, do not forget to create a **ResponsiveLayout**, its code remains the same for almost all the projects. Define the **HomeScreen** widget as a StatefulWidget that manages a list of articles fetched from a static method **Article.fetchAll()**. In its state, the widget builds a **ResponsiveLayout** that adapts to different screen sizes. For mobile and tablet layouts, it uses **Placeholder** widgets as placeholders, while for the web layout, it displays the **HomeWeb** widget with the fetched articles passed as a parameter. Write it as shown:

```
// screens/home/home_screen.dart
import 'package:flutter/material.dart';
import 'package:hero_animation/models/Article.dart';
import 'package:hero_animation/screens/home/home_web.dart';
import 'package:hero_animation/screens/responsive_layout.dart';

class HomeScreen extends StatefulWidget {
  const HomeScreen({super.key});

  @override
  State<HomeScreen> createState() => _HomeScreenState();
}

class _HomeScreenState extends State<HomeScreen> {
  final List<Article> articles = Article.fetchAll();

  @override
  Widget build(BuildContext context) {
    return ResponsiveLayout(
        mobileLayout: Placeholder(),
        tabletLayout: Placeholder(),
        webLayout: HomeWeb(articles: articles));
  }
}
```

Now, define the **HomeWeb** widget as a **StatelessWidget** that represents a web screen displaying a list of articles. It uses a **Scaffold** with a **HeroAppBar** at the top and a **Row** in the body. The **Row** contains three **Expanded** widgets: two empty containers on the left and right sides, and a central container with padding that holds a **GridView**. The **GridView** arranges the articles in a grid with a maximum cross-axis extent of 400 pixels and displays each article using the **ArticleItem** widget. The articles are passed to the **HomeWeb** widget as a list, as shown in the following snippet:

```dart
// screens/home/home_web.dart
import 'package:flutter/material.dart';
import 'package:hero_animation/models/Article.dart';
import '../../widgets/article_item.dart'; // relative import
import '../../widgets/hero_app_bar.dart'; // relative import

class HomeWeb extends StatelessWidget {
  final List<Article> articles;

  const HomeWeb({super.key, required this.articles});

  @override
  Widget build(BuildContext context) {
    return Scaffold(
        appBar: HeroAppBar(),
        body: Row(children: [
          // create an empty container on left side
          Expanded(child: Container()),
          Expanded(
              flex: 3,
              child: Container(
                  padding: const EdgeInsets.all(16),
                  // Display the articles in a grid
                  child: GridView(
                    // Create a grid with 400 pixels
                    // as the maximum cross-axis extent
                    gridDelegate:
                        const SliverGridDelegateWithMaxCrossAxisExtent(
                      maxCrossAxisExtent: 400,
                    ),
                    // map each article to an ArticleItem widget
                    children: articles
                        .map((article) => ArticleItem(article: article))
                        .toList(),
                  ))),
          // create an empty container on right side
```

```
          Expanded(child: Container())
        ]));
  }
}
```

6. **Create DetailScreen and DetailWeb widgets:** Next, define the **`DetailScreen`** widget as a **`StatelessWidget`** that displays detailed information about an article. It retrieves the **`Article`** object from the route's arguments using **`ModalRoute.of(context)?.settings.arguments`**. The code is similar to **`HomeScreen`** widget, write the code shown as follows:

```
// screens/detail/detail_screen.dart
import 'package:flutter/material.dart';
import 'package:hero_animation/models/Article.dart';
import 'package:hero_animation/screens/detail/detail_web.dart';
import 'package:hero_animation/screens/responsive_layout.dart';

class DetailScreen extends StatelessWidget {
  const DetailScreen({super.key});

  @override
  Widget build(BuildContext context) {
    final Article article =
        ModalRoute.of(context)?.settings.arguments as Article;
    return ResponsiveLayout(
      mobileLayout: Placeholder(),
      tabletLayout: Placeholder(),
      webLayout: DetailWeb(article: article),
    );
  }
}
```

Create the **`DetailWeb`** widget as a **`StatelessWidget`** designed to display detailed information about an article. It uses a **`Scaffold`** with a **`HeroAppBar`** at the top. The body of the Scaffold centers a **`Column`** that includes a **`Hero`** widget for the article's image, displayed with a circular clipping and a fixed size of 512 pixels. Below the image, the article's title and description are shown in text widgets with specified font sizes and a vertical space between them.

```
// screens/detail/detail_web.dart
import 'package:flutter/material.dart';
import 'package:hero_animation/models/Article.dart';
```

```
import 'package:hero_animation/widgets/hero_app_bar.dart';

class DetailWeb extends StatelessWidget {
  final Article article;

  const DetailWeb({super.key, required this.article});

  @override
  Widget build(BuildContext context) {
    return Scaffold(
        appBar: HeroAppBar(),
        body: Center(
            child:
                Column(mainAxisAlignment: MainAxisAlignment.center,
          children: [
            Hero(
              // should match with the selected article image
              // for animation to take place
              tag: article.image,
              // Display the image in a circular shape
              child: ClipRRect(
                  borderRadius: BorderRadius.circular(20),
                  child: Image.asset(
                    article.image,
                    width: 512,
                    height: 512,
                    fit: BoxFit.cover,
                  ))),
            Text(article.title, style: const TextStyle(fontSize: 24)),
            const SizedBox(height: 16),
            Text(article.description, style: const TextStyle(fontSize: 16)),
          ])));
  }
}
```

7. **Integration to main.dart**: Finally, the **main.dart** file defines the entry point of the application by running the **MyHeroApp** widget. This **StatelessWidget** sets up a **MaterialApp** with no debug banner, titles it "Hero Animation," and specifies the initial route as "/". It configures two routes: the **root ("/")** leads to the **HomeScreen**, and **/detail** leads to the **DetailScreen**. Update the **main.dart** as shown:

```
// main.dart
import 'dart:ui';

import 'package:flutter/material.dart';

import 'screens/detail/detail_screen.dart';
import 'screens/home/home_screen.dart';

void main() {
  runApp(const MyHeroApp());
}

class MyHeroApp extends StatelessWidget {
  const MyHeroApp({super.key});

  @override
  Widget build(BuildContext context) {
    return MaterialApp(
        debugShowCheckedModeBanner: false,
        title: 'Hero Animation',
        initialRoute: "/",
        routes: {
          '/': (context) => const HomeScreen(),
          '/detail': (context) => const DetailScreen(),
        },
        scrollBehavior: const MaterialScrollBehavior().
copyWith(dragDevices: {
          PointerDeviceKind.touch,
          PointerDeviceKind.mouse,
          PointerDeviceKind.unknown,
        }));
  }
}
```

Finally, run the app, and check the output.

Practical: Adding theme and style to DartByte

For the final practical, you are going to open and update the previous DartByte project, from *Chapter 3, Designing Stunning UIs for the Web* and add theme and style to it. The final output should be similar to the following figure:

Figure 4.10: *DartByte app with theme and style applied*

To make changes in theme, the first step is to create a custom theme. Inside the project's **`lib/`** folder add a new subfolder called **`utils`**. Create a new dart file and name it **`db_theme.dart`**. Inside it, define the **`CustomTheme`** class. It will have two distinct themes for the application: **`lightTheme`** and **`darkTheme`**. Write the code as shown:

```
// utils/db_theme.dart
import 'package:flutter/material.dart';

class CustomTheme {
  static ThemeData get lightTheme {
    return ThemeData(
      primaryColor: Colors.grey,
      useMaterial3: true,
      scaffoldBackgroundColor: Colors.white,
      textTheme: const TextTheme(
        bodyMedium: TextStyle(
          color: Colors.black,
          fontSize: 16,
        ),
        bodySmall: TextStyle(
          color: Colors.black54,
          fontSize: 14,
        ),
        headlineMedium: TextStyle(
          color: Colors.black45,
          fontSize: 22,
          fontWeight: FontWeight.bold,
        ),
      ),
      appBarTheme: const AppBarTheme(
        backgroundColor: Colors.white,
        titleTextStyle: TextStyle(
          color: Colors.black38,
          fontSize: 25,
          fontWeight: FontWeight.bold,
        ),
      ),
      cardColor: Colors.white,
    );
  }

  static ThemeData get darkTheme {
```

```
    return ThemeData(
      primaryColor: Colors.blue,
      useMaterial3: true,
      scaffoldBackgroundColor: Colors.black,
      textTheme: const TextTheme(
        bodyMedium: TextStyle(
          color: Colors.white,
          fontSize: 16,
        ),
        bodySmall: TextStyle(
          color: Colors.white54,
          fontSize: 14,
        ),
        headlineMedium: TextStyle(
          color: Colors.white60,
          fontSize: 22,
          fontWeight: FontWeight.bold,
        ),
      ),
      appBarTheme: const AppBarTheme(
        backgroundColor: Colors.black,
        titleTextStyle: TextStyle(
          color: Colors.white38,
          fontSize: 25,
          fontWeight: FontWeight.bold,
        ),
      ),
      cardColor: Colors.blueGrey,
    );
  }
}
```

In the above code, the **lightTheme** provides a bright, clean look with a white scaffold background, black text, and grey primary color. Text styles are set for different contexts, with **bodyMedium** and **bodySmall** providing black and grey colors respectively. The **headlineMedium** text style is bold and slightly lighter black. The **AppBar** has a white background with black text, ensuring a clear and bright appearance. Cards also use a white background for consistency with the overall light theme.

The **darkTheme** provides a darker aesthetic with a black scaffold background and blue primary color. Text colors are adjusted for readability on dark backgrounds, with white and grey hues for different text styles. The **headlineMedium** text is slightly off-white for better contrast. The **AppBar** features a black background with white text, creating a cohesive dark theme. Cards use a blue-grey color to maintain visibility and contrast with the dark background.

Note: When styling text in your custom widgets, it is best to use the predefined sizes in Flutter's TextTheme for consistency. Adjusting font sizes arbitrarily may disrupt the standard look and feel of Material widgets. Always align with the TextTheme conventions to ensure your design remains cohesive and maintains compatibility with other Material components.

Next thing is to make the changes to **main.dart** file. Follow the steps given below to update the app:

1. **Apply theme switching with Stateful widget**: Change the **DartByteApp** class into StatefulWidget to handle theme switching. Add a **_isDarkTheme** Boolean state to toggle between light and dark themes as shown:

```
class DartByteApp extends StatefulWidget {
  const DartByteApp({super.key});

  @override
  State<DartByteApp> createState() => _DartByteAppState();
}

class _DartByteAppState extends State<DartByteApp> {
  bool _isDarkTheme = false;

  void _toggleTheme() {
    setState(() {
      _isDarkTheme = !_isDarkTheme;
    });
  }

  @override
  Widget build(BuildContext context) {
    return MaterialApp(
      // other properties...
      theme: CustomTheme.lightTheme,
      darkTheme: CustomTheme.darkTheme,
```

```
        themeMode: _isDarkTheme ? ThemeMode.dark : ThemeMode.
light,
        // other properties...
      );
    }
  }
```

2. **Add theme toggle button to AppBar:** For this add an **`IconButton`** in the **`AppBar`** to toggle the theme on click, as shown:

```
AppBar(
  // other properties...
  actions: [
    // other actions...
    IconButton(
      onPressed: toggleTheme,
      icon: const Icon(Icons.brightness_4),
    ),
    const SizedBox(width: 10),
  ],
)
```

3. **Update theme usage in widgets**: For this, widgets now should use **`Theme.of(context)`** to apply colors and text styles from the theme data as shown in the following snippet:

```
class ByteNewsCard extends StatelessWidget {
  @override
  Widget build(BuildContext context) {
    return Card(
      color: Theme.of(context).cardColor,
      // other properties...
    );
  }
}

class RecommendedNews extends StatelessWidget {
  @override
  Widget build(BuildContext context) {
    return Padding(
      padding: const EdgeInsets.all(4.0),
```

```
      child: Row(
        children: List.generate(4, (index) {
          return Expanded(
            child: Card(
              color: Theme.of(context).cardColor,
              // other properties...
            ),
          );
        }),
      ),
    );
  }
}

class NewsArticleItem extends StatelessWidget {
  @override
  Widget build(BuildContext context) {
    return Card(
      color: Theme.of(context).cardColor.withOpacity(0.6),
      // other properties...
    );
  }
}
```

4. **Change ByteNewsCard text styles**: Update **ByteNewsCard** to use theme-specific text styles for title and author as shown in snippet:

```
Text(
  title,
  style: Theme.of(context).textTheme.headlineMedium,
),
Text('by $author', style: Theme.of(context).textTheme.
bodySmall),
```

5. **Change RecommendedNews widget:** Update **RecommendedNews** card to have a custom shape with rounded corners as shown:

```
shape: const RoundedRectangleBorder(
  borderRadius: BorderRadius.only(
    topLeft: Radius.circular(50),
    topRight: Radius.circular(10),
```

```
      bottomLeft: Radius.circular(10),
    ),
  ),
```

6. **Update NewsArticleItem widget**: Modify the shape of **`NewsArticleItem`** cards and adjust the background color with opacity as shown in the snippet:

```
shape: const RoundedRectangleBorder(
  borderRadius: BorderRadius.only(
    bottomLeft: Radius.circular(50),
    topLeft: Radius.circular(50),
    bottomRight: Radius.circular(20),
    topRight: Radius.circular(20),
  ),
),
color: Theme.of(context).cardColor.withOpacity(0.6),
```

The preceding changes include theme management improvements and updates to widget styling to better align with the app's theme. Run the app to see the output.

Conclusion

In this chapter, you have learned the art of creating stunning and interactive UIs with Flutter, diving into advanced concepts like custom widgets and animations. By applying performance optimization techniques and exploring practical implementations such as Hero Animation and Staggered Menu animations, you are now equipped to build dynamic and responsive web applications.

As we move forward to the next chapter, we will explore the integration of machine learning and AI into your Flutter applications, enabling you to enhance functionality and create intelligent, data-driven experiences.

Point to remember

- **Understand responsiveness**: Create interfaces that adapt seamlessly to different screen sizes and orientations.

Multiple choice questions

1. When optimizing animations for performance in Flutter, which technique can help ensure smooth rendering and responsiveness?

a. Using `AnimationController` without `TickerProvider`
b. Minimizing the number of animated properties
c. Increasing the animation frame rate
d. Avoiding the use of `FadeTransition`

2. Which of the following Flutter concepts is essential for creating reusable components with customizable behavior and appearance?
   a. Stateful Widgets
   b. Custom Widgets
   c. Layout Widget

Answer

1	b
2	b

Questions

1. Add the dark mode functionality to all the apps you have created.
2. Create a hero animation-based navigation inside Staggered Menu application.

Additional resources

1. **https://docs.flutter.dev/ui/animations**
2. **https://docs.flutter.dev/cookbook/design/themes**
3. **https://docs.flutter.dev/ui/adaptive-responsive/best-practices**

Join our book's Discord space

Join the book's Discord Workspace for Latest updates, Offers, Tech happenings around the world, New Release and Sessions with the Authors:

https://discord.bpbonline.com

CHAPTER 5
Incorporating Machine Learning and AI

Introduction

In today's digital landscape, the integration of **machine learning (ML)** and **artificial intelligence (AI)** has become increasingly vital for creating smarter, more responsive web applications. These technologies enable developers to provide enhanced user experiences, ranging from personalized recommendations to intelligent chatbots and accurate predictions. Flutter, known for its flexibility and ease of use, is an ideal framework for incorporating these advanced capabilities into web applications. This chapter will guide you through the essential steps to leverage ML and AI using powerful tools like ml_algo, Tensorflow and google_generative_ai, demonstrating how to build practical solutions directly within your Flutter web projects.

Structure

The chapter covers the following topics:

- Introduction to ML and AI in Flutter
- ML and AI in real world
- Common setup for the projects
- Project 1: Diabetes classifier
- Project 2: House Price Prediction

- Project 3: Flower species clustering
- Project 4: Creating a chatbot
- Project 5: Image recognition

Objectives

The primary goal of this chapter is to equip you with the knowledge and skills needed to integrate ML and AI features into your Flutter web applications. Through a series of hands-on projects, you will gain experience with key ML techniques such as classification, regression, and clustering, while also exploring real-world AI applications like image recognition and chatbots. Every app will have different ui and approach so that you get to explore various methodologies and technique. By the end of the chapter, you will be able to build intelligent, data-driven features that enhance the functionality and user engagement of your web applications.

Introduction to ML and AI in Flutter

ML and AI have revolutionized how modern web applications are built and interact with users. Flutter's flexibility, combined with the availability of ML and AI libraries, makes it a powerful tool for integrating intelligent features into web applications. In this section, we will explore fundamental concepts of ML and AI, their importance in today's web development landscape and how Flutter, with its wide range of supporting libraries like **ml_algo**, **tflite**, **google_generative_ai** and **huggingface_client**, can help you build cutting edge applications.

Overview of ML and AI concepts

ML is a subset of AI that enables computers to learn patterns from data without being explicitly programmed. This learning allows systems to make predictions or take actions based on new data, which is crucial for applications like recommendation engines, chatbots, and image recognition. AI goes beyond ML by incorporating reasoning, problem-solving, and understanding natural language, enabling applications to simulate human intelligence. AI-powered applications can not only learn but also adapt and improve based on user interactions.

The key ML concepts include:

- **Supervised learning**: Involves training a model on labeled data to make predictions. Common examples include classification (e.g., predicting if an email is spam or not) and regression (e.g., predicting house prices based on features).
- **Unsupervised learning**: Deals with finding patterns in unlabeled data. One common use case is clustering, where the model groups similar data points without knowing the labels beforehand (e.g., customer segmentation).

- **Reinforcement learning**: This is a type of learning where an agent interacts with an environment and learns to make decisions by receiving feedback in the form of rewards or penalties. Over time, the agent optimizes its actions to maximize cumulative rewards. Reinforcement learning is used in fields like robotics, gaming, and automated trading.
- **Deep learning**: A more advanced form of ML that uses neural networks with multiple layers (hence *deep*). It is especially useful for complex tasks like image recognition, **natural language processing** (**NLP**), and speech recognition.

The following figure summarizes the key components:

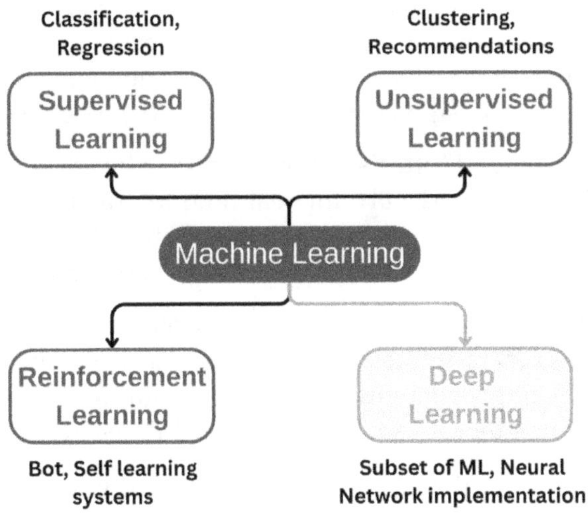

***Figure 5.1:** Show the different areas in ML*

Flutter's role in building intelligent web apps

Flutter has emerged as a powerful framework for building modern web applications, and its versatility extends to integrating ML and AI capabilities. With its fast-rendering engine, customizable widgets, and cross-platform support, Flutter provides a seamless environment for embedding intelligent features into web apps, making it an ideal choice for developers looking to build AI-driven applications. We can summarize Flutter's role in building intelligent web apps as:

- **Cross-platform consistency**: Flutter allows developers to build web applications with a single codebase that runs efficiently on different platforms, including desktop and mobile. When integrating ML and AI, this means that models or features can work consistently across all platforms without needing separate implementations.

- **Fast development cycle**: Flutter's *hot reload* feature accelerates the development process by instantly reflecting code changes in the running app. This is especially beneficial when experimenting with different ML models or AI features, allowing developers to quickly test and refine algorithms in real-time.
- **Integration with ML/AI libraries**: Flutter can easily integrate with powerful ML and AI frameworks like **ml_algo**, **tflite**, **google_generative_ai**, and **huggingface_client**. These libraries provide pre-built models and tools for tasks such as NLP, image recognition, and generative AI, making it easier to bring ML into web applications.
- **Customizable user interfaces for AI**: Flutter's rich set of customizable widgets makes it possible to design intuitive and responsive user interfaces that enhance AI-driven features. For instance, you can create interactive dashboards to visualize ML model results or design chat interfaces for AI-powered virtual assistants.
- **Efficient performance**: Flutter's performance is critical when deploying ML models in web applications, especially for real-time interactions like voice commands, image processing, or chatbot conversations. With its optimized rendering engine, Flutter ensures that AI features run smoothly, even in complex applications.
- **Scalability and maintainability:** As ML/AI-powered apps grow more complex, Flutter's architecture facilitates scalability. You can modularize AI features, allowing easy updates or improvements without overhauling the entire application. This makes it easier to integrate additional AI capabilities over time.

By leveraging Flutter's strengths, developers can efficiently incorporate ML and AI into their web applications, creating intelligent, scalable, and visually appealing experiences across platforms.

Brief introduction to ML and AI libraries in Flutter

To bring ML and AI capabilities to Flutter web applications, several libraries provide ready-to-use models and tools for implementing complex features like NLP, image recognition, and classification. The following section provides a brief overview of some essential ML/AI libraries compatible with Flutter:

ml_algo

`ml_algo` is a Dart library specifically designed for building ML models. It includes a range of supervised and unsupervised learning algorithms like regression, classification, and clustering. Its primary advantage is the ability to run ML models directly in the Flutter app, without needing an external server or backend. It supports algorithms such as linear regression, decision trees, k-means clustering, and more. It is completely Dart-based, allowing for seamless integration with Flutter applications.

tflite_web

`tflite_web` is a web-optimized version of **TensorFlow Lite** (**TFLite**), allowing developers to deploy lightweight ML models directly in the browser. This version of **TFLite** is tailored to run efficiently within web applications, making it ideal for integrating ML capabilities into Flutter web projects without the need for heavy backend computation. It enables on-device inference, ensuring low-latency and real-time AI experiences within web apps.

google_generative_ai

`google_generative_ai` is a cutting-edge library that enables developers to integrate advanced AI models from Google, especially those focused on generative tasks like text generation, chatbot creation, and conversational AI. It simplifies the process of creating interactive and conversational agents within Flutter applications.

huggingface_client

`huggingface_client` is a Dart package that connects Flutter apps with Hugging Face's extensive repository of pre-trained models. Hugging Face is a popular platform for NLP and AI models, offering solutions for tasks like sentiment analysis, translation, and text summarization.

ML and AI in real world

ML and AI are transforming the way web applications operate across various industries, offering intelligent, data-driven solutions that can analyze patterns, automate processes, and enhance user experiences. The following are some practical use cases of ML/AI in web applications across healthcare, e-commerce, and education as summarized in the illustration in *Figure 5.2* also:

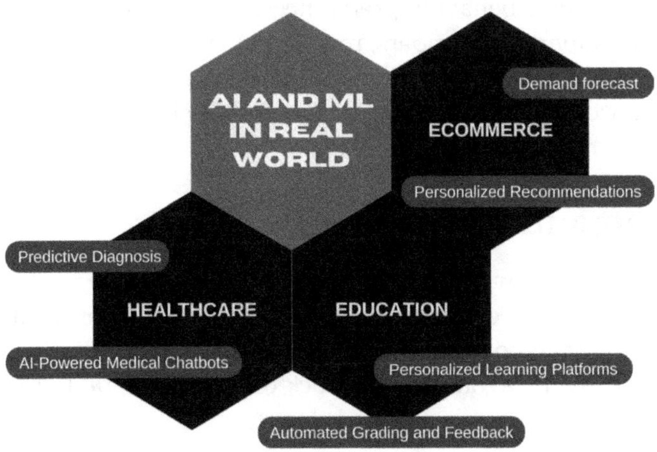

Figure 5.2: *Few examples of AI and ML in real world implementation*

Healthcare

In healthcare, ML and AI have opened the doors to more accurate diagnoses, predictive analytics, and personalized treatments. Web applications powered by AI can help medical professionals and patients access critical insights more efficiently.

Use case: Predictive diagnosis

ML algorithms can analyze patient data to predict the likelihood of certain diseases, such as diabetes or heart conditions, based on medical history, symptoms, and genetic factors. A web-based healthcare app could use ML models to predict the onset of diabetes based on patient lifestyle, family history, and current health metrics. The app can provide personalized recommendations to reduce risk factors and track patient progress over time.

Use case: AI-powered medical chatbots

AI chatbots can offer 24/7 assistance by answering medical questions, scheduling appointments, and triaging symptoms. A virtual assistant integrated into a healthcare web app can help patients understand their symptoms by asking relevant questions and providing suggestions for next steps, such as visiting a doctor or taking medication.

E-commerce

AI and ML technologies are widely used in the e-commerce sector to enhance customer experiences, streamline operations, and boost sales through personalized recommendations and smart automation.

Use case: Personalized product recommendations

ML models can analyze user behavior, preferences, and purchasing history to recommend products tailored to individual shoppers, improving customer satisfaction and increasing sales. An e-commerce website could use ML algorithms to recommend clothing items based on past purchases and browsing patterns, resulting in a more personalized shopping experience for the user.

Use case: Demand forecasting

AI models help businesses predict inventory demand by analyzing historical sales data, seasonal trends, and customer preferences. An online retailer could use ML-driven forecasting to optimize inventory levels for the holiday season, ensuring they have enough stock of popular items while avoiding overstock of less-demanded products.

Education

In the education sector, AI and ML are transforming traditional learning methods by enabling personalized learning experiences, automating administrative tasks, and providing real-time feedback to students and teachers.

Use case: Personalized learning platforms

AI-powered learning platforms analyze student performance and adapt the content to suit each student's learning pace and style, helping students learn more effectively. A web-based learning app could use ML to recommend personalized lessons or exercises to students based on their strengths and weaknesses, thereby improving their learning outcomes.

Use case: Automated grading and feedback

AI models can be used to grade assignments and exams, providing immediate and consistent feedback to students while reducing the workload for educators. An online education platform could use AI to automatically grade quizzes and offer feedback on essay submissions, highlighting areas where the student can improve.

These real-world examples highlight the vast potential of ML and AI in web applications across various domains. By integrating these technologies into Flutter web applications, developers can build more intelligent, responsive, and user-friendly solutions tailored to industry-specific needs.

Common setup for the projects

In this section, we will focus on preparing your Flutter development environment for building web applications that incorporate ML and AI features. This setup is designed to streamline the development process and ensure that your applications run efficiently on the web.

Focusing on web implementation

For the purpose of this book, we will concentrate exclusively on implementing features for web applications. Mobile and tablet layouts are not covered in this chapter and a **`Placeholder`** widget will be provided instead. This focus allows us to explore the web-specific challenges and solutions, ensuring that you can effectively build and deploy ML and AI-powered features on the web.

Structuring the application

Each app example will be structured around a main screen, referred to as the **prediction screen** or a similar name, and a responsive layout that adjusts based on screen size. This approach ensures that your web application maintains a consistent and user-friendly interface across different screen sizes. The following figure shows the basic project structure of the apps:

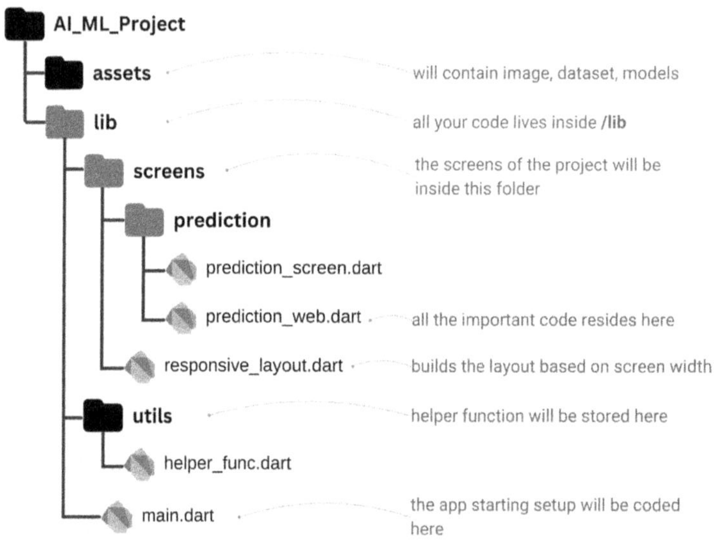

***Figure 5.3:** Suggested project structure of the project in this chapter*

Utilizing asynchronous programming techniques

Most applications in this section will use asynchronous programming to handle tasks such as data fetching and processing ML predictions. Understanding **`Future`**, **`async`**, and **`await`** is essential for managing asynchronous operations efficiently. Here is the summary:

- **Future**: Represents a value that will be available in the future. It is used to handle operations that take time, like network requests or file I/O.
- **async**: Marks a function as asynchronous, allowing it to use await to pause execution until a Future completes.
- **await**: Waits for a Future to complete and retrieves the result.

The following code shows the outline of an asynchronous function:

```
Future<void> fetchPrediction() async {
  try {
    final prediction = await fetchFromServer();
    // Use the prediction
```

```
    } catch (e) {
        // Handle errors
    }
}
```

Working with third-party libraries

Many applications will rely on third-party libraries for added functionality, such as managing user preferences, form validation, or image selection. Knowing how to add and use these packages is crucial for efficient development. There are two ways to add a package (library):

- **Using the pubspec.yaml file**: Update your **`pubspec.yaml`** file to include the desired packages and run the **`pub get`** command in the terminal
- **Add the package from terminal directly**: Open the terminal and then type **`flutter pub add library-name`** and press enter. It will download and add the package to your project.

In the next section, we are going to jump into the first ML practical implementation, the diabetes prediction app.

Project 1: Diabetes classifier

In this project, you will create a web application that predicts the likelihood of diabetes based on user input. The goal is to build a tool that leverages ML to analyze health metrics and provide a predictive outcome. This application will help users understand their risk factors for diabetes by inputting various health indicators into a form. The following figure shows how the user interface will look like:

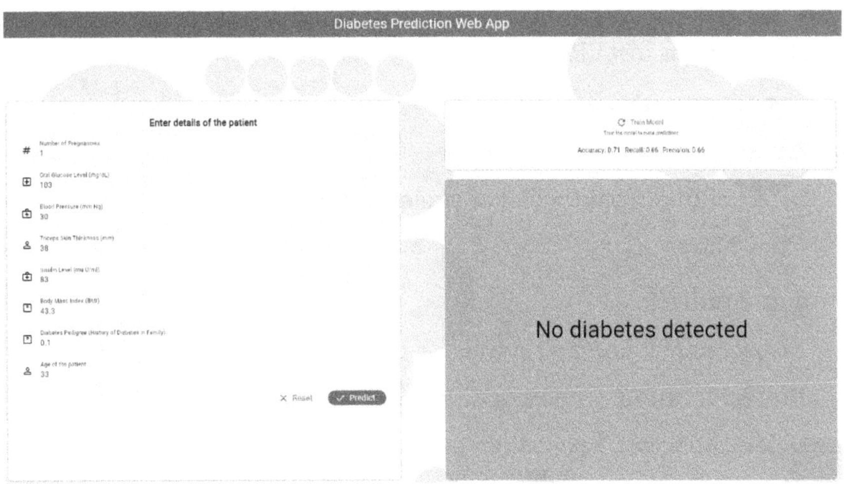

***Figure 5.4:** Diabetes prediction app UI*

The project will involve several steps:

1. **Setting up the environment**: You will configure your Flutter project for web development, ensuring you have all necessary dependencies and libraries to handle ML tasks and build a responsive user interface.
2. **Building the application**: You will create a responsive layout to accommodate different screen sizes and implement a prediction screen where users can input their health data. The application will use a **K-Nearest Neighbors (KNN)** classifier to make predictions based on the input data.
3. **Implementing ML functionalities**: The project includes training a ML model with a dataset, making predictions based on user input, and displaying the results. You will also learn how to save and load the trained model using local storage.
4. **User interface design**: The application will feature a form for data input, including fields for key health indicators such as glucose levels and BMI. The results of the prediction will be displayed with clear, color-coded feedback to help users easily understand their risk level.

Configuring the project

You have to prepare your development environment for building the Diabetes Classifier web application using Flutter in IntelliJ IDEA. The setup process includes creating the project, organizing the folder structure, adding necessary assets, and configuring dependencies.

Creating a new Flutter project

Follow the given steps to create the Diabetes Classifier app:

1. **Open IntelliJ IDEA**: Launch IntelliJ IDEA and ensure that you have the Flutter and Dart plugins installed.
2. **Start a new project**:
    a. Go to **File | New | Project**.
    b. Select Flutter from the list of project types.
    c. Click **Next**.
3. **Configure project**:
    a. **Project name**: Enter **`diabetes_classifier_app`**.
    b. **Project location**: Choose a directory for your project (optional).
    c. **Select devices**: Choose **Web** and **Desktop** only.
    d. Click **Finish** to create the project.

Set up folder structure

The Diabetes Classifier project is organized into folders and files for easier understanding. Follow the given steps to set up the folders and files:

1. **Navigate to lib directory**: In the `lib` directory, create the following subdirectories:
   - `ml_utils` for ML utilities.
   - `screens` for the different screens of the application.
2. **Create subdirectories in screens**:
   - Inside the `screens` directory, create `prediction` for the prediction-related screens:
     - Create `prediction_screen.dart` file
     - Create `prediction_web.dart` file, where the UI will reside
   - `responsive_layout.dart` for handling responsive layouts.
3. **Add asset folder**: Create an `images` directory under the `assets` folder in the root directory of your project. Place the `bg.png` image inside this folder, it can be any image you want to put in the background.

Configure dependencies

The project requires various libraries for the implementation of ML tasks. Follow the given steps to add the required dependencies to the project:

1. **Update pubspec.yaml:**
   - Open `pubspec.yaml` in the root directory of your project
   - Add the following dependencies:

     ```
     ml_dataframe: ^1.6.0
     ml_preprocessing: ^7.0.2
     ml_algo: ^16.17.12
     shared_preferences: ^2.3.2
     flutter_form_builder: ^9.4.1
     form_builder_validators: ^11.0.0
     ```
2. **Open terminal**: In IntelliJ IDEA, run `flutter pub get` to install the listed dependencies. Remember internet connection is required to download the dependencies.

Implementing the Diabetes Classifier

In this section, you will develop the Diabetes Classifier application. This includes coding the ML functionality, setting up the user interface for both the web and responsive layouts, and integrating form handling and prediction logic.

Creating the classifier

The **`ml_utils/classifier.dart`** file contains essential functionalities for the Diabetes Classifier application. The code is divided into four functions for training and prediction, and saving/loading the trained algorithm in and out of the memory for easy operations. Follow the given steps to complete the **`classifier.dart`** file:

1. **Imports and dependencies:** Add the following code to the **`classifier.dart`** file

    ```
    import 'dart:convert';
    import ‘package:ml_algo/ml_algo.dart’;
    import 'package:ml_dataframe/ml_dataframe.dart';
    import 'package:shared_preferences/shared_preferences.dart';
    ```

    In the preceding code snippet, **`dart:convert`** provides JSON encoding and decoding capabilities. The **`ml_algo`** is a package for ML algorithms, including classifiers. **`ml_dataframe`** handles data structures and manipulation for ML. And **`shared_preferences`** manages local storage for persisting data.

2. **Saving and retrieving model from local storage:** Create the methods for save and load the models, shown as follows:

    ```
    Future<void> saveJsonToLocalStorage(String key, Map<String, dynamic> jsonData) async {
      SharedPreferences prefs = await SharedPreferences.getInstance();
      String jsonString = jsonEncode(jsonData);
      await prefs.setString(key, jsonString);
    }

    Future<String?> getJsonFromLocalStorage(String key) async {
      SharedPreferences prefs = await SharedPreferences.getInstance();
      return prefs.getString(key);
    }
    ```

    In the preceding functions, the **`saveJsonToLocalStorage()`** function converts a JSON object into a string and saves it in local storage under the specified key. While the **`getJsonFromLocalStorage()`** retrieves the JSON string from local storage based on the provided key. These function help store the trained model and then load it when prediction task is needed to be executed.

3. **Making predictions:** The following code will be used for taking the user input from the app and then making the prediction:

```
Future<String> makePrediction(Map<String, dynamic> formData) async {
  final inputData = [
    [
      'Pregnancies',
      'Glucose',
      'BloodPressure',
      'SkinThickness',
      'Insulin',
      'BMI',
      'DiabetesPedigreeFunction',
      'Age'
    ],
    [
      double.parse(formData['Pregnancies'].toString()),
      double.parse(formData[‘Glucose’].toString()),
      double.parse(formData['BloodPressure'].toString()),
      double.parse(formData['SkinThickness'].toString()),
      double.parse(formData['Insulin'].toString()),
      double.parse(formData['BMI'].toString()),
      double.parse(formData['DiabetesPedigreeFunction'].toString()),
      double.parse(formData[‘Age’].toString()),
    ]
  ];
  final dataFrame = DataFrame(inputData);
  var modelJson = await getJsonFromLocalStorage('diabetes_model');
  if (modelJson == null) {
    return 'Model not found! Please train the model first.';
  }
  final model = KnnClassifier.fromJson(modelJson);
  final prediction = model.predict(dataFrame);
  return prediction.series.first.data.first.toString();
}
```

The **makePrediction** function processes user input by converting it into a DataFrame. It then loads the trained model from local storage and uses it to predict whether diabetes is present based on the input data. This function is essential for providing real-time predictions to users.

4. **Training the model:** Add the following function to **classifier.dart** file:

```
Future<Map<String, double>> trainModel() async {
  final data = getPimaIndiansDiabetesDataFrame().shuffle();
  final splits = splitData(data, [.8]);
  final model = KnnClassifier(splits.first, 'Outcome', 5);

  var accuracy = model.assess(splits.last, MetricType.accuracy);
  var recall = model.assess(splits.last, MetricType.recall);
  var precision = model.assess(splits.last, MetricType.precision);

  await saveJsonToLocalStorage(‘diabetes_model’, model.toJson());
  return {
    'accuracy': accuracy,
    'recall': recall,
    'precision': precision,
  };
}
```

   The **trainModel** function preceding prepares the dataset, trains the KNN classifier, and evaluates its performance. By saving the trained model, this function ensures that users can make predictions based on a model that has been tailored to their data. The accuracy, recall, and precision metrics provide insights into the model's performance.

The **classifier.dart** file is crucial for managing ML operations in the Diabetes Classifier app.

Creating the responsive_layout.dart file

The **responsive_layout.dart** file defines a **ResponsiveLayout** widget, which dynamically adjusts the user interface based on the screen size. This widget takes three parameters: **mobileLayout**, **tabletLayout**, and **webLayout**, which represent different UI layouts for mobile, tablet, and web screens respectively. In the build method, the **LayoutBuilder** widget is used to determine the maximum width of the available space. Depending on the width, it returns the appropriate layout, such as:

- **Mobile layout**: Used for screens narrower than 600 pixels.
- **Tablet layout**: Applied for screens between 600 and 1200 pixels.
- **Web layout**: Used for screens wider than 1200 pixels.

This approach ensures that the app's interface is responsive and adapts to various devices, providing a user-friendly experience across different screen sizes. All the five app use this same code for the **responsive_layout.dart** file. Write the following code:

```
import 'package:flutter/material.dart';

class ResponsiveLayout extends StatelessWidget {
  final Widget mobileLayout;
  final Widget tabletLayout;
  final Widget webLayout;

  const ResponsiveLayout({
    super.key,
    required this.mobileLayout,
    required this.tabletLayout,
    required this.webLayout,
  });

  @override
  Widget build(BuildContext context) {
    return LayoutBuilder(builder: (context, constraints) {
      if (constraints.maxWidth < 600) {
        return mobileLayout;
      } else if (constraints.maxWidth < 1200) {
        return tabletLayout;
      } else {
        return webLayout;
      }
    });
  }
}
```

Creating the prediction_screen.dart file

The **prediction_screen.dart** file defines the **PredictionScreen** widget, which serves as the main screen for the prediction functionality. It utilizes the **ResponsiveLayout** widget to display the appropriate layout based on the screen size. Write the code shown as follows:

```
import 'package:diabetes_classifier_app/screens/prediction/prediction_web.dart';
import 'package:diabetes_classifier_app/screens/responsive_layout.dart';
import 'package:flutter/material.dart';

class PredictionScreen extends StatelessWidget {
  const PredictionScreen({super.key});

  @override
  Widget build(BuildContext context) {
    return const ResponsiveLayout(
      mobileLayout: Placeholder(),
      tabletLayout: Placeholder(),
      webLayout: PredictionWeb(),
    );
  }
}
```

In the preceding code, for mobile and tablet layouts, placeholders are used, while the **PredictionWeb** widget is specified for web screens. This design allows the app to render a specific UI component for web users, ensuring that the prediction interface is optimized for larger screens. The chapter uses the same logic for the other apps to, which helps us to focus on web layout and logic.

Integration into main.dart code

This is the entry point for our application. The **main()** function runs the **DiabetesClassifier** widget, which is a stateless widget representing the root of the application. Inside **DiabetesClassifier**, the **MaterialApp** widget is used to define the app's structure and theme. As discussed in *Chapter 3, Designing Stunning UIs for the Web*, the **MaterialApp** is a core widget in Flutter that wraps the entire application, providing navigation, theming, and localization. The title is set to *Diabetes Classifier App*, and a custom color scheme is applied using a purple color as the primary swatch. The app is set to use Material 3 design principles with **useMaterial3: true**. Additionally, the debug banner, usually visible during development, is disabled by setting **debugShowCheckedModeBanner: false**. The following code shows the updated **main.dart** file:

```
// main.dart
import 'package:diabetes_classifier_app/screens/prediction/prediction_screen.dart';
import 'package:flutter/material.dart';

void main() {
  runApp(const DiabetesClassifier());
}

class DiabetesClassifier extends StatelessWidget {
  const DiabetesClassifier({super.key});
  @override
  Widget build(BuildContext context) {
    return MaterialApp(
      title: 'Diabetes Classifier App',
      theme: ThemeData(
        colorScheme: ColorScheme.fromSwatch(primarySwatch: Colors.purple),
        useMaterial3: true,
      ),
      home: const PredictionScreen(),
      debugShowCheckedModeBanner: false,
    );
  }
}
```

The **home** parameter in the **MaterialApp** is assigned to **PredictionScreen**, which is a screen that will be displayed when the app is launched. The **PredictionScreen** widget is imported from the **prediction_screen.dart** file, likely containing the user interface for predicting diabetes based on the user's input data. This clean and minimal setup separates concerns by ensuring that the application structure, theming, and core navigation are handled within **DiabetesClassifier**, while the specific functionality and layout of the prediction screen are managed in a different file.

Creating the prediction_web.dart file

To create the UI for the application, we will be creating a stateful widget called **PredictionWeb** and **_PredictionWebState** class that will manage the state. We also need a form that the user can fill. It will contain the details of patient. For this we will create a class called **DiabetesPredictionForm** as a stateless widget. The following class figure shows what properties and methods each class will have:

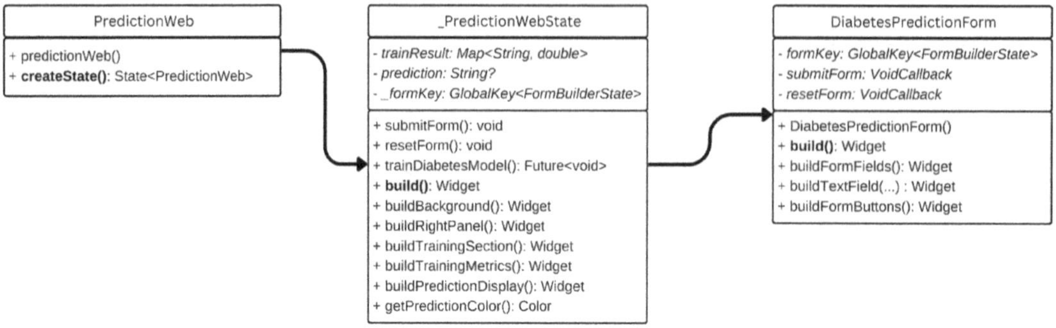

***Figure 5.5:** Class diagram for prediction_web.dart file*

Class: PredictionWeb

The **PredictionWeb** class is a **StatefulWidget** that forms the core structure of the diabetes prediction web app. It acts as a parent widget, managing the creation of the state object which will control how the user interface behaves and reacts to interactions.

The **createState()** method is responsible for returning an instance of the **_PredictionWebState** class, which will handle all the state-related logic for the widget. By using **createState()**, **PredictionWeb** maintains its mutable state, which is essential for dynamic interaction such as form submission and model training. The following code snippet shows the code for writing this class:

```
// screens/prediction/prediction_web.dart
import 'package:flutter/material.dart';
import 'package:flutter_form_builder/flutter_form_builder.dart';
import 'package:form_builder_validators/form_builder_validators.
dart';
import '../../ml_utils/classifier.dart';

class PredictionWeb extends StatefulWidget {
  const PredictionWeb({super.key});

  @override
  State<PredictionWeb> createState() => _PredictionWebState();
}
```

The app requires using the **form_builder** package for creating form and **form_builder_validators** package for form input validation.

Class: _PredictionWebState

The **_PredictionWebState** class is where all the logic for the page resides. It manages everything from handling the form input, training the model, making predictions, and updating the user interface accordingly. The class is part of the **State<PredictionWeb>** and it actively monitors and reacts to changes in state.

State variables

To manage the state and data in the Diabetes Classifier, we define several important state variables that store model results, prediction outcomes, and form states and are described as follows:

- **trainResult** is a **Map** that stores the results of model training, including metrics like accuracy, recall, and precision.
- **prediction** is a nullable **String** that stores the outcome of the prediction, such as "Diabetes detected" or "No diabetes detected."
- **_formKey** is a **GlobalKey<FormBuilderState>** that manages the state of the form, allowing validation, saving, and resetting of form fields.

Method: submitForm()

This function validates the form fields and submits the form. It first checks if the form data is valid using **saveAndValidate()**. Once validated, the form data is extracted and passed to the **makePrediction()** function, which will return a prediction result (either "1" for diabetes or "0" for no diabetes). Based on this result, the prediction state is updated, triggering a UI update to display the result to the user.

Method: resetForm()

This function resets the form to its initial state, clearing all the fields and resetting the prediction value to null. The method uses the form key to reset the form state and ensures that the UI is refreshed accordingly.

Method: trainDiabetesModel()

This method handles the model training process. When the user clicks the **Train Model** button, this function is called to train the diabetes prediction model. The function updates the **trainResult** variable with the training metrics, such as accuracy, recall, and precision, which are then displayed on the UI. Write the following code to create this class:

```
class _PredictionWebState extends State<PredictionWeb> {
  Map<String, double> trainResult = {};
  String? prediction;
  final _formKey = GlobalKey<FormBuilderState>();

  void submitForm() {
    if (_formKey.currentState?.saveAndValidate() ?? false) {
      final formData = _formKey.currentState!.value;
      makePrediction(formData).then((value) {
        setState(() {
```

```
          prediction =
              value == '1'?'Diabetes detected' : 'No diabetes detected';
        });
      });
    }
  }

  void resetForm() {
    _formKey.currentState?.reset();
    setState(() => prediction = null);
  }

  Future<void> trainDiabetesModel() async {
    final result = await trainModel();
    setState(() => trainResult = result);
  }
}
```

These are the variables and methods that will help in background processing. The other methods are widgets that will help to build UI of the app in a dynamic interactive way. Let us begin with the **`build()`** method that is the starting point of class.

Method: build()

This is the main build method of the widget, responsible for rendering the entire user interface. It builds the page layout, including the app bar, background image, form section, and prediction display. The method is divided into multiple smaller functions to manage different sections of the UI, like the form and the prediction result panel. Update the method shown as follows:

```
@override
 Widget build(BuildContext context) {
   return Scaffold(
     appBar: AppBar(
       title: const Text(
         'Diabetes Prediction Web App',
         style: TextStyle(color: Colors.white, fontSize: 30),
       ),
       centerTitle: true,
       flexibleSpace: Container(
```

```
          decoration: const BoxDecoration(
            gradient: LinearGradient(
              colors: [Colors.purple, Colors.deepPurpleAccent],
            ),
          ),
        ),
      ),
      body: Stack(
        children: [
          buildBackground(),
          Row(
            crossAxisAlignment: CrossAxisAlignment.stretch,
            children: [
              Expanded(
                child: DiabetesPredictionForm(
                  formKey: _formKey,
                  submitForm: submitForm,
                  resetForm: resetForm,
                ),
              ),
              Expanded(
                child: buildRightPanel(),
              ),
            ],
          )
        ],
      ),
    );
  }
```

You should run your app in the browser, but replace the methods that are not yet created with a **Placeholder()** or **Container()**. This will help you visualize your app at each step.

Method: buildBackground()

This function builds the background of the application. It uses an image asset with a purple color overlay to create a visually appealing background for the app. The image stretches to fill the entire screen and adds a gradient effect to make the UI more engaging. Write the method given below:

```
Widget buildBackground() {
  return Image.asset(
    "images/bg.png",
    fit: BoxFit.cover,
    height: double.infinity,
    width: double.infinity,
    colorBlendMode: BlendMode.modulate,
    color: Colors.purple.withOpacity(0.1),
  );
}
```

Method: buildRightPanel()

The right panel contains the model training section and the prediction display. This section of the UI is displayed alongside the form. It is structured with two key components: a section for training the model and a section to display the prediction. Add this method to the class:

```
Widget buildRightPanel() {
  return FractionallySizedBox(
    heightFactor: .75,
    widthFactor: .90,
    child: Column(
      children: [
        buildTrainingSection(),
        const SizedBox(height: 20),
        buildPredictionDisplay(),
      ],
    ),
  );
}
```

Method: buildTrainingSection()

This function renders the training section, where users can click a button to trigger the model training process. It also displays the metrics from the training (accuracy, recall, precision). If the model has not been trained yet, it prompts the user to train the model. Write the following method:

```
Widget buildTrainingSection() {
  return Container(
    padding: const EdgeInsets.all(32.0),
```

```
      decoration: BoxDecoration(
        border: Border.all(color: Colors.grey),
        color: Colors.white.withAlpha(250),
        borderRadius: BorderRadius.circular(10),
      ),
      child: Column(
        mainAxisAlignment: MainAxisAlignment.center,
        children: [
          OutlinedButton.icon(
            icon: const Icon(Icons.refresh_rounded),
            onPressed: trainDiabetesModel,
            label: const Text('Train Model'),
          ),
          const Text(
            "Train the model to make predictions",
            style: TextStyle(fontSize: 10, fontWeight: FontWeight.w100),
          ),
          const SizedBox(height: 20),
          buildTrainingMetrics(),
        ],
      ),
    );
  }
```

Method: buildTrainingMetrics()

This function is responsible for displaying the model training metrics. If the model has been trained, it shows the values for accuracy, recall, and precision. If not, a message is shown prompting the user to train the model to obtain metrics. Add the method to the class:

```
Widget buildTrainingMetrics() {
    if (trainResult.isEmpty) {
      return const Text('Train the model to get metrics');
    }
    return Row(
      mainAxisAlignment: MainAxisAlignment.center,
      children: [
        Text("Accuracy: ${trainResult['accuracy']?.
```

```
toStringAsFixed(2)}"),
          const SizedBox(width: 10),
          Text("Recall: ${trainResult['recall']?.
toStringAsFixed(2)}"),
          const SizedBox(width: 10),
          Text("Precision: ${trainResult['precision']?.
toStringAsFixed(2)}"),
        ],
      );
    }
```

Method: buildPredictionDisplay()

This function builds the prediction display section. It uses an animated container that changes its color based on the prediction result (red for diabetes, green for no diabetes, grey for no result). The container displays the prediction result, which is updated dynamically after form submission. Add this method to show the prediction:

```
Widget buildPredictionDisplay() {
    return Expanded(
      child: AnimatedContainer(
        width: double.infinity,
        padding: const EdgeInsets.all(32.0),
        decoration: BoxDecoration(
          border: Border.all(color: Colors.white),
          borderRadius: BorderRadius.circular(10),
          color: getPredictionColor(),
        ),
        duration: const Duration(seconds: 1),
        child: Center(
          child: Text(
            prediction ?? 'Prediction will appear here',
            style: const TextStyle(fontSize: 25),
          ),
        ),
      ),
    );
  }
```

Method: getPredictionColor()

This helper function determines the color of the prediction display based on the value of the prediction variable. If the prediction indicates **Diabetes detected**, it returns a red color. If the prediction is **No diabetes detected**, it returns green. Otherwise, the default color is grey. Write this method for displaying color based on the results:

```
Color getPredictionColor() {
    if (prediction == 'Diabetes detected') {
      return Colors.red.withAlpha(200);
    } else if (prediction == 'No diabetes detected') {
      return Colors.green.withAlpha(200);
    } else {
      return Colors.grey.withAlpha(200);
    }
}
```

This completes the **_PredictionWebState** class, please be sure to check the names of variables, methods and widget for spelling mistakes.

Class: DiabetesPredictionForm

The **DiabetesPredictionForm** class is a **StatelessWidget** that manages the input form where the user enters patient data. This class is responsible for creating the fields, handling form submission, and resetting the form. The constructor takes three parameters: **formKey**, **submitForm**, and **resetForm**. These are required to manage the form's state and interaction logic. **formKey** is used to validate and access form data, while **submitForm** and **resetForm** are callbacks that handle submission and resetting. The code for the class is shown as follows:

```
class DiabetesPredictionForm extends StatelessWidget {
  final GlobalKey<FormBuilderState> formKey;
  final VoidCallback submitForm;
  final VoidCallback resetForm;

  const DiabetesPredictionForm({
    super.key,
    required this.formKey,
    required this.submitForm,
    required this.resetForm,
  });
}
```

Method: build()

The **`build()`** method constructs the UI for the form. The form is housed within a container and has various input fields for the patient's medical data. The form is built using the **`FormBuilder`** widget, which simplifies form validation and data handling. Update the method shown as follows:

```
@override
Widget build(BuildContext context) {
  const gapBwInput = 20.0;
  return FractionallySizedBox(
    heightFactor: .75,
    widthFactor: .90,
    child: Container(
      decoration: BoxDecoration(
        border: Border.all(color: Colors.grey),
        color: Colors.white.withAlpha(250),
        borderRadius: BorderRadius.circular(10),
      ),
      child: Padding(
        padding: const EdgeInsets.all(32.0),
        child: SingleChildScrollView(
          child: FormBuilder(
            key: formKey,
            child: Column(
              children: [
                const Text(
                  'Enter details of the patient',
                  style: TextStyle(
                    fontSize: gapBwInput,
                    fontWeight: FontWeight.bold,
                  ),
                ),
                const SizedBox(height: gapBwInput),
                buildFormFields(),
                const SizedBox(height: gapBwInput),
                buildFormButtons(),
                const SizedBox(height: gapBwInput),
              ],
```

```
            ),
          ),
        ),
      ),
    ),
  );
}
```

Method: buildFormFields()

This function constructs all the input fields required to capture the patient's medical data. The fields include input for parameters like glucose level, BMI, blood pressure, and age. Each field has a label and an icon to make the form intuitive. Create the form in the method shown as follows:

```
Widget buildFormFields() {
    return Column(
      children: [
        buildTextField(
            'Pregnancies', 'Number of Pregnancies', Icons.numbers_outlined),
        buildTextField('Glucose', 'Oral Glucose Level (mg/dL)',
            Icons.local_hospital_outlined),
        buildTextField('BloodPressure', 'Blood Pressure (mm Hg)',
            Icons.medical_services_outlined),
        buildTextField('SkinThickness', 'Triceps Skin Thickness (mm)',
            Icons.person_outline),
        buildTextField('Insulin', 'Insulin Level (mu U/ml)',
            Icons.medical_services_outlined),
        buildTextField(
            'BMI', 'Body Mass Index (BMI)', Icons.monitor_weight_outlined),
        buildTextField(
            'DiabetesPedigreeFunction',
            'Diabetes Pedigree (History of Diabetes in Family)',
            Icons.monitor_weight_outlined,
            hintText: "Enter 0 or 1 only"),
        buildTextField('Age', 'Age of the patient', Icons.person_outline),
```

```
        ],
      );
    }
```

Method: buildTextField()

This helper method creates individual text fields within the form. It takes a name (used to identify the field in the form state), a label (describing the input), and an icon to visually represent the field. The **`hintText`** is optional but helps guide the user on what to enter in certain fields. Add this code to the class:

```
  Widget buildTextField(String name, String label, IconData icon,
      {String? hintText}) {
    return Padding(
      padding: const EdgeInsets.only(bottom: 20.0),
      child: FormBuilderTextField(
        name: name,
        decoration: InputDecoration(
          labelText: label,
          icon: Icon(icon),
          hintText: hintText,
        ),
        validator: FormBuilderValidators.compose([
          FormBuilderValidators.numeric(),
          if (name == 'DiabetesPedigreeFunction') ...[
            FormBuilderValidators.max(3),
            FormBuilderValidators.min(0),
          ],
        ]),
      ),
    );
  }
```

Method: buildFormButtons()

This method builds the buttons for form interaction. It includes a **Reset** button to clear the form and a **Predict** button to submit the form. The buttons trigger the **`resetForm`** and **`submitForm`** callbacks passed from the parent widget. Create this method to complete you code:

```
Widget buildFormButtons() {
    return Row(
      mainAxisAlignment: MainAxisAlignment.end,
      children: [
        OutlinedButton.icon(
          icon: const Icon(Icons.clear),
          onPressed: resetForm,
          label: const Text('Reset', style: TextStyle(fontSize: 18)),
        ),
        const SizedBox(width: 10),
        FilledButton.icon(
          icon: const Icon(Icons.check),
          onPressed: submitForm,
          label: const Text('Predict', style: TextStyle(fontSize: 18)),
        ),
      ],
    );
  }
```

After you complete the code, try to run it. The first step will be to train the model. After that fill the form and see the output. Depending on the form input the results be displayed on the right container. The following figure shows how the output will look:

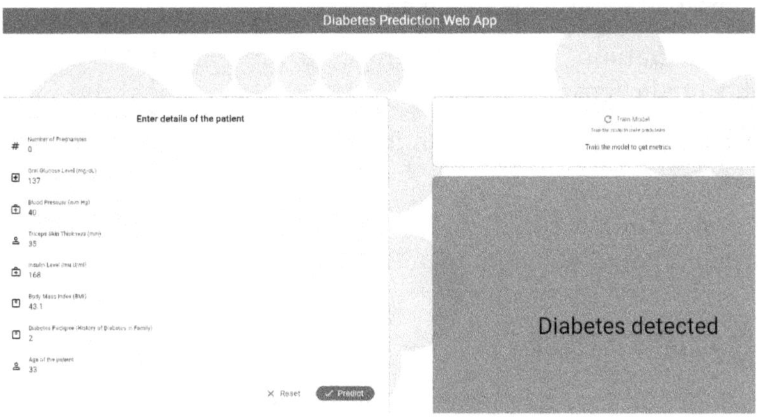

Figure 5.6: *Output of the completed diabetes prediction app*

Project 2: House Price Prediction

The House Price Prediction App leverages cutting-edge ML techniques to provide an easy and intuitive way for users to estimate house prices based on key features such as the number of bedrooms, bathrooms, square footage, number of floors, and the overall condition of the house. Powered by a neural network model, the app is designed to streamline the process of price prediction for users interested in real estate or those making informed decisions in the housing market. The following figure shows how the app looks like when completed:

Figure 5.7: *Completed House price prediction app interface*

This app highlights include:

- **Interactive input sliders**: Users can quickly adjust the house features like bedrooms, bathrooms, and living area.
- **TFLite integration**: The app leverages a pre-trained ML model (**`TFLite`**) to compute predictions.
- **Real-time predictions**: Users can instantly predict house prices based on input data.
- **Clear and intuitive UI**: A simple and clean interface built using Flutter with responsive layouts that work seamlessly across web platforms.

Training the model

The house price prediction model was trained using Python and the TensorFlow deep learning library. By leveraging a comprehensive dataset containing house pricing information, the model was built to predict house prices based on various input features like square footage, number of bedrooms, bathrooms, and more. Since training a model of this scale requires substantial computational resources, it cannot be performed directly on the web or mobile devices. Instead, the model was trained offline, ensuring optimal accuracy and performance through multiple iterations and hyperparameter tuning. You can find the dataset and training code inside the books github repository.

Once the model was trained, it was converted into a TFLite format, which is specifically designed for deployment on edge devices like mobile and web platforms. The **TFLite** model is lightweight and optimized for performance, making it ideal for use in resource-constrained environments. By utilizing the **`tflite_web`** library, this model can be efficiently integrated into web applications, enabling real-time house price predictions with minimal latency while maintaining accuracy.

Setting up the project

Create a new Flutter project, name it, **`house_price_prediction`**. Create the folder structure for the responsive web app, as done in previous project. this app leverages the **Cupertino** design system, which is Apple's style for building user interfaces. This gives the app a sleek and familiar appearance for iOS users. Before getting started, you will need to add the necessary dependencies to your **`pubspec.yaml`** file. Update the code shown as follows:

```
dependencies:
  ...
  tflite_web: ^0.2.2
  flutter_form_builder: ^9.4.1
  form_builder_validators: ^11.0.0
  form_builder_cupertino_fields: ^0.4.0
```

Download the pre-trained model file (**`house_price_prediction.tflite`**) from books project repository and then store it inside the **`web/models`** folder. Download the tflite zip required for the web app to work from the following link **https://github.com/hoomanmmd/tflite-web/releases/download/0.2.0/tflite.zip**. To implement TFLite using the **`tflite_web`** package, the model is packaged as a WebAssembly binary, which enables it to run efficiently in a browser. After downloading and unpacking the necessary files from the tflite-web release into the **`web/tflite`** folder, your project structure should include various **`.js`** and **`.wasm`** files as shown in the following figure:

Figure 5.8: The web folder contents

Setting up the main.dart

The main.dart file establishes the foundation for a Flutter application by utilizing the **CupertinoApp** widget to create an iOS-style interface. It begins with the main function, which launches the app by invoking **runApp** with the **HousePricePredictionApp** widget as the root. This widget configures the app's title, initial screen (**HppScreen**), and visual theme using **CupertinoThemeData** for a cohesive iOS aesthetic. Additionally, the **scrollBehavior** property is tailored to handle input from various devices, including touch and mouse, enhancing the app's adaptability and usability. Write the following code to update your **main.dart** file:

```
import 'dart:ui';
import 'package:flutter/cupertino.dart';
import 'screens/price_prediction/hpp_screen.dart';

void main() {
  runApp(const HousePricePredictionApp());
}

class HousePricePredictionApp extends StatelessWidget {
  const HousePricePredictionApp({super.key});

  @override
```

```
  Widget build(BuildContext context) {
    return CupertinoApp(
      title: 'House Price Prediction App',
      home: const HppScreen(),
      debugShowCheckedModeBanner: false,
      theme: const CupertinoThemeData(
        brightness: Brightness.light,
        primaryColor: CupertinoColors.systemBlue,
      ),
      scrollBehavior: const CupertinoScrollBehavior().copyWith(
        dragDevices: {
          PointerDeviceKind.unknown,
          PointerDeviceKind.touch,
          PointerDeviceKind.mouse,
        },
      ),
    );
  }
}
```

Creating the hpp_screen.dart file

The **hpp_screen.dart** file defines the **HppScreen** widget, which serves as a crucial component of the Flutter application. This widget, extending **StatelessWidget**, is responsible for displaying different layouts based on the device type. Within the build method, it utilizes the **ResponsiveLayout** widget to adapt the UI for various screen sizes. For web platforms, it uses the **HppWeb** widget to provide a tailored web experience, while **Placeholder** widgets are used for mobile and tablet layouts, indicating where specific content or functionality will be implemented. This approach ensures that the application delivers an optimized user experience across diverse devices. Write the code shown as follows:

```
// screens/price_prediction/hpp_screen.dart
import 'package:flutter/cupertino.dart';
import '../responsive_layout.dart';
import 'hpp_web.dart';

class HppScreen extends StatelessWidget {
  const HppScreen({super.key});

```

```
  @override
  Widget build(BuildContext context) {
    return const ResponsiveLayout(
      webLayout: HppWeb(),
      mobileLayout: Placeholder(),
      tabletLayout: Placeholder(),
    );
  }
}
```

Note: You have to create the responsive_layout.dart file inside the screens folder. The code is sample as the previous app.

Creating HppWeb.dart file

The **`hpp_web.dart`** file defines the **`HppWeb`** widget for the web version of the House Price Prediction application. This widget, implemented as a stateful widget, integrates with the TFLite Web library to perform ML predictions. The **`HppWeb`** widget initializes the TensorFlow model on startup, manages the state of the model, and handles user interactions for predicting house prices based on input data. The following is the class figure to help you the code logic:

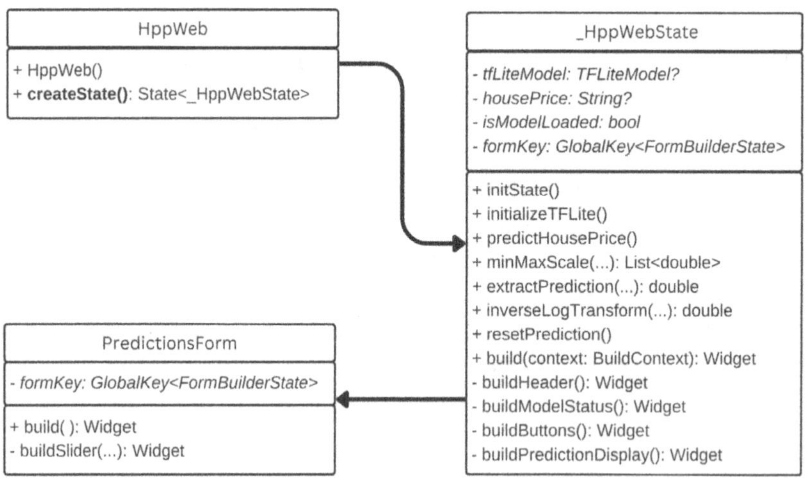

Figure 5.9: *Class diagram of hpp_web.dart file*

The UI is built using Cupertino widgets, featuring a responsive design with a header, model status indicator, a form for user input, and buttons for prediction and resetting. The form, constructed with **`FormBuilder`** and **`FormBuilderCupertinoSlider`**, collects data on house features, processes it through the model, and displays the predicted price, ensuring a seamless and interactive experience for users.

Class: HppWeb

The **HppWeb** class is a **StatefulWidget** that forms the core structure of the house price prediction web app. It acts as a parent widget, managing the creation of the state object which will control how the user interface behaves and reacts to interactions. Write the following code to create it:

```
// screens/price_prediction/hpp_web.dart
import 'dart:math';

import 'package:flutter/cupertino.dart';
import 'package:flutter_form_builder/flutter_form_builder.dart';
import 'package:form_builder_cupertino_fields/form_builder_cupertino_
fields.dart';
import 'package:tflite_web/tflite_web.dart';

class HppWeb extends StatefulWidget {
  const HppWeb({super.key});

  @override
  State<HppWeb> createState() => _HppWebState();
}
```

The **form_builder_cupertino_fields** package is added to use Cupertino themed widgets for the form.

Class: _HppWebState

The **_HppWebState** class manages the state and behavior of the **HppWeb** widget. It handles loading the TensorFlow Lite model, processing predictions, and managing user interactions. The class maintains key variables such as:

- **tfLiteModel**: An instance of **TFLiteModel?** to store the loaded model.
- **housePrice**: A **String?** to store the predicted house price.
- **isModelLoaded**: A bool indicating whether the model has been successfully loaded.
- **formKey**: A **GlobalKey<FormBuilderState>** to manage the form state.

The **initState()** method is overridden to initialize the TensorFlow Lite model when the widget is first created. The following code defines the **_HppWebState** class:

```
class _HppWebState extends State<HppWeb> {
  TFLiteModel? tfLiteModel;
  String? housePrice;
  bool isModelLoaded = false;
  final formKey = GlobalKey<FormBuilderState>();

  @override
  void initState() {
    super.initState();
    initializeTFLite();
  }
}
```

Method: initializeTFLite()

In the **initState()** method, the widget's state is initialized, and the **initializeTFLite()** method is called to load the TFLite model. The **initializeTFLite()** method is asynchronous and initializes the TFLite Web library, loading the model from a specified URL. Upon successful loading, it sets the **isModelLoaded** flag to **true**. Write the following code for creating the method:

```
Future<void> initializeTFLite() async {
    try {
      await TFLiteWeb.initialize();
      tfLiteModel =
         await TFLiteModel.fromUrl('/models/house_price_model.tflite');
      setState(() => isModelLoaded = true);
    } catch (e) {
      print('Failed to initialize TFLite: $e');
    }
  }
```

Method: predictHousePrice()

This method performs the prediction of house prices. It first checks if the model is loaded. It retrieves input data from the form, scales the inputs, and creates a tensor for prediction. It then calls the model's **predict** method to get the prediction and updates the UI with the result. Add the method code as shown:

```
Future<void> predictHousePrice() async {
    if (!isModelLoaded) return;

    final houseData = formKey.currentState!.value;
    final inputs = [
      houseData['bedrooms'],
      houseData['bathrooms'],
      houseData['sqft_living'],
      houseData['floors'],
      houseData['condition'],
    ].map((e) => e as double).toList();

    final scaledInputs = minMaxScale(inputs);
    final inputTensor =
        createTensor(scaledInputs, shape: [1, 5], type: TFLiteData-
Type.float32);

    try {
      final prediction =
          await tfLiteModel!.predict<NamedTensorMap>([inputTensor]);
      final result = extractPrediction(prediction);
      setState(
        () => housePrice = inverseLogTransform(result).
toStringAsFixed(2));
    } catch (e) {
      print('Prediction failed: $e');
    }
  }
```

Method: minMaxScale()

This method normalizes the input data using min-max scaling to fit within a range of zero to one. The maximum and the minimum values for each column are taken from the dataset into to list. It uses predefined minimum and maximum values for each feature. Add the code to your file:

```
List<double> minMaxScale(List<double> data) {
    const maxValues = [33.0, 8.0, 12050.0, 3.5, 13.0];
    const minValues = [0.0, 0.0, 290.0, 1.0, 1.0];
    return List.generate(data.length,
        (i) => (data[i]-minValues[i])/(maxValues[i]-minValues[i]));
}
```

Method: extractPrediction()

This method extracts the prediction result from the **NamedTensorMap** output of the model. It processes the string representation of the prediction to retrieve the numerical value. Write the following code to create the method:

```
double extractPrediction(NamedTensorMap prediction) {
  final parts = prediction.toString().split(RegExp(r'\[\[|\],\]'));
  if (parts.length > 1) {
    return double.parse(parts[1].trim());
  }
  throw Exception('Invalid prediction format');
}
```

Method: inverseLogTransform()

This one line of method applies an inverse log transformation to the predicted value to convert it back to its original scale. Add this line to your code:

```
double inverseLogTransform(double value) => exp(value) - 1;
```

Method: resetPrediction()

This method resets the displayed house price by setting it to null. It is used to clear any previous predictions. Add the following method to your code:

```
void resetPrediction() => setState(() => housePrice = null);
```

Method: build()

This method builds the entire widget tree for the **HppWeb** screen. It uses a **CupertinoPageScaffold** as the main structure, with a centered **SingleChildScrollView** containing a column of widgets. These widgets include a header, model status display, the prediction form, buttons, and the prediction result display. Add the following code to build method:

```
@override
Widget build(BuildContext context) {
  return CupertinoPageScaffold(
    backgroundColor: CupertinoColors.systemBackground,
    child: Center(
      child: SizedBox(
        width: 1200,
        child: SingleChildScrollView(
          child: Column(
            children: [
              buildHeader(),
              buildModelStatus(),
              PredictionsForm(formKey: formKey),
              const SizedBox(height: 16),
              buildButtons(),
              buildPredictionDisplay(),
            ],
          ),
        ),
      ),
    ),
  );
}
```

Method: buildHeader()

This method creates a header widget for the page. It uses padding and a Text widget to display a welcome message with bold styling. This header appears at the top of the screen. Add the given code to create the method:

```
Widget buildHeader() {
    return const Padding(
      padding: EdgeInsets.all(16),
      child: Text(
        'Welcome to the House Price Prediction App',
        style: TextStyle(fontSize: 25, fontWeight: FontWeight.bold),
      ),
    );
}
```

Method: buildModelStatus()

This method displays the status of the TFLite model. If the model has been successfully loaded (**`isModelLoaded`** is true), it shows a success message with a green color. If the model is still loading, it shows a loading spinner with a pink color message indicating that the model is being loaded.

```
Widget buildModelStatus() {
    return isModelLoaded
        ? const Padding(
            padding: EdgeInsets.all(16),
            child: Text(
              'Neural Network Model Loaded Successfully!',
              style:
               TextStyle(fontSize: 16, color: CupertinoColors.systemGreen),
            ),
          )
        : const Padding(
            padding: EdgeInsets.all(16),
            child: Column(
              children: [
                CupertinoActivityIndicator(),
                SizedBox(height: 16),
                Text(
                  'Loading Model...',
                  style: TextStyle(
                      fontSize: 16, color: CupertinoColors.systemPink),
                ),
              ],
            ),
          );
  }
```

Method: buildButtons()

This method creates a row of buttons for interacting with the app. It includes a **Predict House Price** button, which is enabled only if the model is loaded, and a **Clear** button to reset the prediction. The buttons are centered horizontally. Write the following code to add the method:

```
Widget buildButtons() {
    return Row(
      mainAxisAlignment: MainAxisAlignment.center,
      children: [
        CupertinoButton.filled(
          onPressed: isModelLoaded
              ? () {
                  formKey.currentState!.save();
                  predictHousePrice();
                }
              : null,
          child: const Text('Predict House Price'),
        ),
        const SizedBox(width: 16),
        CupertinoButton(
          color: CupertinoColors.systemRed,
          onPressed: resetPrediction,
          child: const Text("Clear"),
        ),
      ],
    );
  }
```

Method: buildPredictionDisplay()

This method constructs the widget that displays the prediction result. It uses **AnimatedCrossFade** to smoothly transition between showing a placeholder message when no prediction is available and displaying the actual predicted house price when it is available. The prediction is shown in a larger, bold, green text. Write the following code:

```
Widget buildPredictionDisplay() {
    return Padding(
      padding: const EdgeInsets.all(16.0),
      child: AnimatedCrossFade(
        duration: const Duration(milliseconds: 100),
        firstChild: const Text('Click the button to predict price'),
        secondChild: Column(
          children: [
            const Text('The predicted house price is'),
```

```
                const SizedBox(height: 8),
                Text(
                  "\$$housePrice",
                  style: const TextStyle(
                    fontSize: 25,
                    fontWeight: FontWeight.bold,
                    color: CupertinoColors.systemGreen,
                  ),
                ),
              ],
            ),
            crossFadeState: housePrice == null
                ? CrossFadeState.showFirst
                : CrossFadeState.showSecond,
          ),
        );
      }
```

Class PredictionForm

The **PredictionsForm** class is a StatelessWidget that provides a form for users to input data related to house features for prediction purposes. It uses Flutter's **FormBuilder** to manage form state and includes several sliders to gather input values. This constructor initializes the **PredictionsForm** widget. It requires a **GlobalKey<FormBuilderState>** as an argument to manage and validate the form state. The key parameter is passed to the superclass to maintain widget identity. Write the following code to create the class:

```
// screens/price_prediction/hpp_web.dart
class PredictionsForm extends StatelessWidget {
  const PredictionsForm({Key? key, required this.
formKey}):super(key: key);

  final GlobalKey<FormBuilderState> formKey;
}
```

Method: build()

This method constructs the form using **FormBuilder** from the **flutter_form_builder** package. It creates a **Column** containing multiple sliders for user input. Each slider is used to input different house features like bedrooms, bathrooms, and square footage. Update the code of the build method of **PredictionForm** shown as follows:

```
@override
  Widget build(BuildContext context) {
    return FormBuilder(
      key: formKey,
      child: Column(
        children: [
          buildSlider('bedrooms', 0, 30, 4, "bedrooms"),
          buildSlider('bathrooms', 0, 8, 3, "bathrooms"),
          buildSlider('sqft_living', 290, 12050, 5420, "sqft"),
          buildSlider('floors', 1, 5, 1, "floors", divisions: 4),
          buildSlider('condition', 1, 13, 11, "Condition: ", divisions: 12),
        ],
      ),
    );
  }
```

Method: buildSlider()

This method creates a **FormBuilderCupertinoSlider** for a specific form field. The slider allows users to input a numerical value between min and max. It also sets an initial value and displays a label with the current value. The optional divisions parameter defines the number of discrete values the slider can take. Add the method to the class:

```
Widget buildSlider(
      String name, double min, double max, double initialValue, String label,
      {int? divisions}) {
    return FormBuilderCupertinoSlider(
      name: name,
      min: min,
      max: max,
      initialValue: initialValue,
      divisions: divisions,
      valueWidget: (value) => Text("$value $label"),
    );
  }
```

After complete the last method, run the app to test it. Overall, this project demonstrates the effective combination of Flutter's UI capabilities with TFLite's ML models, creating a practical and interactive tool for predicting house prices. The next project is based on clustering, which is handled in the next section.

Project 3: Flower species clustering

The Flower Species Clustering Project is a dynamic web application designed to showcase the synergy between ML and data visualization using Flutter. Leveraging the classic Iris dataset, this project illustrates the application of the K-means clustering algorithm to categorize flower species based on their attributes. The final output would look like the following figure:

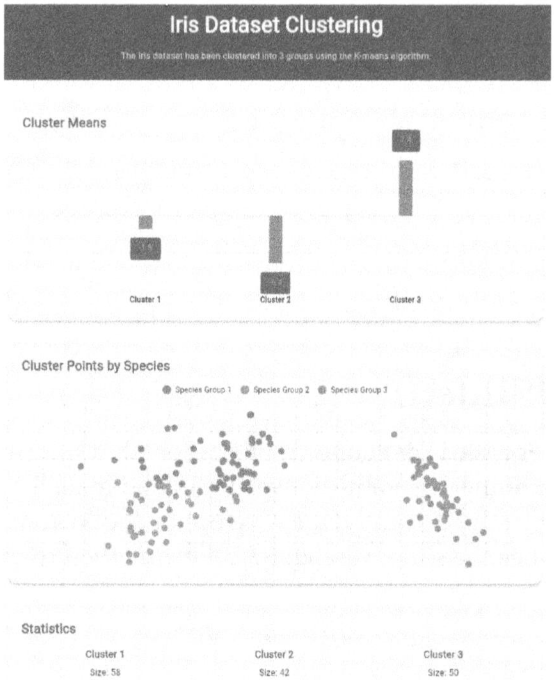

***Figure 5.10:** Preview of flower species clustering app*

The Iris dataset, a staple in data science introduced by *Ronald Fisher* in 1936, is used here to demonstrate clustering techniques. By applying K-means, a popular unsupervised learning algorithm, the application groups iris flowers into distinct clusters based on their characteristics. The result is an engaging and interesting experience that provides clear insights into data clustering.

Setting up the flower species clustering project

To set up the flower species clustering project, follow these steps:

1. Create a new project in IntelliJ IDEA and name is **`flower_species_clustering_app`**.
2. Open the **`pubspec.yaml`** file located in the project's root directory and add the required libraries for clustering and charts, as shown below:

```
fl_chart: ^0.69.0
kmeans: ^1.0.0
```

3. Run the following command to install the dependencies:

   flutter pub get

4. Add the iris dataset (**iris_lda.csv**) provided in the books github repository, to **assets/data/** folder, within the root folder of the project. Declare it in **pubspec.yaml** file under assets, so Flutter knows where the dataset it.

5. Set up the project structure, create the required folders and files in the project:
   - **lib/screens/home/flower_screen.dart**
   - **lib/screens/flower_web.dart**
   - **lib/screens/responsive_layout.dart**

Note: The responsive_layout.dart is same as the previous app. So just write the same code from the previous app.

Setting up the main.dart

The **main.dart** file in the Flower Species Clustering project serves as the entry point for the application. It begins by importing essential libraries, including **MaterialApp** and **FlowerScreen**, which represent the UI and core functionality. The **main()** function calls **runApp()**, which launches the application with the root widget, **FlowerClusteringApp**. Update the **main.dart** as shown:

```
// main.dart
import 'dart:ui';
import 'package:flower_species_clustering_app/screens/home/flower_
screen.dart';
import 'package:flutter/material.dart';

void main() {
  runApp(const FlowerClusteringApp());
}

class FlowerClusteringApp extends StatelessWidget {
  const FlowerClusteringApp({super.key});

  // This widget is the root of your application.
  @override
  Widget build(BuildContext context) {
```

```
    return MaterialApp(
      title: 'Flower Clustering',
      theme: ThemeData(
        primarySwatch: Colors.green,
      ),
      home: const FlowerScreen(title: 'Flower species clustering'),
      debugShowCheckedModeBanner: false,
      scrollBehavior: const MaterialScrollBehavior().copyWith(dragDevices: {
        PointerDeviceKind.touch,
        PointerDeviceKind.mouse,
        PointerDeviceKind.unknown,
      }),
    );
  }
}
```

The **FlowerClusteringApp** is a stateless widget that defines the structure of the app. Inside its **build()** method, a **MaterialApp** widget is created with the title **Flower Clustering** and a green primary theme color. The home screen of the app is set to the **FlowerScreen** widget, which accepts the title **Flower species clustering**. Additionally, the **debugShowCheckedModeBanner** is set to false to hide the debug banner, and a custom **scrollBehavior** is implemented to support scrolling on various devices, including touch and mouse input. This structure ensures that the app is set up with a responsive and user-friendly interface from the start.

Creating the flower_screen.dart file

The **FlowerScreen** widget is a stateless widget that serves as the main screen for the Flower Species Clustering app. It takes a **title** parameter, which is displayed on the screen, and utilizes the **ResponsiveLayout** widget to manage the layout across different devices, such as mobile, tablet, and web. Write the following code:

```
import '../responsive_layout.dart';
import 'package:flutter/material.dart';
import 'flower_web.dart';

class FlowerScreen extends StatelessWidget {
  const FlowerScreen({super.key, required this.title});

  final String title;
```

```

  @override
  Widget build(BuildContext context) {
    return ResponsiveLayout(
      webLayout: FlowerWeb(title: title),
      mobileLayout: const Placeholder(),
      tabletLayout: const Placeholder(),
    );
  }
}
```

Creating the flower_web.dart file

In this section, we will define the **`FlowerWeb`** class, which will serve as the main interface for visualizing flower species clustering on the web.

Class: FlowerWeb

The **`FlowerWeb`** class is a stateful widget that serves as the main interface for the flower species clustering visualization on the web layout. The following class figure summarize the classes in the code:

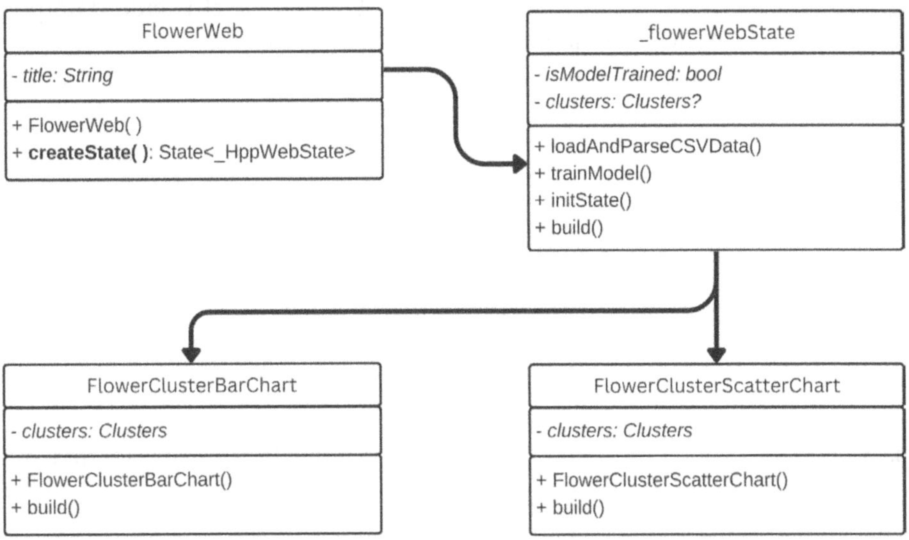

***Figure 5.11:** Class diagram showing classes of flower_web.dart file*

It takes a title parameter and manages the clustering process by loading data and training a **K-means** model on the Iris dataset. The state logic is handled by the associated **`_FlowerWebState`** class. Write the following code:

```
// screens/home/flower_web.dart
import 'package:fl_chart/fl_chart.dart';
import 'package:flutter/material.dart';
import 'package:flutter/services.dart';
import 'package:kmeans/kmeans.dart';

class FlowerWeb extends StatefulWidget {
  const FlowerWeb({super.key, required this.title});

  final String title;

  @override
  State<FlowerWeb> createState() => _FlowerWebState();
}
```

Class: _FlowerWebState

The **_FlowerWebState** class manages the core logic of the flower clustering feature. It handles loading the dataset, training the K-means model, and rendering the clustered data using various charts. The class tracks whether the model is trained and stores the clusters. **isModelTrained** is a boolean that indicates whether the K-means model has completed training. **clusters** is a nullable Clusters object that stores the clustered data points and means after training. Write the following code to create the class:

```
class _FlowerWebState extends State<FlowerWeb> {
  bool isModelTrained = false;
  Clusters? clusters;
  @override
  void initState() {
    super.initState();
    trainModel();
  }
}
```

The **initState()** method is automatically called the when the screen is loaded and it calls the **trainModel()** method.

Method: loadAndParseCSVData()

This asynchronous method loads and parses the CSV data containing the Iris dataset. It reads the CSV file from assets, splits the data into rows, and converts it into a list of numerical values, excluding the class labels. Add the method to the class with following code:

```
Future<List<List<double>>> loadAndParseCSVData(String path) async {
    final String csvData = await rootBundle.loadString(path);
    return csvData.split('\n').sublist(1).map((String line) {
      var list = line.split(',').map((String x) => x.trim()).toList();
      return list.sublist(0, list.length - 1).map(double.parse).toList();
    }).toList();
}
```

Method: trainModel()

This method triggers the K-means training process by passing the parsed data to the K-means algorithm. It trains the model with a default of three clusters and simulates a delay before updating the state to mark the model as trained. Write the following code given:

```
Future<void> trainModel({int k = 3}) async {
    var irisTrainingData =
        await loadAndParseCSVData('assets/data/iris_lda.csv');
    var model = KMeans(irisTrainingData);
    var clusters = model.fit(k);
    await Future.delayed(const Duration(seconds: 3)); // Simulate delay
    setState(() {
      isModelTrained = true;
      this.clusters = clusters;
    });
  }
```

Method: build()

The **build** method creates a **Scaffold** widget that displays different content based on whether a model has been trained. If the model is trained (**isModelTrained** is true), it shows a scrollable view with a **Column** containing:

- A header section with a title and description about clustering the Iris dataset using the K-means algorithm.
- A section displaying cluster means using a **FlowerClusterBarChart**.
- A section with a scatter chart of cluster points by species and a legend.
- A section showing statistics.

If the model is not yet trained, it displays a **CircularProgressIndicator** in the center of the screen. Write the following code for the build method:

```
@override
  Widget build(BuildContext context) {
    return Scaffold(
      body: isModelTrained
          ? SingleChildScrollView(
              child: Column(
                children: [
                  Container(
                    color: Colors.indigo,
                    width: double.infinity,
                    padding: const EdgeInsets.all(32),
                    child: const Column(
                      children: [
                        Text(
                          'Iris Dataset Clustering',
                          style: TextStyle(
                              fontSize: 40,
                              fontWeight: FontWeight.bold,
                              color: Colors.white),
                        ),
                        SizedBox(height: 16),
                        Text(
                          'The Iris dataset has been clustered into 3 groups using the K-means algorithm.',
                          style: TextStyle(fontSize: 16, color: Colors.white70),
                          textAlign: TextAlign.center,
                        ),
                      ],
                    ),
                  ),
                  const SizedBox(height: 32),
                  buildSection(
                    'Cluster Means',
                    FlowerClusterBarChart(clusters: clusters!),
                  ),
```

```
                    const SizedBox(height: 32),
                    buildSection(
                      'Cluster Points by Species',
                      Column(
                        children: [
                          buildSpeciesLegend(),
                          const SizedBox(height: 16),
                          FlowerClusterScatterChart(clusters!),
                        ],
                      ),
                    ),
                    const SizedBox(height: 32),
                    buildSection(
                      'Statistics',
                      buildStatisticsContainer(),
                    ),
                    const SizedBox(height: 32),
                  ],
                ),
              )
            : const Center(
                child: CircularProgressIndicator(),
              ),
    );
  }
```

Method: buildSection()

A helper method that builds a UI section containing a title and a widget. It returns a **Card** widget wrapped in padding and margin, used to display clustered data like bar charts and scatter plots. Add this method to create the top section as shown in the following code:

```
Widget buildSection(String title, Widget content) {
  return Container(
    width: 1000,
    margin: const EdgeInsets.symmetric(horizontal: 16),
    child: Card(
      elevation: 4,
      shape: RoundedRectangleBorder(borderRadius: BorderRadius.circular(16)),
```

```
        child: Padding(
          padding: const EdgeInsets.all(24),
          child: Column(
            crossAxisAlignment: CrossAxisAlignment.start,
            children: [
              Text(
                title,
                style: const TextStyle(
                    fontSize: 24,
                    fontWeight: FontWeight.bold,
                    color: Colors.indigo),
              ),
              const SizedBox(height: 16),
              content,
            ],
          ),
        ),
      ),
    );
  }
```

Method: buildSpeciesLegend()

Creates a legend to represent the different species clusters, using colored circles to distinguish between the groups. Update the **_FlowerWebState** class with the following code:

```
Widget buildSpeciesLegend() {
  return Row(
    mainAxisAlignment: MainAxisAlignment.center,
    children: [
      buildLegendItem("Species Group 1", Colors.red),
      const SizedBox(width: 16),
      buildLegendItem("Species Group 2", Colors.green),
      const SizedBox(width: 16),
      buildLegendItem("Species Group 3", Colors.blue),
    ],
  );
}
```

Method: buildLegendItem()

A helper function that creates a single item in the species legend, consisting of a colored circle and text label. Add this method to the class with the following code:

```
Widget buildLegendItem(String text, Color color) {
    return Row(
      children: [
        Container(
          width: 16,
          height: 16,
          decoration: BoxDecoration(
            color: color,
            shape: BoxShape.circle,
          ),
        ),
        const SizedBox(width: 8),
        Text(text, style: const TextStyle(fontSize: 14)),
      ],
    );
  }
```

Method: buildStatisticsContainer()

Displays the statistics for each cluster, such as the number of points in each cluster, inside a row of cards. It loops through the clusters and shows the cluster size. Write the following code:

```
Widget buildStatisticsContainer() {
    return Row(
      mainAxisAlignment: MainAxisAlignment.spaceAround,
      children: List.generate(3, (index) {
        return Column(
          children: [
            Text(
              'Cluster ${index + 1}',
              style: const TextStyle(
                  fontSize: 18,
                  fontWeight: FontWeight.bold,
                  color: Colors.indigo),
            ),
```

```
              const SizedBox(height: 8),
              Text(
                'Size: ${clusters!.clusterPoints[index].length}',
                style: const TextStyle(fontSize:16,color:Colors.black87),
              ),
            ],
          );
        }),
      );
    }
```

Class: FlowerClusterBarChart

The **FlowerClusterBarChart** is a stateless widget that displays a bar chart representing the mean values of each cluster generated by the K-means algorithm. The widget takes the **Clusters** object and visualizes the cluster means using the **BarChart** component from the **fl_chart** package. Write the following class:

```
// screens/home/flower_web.dart
class FlowerClusterBarChart extends StatelessWidget {
  const FlowerClusterBarChart({super.key, required this.clusters});
  final Clusters clusters;
}
```

Method: build( )

Renders a **BarChart** widget, where each bar represents the average of the features in each cluster. It customizes the chart with titles, grid lines, and other styling options, like the bar's color and size. The x-axis shows the cluster numbers, and the y-axis represents the average feature value. Update the build method of **FlowerClusterBarChart** as shown:

```
@override
  Widget build(BuildContext context) {
    return SizedBox(
      height: 300,
      child: BarChart(
        BarChartData(
          titlesData: FlTitlesData(
            bottomTitles: AxisTitles(
              sideTitles: SideTitles(
                showTitles: true,
```

```
                  reservedSize: 32,
                  getTitlesWidget: (value, meta) => SideTitleWidget(
                    axisSide: meta.axisSide,
                    child: Text(
                      'Cluster ${value.toInt() + 1}',
                      style: const TextStyle(
                          color: Colors.black87,
                          fontWeight: FontWeight.bold,
                          fontSize: 14),
                    ),
                  ),
                ),
              ),
              leftTitles:
                 const AxisTitles(sideTitles: SideTitles(showTitles: false)),
              rightTitles:
                 const AxisTitles(sideTitles: SideTitles(showTitles: false)),
              topTitles:
                 const AxisTitles(sideTitles: SideTitles(showTitles: false)),
            ),
            gridData: FlGridData(
              show: true,
              drawVerticalLine: false,
              getDrawingHorizontalLine: (value) => FlLine(
                color: Colors.black12,
                strokeWidth: 1,
              ),
            ),
            borderData: FlBorderData(show: false),
            barGroups: clusters.means.asMap().entries.map((entry) {
              return BarChartGroupData(
                x: entry.key,
                barRods: [
                  BarChartRodData(
                    toY: double.parse(
```

```
                          entry.value.reduce((a, b) => a + b).
toStringAsFixed(1)),
                      width: 25,
                      color: Colors.indigo.shade300,
                      borderRadius:
                          const BorderRadius.vertical(top: Radius.
circular(4)),
                    ),
                  ],
                  showingTooltipIndicators: [0],
                );
              }).toList(),
              maxY: 10,
              minY: -10,
            ),
          ),
        );
      }
```

Class: FlowerClusterScatterChart

The **FlowerClusterScatterChart** is a stateless widget that visualizes the cluster points on a scatter plot. The widget takes the **Clusters** object and plots the clustered points on a 2D chart, where different colors represent different species groups. Create the class as shown in the following code:

```
// screens/home/flower_web.dart
class FlowerClusterScatterChart extends StatelessWidget {
  const FlowerClusterScatterChart(this.clusters, {super.key});
  final Clusters clusters;
}
```

Method: build()

It renders a **ScatterChart** widget with the clustered data points. Each point corresponds to a data sample, and its position is determined by two of the feature dimensions from the Iris dataset. Update the method shown in the following code:

```
  @override
  Widget build(BuildContext context) {
    return SizedBox(
      height: 300,
```

```
        child: ScatterChart(
          ScatterChartData(
            scatterSpots: clusterSpots(clusters.clusterPoints),
            minY: -3,
            maxY: 3,
            minX: -12,
            maxX: 12,
            titlesData: const FlTitlesData(show: false),
            borderData: FlBorderData(show: false),
            gridData: FlGridData(
              show: true,
              drawHorizontalLine: true,
              drawVerticalLine: true,
              getDrawingHorizontalLine: (value) =>
                  FlLine(color: Colors.black12, strokeWidth: 1),
              getDrawingVerticalLine: (value) =>
                  FlLine(color: Colors.black12, strokeWidth: 1),
            ),
          ),
        ),
      );
    }
```

Method: clusterSpots()

It converts the clustered points into a list of **ScatterSpot** objects, each representing a point on the scatter plot. It assigns different colors to the points based on their respective clusters, using red, green, and blue for the three species groups. Add the method by writing the given code:

```
List<ScatterSpot> clusterSpots(List<List<List<double>>> clusterPoints) {
    const colorList = [Colors.red, Colors.green, Colors.blue];
    return clusterPoints.asMap().entries.expand((entry) {
      final color = colorList[entry.key];
      return entry.value.map((point) {
        return ScatterSpot(
          point[0],
          point[1],
          dotPainter: FlDotCirclePainter(
```

```
                radius: 6,
                color: color,
                strokeWidth: 0,
              ),
            );
          });
        }).toList();
      }
```

Run the application to view the output in the form of graph and charts in the web app. Our results demonstrate that clustering algorithms can effectively group flower species with high accuracy, revealing natural groupings that align well with known classifications. In the next section, you will learn how to make a chatbot using generative ai implementation:

Project 4: Creating a chatbot

This project is going to be a chatbot application designed to provide an interactive and engaging user experience. The application leverages Google's generative AI to simulate human-like conversations, making it a versatile tool for various use cases, from customer support to personal assistance. The key features of the project include:

- **Responsive design**: The app adapts seamlessly to different screen sizes, providing optimized layouts for mobile, tablet, and web platforms.
- **Interactive chat interface**: Users can engage in conversations with the AI, which responds in real-time, creating a dynamic and interactive experience.
- **Markdown support**: The chat interface supports Markdown, allowing for rich text formatting in the messages.
- **Loading animations**: The app includes visually appealing loading animations to enhance the user experience during data processing.
- **Error handling**: The application is equipped with robust error handling mechanisms to ensure smooth operation and provide informative feedback to users.

By combining advanced AI capabilities with a user-friendly interface, this project aims to deliver a powerful and enjoyable chatbot experience. The output of the project is shown in the following figure:

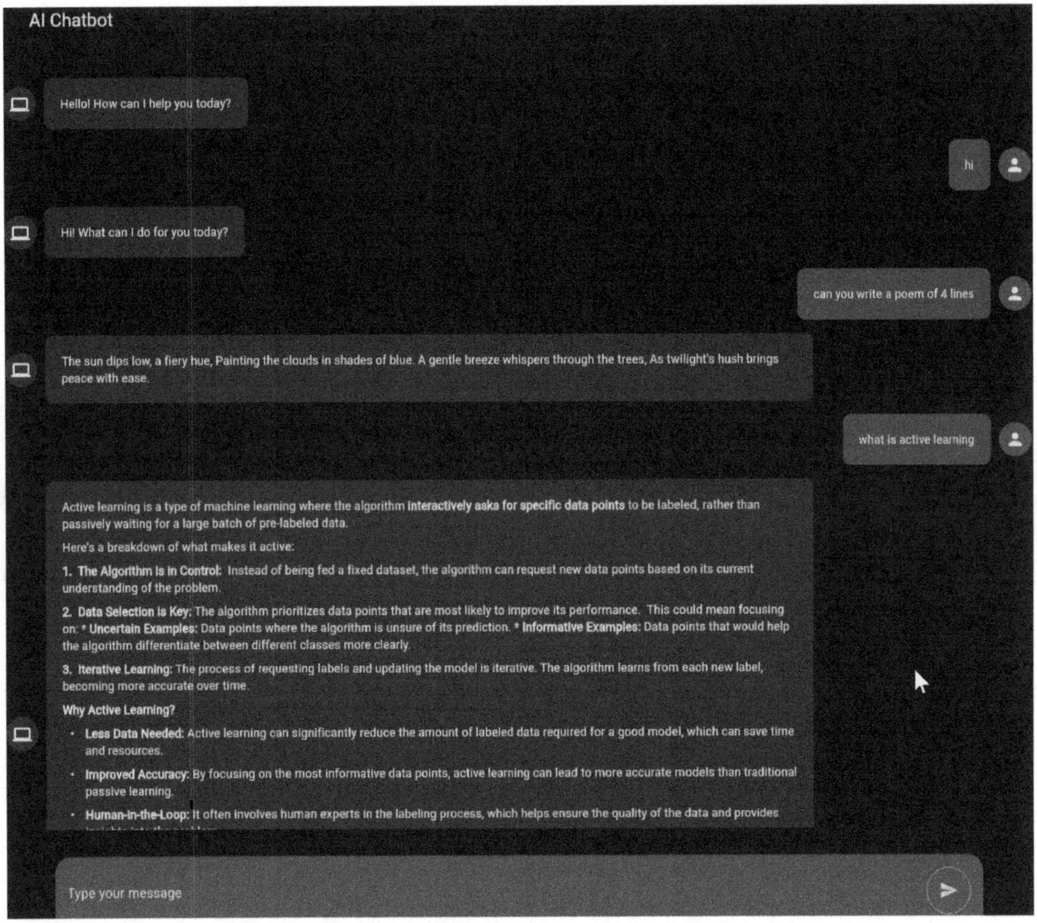

Figure 5.12: *The completed chatbot application*

Understanding Generative AI

Generative AI refers to a subset of AI that focuses on creating new content, such as text, images, music, or even code, by learning patterns from existing data. Unlike traditional AI, which typically classifies or predicts based on input data, generative AI models can produce novel outputs that resemble the training data.

Google *Gemini* is a suite of generative AI models developed by Google. These models are designed to generate human-like text, images, and other forms of content by learning patterns from large datasets. Gemini models are part of Google's broader AI initiatives and are used in various applications, including chatbots, content creation, and more. This project requires an API key from Google AI Studio, follow the steps to get it:

1. Visit **https://aistudio.google.com/**
2. Sign In to Google AI Studio
3. In the project dashboard, click on the button on top left **Get Api Key**.
4. Click on **Create Api Key** and follow the steps to get the key.
5. Save the key on your system or notes and do not share it with anyone.

Setting up the project

To setup this project, follow the given steps:

1. **Create a new project**: Open IntelliJ IDEA or your preferred IDE. And create a new Flutter project and name it **`chatbot_app`**.
2. **Add required libraries**: Open the **`pubspec.yaml`** file located in the project's root directory. Then, add the following dependencies under dependencies

```
flutter_markdown: ^0.7.3+1
lottie: ^3.1.2
dio: ^5.7.0
google_generative_ai: any
```

3. **Install dependencies**: Run the following command in your terminal to install the dependencies

```
flutter pub get
```

4. **Add Lottie file**: Place the **`animated_loader.json`** file from the books github repository and put it inside the assets folder in your project's root directory. If the assets folder does not exist, create it. Update the **`pubspec.yaml`** file to include the assets as shown:

```
flutter:
  assets:
    - assets/animated_loader.json
```

5. **Set up project structure**: Create the required folders and files in your project structure
   - `screens/chat/chat_screen.dart`
   - `screens/chat/chatbot_web_interface.dart`
   - `screens/responsive_layout.dart`
   - `widgets/chat_widgets.dart`
6. Create the **`responsive_layout.dart`**, with the same code from the previous apps.

Creating main.dart

The **main.dart** file contains the entry point for the **ChatBot** application. It defines the **ChatBotApp** class, which extends **StatelessWidget** and serves as the root of the application. In this class, the build method sets up the **MaterialApp** with a dark theme and customized color scheme, using **Material3** design principles. The home parameter is set to **ChatScreen**, which is the main screen of the app. The code is similar to previous apps in the chapter. Update the following code:

```
import 'dart:ui';

import 'package:chatbot/screens/chat/chat_screen.dart';
import 'package:flutter/material.dart';

void main() {
  runApp(const ChatBotApp());
}

class ChatBotApp extends StatelessWidget {
  const ChatBotApp({super.key});

  // This widget is the root of your application.
  @override
  Widget build(BuildContext context) {
    return MaterialApp(
        title: "ChatBot",
        theme: ThemeData(
          brightness: Brightness.dark,
          useMaterial3: true,
        ),
        darkTheme: ThemeData.dark().copyWith(
            colorScheme: ThemeData.dark().colorScheme.copyWith(
                  primary: Colors.deepPurple.shade800,
                  secondary: const Color(0xFF2C282F))),
        home: const ChatScreen(),
        debugShowCheckedModeBanner: false,
        scrollBehavior: const MaterialScrollBehavior().copyWith(dragDevices: {
          PointerDeviceKind.touch,
          PointerDeviceKind.mouse,
```

```
              PointerDeviceKind.unknown,
            }));
    }
  }
```

Creating chat_screen.dart file

The **chat_screen.dart** file will contain the **ChatScreen** class, which extends **StatelessWidget**. Within the build method, it utilizes the **ResponsiveLayout** widget to provide different layouts based on the device type. For mobile and tablet devices, it displays a **Placeholder** widget, while for web devices, it shows the **ChatbotWebInterface** widget, passing an **API key** as a parameter. This setup allows the **ChatScreen** to adapt its layout depending on the platform. Update the variable **_apiKey** with your API key from Google. Write the following code to create the class:

```
import 'package:chatbot/screens/chat/chatbot_web_interface.dart';
import 'package:chatbot/screens/responsive_layout.dart';
import 'package:flutter/material.dart';

class ChatScreen extends StatelessWidget {
  const ChatScreen({super.key});
  // visit https://aistudio.google.com/app/apikey
  final String _apiKey = "YOUR_API_KEY";

  @override
  Widget build(BuildContext context) {
    return ResponsiveLayout(
      mobileLayout: const Placeholder(),
      tabletLayout: const Placeholder(),
      webLayout: ChatbotWebInterface(_apiKey),
    );
  }
}
```

Creating chat_widget.dart file

The **chat_widget.dart** file will define the **ChatWidget** class, which extends **StatelessWidget**. This widget represents a chat message and displays it with different styles depending on whether the message is from the user or not. The **ChatWidget** takes two parameters: **text** (the message content) and **isFromUser** (a boolean indicating if the message is from the user). Write the following code for the widget:

```
// widgets/chat_widget.dart
import 'package:flutter/material.dart';
import 'package:flutter_markdown/flutter_markdown.dart';

class ChatWidget extends StatelessWidget {
  final String? text;
  final bool isFromUser;

  const ChatWidget({
    this.text,
    this.isFromUser = false,
    super.key,
  });

  @override
  Widget build(BuildContext context) {
    return Padding(
        padding: const EdgeInsets.all(8),
        child: Row(
            mainAxisAlignment:
                isFromUser ? MainAxisAlignment.
end : MainAxisAlignment.start,
            children: [
              if (!isFromUser)
                CircleAvatar(
                    backgroundColor: Theme.of(context).colorScheme.
secondary,
                    child: const Icon(Icons.computer)),
              const SizedBox(width: 10),
              if (text != null)
                Container(
                    constraints: BoxConstraints(
                      // 70% of the screen width
                      maxWidth: MediaQuery.of(context).size.
width * 0.7,
                    ),
                    padding: const EdgeInsets.all(20),
                    decoration: BoxDecoration(
```

```
                      color: isFromUser
                          ? Theme.of(context).colorScheme.primary
                          : Theme.of(context).colorScheme.secondary,
                      borderRadius: BorderRadius.circular(10)),
                  child: MarkdownBody(
                    data: text!,
                  )),
            const SizedBox(width: 10),
            if (isFromUser)
              const CircleAvatar(
                child: Icon(Icons.person),
              )
          ]));
  }
}
```

In the **build** method, a **Row** is used to align the message and avatar based on the sender. Messages from the user are aligned to the end and have a different background color compared to those from other sources. The message text is rendered using the **MarkdownBody** widget for formatted content, and avatars are displayed accordingly.

Creating chatbot_web_interface.dart file

In this section, we will define the **ChatbotWebInterface** class, which acts as the entry point for the chatbot's user interface on the web. The class extends **StatefulWidget** and requires an API key for functionality. This key is essential for initializing the mutable state and enabling communication with the Google Generative AI service. The associated state class, **_ChatbotWebInterfaceState**, handles chat interactions, UI updates, and API calls to generate responses. In the following section, we will walk through the structure and code needed to implement the chatbot interface effectively.

Class: ChatbotWebInterface

The **chatbot_web_interface.dart** file defines the **ChatbotWebInterface** class, which extends StatefulWidget, and its associated state class **_ChatbotWebInterfaceState**. The **ChatbotWebInterface** class serves as the main entry point for the chatbot interface, requiring an API key to function. This key is used to initialize the mutable state of the widget. Write the following code to create the class:

```
// screens/chat/chatbot_web_interface.dart
import 'package:flutter/material.dart';
import 'package:google_generative_ai/google_generative_ai.dart';
import 'package:lottie/lottie.dart';

import '../../widgets/chat_widget.dart';

class ChatbotWebInterface extends StatefulWidget {
  final String apiKey;

  const ChatbotWebInterface(this.apiKey, {super.key});

  @override
  State<ChatbotWebInterface> createState() => _
ChatbotWebInterfaceState();
  }
}
```

Class: _ChatbotWebInterfaceState

The **`_ChatbotWebInterfaceState`** class, which manages the state and logic for ChatbotWebInterface, handles chat interactions, UI updates, and API communications. It contains several state variables including:

- **_model**: An instance of **`GenerativeModel`** from the Google Generative AI package.
- **_chat**: A **`ChatSession`** object for managing conversations.
- **_textController**: A **`TextEditingController`** for the input text field.
- **_scrollController**: A **`ScrollController`** for managing chat scrolling.
- **_textFieldFocus**: A **`FocusNode`** for managing text field focus.
- **_generatedConten**: A list of tuples for chat messages and their sources.
- **_loading**: A Boolean flag indicating whether the AI is processing a response. The getter **`loading`** simply returns the current value of **`_loading`**, while the setter **`loading`** updates **`_loading`** and calls **`setState`** to ensure the UI is refreshed to reflect the new state.

The **`initState()`** lifecycle method initializes the **`GenerativeModel`** with the provided API key and starts a new chat session when the state object is inserted into the widget tree. Write the code for the class as shown:

```
class _ChatbotWebInterfaceState extends State<ChatbotWebInterface> {
  late final GenerativeModel _model;
  late final ChatSession _chat;
  final TextEditingController _textController=TextEditingController();
  final ScrollController _scrollController = ScrollController();
  final FocusNode _textFieldFocus = FocusNode();
  final List<({bool fromUser, String? text})> _generatedContent =
      <({bool fromUser, String? text})>[
    (text: 'Hello! How can I help you today?', fromUser: false),
  ];

  bool _loading = false;
  bool get loading => _loading;
  set loading(bool set) => setState(() => _loading = set);

  @override
  void initState() {
    super.initState();
    _model = GenerativeModel(
      model: 'gemini-1.5-flash-latest',
      apiKey: widget.apiKey,
    );
    _chat = _model.startChat();
  }
}
```

The **_scrollDown** method ensures the chat view scrolls to the most recent message by using a post-frame callback. Add the following code:

```
void _scrollDown() {
    WidgetsBinding.instance.addPostFrameCallback(
      (_) => _scrollController.animateTo(
        _scrollController.position.maxScrollExtent,
        duration: const Duration(
          milliseconds: 750,
        ),
        curve: Curves.easeOutCirc,
      ),
    );
  }
```

Next, the **_sendChatMessage** method handles sending a user message to the AI, processing the response, updating the UI, handling errors, and clearing the text field in an asynchronous manner. Add it to the following class:

```
Future<void> _sendChatMessage(String message) async {
    setState(() {
      loading = true;
    });
    try {
      _generatedContent.add((text: message, fromUser: true));
      final response = await _chat.sendMessage(
        Content.text(message),
      );
      final text = response.text;
      _generatedContent.add((text: text, fromUser: false));
      if (text == null) {
        _showError('No response from API.');
        setState(() {
          _loading = false;
        });
        return;
      } else {
        setState(() {
          _loading = false;
          _scrollDown();
        });
      }
    } catch (e) {
      _showError(e.toString());
      setState(() {
        _loading = false;
      });
    } finally {
      _textController.clear();
      setState(() {
        _loading = false;
      });
      _textFieldFocus.requestFocus();
    }
  }
```

The **_showError** method displays an error dialog with the error message and an **OK** button for dismissal. Add it to the class, shown as follows:

```
void _showError(String message) {
    showDialog<void>(
      context: context,
      builder: (context) {
        return AlertDialog(
          title: const Text('Something went wrong'),
          content: SingleChildScrollView(
            child: SelectableText(message),
          ),
          actions: [
            TextButton(
              onPressed: () {
                Navigator.of(context).pop();
              },
              child: const Text('OK'),
            )
          ],
        );
      },
    );
  }
```

Finally, the **build** method constructs the UI, which includes an **AppBar**, a scrollable **ListView** for chat history, a loading animation displayed during processing, a text input field, and a send button that transforms into a loading indicator when processing messages. Write the following code to complete the app:

```
@override
  Widget build(BuildContext context) {
    return Scaffold(
      appBar: AppBar(
        title: const Text('AI Chatbot'),
        leading: Icon(Icons.mark_chat_unread_sharp),
        actions: [
          IconButton(
            icon: const Icon(Icons.restart_alt_outlined),
            onPressed: () {
```

```
          setState(() {
            _generatedContent.clear();
          });
        },
      ),
    ],
  ),
  body: Padding(
    padding: const EdgeInsets.all(32.0),
    child: Column(children: [
      Expanded(
          child: widget.apiKey.isNotEmpty
              ? Align(
                  alignment: Alignment.bottomCenter,
                  child: SingleChildScrollView(
                    reverse: true,
                    child: ListView.builder(
                      itemBuilder: (context, idx) {
                        final content = _generatedContent[idx];
                        return ChatWidget(
                          text: content.text,
                          isFromUser: content.fromUser,
                        );
                      },
                      shrinkWrap: true,
                      physics: const NeverScrollableScrollPhysics(),
                      controller: _scrollController,
                      itemCount: _generatedContent.length,
                      reverse: false,
                    ),
                  ),
                )
              : ListView(
                  children: const [
                    Text(
                      'No API key found. Please provide API Key',
```

```
                          ),
                        ],
                      )),
            if (loading)
              SizedBox(
                width: 150,
                height: 150,
                child: Lottie.asset('animated_loader.json'),
              ),
          ]),
        ),
        bottomNavigationBar: Padding(
          padding: const EdgeInsets.symmetric(horizontal: 100),
          child: Container(
            width: double.infinity,
            decoration: BoxDecoration(
              color: Theme.of(context).colorScheme.primaryContainer,
              borderRadius: const BorderRadius.vertical(
                top: Radius.circular(20),
              ),
            ),
            padding: const EdgeInsets.all(15),
            child: Row(
              children: [
                Expanded(
                  child: TextField(
                    controller: _textController,
                    focusNode: _textFieldFocus,
                    decoration: const InputDecoration(
                      hintText: 'Type your message',
                      border: InputBorder.none,
                    ),
                    canRequestFocus: true,
                    textInputAction: TextInputAction.send,
                    maxLines: 10,
                    minLines: 1,
                    onSubmitted: _sendChatMessage,
```

```
                ),
              ),
              const SizedBox(width: 10),
              Container(
                height: 56,
                width: 56,
                decoration: BoxDecoration(
                  borderRadius: BorderRadius.circular(20),
                ),
                child: !loading
                    ? IconButton.outlined(
                        onPressed: () async {
                          _sendChatMessage(_textController.text);
                        },
                        icon: const Icon(Icons.send),
                      )
                    : const CircularProgressIndicator(),
              ),
            ],
          ),
        ),
      ),
    );
  }
```

Run the app in the browser and test it by entering message, the chatbot should reply quickly, with a beautiful loading status which processing request. This completes the chatbot app. In the final section, you are going to make an image recognition app.

Project 5: Image recognition

This Flutter application demonstrates how to create a web-based image recognition tool using the Hugging Face API. Users can select an image from their device, and the app will analyze it using a pre-trained vision model to identify objects and concepts within the image. The app showcases Flutter's capabilities for building interactive UIs and integrating with external APIs for ML tasks. The UI will look like the following figure:

Figure 5.13: *The finished user interface of image recognition app*

Understanding Hugging Face

Hugging Face is an open-source platform specializing in ML, particularly NLP and computer vision. It offers a vast array of pre-trained models and tools for AI tasks. The **google/vit-base-patch16-224** model used in this Flutter app is one such offering. It is a **Vision Transformer (ViT)** model developed by Google, designed for image classification tasks. The *base* version balances performance and efficiency, processes images in 16x16 pixel patches, and is optimized for 224x224 pixel input images. This model enables the app to analyze uploaded images and identify objects or concepts within them, showcasing the integration of advanced AI capabilities in a user-friendly mobile application. Next step is to set up the new project.

Setting up the project

To setup this project, follow the given steps:

1. **Create a new project**: Create a new Flutter web project - **image_recognition_app**.
2. **Add required libraries**: Open the **pubspec.yaml**, add the following dependencies.
   ```
   image_picker: ^1.1.2
   image_picker_for_web: ^3.0.5
   huggingface_client: ^1.2.3
   ```
3. **Install dependencies**: Run flutter pub get in the terminal.

4. **Set up project files**: Create the required folders and files in your project structure
   - **`screens/image_selection/image_selection_screen.dart`**
   - **`screens/image_selection/image_selection_web.dart`**
   - **`screens/responsive_layout.dart`**

Creating main.dart file

In the **`main.dart`** file, our app's main entry point is the **`ImageRecognitionApp`** widget, which is a stateless widget. It uses **`MaterialApp`** to set up the application's title, light and dark themes, and a home screen, which is defined by the **`ImageSelectionScreen`**. The app also hides the debug banner. The **`ColorScheme`** is customized using the **`fromSwatch`** method for both light and dark themes, providing a structured appearance for the app's user interface. Write the code as shown in **`main.dart`**:

```
import 'package:flutter/material.dart';

import 'screens/image_selection/image_selection_screen.dart';

void main() {
  runApp(const ImageRecognitionApp());
}

class ImageRecognitionApp extends StatelessWidget {
  const ImageRecognitionApp({super.key});
  @override
  Widget build(BuildContext context) {
    return MaterialApp(
          title: 'Image Recognition App',
          theme: ThemeData(
              colorScheme: ColorScheme.fromSwatch(
            brightness: Brightness.light,
          )),
          darkTheme: ThemeData(
              colorScheme: ColorScheme.fromSwatch(
            brightness: Brightness.dark,
          )),
          home: const ImageSelectionScreen(),
          debugShowCheckedModeBanner: false);
    }
}
```

In the previous four projects, you have learned that the code for **responsive_layout.dart** and the **app_screen** files is similar for almost all projects. For this project, create the **ImageSelectionScreen** stateless widget in the **image_selection_screen.dart** file and set the **webLayout** to be **ImageSelectionWeb()**.

Creating the image_selection_web.dart file

This file implements an **ImageSelectionWeb** stateful widget which allows users to upload an image from their device, and upon selection, the app interacts with the **Hugging Face API** to classify the contents of the image. The application displays the selected image and provides a button to trigger the recognition process. Once the image is analyzed, it shows the results, including labels and confidence scores for the detected items. Users can reset the image and try again, with the app updating its state dynamically based on user actions and the recognition process. The class diagram for this file is shown in the following figure:

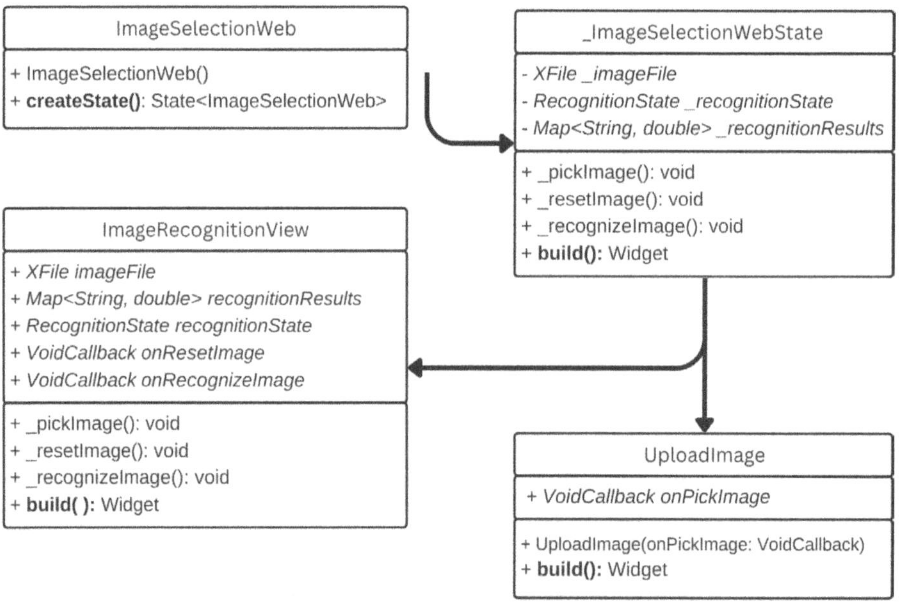

Figure 5.14: *Class diagram for the image_selection_web.dart file*

Class: ImageSelectionWeb

ImageSelectionWeb is the main widget that provides the user interface for selecting and recognizing images. The code for the class is given as follows:

```
// screens/image_selection/image_selection_web.dart
import 'package:flutter/material.dart';
import 'package:huggingface_client/huggingface_client.dart';
import 'package:image_picker/image_picker.dart';
```

```
import 'package:image_picker_for_web/image_picker_for_web.dart';

// get your Access Token from https://huggingface.co/settings/tokens
const inferenceApiKey = '<YOUR_HUGGINGFACE_ACCESS_TOKEN>';
enum RecognitionState { idle, loading, success, error }

class ImageSelectionWeb extends StatefulWidget {
  const ImageSelectionWeb({super.key});

  @override
  State<ImageSelectionWeb> createState() => _ImageSelectionWebState();
}
```

Class: _ImageSelectionWebState

The **`_ImageSelectionWebState`** class manages the state of the **`ImageSelectionWeb`** widget, allowing users to select an image from their device, reset the image, and send it for recognition using **Hugging Face's API**. It stores the selected image, handles the recognition process, and updates the UI based on the recognition state (**`idle`**, **`loading`**, **`success`**, or **`error`**). The code for the class is given as follows:

```
class _ImageSelectionWebState extends State<ImageSelectionWeb> {
  XFile? _imageFile;
  RecognitionState _recognitionState = RecognitionState.idle;
  Map<String, double> _recognitionResults = {};

  Future<void> _pickImage() async {
    final ImagePickerPlugin imagePicker = ImagePickerPlugin();
    final pickedFile =
        await imagePicker.getImageFromSource(source:ImageSource.gallery);
    if (pickedFile != null) {
      setState(() {
        _imageFile = pickedFile;
        _recognitionResults.clear();
        _recognitionState = RecognitionState.idle;
      });
    }
  }
```

```

  void _resetImage() {
    setState(() {
      _imageFile = null;
      _recognitionResults.clear();
      _recognitionState = RecognitionState.idle;
    });
  }

  Future<void> _recognizeImage() async {
    if (_imageFile == null) return;

    setState(() => _recognitionState = RecognitionState.loading);

    try {
      final client = HuggingFaceClient.getInferenceClient(
          inferenceApiKey, HuggingFaceClient.inferenceBasePath);
      final apiInstance = InferenceApi(client);
      final imageFileContent = await _imageFile!.readAsBytes();

      final result = await apiInstance.queryVisionImageClassification(
        imageFile: imageFileContent,
        model: 'google/vit-base-patch16-224',
      );

      setState(() {
        _recognitionResults = {
          for (var item in result!)
            if (item != null) item.label: item.score
        };
        _recognitionState = RecognitionState.success;
      });
    } catch (e) {
      // print('Exception when calling InferenceApi->inferenceImage: $e');
      setState(() => _recognitionState = RecognitionState.error);
    }
```

```
  }

  @override
  Widget build(BuildContext context) {
    return Scaffold(
        body: Center(
            child: SingleChildScrollView(
      padding: const EdgeInsets.all(16.0),
      child: _imageFile == null
          ? UploadImage(onPickImage: _pickImage)
          : ImageRecognitionView(
              imageFile: _imageFile!,
              recognitionResults: _recognitionResults,
              recognitionState: _recognitionState,
              onResetImage: _resetImage,
              onRecognizeImage: _recognizeImage,
            ),
    )));
  }
}
```

Class: UploadImage

The **UploadImage** class is a stateless widget that provides the UI for selecting an image. It displays a title, **Image Recognition App**, styled with bold yellow text and shadows, and includes a button labeled **Select Image**. When the button is pressed, it triggers the **onPickImage** callback, which allows the user to choose an image from their device. This class focuses solely on presenting the interface for image selection. The following code creates the class:

```
class UploadImage extends StatelessWidget {
  final VoidCallback onPickImage;

  const UploadImage({super.key, required this.onPickImage});

  @override
  Widget build(BuildContext context) {
    return Column(mainAxisSize: MainAxisSize.min, children: [
      const Text('Image Recognition App',
          style: TextStyle(
```

```
                fontSize: 50,
                fontWeight: FontWeight.bold,
                color: Colors.yellow,
                shadows: [
                  BoxShadow(spreadRadius: 3, color: Colors.black, blurRadius: 2)
                ])),
        const SizedBox(height: 16),
        FilledButton.icon(
            style: ButtonStyle(
                backgroundColor: WidgetStateProperty.all(Colors.orange),
                foregroundColor: WidgetStateProperty.all(Colors.white),
                padding: WidgetStateProperty.all(
                    const EdgeInsets.symmetric(horizontal: 20.0, vertical: 16.0)),
                textStyle: WidgetStateProperty.all(const TextStyle(
                    fontSize: 16.0, fontWeight: FontWeight.bold))),
            icon: const Icon(Icons.upload),
            onPressed: onPickImage,
            label: const Text('Select Image'))
      ]);
  }
}
```

Class: ImageRecognitionView

The **ImageRecognitionView** class is a stateless widget that displays the selected image and handles image recognition results. It shows the image in a container with a clear button to reset it, and a button labeled **Recognize Contents** to trigger the image recognition process. It also displays the recognition results in a list format. Depending on the recognition state, it either shows a loading spinner, the results of the image recognition with confidence scores, or an error message if the recognition fails.

```
class ImageRecognitionView extends StatelessWidget {
  final XFile imageFile;
  final Map<String, double> recognitionResults;
  final RecognitionState recognitionState;
  final VoidCallback onResetImage, onRecognizeImage;

```

```
  const ImageRecognitionView({
    super.key,
    required this.imageFile,
    required this.recognitionResults,
    required this.recognitionState,
    required this.onResetImage,
    required this.onRecognizeImage,
  });

  @override
  Widget build(BuildContext context) {
    return Row(crossAxisAlignment: CrossAxisAlignment.start, children: [
      Expanded(
          child: Column(children: [
        Stack(children: [
          Container(
            width: 512,
            height: 512,
            decoration: BoxDecoration(
                color: Colors.white,
                boxShadow: const [
                  BoxShadow(spreadRadius: 1, color: Colors.black, blurRadius: 2)
                ],
                borderRadius: BorderRadius.circular(8.0)),
            child: ClipRRect(
                borderRadius: BorderRadius.circular(8.0),
                child: Image.network(imageFile.path, fit: BoxFit.cover)),
          ),
          Positioned(
              top: 5,
              right: 5,
              child: IconButton(
                icon: const Icon(Icons.clear),
                onPressed: onResetImage,
                color: Colors.red,
              ))
```

```
        ]),
        const SizedBox(height: 16.0),
        Text("Image selected: ${imageFile.name}"),
        const SizedBox(height: 16.0),
        FilledButton.icon(
            onPressed: onRecognizeImage,
            icon: const Icon(Icons.image_search),
            label: const Text("Recognize Contents"))
      ])),
      const SizedBox(width: 16.0),
      Expanded(
        child: _buildRecognitionResults(),
      )
    ]);
  }

  Widget _buildRecognitionResults() {
    switch (recognitionState) {
      case RecognitionState.loading:
        return const Center(child: CircularProgressIndicator());
      case RecognitionState.success:
        return Column(
          children: recognitionResults.entries
              .map((entry) => ListTile(
                  title: Text(entry.key,
                      style: const TextStyle(
                          fontWeight: FontWeight.bold, fontSize: 16.0)),
                  subtitle:
                      Text('Score: ${(entry.value * 100).toStringAsFixed(2)}%'),
                  leading: Icon(
                      entry.value > .7 ? Icons.image_outlined : Icons.image)))
              .toList(),
        );
      case RecognitionState.error:
        return const Text('Error recognizing image');
```

```
        default:
          return const SizedBox.shrink();
      }
    }
  }
```

This completes the Image Recognition App, run this app in the browser to test it.

Conclusion

This chapter has equipped you with the foundational knowledge and practical experience needed to seamlessly integrate ML and AI into your Flutter web applications. By exploring a variety of real-world projects—ranging from Diabetes Classifiers and house price predictors to image recognition and chatbots—you've learned how to harness the power of ML and AI to build more intelligent, responsive, and engaging web solutions. With the tools and techniques covered, you are now prepared to apply these advanced capabilities to create innovative applications that meet the evolving needs of users and enhance their overall experience.

In the next chapter, you will learn how to debug your app effectively.

Points to remember

- Optimize Flutter app performance when using ML models, including efficient model loading and inference.
- Always use stateful widgets to manage the state of ML model interactions within your Flutter app.
- Handle asynchronous operations effectively when running ML models to keep the UI responsive.
- Use package like flutter_form_builder, fl_charts, image_picker to capture and display data.

Multiple choice questions

1. **Which Flutter plugin can be used to integrate TFLite models into a Flutter web application?**
   a. Flutter_tflite
   b. tf_lite
   c. flutter_markdown
   d. tflite_web

2. **When integrating ML models into a Flutter application, why is it important to handle asynchronous operations effectively?**
   a. To improve app security
   b. To ensure the model's accuracy
   c. To keep the UI responsive
   d. To reduce the app size

Answer

1	d
2	c

Questions

1. Create a new AI web app using Hugging Face NLP models.
2. Create the mobile and tablet layout for Diabetes Prediction App.
3. Create the mobile and tablet layout for the chatbot app.

Additional resources

- **https://pub.dev/packages/tflite_web**
- **https://huggingface.co/docs**
- **https://pub.dev/documentation/google_generative_ai/latest/**
- **https://github.com/flutter-form-builder-ecosystem**

Join our book's Discord space

Join the book's Discord Workspace for Latest updates, Offers, Tech happenings around the world, New Release and Sessions with the Authors:

https://discord.bpbonline.com

CHAPTER 6
Effective Debugging Techniques

Introduction

In this chapter, we understand the art of effective debugging techniques. Debugging is an essential skill for any developer, as it allows us to identify and resolve issues in our code efficiently. Moreover, we will explore various strategies and tools specifically designed to help you pinpoint and fix errors in your Flutter applications. By mastering these techniques, you will be able to troubleshoot problems with confidence and deliver high-quality, bug-free software.

Structure

The chapter covers the following topics:

- Introduction to debugging in Flutter
- Common debugging scenarios
- Debugging techniques in Flutter
- Using Flutter DevTools
- Handling exceptions
- Logging and monitoring
- Testing in Flutter

- Practical: Adding tests to DartByte project
- Tips and tricks for proactive debugging

Objectives

By the end of this chapter, you will have a solid understanding of effective debugging techniques in Flutter. You will be able to identify common debugging scenarios, leverage Flutter DevTools for in-depth analysis, handle exceptions gracefully, implement effective logging and monitoring, write unit and widget tests, and apply practical tips for proactive debugging. This knowledge will empower you to troubleshoot issues efficiently and deliver high-quality Flutter applications.

Introduction to debugging in Flutter

Debugging is a crucial aspect of software development, ensuring that applications run smoothly and as intended. In Flutter, debugging takes on unique dimensions due to its declarative UI framework, which allows developers to quickly identify and resolve issues across various platforms such as mobile, web, and desktop.

Overview of debugging

Debugging is an integral part of the software development process, and its importance cannot be overstated. In Flutter development, debugging plays a critical role in ensuring that applications run efficiently, without crashes, performance bottlenecks, or unexpected behaviors. Understanding the importance of debugging enables developers to tackle problems effectively, resulting in a smoother development cycle and a more stable, high-quality application. The following figure summarizes the importance of debugging:

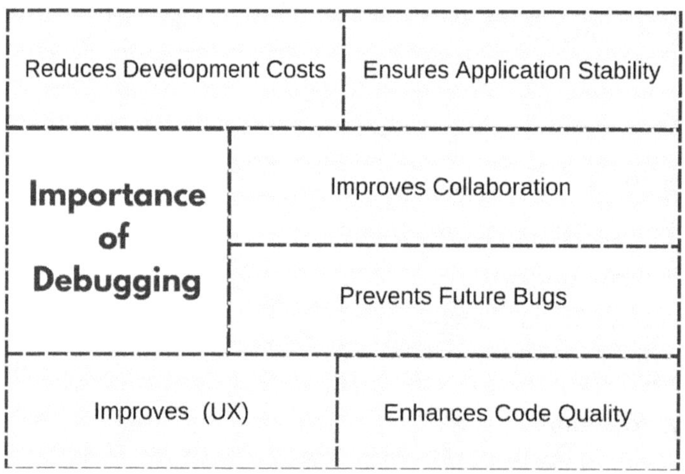

Figure 6.1: *Importance of debugging in projects*

Ensures application stability

One of the primary goals of debugging is to maintain the stability of the application. Flutter applications, due to their complex widget trees and reliance on reactive programming, can encounter a wide range of issues, such as layout glitches, incorrect state management, or asynchronous programming errors. Proper debugging practices ensure that these issues are caught early and fixed before they escalate into bigger problems that might cause the app to crash or misbehave. By identifying and resolving bugs during the development phase, developers can ensure the app performs as intended across multiple platforms (mobile, web, and desktop). Stable applications result in fewer user complaints, better reviews, and a stronger reputation for the development team.

Improves user experience

A critical aspect of debugging is improving the **user experience (UX)**. Bugs such as UI glitches, slow load times, or unexpected behavior in Flutter applications can frustrate users. For instance, an app that freezes or crashes when interacting with certain widgets or screens can lead to user abandonment. Debugging allows developers to fine-tune the application's responsiveness, ensuring smooth transitions, proper animations, and quick feedback to user inputs.

Flutter applications, known for their expressive UIs and fluid animations, rely heavily on maintaining performance at all times. Debugging performance issues, such as laggy scrolling or unresponsive buttons, helps create a more engaging and enjoyable user experience, which is vital for retaining users and gaining positive feedback.

Reduces development costs and time

Efficient debugging significantly reduces both time and costs associated with app development. Unaddressed bugs can lead to more complex issues later in the development cycle or, worse, after the app has been deployed. The cost of fixing bugs increases the longer they remain undetected. For example, a memory leak that is not caught early might cause major performance issues in production, requiring extensive post-release patches, downtime, and possibly even a complete overhaul of certain parts of the application.

By identifying and resolving issues during development through debugging, developers avoid costly rework and minimize the time spent chasing bugs. This makes the overall development process more efficient, enabling teams to meet deadlines and deliver applications faster.

Enhances code quality

Debugging is not just about fixing errors—it also improves the overall quality of the code. During the debugging process, developers often discover areas where the code could be cleaner, more efficient, or easier to maintain. For example, frequent debugging of state management logic in Flutter can highlight the need for refactoring the code to better handle asynchronous data or implement a more structured state management solution like Provider, Bloc, or Riverpod.

This process also helps developers write more robust code by prompting them to implement better error handling, logging, and testing practices. Debugging encourages developers to anticipate and handle edge cases, ensuring that the app behaves correctly in a variety of situations.

Prevents future bugs

Effective debugging not only resolves current issues but also helps prevent future bugs. When developers take the time to fully understand the root cause of a bug and the conditions that triggered it, they can implement solutions that avoid similar issues in the future. This proactive approach helps create more resilient applications that can handle different scenarios without breaking.

In Flutter, where widgets are rebuilt frequently, understanding how and why certain bugs occur helps developers write code that minimizes unexpected behaviors during rebuilds or state transitions. Additionally, writing test cases for fixed bugs ensures that they do not reappear when future features or updates are added.

Fosters learning and skill development

Debugging is also a powerful learning tool. By exploring the code to find and resolve bugs, developers enhance their understanding of Flutter's framework, including its widget tree, state management, rendering pipeline, and asynchronous behavior. Debugging encourages problem-solving and critical thinking, helping developers build a more intuitive grasp of how different parts of the codebase interact. As developers encounter and fix bugs, they also become familiar with debugging tools, like Flutter DevTools, breakpoints, and log analysis. Mastery of these tools not only makes them more efficient at resolving issues but also improves their overall development workflow.

Improves collaboration and team productivity

In larger development teams, debugging plays a crucial role in maintaining collaboration and productivity. When a bug is identified, especially in shared codebases, effective debugging practices like clear logging, meaningful error messages, and structured exception handling make it easier for team members to trace the issue and contribute to a solution.

Debugging helps ensure that one developer's changes do not inadvertently break another part of the application, fostering smoother collaboration. Moreover, by implementing best practices like unit and widget testing as part of the debugging process, teams can detect bugs early through continuous integration pipelines. This reduces the amount of time spent tracking down errors during code reviews or in production environments, leading to increased overall team productivity. In the next section we are going to look at the common debugging scenarios.

Common debugging scenarios

In any Flutter project, developers often face various debugging challenges that can affect the functionality, performance, and user experience of the application. These common scenarios involve issues such as incorrect state management, layout inconsistencies, and asynchronous errors. Understanding these typical issues helps in efficiently diagnosing and resolving bugs, ensuring a smoother development process and a high-quality end product.

Typical issues faced in Flutter projects

Let us discuss some common issues that you can face in your Flutter projects. The following figure summarizes the common issues:

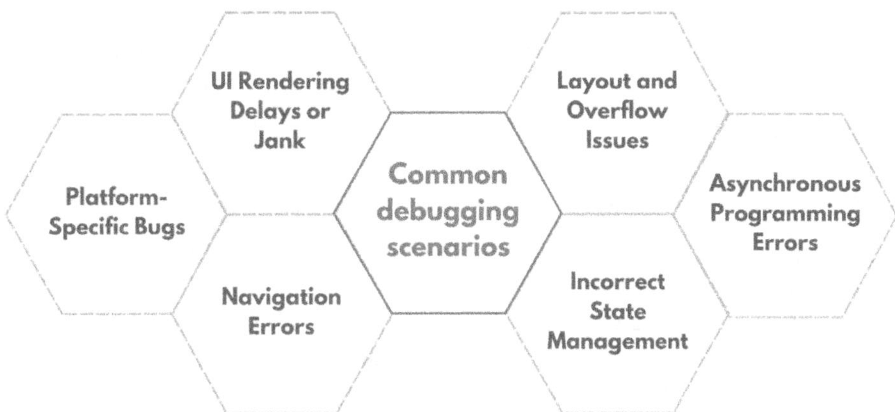

Figure 6.2: *Common debugging scenarios in Flutter projects*

Incorrect state management

State management is a core aspect of Flutter applications and mishandling it can lead to bugs such as improper UI updates or data inconsistencies. For example, using `setState` in the wrong widget or managing the state of a complex application without a proper structure like **Provider** or **Bloc** can cause unpredictable UI behavior. This can result in widgets not rebuilding correctly when the state changes, or the app displaying outdated data. A common scenario is when a form's input fields do not reflect the latest values due to incorrect state handling, leading to a frustrating user experience.

Layout and overflow issues

Flutter's flexible layout system allows for rich UIs, but it can also lead to common layout problems such as widget overflow or incorrect alignment. One frequent issue is the **RenderFlex overflowed** error, which happens when a widget's size exceeds the available space in the viewport, causing layout distortion.

For example, placing a **Row** inside a container without constraints can cause horizontal overflow, particularly when there are too many child widgets to fit on the screen. Similarly, widgets may not be centered or aligned as expected if the layout hierarchy is incorrectly structured, causing inconsistent designs across devices.

Asynchronous programming errors

Flutter heavily relies on asynchronous programming to handle tasks like fetching data from the network or reading from a local database. However, failing to manage **Future** and **Stream** properly can lead to errors such as unhandled exceptions or inconsistent data fetching. For instance, when using a **FutureBuilder** to load data asynchronously, a common bug occurs when developers neglect to handle the **null** or loading state properly, leading to crashes or blank screens. Additionally, issues like racing conditions can arise if asynchronous tasks are not handled in the correct sequence, causing unexpected app behavior.

UI rendering delays or jank

Poor performance in Flutter applications often manifests as **jank** (laggy animations or slow rendering). This issue occurs when widgets take too long to rebuild, typically due to inefficient code in the **`build`** method. For example, rebuilding an entire widget tree instead of optimizing it by using stateless widgets or **memoizing** expensive computations can lead to frame drops. Similarly, performing heavy calculations or network requests directly in the **`build`** method can cause the UI to freeze momentarily, resulting in poor user experience.

Navigation errors

Handling navigation and route management in Flutter can sometimes lead to issues, especially in more complex applications with nested navigation flows. A typical scenario is when the back button behavior is not handled properly, leading to crashes or incorrect navigation paths. For example, if the navigator stack is not correctly managed (e.g., multiple **`Navigator.push`** without proper pops), users may get stuck in the app, unable to go back to the previous screen. Another issue arises when deep linking is used and the app's navigation state does not synchronize correctly with the deep link path, leading to incorrect screens being shown.

Platform-specific bugs

Since Flutter is a cross-platform framework, bugs may arise that are specific to the platform on which the app is running. For instance, an app may behave perfectly on Android but exhibit issues on iOS due to differences in platform APIs or widget implementations. A common example is the inconsistent behavior of the **Cupertino** widgets on Android devices, or permission-related issues that vary between iOS and Android. Developers need to be aware of these platform-specific nuances and handle them properly by using conditional code or platform-specific configurations.

By identifying and understanding these typical issues, developers can anticipate potential problems early in the development process and apply the correct debugging techniques to address them efficiently.

Note: Memoizing is an optimization technique where the results of expensive function calls are cached, so when the function is called again with the same inputs, the cached result is returned instead of recalculating. This helps improve performance, especially in Flutter's widget rebuilding process.

Typical debugging issues in Flutter web projects

When developing Flutter web applications, certain debugging challenges can be unique compared to mobile or desktop environments. These challenges stem from the differences in how the browser handles rendering, performance, and interactions. We have already solved some of them, by creating project with proper responsive system and adding extra setting to Material app in *Chapter 4, Advanced UI Design and Animation*. The following figure summarizes the issues that occur in Flutter web projects:

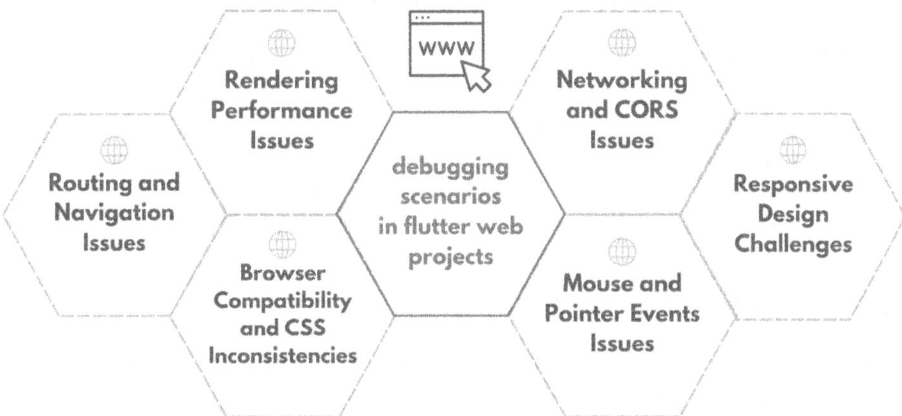

***Figure 6.3**: Debugging issues faced in Flutter web*

Rendering performance issues

Flutter web applications often face rendering performance challenges, especially on complex or animation-heavy pages. This can manifest as slow page loads, laggy animations, or unresponsive interfaces. For instance, heavy reliance on custom widgets or deeply nested structures can result in slow frame rates and jittery animations in web browsers.

Browser compatibility and CSS inconsistencies

Unlike mobile apps, Flutter web projects must account for browser compatibility across different platforms (e.g., **Chrome**, **Firefox**, **Safari**, **Edge**). Occasionally, certain widgets or layouts might behave differently in one browser compared to another. For example, **Cascading Style Sheet (CSS)** based behaviors, such as how elements are positioned or sized within containers, can lead to misalignments or clipping issues that appear only in certain browsers. This can be particularly frustrating when working with responsive layouts where dynamic resizing may cause unexpected results on web pages.

Networking and CORS issues

Network-related bugs, particularly **Cross-Origin Resource Sharing** (**CORS**) issues, are common in Flutter web applications. Since web apps interact with external APIs or databases, CORS policies can restrict access if not properly configured. For instance, an API call that works perfectly in a mobile Flutter app might fail in a web environment due to restrictive CORS settings on the server.

Mouse and pointer events issues

Unlike mobile apps, where touch events dominate, Flutter web applications must handle mouse, keyboard, and other pointer events. Debugging issues related to mouse clicks, hover states, or focus management can be tricky, as some widgets designed for touch interactions may not respond as expected in a web environment. For example, interactive widgets like buttons or forms might not register click events correctly, or hover effects may not behave as anticipated.

Routing and navigation issues

Bugs often occur when navigation flows do not synchronize properly with the URL changes, causing unexpected page reloads or incorrect route rendering. For instance, if a user navigates to a specific URL, the app may not correctly load the corresponding screen, especially in **Single Page Applications (SPAs)**. Debugging these routing issues requires a deep understanding of both Flutter's navigation system and web-specific routing mechanics.

Responsive design challenges

One of the most common issues in Flutter web projects is ensuring that the UI is responsive and adaptable to different screen sizes, from small mobile screens to large desktop monitors. Layout bugs can arise when widgets do not resize or reposition correctly, especially in dynamic layouts where screen dimensions are constantly changing.

Debugging techniques in Flutter

Flutter offers a robust set of tools and techniques that simplify the process of identifying and fixing bugs. Whether it is using the quick feedback features like hot reload, managing breakpoints, or stepping through the code execution process, mastering these techniques can significantly improve a developer's efficiency.

Hot reload and hot restart

Hot reload and hot restart are two of the most commonly used debugging techniques in Flutter. Both are integral to Flutter's development process, but they differ in terms of what they refresh during debugging. The following figure shows IntelliJ IDEA run panel that contains both options:

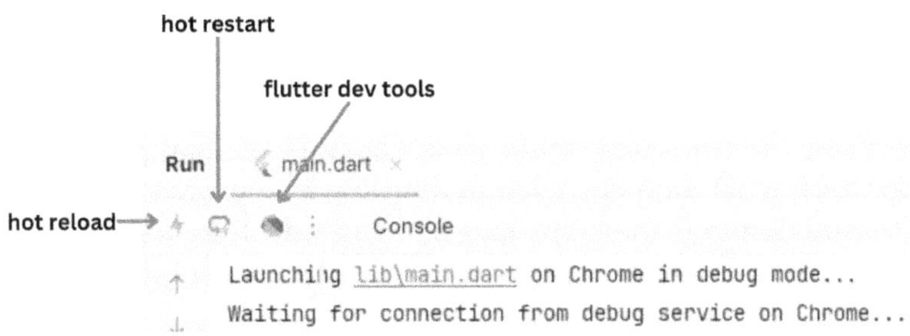

Figure 6.4: *IntelliJ IDEA's run panel with hot reload and hot restart options*

Hot reload

Hot reload allows you to instantly inject changes into a running app without losing the current state of the application. When you make modifications to the UI or the logic in your Dart code, Flutter refreshes the parts of the code that have been modified and re-renders them on the screen. Hot reload is best used when you are iterating on the look and feel of your app or tweaking functionality without wanting to lose the app's current state. For instance, if you change the layout of a widget, hot reload will update it in real-time without resetting the app, preserving data like form inputs or navigation history.

Note: Hot reload will not work for structural changes like modifying main() or changing global variables. In these cases, you would need to use a hot restart.

Hot restart

Hot restart restarts the entire application from scratch but does so much faster than a full rebuild. It resets the app's state, reinitializes global variables, and restarts the `main()` method. The entire app goes back to its initial launch state. You should use hot restart when you make significant changes that affect the app's state or overall structure, such as modifying initialization logic, state management, or third-party integrations. Although hot restart resets the state, it takes slightly more time than hot reload. It also clears any unsaved user input or state changes from the app.

Note: In IntelliJ IDEA, use CTRL + \ on windows or CMD + \ on mac for Flutter hot reload and CTRL + SHIFT + \ on windows or CMD + SHITFT+ \ on mac for Flutter hot restart.

Using breakpoints in IntelliJ IDEA

Breakpoints are one of the most powerful debugging tools available in IntelliJ IDEA. They allow developers to pause the execution of a program at specific points, making it possible to inspect the current state of variables and the flow of the application in real time.

Setting breakpoints

To set a breakpoint in IntelliJ IDEA, click on the left margin next to the line number (**gutter area**) where you want the execution to pause, or right-click and select **Add Breakpoint** This is useful when you want to monitor what happens at a particular point in the code. If you need to check what happens when a user logs in, you can set a breakpoint in the **authentication function** to inspect the values of **variables like username and password** as they are processed. Look at the following figure which show breakpoint options:

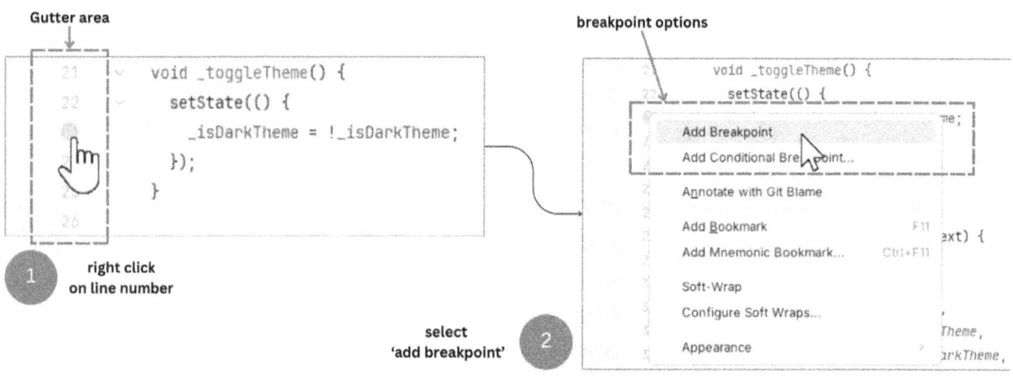

Figure 6.5: Adding a breakpoint in IntelliJ IDEA

Conditional breakpoints

IntelliJ IDEA allows you to set conditional breakpoints, which only activate when certain conditions are met. This feature is handy when you are trying to catch specific scenarios without pausing execution at every instance of the breakpoint. You can right-click on a breakpoint and select **Add Conditional Breakpoint** then define a condition like if (**`user.isloggedIn = false`**). If you are debugging a function that processes a list of users, and you only want to stop the execution when a **user is over 18 years old**, you can set a conditional breakpoint to only trigger when this condition is true. The following figure shows setting up of a conditional breakpoint:

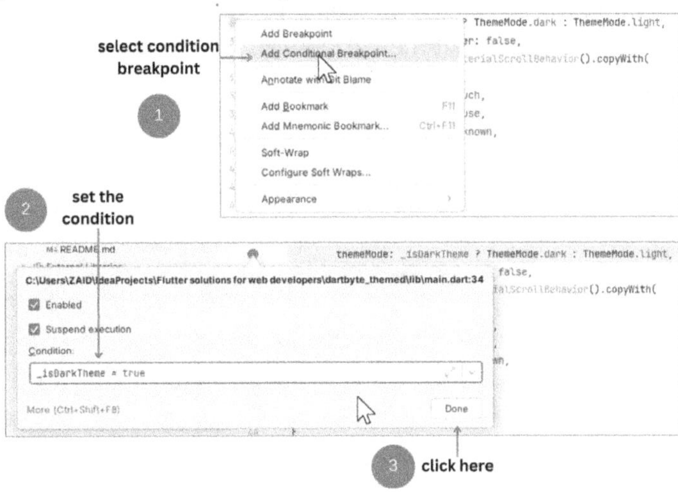

Figure 6.6: Setting up a conditional breakpoint in IntelliJ IDEA

Note: To quickly add/remove breakpoints, simply click on the line number in gutter area to add breakpoint and click on it again to remove it.

Running in debug mode

To make use of breakpoints, you need the app to run in debug mode. For this you can follow the following *Figure 6.7* or use shortcut *SHIFT + F9*:

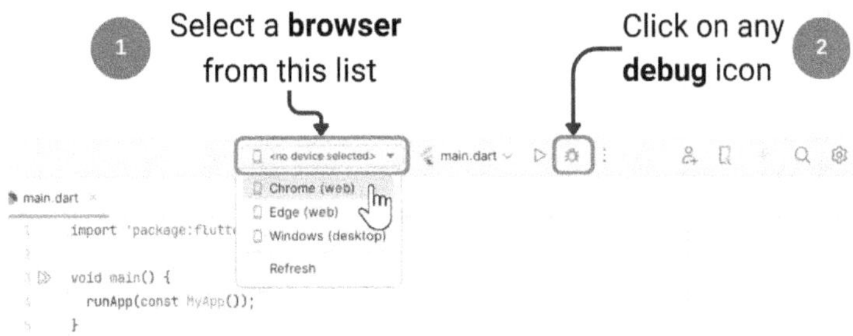

Figure 6.7: Running project in debug mode in IntelliJ IDEA

When the app executes in the browser, it will pause before Flutter executes the breakpoint and launches the debug panel where you can see all the values that are in the memory and all the methods that have been executed.

Inspecting variables

When your app pauses at a breakpoint, you can inspect variables and objects in real time. Both VS Code and Android Studio display the current state of all local and global variables, allowing you to check if their values are what you expect. For example, when debugging a function that calculates a user's shopping cart total, you can inspect the value of each item's price and quantity to ensure they are being processed correctly. The following figure shows the debug toolbar showing all the variable and their values:

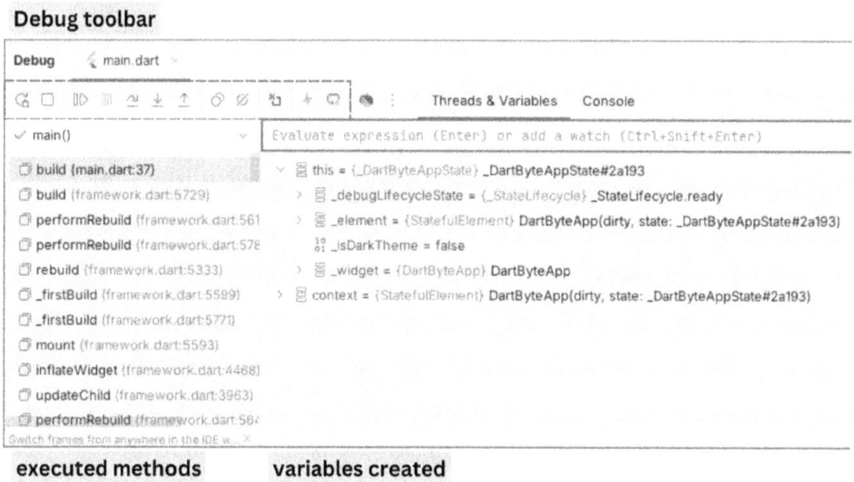

Figure 6.8: Debug panel with threads and variables

Step-by-step debugging process

Once your application is paused at a breakpoint, IntelliJ IDEA provides tools to step through your code line by line, allowing you to closely follow the flow of execution and identify the exact moment when something goes wrong. The following figure shows the options in the debug tollbar:

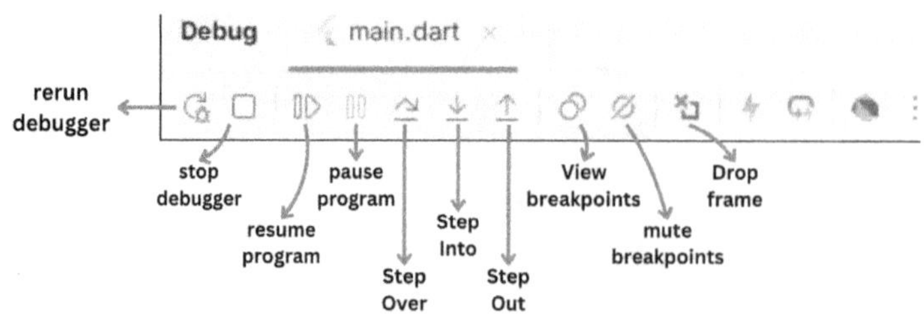

Figure 6.9: Debug toolbar in IntelliJ IDEA showing options for step-by-step debugging

Step over

The Step Over command allows you to **skip over function calls** and proceed to the next line of code. This is useful when you want to focus on the logic outside a particular function without diving into its internal details. For example, if your app is calling a helper function to format a date, and you are confident the function works correctly, you can use Step Over to move past it and continue debugging the rest of the logic.

Step into

The Step Into feature lets you **dive into a function call** and follow its execution. This is useful when you want to explore what happens inside a particular function. For example, if you suspect a bug is occurring inside a function that calculates a discount on an order, Step Into allows you to see the detailed execution of the function, line by line.

Step Out

Once you have stepped into a function, you can use the Step Out feature to **return to the higher-level function that called it**. This is helpful when you have determined the function is working correctly and want to return to the broader context of the code. For example, after stepping into a function that validates a user's input, and confirming that the validation logic is correct, Step Out lets you quickly return to the calling function and continue debugging the overall flow.

Resume Program

The Resume Program feature in debugging allows the **program's execution to continue** after it has been paused at a breakpoint. When you use this option, the program runs until it either finishes or hits another breakpoint. Essentially, it **resumes the normal flow of the program** after you have inspected or made changes at a breakpoint, without stepping through the code line by line. This is useful when you want to skip over sections of code without pausing or stepping through them and quickly move to the next point of interest or potential issue.

Using Flutter DevTools

Flutter DevTools is a suite of performance and debugging tools specifically designed for Flutter applications. It allows developers to gain deep insights into their apps, debug visual issues, monitor network calls, inspect widget trees, and understand rendering layers. While the tool offers many features for performance optimization, its power for diagnosing UI and layout problems is just as important.

Overview of Flutter DevTools

Flutter DevTools can be accessed directly from IDEs like VS Code and IntelliJ IDEA, or from the command line via **`flutter pub global activate devtools`**. Once launched, DevTools provides a comprehensive dashboard where you can inspect various aspects of your Flutter app in real-time. The key features include:

- **Flutter inspector**: Enables you to visually inspect and modify the widget tree.
- **Layout explorer**: Helps visualize widget layout constraints, paddings, margins, and alignment.
- **Rendering layers**: Shows how your app is drawn on the screen, which is useful for understanding visual issues.
- **Debugging console**: Displays real-time logs and helps you spot potential errors or exceptions.
- **Logging and error tracking**: Monitors logs and tracks issues in real-time during app runtime.

The following figure shows the flutter DevTools window opened in the browser using IntelliJ IDEA:

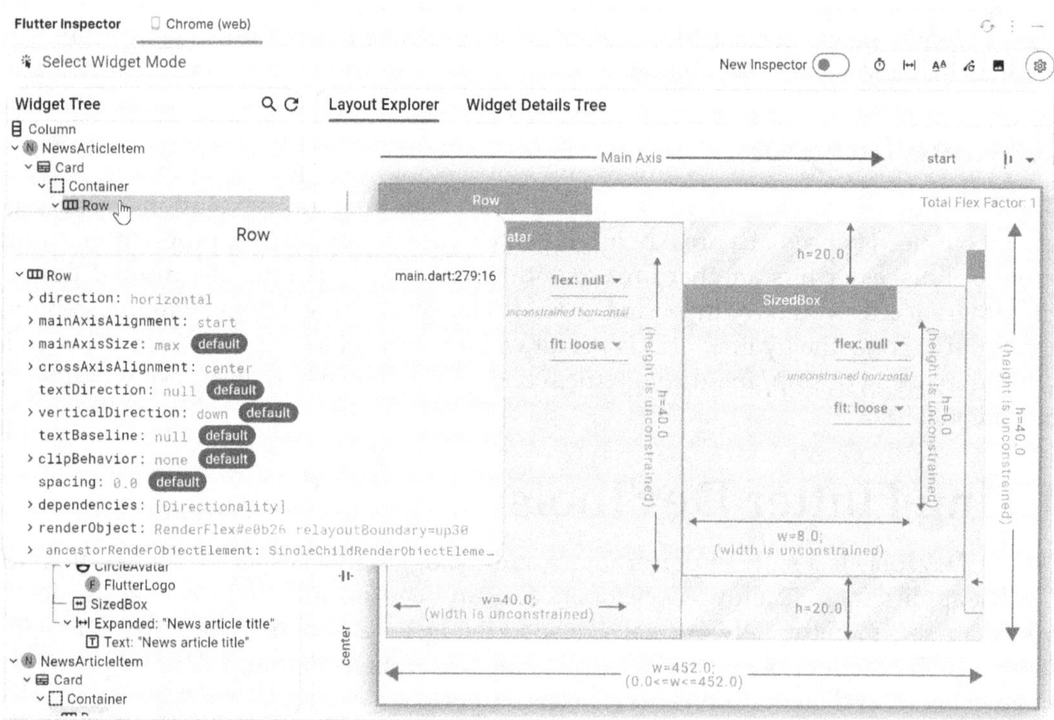

Figure 6.10: Flutter DevTools window with Flutter inspector selected

For the purpose of debugging UI or layout problems, Flutter DevTools offers powerful features like the Flutter Inspector and Layout Explorer, allowing developers to pinpoint where things go wrong visually, rather than focusing on performance metrics.

Inspecting widgets and rendering layers

The **Flutter Inspector** is one of the most frequently used tools for debugging visual and logical bugs. It provides a real-time view of the widget tree that represents your Flutter app's UI structure. When dealing with layout issues or unexpected visual behavior, the Flutter Inspector helps identify which widget is causing the problem. In Flutter, the UI is built as a hierarchical tree of widgets, with parent-child relationships that define layout and behavior. The Flutter Inspector allows you to explore this tree, helping you see which widgets are part of the UI and how they interact. For example, if a button is not appearing where you expect it to, the Flutter Inspector can show you if it is being hidden behind another widget or if it has not been added to the correct container. Flutter draws its UI using layers, which include widgets, canvases, and elements that help create the final visual interface. By inspecting the rendering layers, you can gain insight into the drawing order of widgets, making it easier to debug issues like improper layering, clipping, or widget overlap. The following figure shows the **Flutter Inspector** tab for the project **`DartByteApp`**:

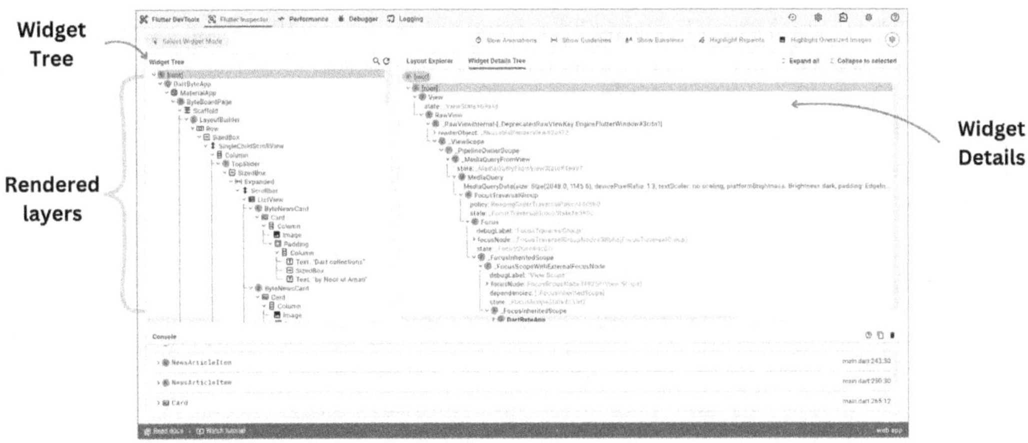

Figure 6.11: *Flutter inspector with widget tree and widget details of DartByte app*

Visual debugging

With DevTools **select a widget mode**, you can select a widget in the UI and simultaneously see where it is located in the code, which makes it easy to jump directly to the relevant part of the widget tree for quick adjustments. The following *Figure 6.12* shows the DartByte app and Flutter DevTools with widget selection example:

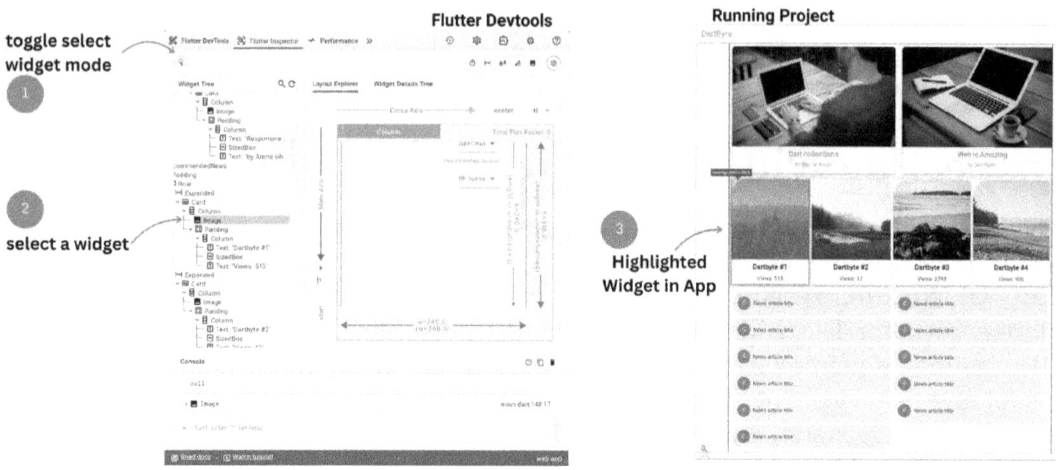

Figure 6.12: Flutter DevTools visual debugging example

Analyzing the widget tree and layout

In Flutter, every visual element on the screen is part of a widget tree, a hierarchical structure that represents how widgets are organized and rendered. Properly analyzing the widget tree and layout is crucial for debugging UI-related issues, especially when elements do not appear as expected, or the layout behaves inconsistently across different devices or screen sizes. Flutter DevTools provides powerful features for inspecting and understanding the widget tree, layout constraints, and how individual widgets are placed relative to one another. Let us explore how you can analyze the widget tree and layout using Flutter DevTools.

Understanding the widget tree

The widget tree forms the backbone of Flutter's UI structure. Every visual element in Flutter is a widget, from the smallest Text widget to larger structures like Rows, Columns, and Scaffold. By inspecting this tree, you can understand how widgets relate to one another, helping you locate issues where the UI might not behave as intended. Two important concepts used in Flutter for understanding widget tree are:

- **Parent-child relationships**: Every widget in Flutter has a parent-child relationship. Parents control how their child widgets are displayed and laid out. By exploring this hierarchy in the Flutter Inspector in DevTools, you can trace how each widget fits into the overall structure of the app. If a button appears outside its container, inspecting the widget tree will help you see if it is misplaced or inside an unexpected parent widget (like a Stack instead of a Column).
- **Widget properties**: Every widget will have multiple properties. When inspecting the widget tree, **DevTools** provides detailed information about the properties of

each widget, such as size, alignment, and constraints. You can see attributes like color, padding, and margins, which can provide you with insight into why certain elements are not rendered as expected.

The following figure shows the widget tree and selected widgets properties:

***Figure 6.13:** Widget Tree in Flutter DevTools showing widget properties*

Analyzing layout constraints

Layout constraints define how widgets in Flutter are sized and positioned. Every widget passes constraints down to its children, which define the maximum or minimum size the children can take. Debugging layout issues often requires analyzing these constraints to ensure they are properly configured. Flutter's Layout Explorer in DevTools allows you to visually inspect layout constraints applied to widgets, making it easy to understand how Flutter is interpreting the **size**, **alignment**, and **positioning** of each widget. The following are some important points to remember:

- **Constraint propagation:** Parent widgets pass down constraints to their children, which in turn apply these constraints to define their size and position. You can use the Layout Explorer to view the exact constraints applied to each widget. For example, if a **`Container`** widget is not expanding to fill available space, you can inspect whether its parent (e.g., a Column or Row) is restricting its size due to constraints.
- **Alignment and spacing:** In many cases, issues like overlapping widgets or incorrect alignment are caused by improper configuration of alignment properties in layout widgets (**`Align`**, **`Center`**, **`Padding`**, etc.). The Layout Explorer makes it easy to see if a widget's alignment, padding, or margin is misconfigured. For example, if a widget is too close to the edge of the screen, inspecting the layout constraints might show that there is insufficient padding, or an **`Align`** widget is forcing the child into a specific corner.
- **Analyzing flexible and expanded widgets**: Widgets like Flexible and Expanded are commonly used to control how space is distributed in layouts like Row and Column. DevTools allows you to see if these widgets are correctly expanding or contracting to fit their available space. For example, if multiple widgets inside a Row are not properly sharing the available space, the Layout Explorer will show how constraints from Expanded or Flexible are being applied, allowing you to identify the issue and adjust accordingly.

The following figure shows the **Layout Explorer**:

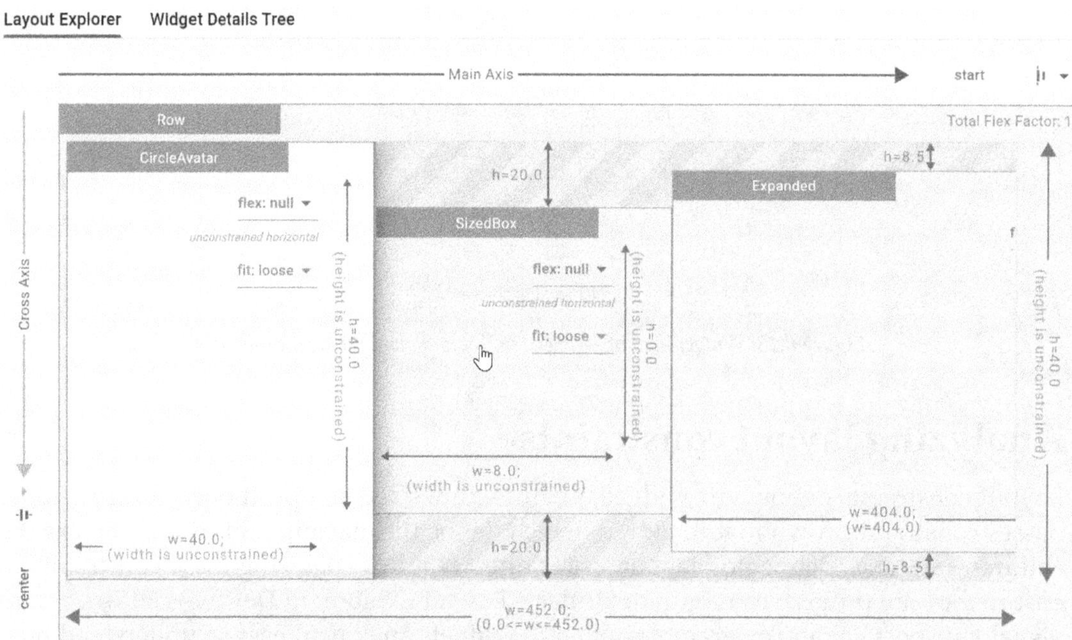

Figure 6.14: Layout inspector in Flutter inspector showing arrangement of widgets

Handling exceptions

Exception handling is a crucial aspect of debugging and building reliable applications. In Flutter, exceptions can occur for a variety of reasons, ranging from invalid inputs, network errors, and file I/O issues to more complex scenarios in asynchronous code. To build a robust Flutter application, developers need to be adept at identifying, categorizing, and handling exceptions.

Identifying and categorizing exceptions in Flutter

In Flutter, exceptions can arise from various parts of the app. It is important to categorize exceptions based on where and why they occur so that they can be handled effectively. The common exception categories include:

- **Input validation errors:** These exceptions arise when user inputs are invalid. For instance, trying to divide by zero, entering invalid date formats, or leaving mandatory fields empty can result in exceptions.
- **Network exceptions:** When your app interacts with an external API or web service, network issues can cause exceptions. Common examples include `SocketException`, `HttpException`, or `TimeoutException`. These typically arise from connectivity problems, invalid requests, or server downtime.
- **File I/O exceptions:** Applications that read from or write to files can encounter issues like missing files, incorrect file paths, or insufficient permissions. Examples include `FileSystemException` and `IOException`.
- **Asynchronous exceptions:** Flutter heavily relies on asynchronous programming for tasks like fetching data from the internet or accessing device storage. Exceptions can arise when handling asynchronous code, such as unhandled promises or failed `Future` operations.
- **Widget and layout exceptions:** These can occur when the app's widget tree contains inconsistencies, such as trying to display `null` where a widget is expected or improperly handling state changes.
- **Third-party library exceptions:** Sometimes, exceptions occur because of issues in third-party packages. These can be harder to debug but can often be traced back to incorrect usage or outdated dependencies.

Custom exception handling

Flutter allows you to create and throw custom exceptions that are specific to your application's business logic. This is useful when you want to provide more meaningful error messages and improve error diagnostics. Look at the following code snippet:

```
class InvalidUserInputException implements Exception {
  final String message;
  InvalidUserInputException(this.message);
  @override
  String toString() => 'InvalidUserInputException: $message';
}

void validateUserInput(String input) {
  if (input.isEmpty) {
    throw InvalidUserInputException("Input cannot be empty.");
  }
}

void main() {
  try {
    validateUserInput('');
  } catch (e) {
    // Output: InvalidUserInputException: Input cannot be empty.
    print(e);
  }
}
```

In this example, a custom exception **InvalidUserInputException** is thrown when the user input is empty, allowing the application to handle the error gracefully.

Using try-catch blocks and Future error handling

Flutter's **try-catch** blocks are the most common way to catch exceptions that occur in synchronous code. For asynchronous code, **Future** has built-in methods to handle errors, such as **catchError**. For example, the following code snippet demonstrates using **try-catch** for synchronous code:

```
void divide(int a, int b) {
  try {
    var result = a ~/ b;
    print(result);
  } catch (e) {
    print('Exception caught: $e');
  }
}
```

```
void main() {
  // Output: Exception caught: IntegerDivisionByZeroException
  divide(10, 0);
}
```

In this example, try-catch is used to handle the exception that occurs when dividing by zero.

Handling errors in asynchronous code

For asynchronous code that involves Future, you can handle errors in the following two ways:

- Using **try-catch** inside **async** functions
- Using **catchError** for a **Future** chain

The code snippet for **try-catch** is as follows:

```
Future<void> fetchData() async {
  try {
    var response = await fetchFromAPI();
    print(response);
  } catch (e) {
    print('Error fetching data: $e');
  }
}
```

Another scenario is using **catchError**, this method allows you to handle any errors that might occur in the future chain. It is often used when chaining multiple asynchronous operations. The code snippet for this is as follows:

```
fetchFromAPI().then((data) {
  print(data);
}).catchError((error) {
  print('Error: $error');
});
```

Debugging asynchronous code

One of the trickiest areas to debug in Flutter is asynchronous code, as operations such as network requests or file I/O can result in exceptions that occur after a delay or in different execution contexts. Here are some common issues and debugging tips for asynchronous code:

- **Unhandled exceptions in futures:** If an exception occurs in an asynchronous function, it will not always be caught unless explicitly handled. It is crucial to use **`try-catch`** blocks or **`catchError`** to handle errors in async code.
- **Isolating problem areas:** If your app crashes without clear information, isolate the problem by logging before and after each asynchronous call. This helps you trace where the code fails. The following snippet shows how to add logs in asynchronous code:

```
try {
  print('Fetching data...');
  var data = await fetchFromAPI();
  print('Data fetched successfully');
} catch (e) {
  print('Error: $e');
}
```

- **Using Flutter DevTools:** Flutter DevTools can help monitor asynchronous operations, inspect logs, and identify which future or stream is failing. You can place breakpoints in async code and step through it just like synchronous code.
- **Handling timeouts:** If a network request takes too long, it might cause the app to freeze or crash. You can handle timeouts by setting a time limit for operations using **`timeout`**, as show in the following code snippet:

```
Future<void> fetchData() async {
  try {
    var result = await fetchFromAPI().timeout(Duration(seconds: 5));
    print(result);
  } catch (e) {
    print('Timeout or Error: $e');
  }
}
```

By understanding the common pitfalls in asynchronous code and using techniques like **`try-catch`** and **`catchError`**, you can make your Flutter applications more reliable and easier to debug when handling network requests, file I/O, and other asynchronous operations.

Logging and monitoring

Logging is a critical tool in debugging and monitoring Flutter applications as it provides visibility into the internal state and behavior of the app at runtime. Proper logging not only aids in debugging during development but also helps in monitoring production applications to catch bugs and performance issues early.

Importance of logging in debugging

Effective logging is essential for identifying and fixing issues that may not immediately crash the app but still result in incorrect behavior. Logging allows developers to:

- **Track application flow**: Logs help to understand the sequence of events leading up to an issue, especially in complex or asynchronous operations.
- **Capture errors and warnings**: Logs provide useful information about exceptions or issues occurring in the application, which might be hard to trace otherwise.
- **Debug without interruption**: While breakpoints and interactive debugging can be intrusive, logging allows developers to observe the application's behavior without interrupting its flow.
- **Monitor performance**: Logging can be used to track performance metrics such as load times, memory consumption, and widget build durations.
- **Analyze production issues**: In production environments where debugging tools are not available, logs offer a way to track down bugs remotely.

Using print statements and debugPrint

The simplest form of logging in Flutter is using print statements. This is often used for quick, temporary logging to track variables, states, or the flow of the application during development. While print is useful for small debugging tasks, it has some limitations, such as:

- Prints everything to the console, which can become overwhelming in larger applications.
- In production builds, **`print`** statements are not removed and can affect performance.
- Print output is also truncated, so long debug messages will not be visible.

To mitigate this, Flutter provides a better alternative: **`debugPrint`**. This function is more efficient for logging in Flutter because it truncates long outputs and can be disabled in production. This is especially useful when you need to log a lot of information but do not want it to clutter your console or slow down performance. The following code snippet shows **`debugPrint`** implementation:

```
debugPrint('Hello debugging.');
debugPrint('This is a long debug message!!');
```

Using log function

Flutter provides a built-in logging utility through the **`dart:developer`** library's **`log()`** function. This method allows you to log detailed information during app development, which can be viewed in the debugging console. The **`log()`** function is especially useful for tracking events, debugging issues, or monitoring app behavior in a structured and readable format. Unlike **print** statements, it offers additional features such as tagging logs with a name, level, and stack trace, making it more versatile for complex debugging scenarios. The following code snippets shows the implementation of **log()** function:

```
import 'dart:developer' as developer;

void main() {
  developer.log('App started');
  developer.log('Fetching user data', name: 'network.request');
  developer.log(Data fetched ✓', name: 'network.response');
}
```

Setting up structured logging with logger package

For more advanced and structured logging, you can use the **logger** package in Flutter. This package provides a more flexible way of logging, allowing developers to log messages at different levels (**info**, **debug**, **warning**, **error**) and format them in a structured manner. You can add it to your project by adding it to **pubspec.yaml** file as shown in the following snippet:

```
dependencies:
  logger: ^1.1.0
```

To use logger in the project, try to implement the following code snippet in your app:

```
import ‘package:logger/logger.dart’;

final logger = Logger();

void fetchData() {
  logger.i('Fetching data...');
  try {
    var data = fetchFromAPI();
    logger.d('Data fetched: $data');
  } catch (e) {
    logger.e('Error fetching data', e);
  }
}
```

The preceding example shows a **fetchData()** function, which when called, uses logger to log messages into the terminal, which can help you understand what part of code has been executed. The logger package offers various log levels, such as:

- **Verbose (v)**: For detailed logs that may not be necessary in production.
- **Debug (d)**: Logs for debugging purposes during development.
- **Info (i)**: Logs for general information about the app's behavior.
- **Warning (w)**: Logs for potential issues that do not necessarily break the app but need attention.
- **Error (e)**: Logs for serious issues or crashes that require immediate attention.

Additionally, logger allows you to customize log formatting, export logs to a file, or send them to external monitoring services. By leveraging simple **`print`** statements, **`debugPrint`**, and advanced logging with the **`logger`** package, Flutter developers can effectively monitor and debug their applications, ensuring better control over both development and production environments.

Testing in Flutter

Testing is an integral aspect of software development, ensuring that code behaves as intended, prevents regressions, and improves overall reliability. In Flutter, testing takes on even greater significance as it helps maintain app performance, UI responsiveness, and correctness across platforms. Flutter supports various types of testing to address different needs, ranging from verifying business logic to ensuring smooth user interactions. By embracing testing, developers can catch bugs early, save time, and deliver higher-quality applications.

While testing in Flutter is a very vast topic, this section covers the basics of testing in Flutter. Flutter supports three types of testing: unit tests, widget tests, and integration tests. Each of these tests serves a specific purpose, from verifying individual pieces of logic to testing entire user flows.

Unit tests: Basics and setup in Flutter

Unit tests are the foundation of a robust testing strategy, allowing developers to ensure individual pieces of logic behave as expected. In Flutter, unit tests focus on verifying isolated functions or classes. These tests run quickly and are an excellent way to catch bugs early in the development process.

To integrate unit testing into your Flutter project, you need to add the test package to the **`pubspec.yaml`** file under **`dev_dependencies`**, as shown:

```
dev_dependencies:
  test: any
```

Writing a unit test

To get started, create a file named **unit_1_test.dart** inside the **test** folder and then write the following code to test a couple of simple math functions:

```
import 'package:test/test.dart';

int add(int a, int b) => a + b;
int divide(int a, int b) => a ~/ b;

void main() {
  test('add 2 numbers', () {
    expect(add(1, 2), 3);
  });

  test('divide 2 numbers', () {
    expect(divide(6, 3), 2);
  });

  test('divide by zero', () {
    expect(() => divide(6, 0), throwsA(isA<Exception>()));
  });
}
```

In this test, code contains unit tests for two functions, add and divide. The first test checks if **add** correctly sums two numbers, while the second test ensures **divide** performs integer division correctly. The third test verifies that dividing by zero throws an exception using the **throwsA(isA<Exception>())** matcher.

Running unit tests

Flutter makes it simple to run unit tests using various tools. IntelliJ Idea and VSCode, both offer integrated support for running tests, providing a seamless experience with quick feedback and debugging capabilities. In IntelliJ Idea follow these steps:

1. Open the **unit_1_test.dart** file.
2. Go to **Run** menu | select **Run** | in the popup select '**tests in unit_1_test.dart**'.
3. Or use the small green play icons shown beside the line numbers to run the test.

Combining multiple tests in a group

In Flutter, when working with unit tests, you might want to organize them into groups for better clarity and management. This can be done using the **`group()`** function, which allows you to combine multiple tests under a common header. Grouping tests can help to logically structure them based on the feature, module, or functionality being tested, making the tests more organized and easier to maintain. Here is a sample snippet:

```
// test/unit_2_test.dart
import 'package:test/test.dart';
// sample functions for the tests
String reverseString(String input)=>input.split('').reversed.
join('');
String toUpperCase(String input) => input.toUpperCase();
int add(int a, int b) => a + b;
int subtract(int a, int b) => a - b;
// main function to run the tests
void main() {
  group('String manipulation tests', () {
    test('Test string reversal', () {
      String reversed = reverseString('hello');
      expect(reversed, equals('olleh'));
    });
    test('Test string to uppercase', () {
      String upper = toUpperCase('hello');
      expect(upper, equals('HELLO'));
    });
  });
  group('Math operations tests', () {
    test('Test addition', () {
      int sum = add(2, 3);
      expect(sum, equals(5));
    });
    test('Test subtraction', () {
      int difference = subtract(5, 3);
      expect(difference, equals(2));
    });
  });
}
```

Running tests in the terminal

To execute tests via the terminal, open the terminal, navigate to the project root.

Running tests

Use **`flutter test`** to execute all the test. This command will discover and run all the test files in the project. Once the tests are run, the terminal will show you the results, indicating how many tests passed or failed.

Running specific test

If you want to run a specific test file you can specify the path, as shown below:

```
flutter test test/unit_1_test.dart
```

Additionally, if you want to see more detailed output or debug the tests, you can use the verbose flag, as given below:

```
flutter test -verbose
```

Above command will provide more information about each test case, helping you to identify issues faster.

Running test in one group

If you want to execute test from a group, use the following command:

```
flutter test --plain-name "Math operations tests"
flutter test --plain-name "String manipulation tests"
```

Widget tests: Ensuring UI behaves correctly

Widget tests verify the behavior of individual widgets. They ensure that UI components are correctly built and respond to user interaction. These tests are most appropriate when you want to validate that a specific widget behaves as expected in isolation, without integrating it with other parts of the application or external dependencies. For example, here is a simple widget test for a widget containing a clickable button in the following code snippet:

```
import 'package:flutter/material.dart';

class WebButtonWidget extends StatelessWidget {
  @override
  Widget build(BuildContext context) {
    return MaterialApp(
        home: Scaffold(
```

```
            body: Center(
              child: ElevatedButton(
      onPressed: () {
        print('Button clicked!');
      },
      child: Text('Click Me'),
    ))));
  }
}
```

Let us create a test that will verify that the button is present and then simulates the button click using he **tap()** function. The code snippet for widget test is as follows:

```
import 'package:flutter_test/flutter_test.dart';
import 'package:sample_app/web_button_widget.dart';

void main() {
  testWidgets('Button is clickable', (WidgetTester tester) async {
    // Build the widget
    await tester.pumpWidget(WebButtonWidget());

    // Find the button by its text
    final buttonFinder = find.text('Login with Google');

    // Verify the button is found
    expect(buttonFinder, findsOneWidget);

    // Tap the button
    await tester.tap(buttonFinder);

    // Rebuild the widget after the button is tapped
    await tester.pump();
  });
}
```

Integration tests: Automating app flows

Integration tests differ from widget tests by focusing on testing the app as a whole, rather than isolated components. They are particularly useful for identifying issues related to app navigation, user interactions, and the combined behavior of various widgets and services.

While widget tests validate the functionality of individual widgets, integration tests ensure that these widgets interact seamlessly within the context of the entire application. Add the **integration_test** package **dev_dependencies** section to **pubspec.yaml** as shown in the following snippet:

```
dev_dependencies:
  ...
  integration_test:
    sdk: flutter
```

Next, create a Dart file inside test folder, and write your integration tests. The following code snippet shows an example integration test:

```
import 'package:integration_test/integration_test.dart';
import 'package:flutter_test/flutter_test.dart';
import 'package:my_app/main.dart';

void main() {
  IntegrationTestWidgetsFlutterBinding.ensureInitialized();

  testWidgets('Full app test', (WidgetTester tester) async {
    await tester.pumpWidget(MyApp());

    await tester.tap(find.text('Login'));
    await tester.pumpAndSettle();

    expect(find.text('Welcome'), findsOneWidget);
  });
}
```

This test simulates a user tapping the **Login** button and checks whether the app correctly navigates to the **Welcome** screen.

Adding mockito for mocking dependencies

To write effective unit tests that involve dependencies, you can use the **mockito** package. Add it to your **pubspec.yaml** file as follows:

```
dev_dependencies:
  mockito: ^5.3.2
  build_runner: ^2.4.0
```

Or you can also use command line to add dependencies using **flutter pub add**:

flutter pub add http dev:mockito dev:build_runner

The **mockito** package helps create mock objects, allowing you to simulate and verify interactions with dependencies. To mock a class, use the **@GenerateMocks** annotation. For example, check the snippet below:

```
import 'package:mockito/mockito.dart';
import 'package:mockito/annotations.dart';
import 'package:test/test.dart';

@GenerateMocks([DatabaseService])
void main() {
  group('DatabaseService Tests›, () {
    late MockDatabaseService mockService;

    setUp(() {
      mockService = MockDatabaseService();
    });

    test('fetchData returns mocked result', () {
      when(mockService.fetchData()).thenReturn('Mocked Data');

      expect(mockService.fetchData(), 'Mocked Data');
      verify(mockService.fetchData()).called(1);
    });
  });
}
```

To generate the mock class, run:

dart run build_runner build

This approach ensures that external dependencies do not impact your test results. For example, if a **DatabaseService** class fetches data from a server, the mock will instead return predefined results. This not only makes your tests more reliable but also segregated. The next section deals with the practical implementation of widget tests in the DartByte project.

Practical: Adding tests to DartByte project

When building and maintaining applications like DartByte, writing tests for UI components ensures that the app behaves as expected under different conditions. First open the DartByte project in IntelliJ IDEA. To write the test, open the test folder, you will find a file with name, **widget_test.dart**. This file contains a sample button click test, but it would show you error, because the sample counter code was deleted from the app. To write you code just remove the existing code and update it.

Creating widget tests for UI components

You are going to create the following two tests:

- **AppBar Test**
- **Theme Toggle Test**

Write the following code in **`widget_test.dart`** for the DartByte project:

```
import 'package:dartbyte/main.dart';
import 'package:flutter/material.dart';
import 'package:flutter_test/flutter_test.dart';

void main() {
  // Test to check if the AppBar is displayed
  testWidgets('Display app bar', (WidgetTester tester) async {
    // Build the DartByte app
    await tester.pumpWidget(const DartByteApp());

    // Verify if AppBar is displayed
    expect(find.byType(AppBar), findsOneWidget);

    // Verify if the AppBar title text is 'DartByte'
    expect(find.text('DartByte'), findsOneWidget);
  });

  // Test to check if the theme toggle (light/dark mode) works
  testWidgets('Toggle light/dark theme', (WidgetTester tester) async {
    // Build the DartByte app
    await tester.pumpWidget(const DartByteApp());

    // Verify the MaterialApp and the default page are present
    expect(find.byType(MaterialApp), findsOneWidget);
    expect(find.byType(ByteBoardPage), findsOneWidget);

    // Find the theme toggle button (icon) and tap it
    expect(find.byIcon(Icons.brightness_4), findsOneWidget);
```

```
      await tester.tap(find.byIcon(Icons.brightness_4));

      // Trigger a frame to reflect the UI change
      await tester.pump();

      // Verify the toggle button is still there after the theme change
      expect(find.byIcon(Icons.brightness_4), findsOneWidget);
    });
  }
```

Running and analyzing test results

To run these tests, execute the following command in your terminal: **`flutter test`** or just use the **play icon on the left side** of the **`main()`** function inside the **`widget_test.dart`** or use the shortcut *Ctrl* + *Shift* + *F10* (*Cmd* + *Shift* + *R* for mac). After running the tests, Flutter will output the results, indicating if the tests passed or failed. If the app's AppBar is correctly displayed and the theme toggle works as expected, the tests will pass. The following figure shows the results of test executed for the DartByte app in IntelliJ IDEA:

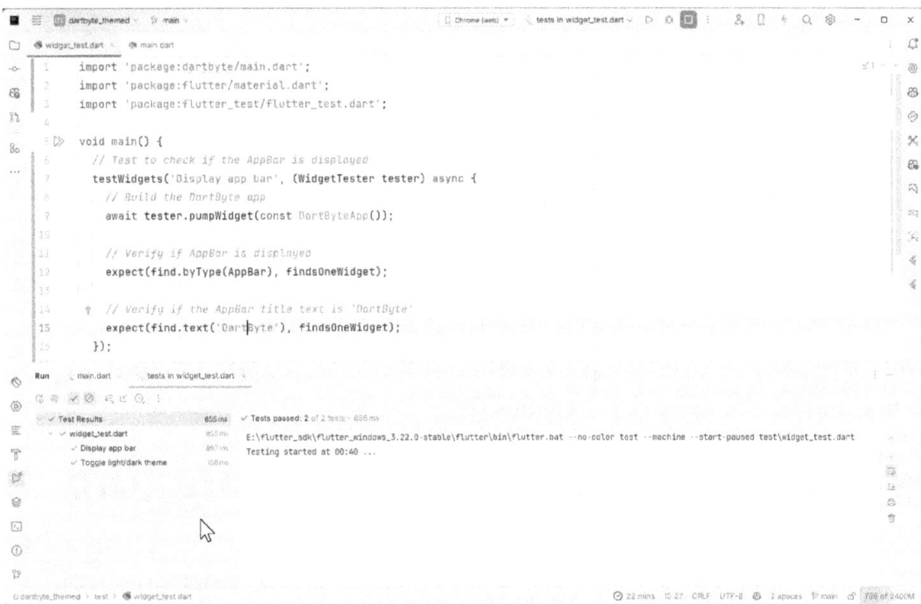

***Figure 6.15:** DartByte app with successfully passed widget tests*

If there are any discrepancies, such as the AppBar not being found or the theme toggle not functioning, Flutter will indicate which test failed, along with details on the issue. For example, if you entered the wrong app title text i.e. **`expect(find.text('DartByte'), findsOneWidget);`** then the first test will fail. The following figure shows the failed test details:

Figure 6.16: *DartByte app showing both passed and failed tests results in IntelliJ IDEA*

The following point show what these tests achieve:

- **AppBar test**: Ensures that the app's main navigation bar, which includes essential components like the title ("DartByte"), is always present in the UI.
- **Theme toggle test**: Validates that the user can switch between light and dark modes seamlessly, a key feature of many modern apps. It checks the button and ensures the UI reflects the theme change appropriately.

By including these tests, you are safeguarding critical aspects of the DartByte app, ensuring consistency and reliability in the user interface.

Tips and tricks for proactive debugging

Proactive debugging involves taking preemptive steps to prevent bugs before they occur, which leads to cleaner code, fewer runtime errors, and smoother development.

Proactive approaches to prevent bugs

Here are some essential tips and tricks to help prevent issues in your Flutter projects. The proactive approaches to prevent bugs are:

- **Thorough code reviews**: Encourage peer reviews of code changes to catch issues early. A fresh set of eyes often spots problems missed by the original developer.

- **Early testing**: Write and run unit tests, widget tests, and integration tests as you develop features. This ensures that each component works as expected and prevents the accumulation of undetected bugs.
- **Regular debugging sessions**: Do not wait until the end to debug. Frequently run debugging sessions during development, making it easier to identify issues as they arise.
- **Static code analysis**: Use tools like Dart's **`dart analyze`** to catch potential issues like unused variables, bad practices, and minor code inconsistencies.
- **Version control for debugging**: Regular commits in Git (or another version control system) make it easier to pinpoint when a bug was introduced and allow you to roll back to a stable state if necessary.

The following are the best practices for clean code to reduce bugs:

- **Keep code modular and readable**: Break down large functions and classes into smaller, reusable components. This makes it easier to track down where bugs are introduced and prevents bloated code.
- **Adopt consistent naming conventions**: Use meaningful names for variables, methods, and classes. This makes the code more understandable and reduces confusion, which can often lead to bugs.
- **Handle exceptions carefully**: Always handle potential exceptions in your code. Utilize **`try-catch`** blocks where applicable, and make sure you provide meaningful error messages to help trace bugs.
- **Document your code**: Well-commented code not only helps others understand your logic but also serves as a reminder of your intentions when debugging or making changes later.

Conclusion

In this chapter, we have explored the essential debugging techniques required for Flutter applications, from identifying common issues to using tools like **Flutter DevTools** to streamline the debugging process. By learning how to handle exceptions, leverage structured logging, and effectively utilize breakpoints and step-by-step debugging, you are now equipped to diagnose and resolve problems efficiently.

Additionally, testing plays a vital role in maintaining code quality, and incorporating unit, widget, and integration tests ensures that your app functions as expected across different scenarios. By adopting proactive debugging strategies and following best practices for clean code, you can prevent many issues from arising in the first place. These combined approaches will not only save time but also improve the reliability and performance of your Flutter applications, leading to a smoother development process and a better end-user experience.

In the next chapter, we will explore advanced architectural patterns and harness the power of Firebase to create scalable, maintainable, and feature-rich applications.

Points to remember

- Utilize techniques like hot reload, breakpoints, and step-by-step debugging to efficiently identify and fix bugs.
- Leverage Flutter DevTools for visual inspection of widgets and layout, making it easier to debug UI-related issues.
- Implement effective exception handling strategies using try-catch blocks, and categorize exceptions to manage errors appropriately.
- Adopt proactive debugging techniques, such as thorough code reviews, static code analysis, and maintaining clean, modular code to minimize bugs.
- Use logging to track application behavior and diagnose issues, employing tools like the logger package for structured logging.
- Regularly review and update your debugging practices as you gain experience, adapting to new tools and methodologies to enhance your skills.

Multiple choice questions

1. **What is the primary purpose of debugging in Flutter applications?**
   a. To add new features to the app
   b. To deploy the app to production
   c. To identify and resolve issues within the application
   d. To improve the app's design

2. **Which tool can be used to visually inspect widgets and diagnose layout issues in Flutter?**
   a. Android Studio
   b. VS Code
   c. DartPad
   d. Flutter DevTools

3. **What is a proactive approach to debugging that can help prevent issues before they occur?**
   a. Ignoring minor bugs until the end of development
   b. Writing unit tests and conducting code reviews

a. Using only print statements for debugging

b. Avoiding documentation

Answer

1	c
2	d
3	b

Questions

1. Write a Flutter function that retrieves data from an API. Implement proper exception handling using try-catch blocks to manage potential errors, such as network issues or data format errors. Include a user-friendly error message to display if an exception occurs.
2. Choose a specific widget in your DartByte application that is not displaying correctly. Use Flutter DevTools to inspect the widget tree and identify any layout issues. Document your debugging process, detailing how you diagnosed the problem and the steps you took to fix it.

Key terms

- **Debugging**: The process of identifying and resolving issues within an application.
- **Flutter DevTools**: A suite of tools for debugging Flutter applications, including widget inspection and performance analysis.
- **Hot reload**: A feature that allows developers to see code changes in real-time without restarting the application.
- **Breakpoints**: Debugging markers that pause the execution of code at specified lines to inspect variables and program flow.
- **Exception handling**: The practice of managing errors and exceptions to prevent crashes and provide user-friendly feedback.
- **Logging**: The process of recording application behavior and errors to assist in debugging and monitoring.
- **Unit testing**: A method of testing individual components or functions in isolation to ensure correctness.
- **Widget testing**: A type of testing that verifies the behavior and appearance of UI components in a Flutter application.

- **Integration testing**: Testing that focuses on the interactions between various components of the application to ensure they work together as expected.
- **Proactive debugging**: Techniques aimed at preventing bugs from occurring in the first place, such as code reviews and static analysis.

Chapter 7
Building Versatile Architectures and Integrating Firebase

Introduction

In this chapter, we explore the core architecture patterns suitable for Flutter applications, such as clean architecture and layered structures. By mastering these, developers can ensure that their apps are not only scalable but also easy to maintain and extend. Alongside architectural foundations, we introduce Firebase—a powerful backend-as-a-service platform that integrates seamlessly with Flutter. Firebase enhances the app's capabilities by providing authentication, real-time database services, and robust security. We will create a project using Firebase and follow a modular app architecture.

Structure

The chapter covers the following topics:

- Introduction to app architecture
- Fundamental architectural principles
- Popular app architectures in Flutter
- Introduction to Firebase
- Visionary: Crafting a digital vision board
- Optimizing Firebase usage
- Asynchronous programming challenges

Objectives

The goal of this chapter is to equip developers with the knowledge to design versatile app architectures that support the growing needs of modern applications. By the end of the chapter, you will have learned how to implement scalable and maintainable structures using Flutter, integrate Firebase for backend functionalities, and address challenges related to asynchronous programming. Through the hands-on project, with Firebase authentication and Firestore, you will understand how to optimize Firebase usage while ensuring your application remains secure and responsive to user needs. This chapter will solidify your architectural foundations and backend skills, enabling you to build robust, real-world applications.

Introduction to app architecture

A well-designed app architecture is crucial for managing complexity, maintaining a clean codebase, and improving performance as an application grows. Flutter does not enforce a specific architecture, providing flexibility for developers to choose the approach that best suits their needs. A clean architecture emphasizes the separation of concerns by dividing an application into independent layers. This separation ensures that changes in one layer, such as updating the UI or modifying external services, do not impact the other layers. Such a design enables better testability, scalability, and maintainability while reducing technical debt. The following figure shows an illustration of layer wise separation:

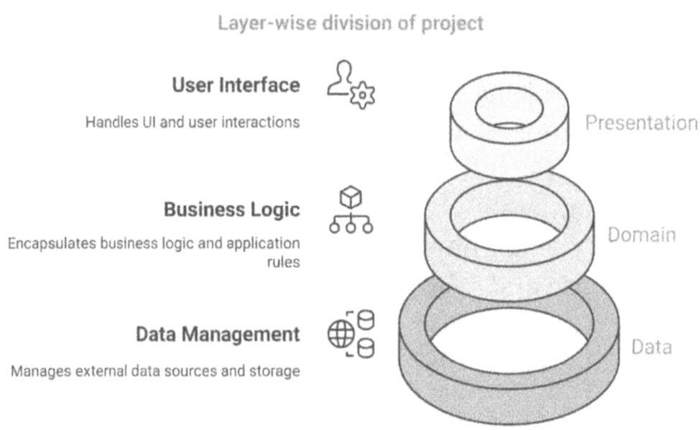

Figure 7.1: *Illustration showing the division of each layer in a clean architecture*

In a Flutter project, making an app architecture (clean project structure) involves splitting the code into several Dart packages or libraries, each focusing on a specific feature or functionality. You can use or mix the following folder organization:

- **Feature-based organization**: Grouping code by feature (e.g., user authentication, profile management) ensures that related components are organized together. This makes it easier to work on a specific feature without searching across the entire codebase.

- **Component-based organization**: Reusable components such as widgets, services, and utilities are organized separately. This allows for better code reuse across different features. The following figure illustrates organization of folders for a clean architecture:
- **Layer-based organization**: Layer-based organization structures code into distinct layers, each with a specific responsibility, such as UI, logic, and data layers. This separation ensures that each layer focuses on its task and communicates only with adjacent layers. It promotes maintainability and scalability by keeping concerns isolated and easily manageable. It is the preferred way for medium to large scale applications.

The following figure shows the project structure organization types:

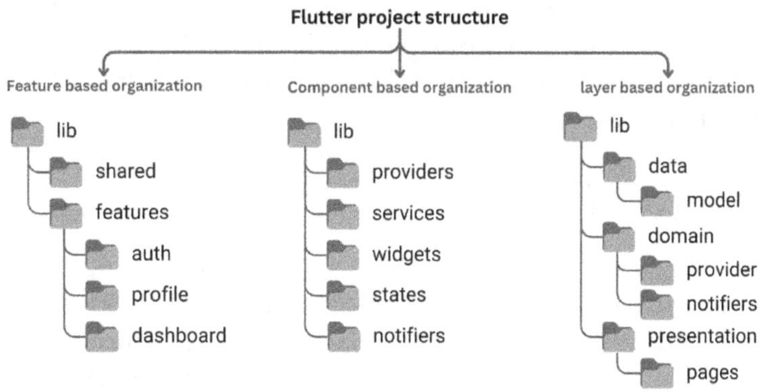

Figure 7.2: *Folder structure organization in Flutter*

Fundamental architectural principles

To make our app adaptable, we should follow a few architecture principles. The key principle includes the following.

Layered architecture

Layered architecture is a software design pattern that organizes an application into multiple layers, each dedicated to specific tasks. Depending on the complexity, an application can have two to three layers. The three primary layers in app architecture are:

- **UI layer**: The UI layer is responsible for displaying data to the user and handling user interactions. It is also known as the **presentation layer**.
- **Logic layer**: The logic layer handles the core business logic of the app and acts as an intermediary between the UI and data layers. It is often referred to as the **domain layer**. This layer is optional and is primarily needed for apps with complex business logic. Simple CRUD apps may not require this layer.

- **Data layer**: The data layer manages interactions with data sources (e.g., databases, API calls) and exposes data and methods to the logic layer.

Each layer can communicate only with the layers directly above or below it. The UI layer should be unaware of the data layer, and vice versa, maintaining clear boundaries between each layer.

Separation of concerns

Separation of concerns is a fundamental principle in app development that promotes modularity and maintainability by dividing an application's functionality into discrete, independent units. In broad terms, this means segregating UI logic from business logic. This approach is typically implemented through a layered architecture, where each layer has a distinct responsibility. For example, authentication logic should be separated from search functionality. In Flutter, this principle applies to the UI layer as well. It is essential to create reusable and lightweight widgets that contain minimal logic, keeping the UI code simple and focused on presentation.

Single source of truth

The principle of a single source of truth states that every data type in the app should be represented by a single authoritative source. This ensures that there is one class responsible for managing and modifying data, which significantly reduces the likelihood of errors and simplifies the codebase. Typically, the **single source of truth** (**SSOT**) for a given type of data resides in a class called a **repository**, part of the data layer. Each type of data in the app should have its own repository class.

Unidirectional data flow

Unidirectional data flow (**UDF**) is a design pattern that helps decouple the state from the UI that displays it. The state flows from the data layer through the logic layer to the UI layer, while user interaction events flow from the UI back to the data layer through the logic layer. The following figure illustrates this concept:

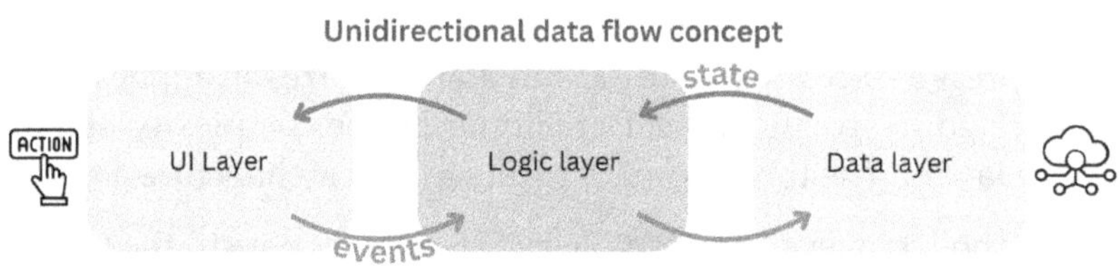

Figure 7.3: *The concept of unidirectional data flow in applications*

If the data originates in the data layer (e.g., an HTTP server response), the flow only goes through the second half. The key concept is that data updates occur exclusively in the SSOT, ensuring that the data remains consistent and easier to manage.

UI is a function of state

Flutter is a declarative framework, meaning that the UI is built to reflect the current state of the application. As the state changes, the UI must be rebuilt to match the updated state. The phrase "UI is a function of state" encapsulates this approach. In Flutter, data should drive the UI, not the other way around. Data should be immutable and persistent, while views should contain minimal logic. This design minimizes the risk of losing data when the app is closed and improves the testability and robustness of the app.

Extensibility

Each architectural component should have clearly defined inputs and outputs. For example, a view model in the logic layer should accept data sources (like repositories) as inputs and should expose only the data or commands that the view needs. This clean separation allows you to swap concrete implementations of classes without needing to modify any code that consumes the interfaces.

Testability

The principles that enhance the extensibility of software also make it easier to test. For instance, you can mock the repository to test the logic of a view model independently, without needing to mock other parts of the application. Similarly, you can test UI logic separately from Flutter widgets themselves. This architecture also enhances flexibility. For instance, adding a new view model will not break any logic in the data or business logic layers.

By adhering to these principles, our application becomes more robust, scalable, and easier to manage over time. The following figure summarizes these principles:

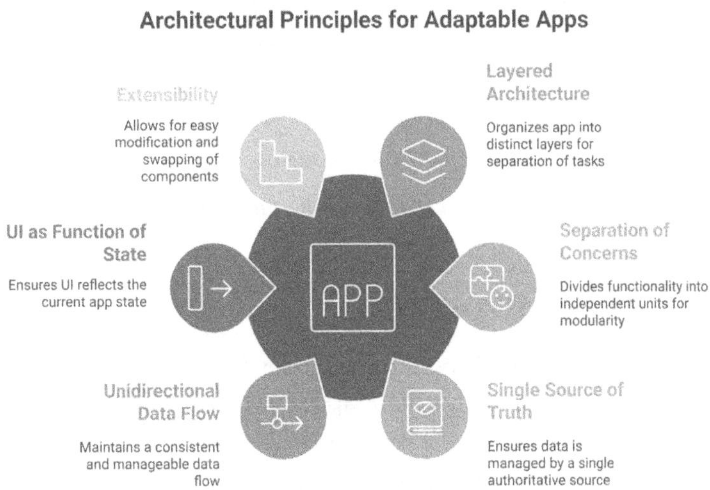

Figure 7.4: Fundamental architectural principles summary

Popular app architectures in Flutter

The following sections discuss widely used architectural patterns to create clean, scalable, and maintainable Flutter applications:

Model-view-viewmodel (MVVM)

The MVVM pattern divides the app into distinct components, making it more scalable and maintainable. This pattern aligns well with the layered architecture as follows:

- **views**: Includes user interface components (e.g., `UserView`).
- **widgets**: Contains reusable UI components used across the app.
- **viewmodels**: Acts as an intermediary between the views and models, handling presentation logic and managing state (e.g., `UserViewModel`).
- **models**: Represents data structures and encapsulates business logic (e.g., `UserModel`).
- **services**: Handles external interactions such as API requests or database operations.

This layered MVVM structure ensures separation of UI, business logic, and data sources, simplifying updates and fostering component reusability. The following figure illustrates MVVM architecture:

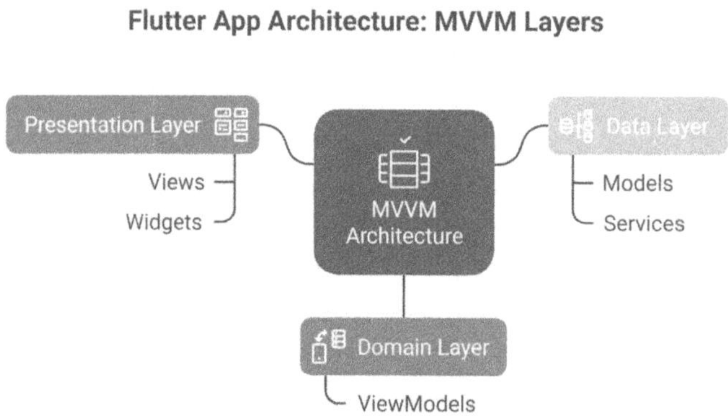

Figure 7.5: The MVVM architecture for a project

Business logic component

The **Business logic component** (**BLoC**) pattern uses Streams to decouple business logic from the UI, making it an excellent choice for applications requiring dynamic data updates or real-time functionality. It aligns with the layered architecture as follows:

- **pages(views)**: Includes UI components (e.g., `UserView`) that consume Stream-based outputs from the BLoC.

- **widgets**: Contains reusable UI components shared across the app.
- **blocs**: Encapsulates business logic and manages the flow of data and events.
- **events**: Represents user actions or app triggers (e.g., **`UserEvent`**) dispatched to the BLoC.
- **states**: Defines the states of the UI (e.g., **`UserState`**) based on the business logic.
- **repositories**: Abstracts data operations, such as API calls or database interactions.
- **models**: Represents the app's data structures (e.g., **`UserModel`**).

This approach allows for better state management, testability, and a clear division between layers. The following figure illustrates the BloC pattern:

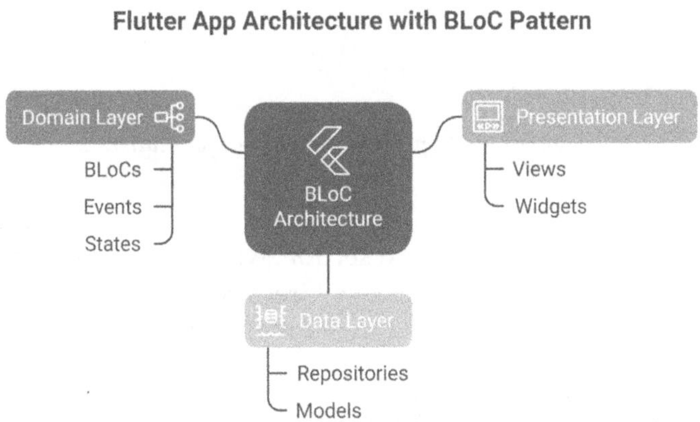

Figure 7.6: The BloC architecture for Flutter

Provider architecture

The provider package simplifies state management by injecting dependencies and efficiently sharing data between different parts of the application. It can be mapped to the following layers:

- **pages**: Contains UI components and screens that react to state changes from the provider.
- **widgets**: Includes reusable UI components.
- **providers**: Manages state and business logic using the provider package (e.g., **`UserProvider`**).
- **notifiers**: Tracks changes in state based on specific events and notifies listeners (e.g., **`AuthNotifier`**).
- **models**: Represents data entities (e.g., **`UserModel`**).
- **services**: Manages external interactions like APIs or databases.

The provider architecture's simplicity and alignment with the layered approach make it an excellent choice for small to medium-sized applications. The following figure illustrates the provider architecture:

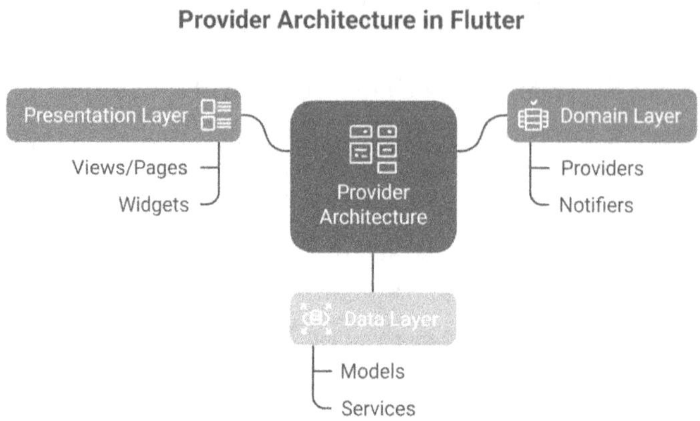

Figure 7.7: The provider architecture for Flutter

After exploring foundational architectural concepts and popular app architectures, the next step is to dive into Firebase. In the next section, we will cover how to integrate Firebase with Flutter app, set up essential services like Firestore and Firebase Authentication, and begin utilizing Firebase's features to enhance your app's functionality.

Introduction to Firebase

Firebase is a powerful platform developed by *Google* that provides a suite of cloud-based services for building, managing, and scaling web and mobile applications. Its comprehensive tools and services simplify the development process, allowing developers to focus on creating high-quality applications without worrying about infrastructure management. This section provides an overview of Firebase, its key features, and the benefits of integrating it into Flutter applications.

Understanding Firebase

Firebase is a **Platform-as-a-Service (PaaS)** that offers a range of backend services that cater to various needs of application development, including:

- **Cloud Firestore**: An advanced, flexible database for mobile, web, and server development. It provides a richer data model than the realtime database and supports advanced querying and offline capabilities.
- **Realtime database (legacy)**: A NoSQL cloud database that allows developers to store and sync data in real-time across all clients. This feature is particularly useful for applications that require live data updates, such as chat applications or collaborative tools.

- **Authentication**: Firebase Authentication simplifies the process of user authentication, providing built-in support for various authentication methods, including email/password, phone numbers, Google, Facebook, and more. This enables developers to quickly implement secure user authentication flows.
- **Cloud functions**: A serverless solution that allows developers to run backend code in response to events triggered by Firebase features and HTTPS requests. This helps to create custom backend functionality without the need to manage servers.
- **Cloud storage**: A robust solution for storing and serving user-generated content, such as images, videos, and audio files. It integrates seamlessly with Firebase Authentication for secure access control.
- **Hosting**: A fast and secure way to host web applications. Firebase Hosting provides a global **content delivery network (CDN)** and supports HTTPS out of the box.
- **Analytics**: Firebase analytics offers insights into app usage and user engagement. This helps developers make informed decisions based on real user behavior.
- **Crashlytics**: A lightweight, real-time crash reporting tool that helps developers identify, prioritize, and fix stability issues in their applications.

Integrating Firebase into Flutter accelerates development by offering pre-built services for authentication, data storage, and analytics, reducing the need for custom backend infrastructure. Its scalability allows handling user loads from a few to millions without major architectural changes. Firebase's real-time capabilities support apps needing data synchronization, like chat and collaborative tools. It simplifies authentication and enhances security with multiple options. Built-in analytics and crash reporting offer insights to improve app performance and user engagement. Firebase's extensive community and documentation provide valuable resources for developers.

Setting up Firebase in a Flutter project

To start using Firebase in a Flutter application, you need to follow these steps:

1. **Create a Firebase project**: Go to the Firebase Console (**https://console.firebase.google.com**) and create a **new project** as shown in the following figure:

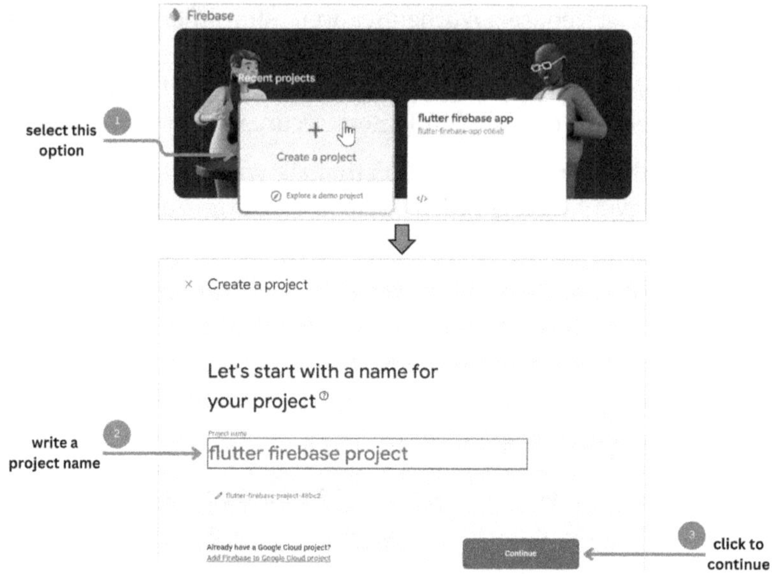

Figure 7.8: Creating a new Firebase project

You can choose to enable or disable the Google analytics in your Firebase project, which is useful for tracking and monitoring of released apps. Click on continue and then wait while the Firebase generates your project, as shown in the following figure:

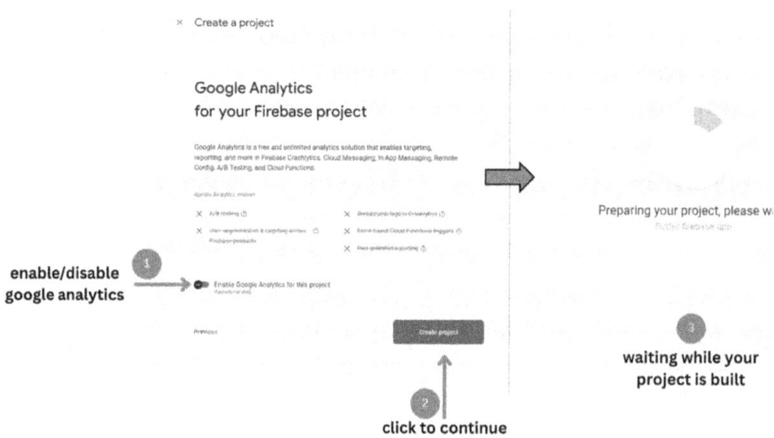

Figure 7.9: Creating the Firebase project

2. **Install the Firebase CLI**: You will need to install **Firebase command line interface (CLI)** program onto your machine, so that you can easily set up the connection configuration for Firebase in your project. To download Firebase CLI visit **https://firebase.google.com/docs/cli** and download the setup for your machine, as show in the following figure:

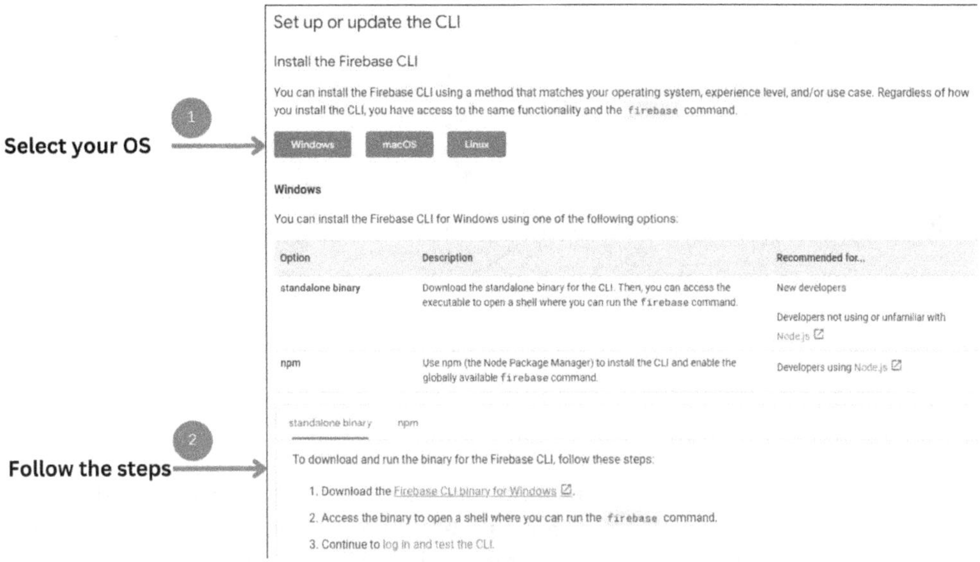

Figure 7.10: Downloading Firebase CLI tool

Alternatively, if you have a node package manager installed, you can install it using the command line by running the following command:

```
npm install -g firebase-tools
```

After installation, you will have to open your terminal (command prompt) and then login to your Firebase account using the following command:

```
firebase login
```

This command will connect your machine to the Firebase website and will provide access to your Firebase projects.

3. **Configure Firebase services**: To effectively integrate Firebase services like Authentication and Firestore into your Flutter application, the first step is setting up these features on the Firebase Console. The following are simplified instructions for configuring Firebase Authentication and Firebase Firestore:

   a. **Firebase authentication configuration**: Firebase Authentication provides secure user authentication for various platforms, supporting methods such as email/password, Google, Facebook, phone numbers, and more. Here is how to configure Firebase Authentication in the Firebase Console:

      i. **Go to Firebase console:** Open your web browser and go to Firebase Console.

      ii. **Navigate to authentication settings:** In the left-hand menu of the Firebase Console, click on **Authentication** under the **Build** section. You will be directed to the **Authentication** page, where you can manage your sign-in methods, as shown in the following figure:

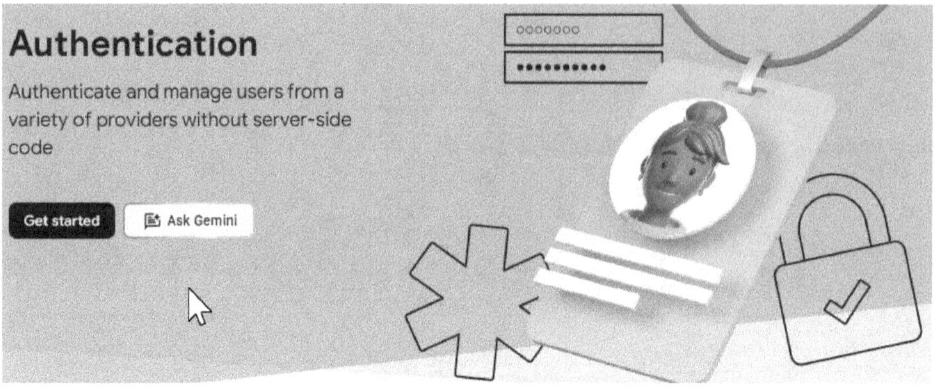

Figure 7.11: The authentication page of the Firebase console

iii. **Enable sign-in methods:** Click on get started button and then you will be redirected to the **Sign-in method** tab at the top of the **Authentication** page. You will see a list of available sign-in providers such as Email/Password, Google, Facebook, Phone, etc., as shown in the following figure:

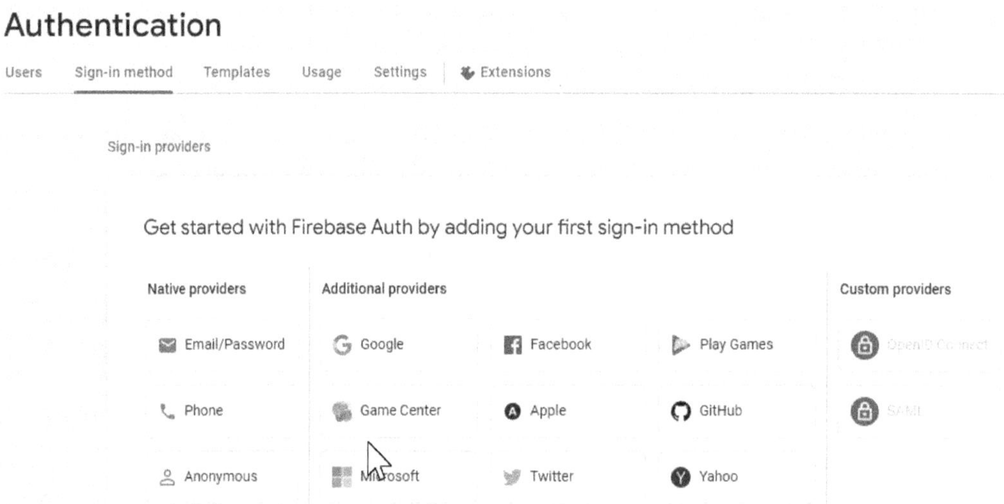

Figure 7.12: Sign-in method tabs displaying various authentication methods

iv. **Configure Google authentication**: For our project, we are going to use Google authentication. Click on the *Google* icon. In the expanded window, click on the radio button, set the support email for the project and update the public facing name of the project as shown in the following figure and click on **Save**:

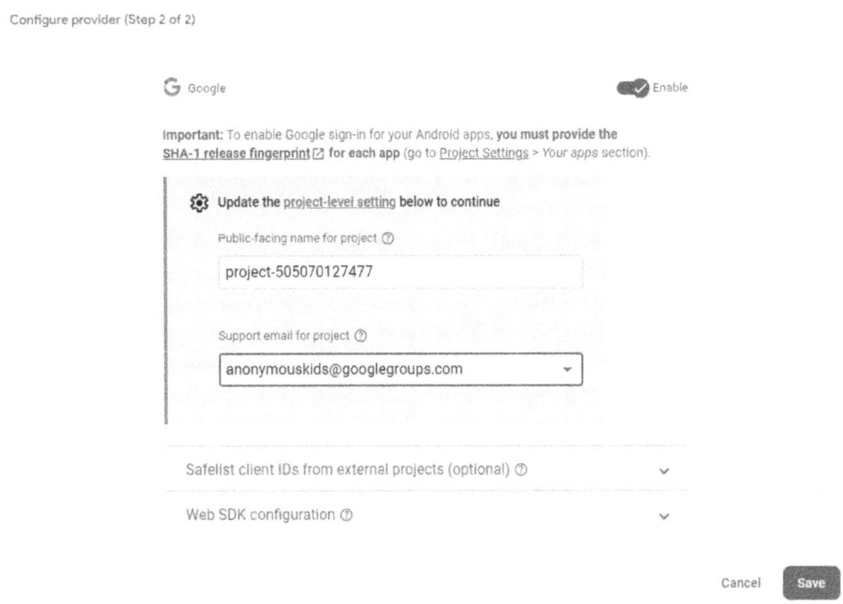

Figure 7.13: Configuration window for Google authentication on Firebase console

Note: Firebase documentation provide very detailed guides on setting up various service and how to integrate it on various platform. Visit the Firebase documentation https://firebase.google.com/docs to learn more about it.

b. **Firebase Firestore configuration**: Firebase Firestore is a flexible, scalable NoSQL cloud database that supports real-time synchronization across clients. To store and manage your app's data securely, follow the steps to configure Firestore:

   i. **Go to Firestore settings**: In the Firebase Console, click on **Firestore Database** from the left-hand menu under the **Build** section. You will be presented with an option to create a Firestore database. Click on the button to create the database as shown in the following figure:

Figure 7.14: Cloud Firestore creation screen on Firebase console

ii. **Set up Firestore database:** After clicking on the **Create database** button. You will be prompted to choose the database's server location and security rules mode, as shown in the following figure:

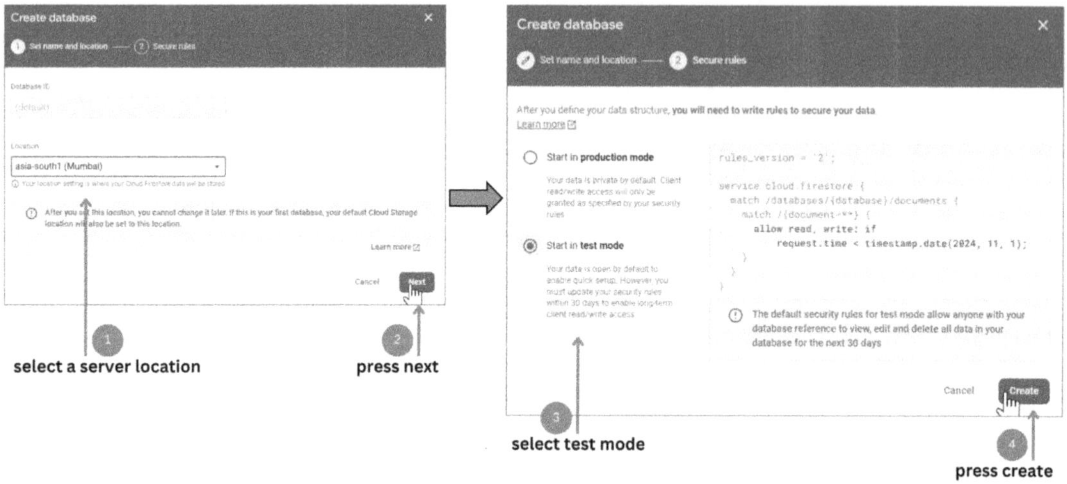

Figure 7.15: *Steps showing how to setup up Firebase Firestore*

After setting up both the authentication and database (Firestore) services, you are now ready to create you flutter project and integrate Firebase into it, which is discussed in detail in the next section.

Note: When you initialize Firebase Cloud Firestore in test mode, it grants open access to the database without authentication checks for 30 days. After this period, the database will be locked. You can visit the Firebase console to reset the timestamp, but it is recommended to implement authentication-based access for better security and control over database access.

Visionary: Crafting a digital vision board

In this section, we will integrate Firebase into the **Visionary** project, transforming it into a fully functional digital vision board with robust backend capabilities. The Visionary app will allow users to create, manage, and organize their goals, visions, and inspirations visually. By adding Firebase Authentication and Firestore to the app, we will enable users to securely sign up, log in, and store their vision board data in a cloud-based environment. The focus of this project will be implementing a modular app architecture. After completing the project, it will look like the following figure:

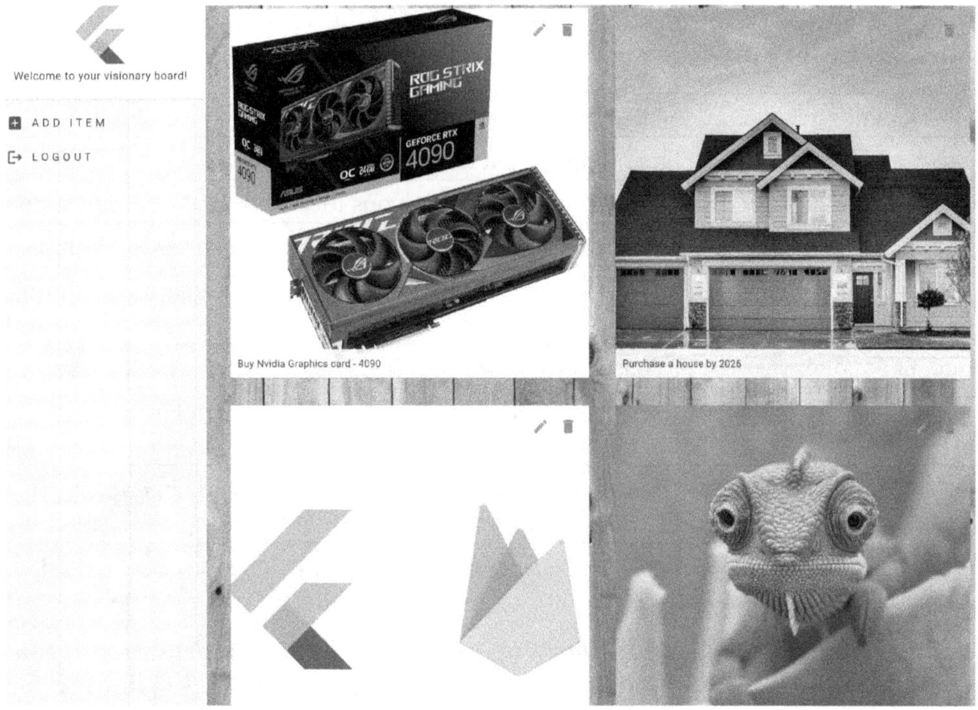

Figure 7.16: The visionary app preview

The first step is to set up the foundation for the Visionary project using IntelliJ IDEA. Open your IDE and create a new Flutter project. Set up the project name as visionary or any relevant project title that fits. Choose the target platforms (Windows, Web), as our focus is on web implementation of the project. Once the project is initialized, ensure that it builds successfully before moving on to installing dependencies.

Adding project dependencies

To enable the features required for Visionary, we need to integrate several third-party packages. These packages provide essential functionalities such as icons, animations, Firebase integration, form building, and state management. In the **`pubspec.yaml`** file, add the following dependencies:

- **`flutter_riverpod`**
- **`font_awesome_flutter`**
- **`firebase_core`**
- **`firebase_auth`**
- **`cloud_firestore`**
- **`flutter_form_builder`**
- **`form_builder_validators`**

These dependencies are integral to the functionality of the Visionary project and the table provides the use for each dependency:

Dependency	Use
`flutter_riverpod`	State management library for managing application state.
`font_awesome_flutter`	Provides Font Awesome icons for use in Flutter applications.
`firebase_core`	Core library for connecting Flutter applications to Firebase.
`firebase_auth`	Firebase library for authentication services (sign-in, sign-up, social authentication).
`cloud_firestore`	Firebase library for accessing Firestore database services.
`flutter_form_builder`	Library for building and managing forms in Flutter applications.
`form_builder_validators`	Provides validation functions for form fields in **`flutter_form_builder`**.

Table 7.1: Flutter dependency and its use

Note: To ensure you are using the most up-to-date versions of dependencies, you can run the following command in your terminal `flutter pub upgrade --major-versions`.

Setting up assets

The Visionary project relies on two static images, which are to be stored in the app's assets folder. To let Flutter know where the files are, you need to add them to **`pubspec.yaml`**. In the **`pubspec.yaml`** file, declare the assets path, shown as follows:

```
flutter:
  assets:
    - assets/images/
```

Setting up the project structure

The file structure of the project is given in the following figure, create the folders and files in IntelliJ IDEA to start:

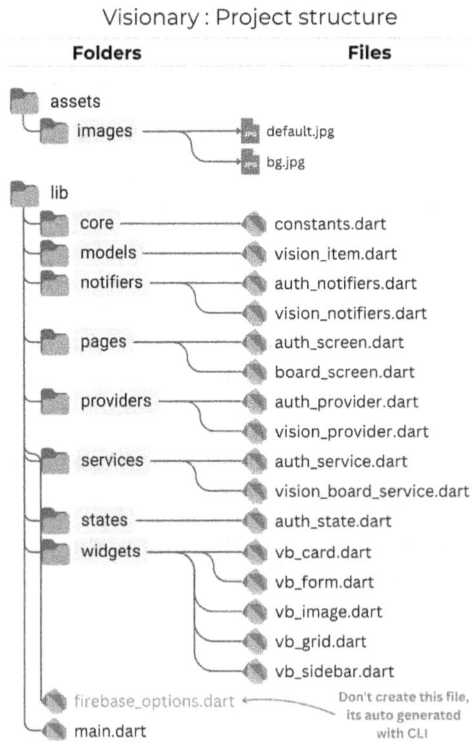

Figure 7.17: *The folder structure of the visionary app*

The Visionary project utilizes a component-based organization approach, leveraging **Riverpod** for state management. Here is a detailed breakdown of its structure, designed to make development streamlined and intuitive:

Assets

The assets folder contains static resources required by the application, such as images and fonts. In this project, the **`assets/images`** subfolder is used to store image files. Following files are kept inside the folder, you can choose to add any image files, but remember to use correct names of files in code:

- **default.jpg**: Serves as a placeholder or fallback image across the app.
- **bg.jpg**: A background image used to enhance the visual appeal of the application.

Core

This folder contains files that define constants and configurations used throughout the app. It contains one file for this project:

- **constants.dart**: Holds application-wide constants such as color codes, API endpoints, and reusable text strings.

Models

The `models` folder is used for data representation. Following file in stored in this folder:

- **vision_item.dart**: Represents the structure of a vision board item, including properties such as title, description, and image URL. Models ensure consistent data structures when working with features like the vision board.

Notifiers

The notifiers folder contains classes responsible for managing the app's state using **Riverpod**. Notifiers serve as the backbone of the state management system, ensuring data consistency across the app. The following files are stored in this folder:

- **auth_notifiers.dart**: Handles state changes related to user authentication, such as login status or user credentials.
- **vision_notifiers.dart**: Manages state changes for the vision board, such as updating or retrieving board items.

Pages

The pages folder will contain the user interface screens. This project has two screens in the following two files respectively:

- **auth_screen.dart:** Displays the user authentication interface, allowing users to sign in or register.
- **board_screen.dart:** Hosts the vision board interface, where users can add or view items.

Providers

The providers folder defines Riverpod providers, which act as bridges between the state (managed by notifiers) and the UI. It will contain two files:

- **auth_provider.dart**: Exposes authentication-related notifiers to the rest of the app.
- **vision_provider.dart**: Connects vision board notifiers with the screens that consume their state.

Services

The services folder encapsulates backend and API-related logic. By isolating service logic, the app remains modular and easier to maintain. It also has two files:

- **auth_service.dart:** Contains methods for user authentication, such as login, registration, and logout.

- **vision_board_service.dart:** Handles operations related to the vision board, such as fetching or saving items to the database.

States

The states folder defines specific state classes used by Riverpod notifiers. It has one file:

- **auth_state.dart**: Represents the various states of authentication, such as loading, authentication, or error.

Widgets

Reusable UI components are housed in the widgets folder, promoting code reusability and consistency. By isolating reusable components, this structure enhances maintainability. For visionary project, it contains the following files:

- **vb_card.dart**: A card widget used to display vision board items.
- **vb_form.dart**: A form widget for adding new items to the vision board.
- **vb_grid.dart**: A grid layout widget for organizing vision board items.
- **vb_image.dart**: A widget to display the background image.
- **vb_sidebar.dart**: A sidebar navigation widget for the app.

Note: In the widgets folder, the characters *'vb_'* are prepended to each generic file names, as they are vision board related files.

By adopting the preceding architecture, the Visionary app ensures a predictable and testable structure, making future enhancements, maintenance, and scaling more efficient.

Project Firebase integration

After completing the project setup, you will now add your project to Firebase website. Before continuing, you have to install Firebase cli, discussed in previous section. When you are ready, visit the Firebase console (**https://console.firebase.google.com**) and then click on add app section in console, given on topmost section, as shown in *Figure 7.13*, a page will slide in showing the three steps for connecting the app.

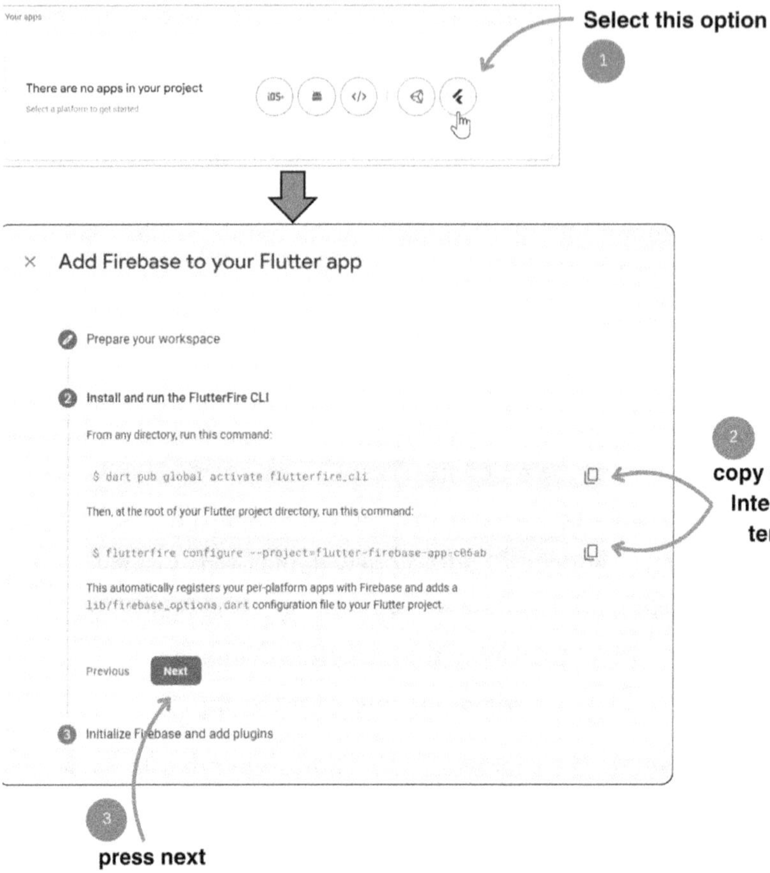

Figure 7.18: Steps to add Firebase with flutter project

To seamlessly integrate Firebase into your Visionary project, follow these guided steps to ensure proper setup and configuration:

- On **step 1,** click **Next** as you have already completed it.
- On **step 2**, switch back to IDE and open the terminal and then run the first and second commands given on website. This will register your app to Firebase console and store the configuration inside a generated file **`firebase_options.dart`**, do not edit/delete the file.
- On **step 3**, read the instructions for initializing the Firebase connection in the **`main.dart`** file. After that, click **Continue to Console** to return to the Firebase project dashboard.

Once the above step is complete, the next task is to implement the authentication and database logic using Firebase. This involves creating five key components, outlined as follows:

Component	File	Purpose
Setting up the constants	**constants.dart**	A centralized location for defining constants.
Authentication state	**auth_state.dart**	Represents the authentication states.
authentication service	**auth_service.dart**	Manages user authentication processes.
Vision board model	**vision_item.dart**	Defines the data structure for vision board items.
Data management service	**vision_board_service.dart**	Handles operations related to vision board data in Firebase.

Table 7.2: Components used for Firebase implementation

Centralizing app constants

The **core/constants.dart** file serves as a centralized location for defining constants used throughout the Visionary app. By consolidating all string literals, collection names, and configuration values in one place, this file enhances maintainability and consistency within the codebase. Add the following code to the **constants.dart** file:

```
// core/constants.dart

class Constants {
  // Firestore Collections
  static const String visionItemsCollection = 'vision_items';

  // Routes (for navigation)
  static const String boardScreen = '/board';
  static const String authScreen = '/auth';

  // UI Strings
  static const String appTitle = 'Visionary';
  static const String addVisionItem = 'Add/Edit your vision here!';
  static const String editVisionItem = 'Edit';
  static const String deleteVisionItem = 'Delete';
  static const String saveVisionItem = 'Save';
  static var itemText = 'Write your vision here';
  static var imageUrl = 'Enter an image URL';
  static const String emptyBoardMessage =
```

```
      'Your vision board is empty. Start adding your dreams!';

  // Firestore Document Fields
  static const String itemTextField = 'itemText';
  static const String imageUrlField = 'imageUrl';

  // Miscellaneous
  static const String googleSignInButtonText = 'Sign in with Google';

  // Image Placeholders
  static const String placeholderImage = "assets/images/default.jpg";

  static String sidebarTitle = 'Welcome to your Vision Board!';

  // Todo: add more constants as needed
}
```

By using constants, you avoid hardcoding values in multiple locations, reducing the risk of errors and making future updates more straightforward.

Handling authentication state

When handling authentication states, it is important to ensure that the app can easily track and respond to changes in the user's authentication status. The **`AuthState`** class simplifies this by representing the current authentication status of the user. It encapsulates key information, such as whether the user is logged in and any error messages that might occur during the authentication process. For example, when a user attempts to log in, the **`AuthState`** can be updated to reflect their login status (**`isLoggedIn`**) and display an appropriate error message (**`errorMessage`**) if the login fails. Add the following code to **`lib/states/auth_state.dart`** in the Visionary project:

```
// lib/states/auth_state.dart
class AuthState {
  final String? errorMessage;
  final bool isLoggedIn;

  AuthState({this.errorMessage, this.isLoggedIn = false});
}
```

The **AuthState** class can be extended to include more details as needed, such as the user's profile information or authentication tokens. For now, focus on the login status and error message, and make sure to update the **AuthState** whenever changes occur, such as during login, logout, or when an error arises. This will ensure a consistent and responsive user experience.

Creating Firebase authentication service

For implementing authentication, it is crucial to handle different scenarios, such as successful sign-ins, errors during authentication, and proper sign-out management. The **AuthService** class will be responsible for managing all Firebase authentication operations in the application. It will use Firebase's **FirebaseAuth** instance to handle tasks like checking if a user is logged in, signing in with Google, and signing out. The code will do the following three tasks:

1. **Checking if the user is logged in**: The **isLoggedIn** method verifies if a user is currently authenticated by checking the presence of **currentUser** from **FirebaseAuth**. It returns a **boolean** indicating the login status.
2. **Signing in with Google**: The **signInWithGoogle** method handles Google sign-ins. It creates a **GoogleAuthProvider**, displays the sign-in dialog, and processes the credentials returned. If the sign-in is successful, it returns an **AuthState** indicating that the user is logged in. If there is an issue, it returns an **AuthState** with an error message.
3. **Signing out the current user**: The **signOut** method signs out the user using FirebaseAuth's **signOut()** method. If successful, it updates the authentication state to reflect that the user is logged out. If an error occurs, it catches the exception and provides an error message.

Add this code in **lib/services/auth_service.dart** to implement Firebase authentication in the Visionary project:

```
// lib/services/auth_service.dart
import 'package:firebase_auth/firebase_auth.dart';
import 'package:flutter/material.dart';
import 'package:visionary_project/states/auth_state.dart';

/// Service class for handling authentication
class AuthService {
  final FirebaseAuth _auth = FirebaseAuth.instance;

  /// Checks if the user is logged in
  Future<bool> isLoggedIn() async {
```

```
    return _auth.currentUser != null;
  }

  /// Signs in the user with Google authentication
  Future<AuthState> signInWithGoogle() async {
    try {
      // Create a Google auth provider
      GoogleAuthProvider googleProvider = GoogleAuthProvider();
      // show the Google sign-in dialog
      var userCredentials = await _auth.
signInWithPopup(googleProvider);
      // If the user is not null, the sign-in was successful
      if (userCredentials.user != null) {
        // update the state to reflect the user's login status
        return AuthState(
          isLoggedIn: true,
        );
      } else {
        return AuthState(errorMessage: 'Sign in failed');
      }
    } on FirebaseAuthException catch (e) {
      debugPrint("FirebaseAuthException: ${e.message}");
      return AuthState(
        errorMessage: "Sign in failed: ${e.message}",
      );
    } catch (e) {
      debugPrint("Unknown error: $e");
      return AuthState(errorMessage: "Unknown error: $e");
    }
  }

  /// Signs out the current user
  Future<AuthState> signOut() async {
    try {
      await _auth.signOut();
      return AuthState(isLoggedIn: false);
    } catch (e) {
```

```
        debugPrint("Error signing out: $e");
        return AuthState(
          isLoggedIn: true,
          errorMessage: "Sign out failed: $e",
        );
      }
    }
  }
```

Note: Always ensure that you catch specific exceptions like FirebaseAuthException to provide meaningful error messages. Additionally, consider adding more authentication methods (e.g., email/password login) to your `AuthService` class in the future for more flexibility.

Defining the vision board item model

In any application, models serve as the backbone for structuring and managing data. They ensure consistency by representing the shape and attributes of the data being handled, whether it is fetched from a database, an API, or user input. For the visionary, the **`VisionItem`** model encapsulates all the necessary attributes for each item displayed on the board, simplifying state management and interactions with Firebase. This approach not only enhances code readability but also makes the app scalable and easier to maintain. The **`VisionItem`**, model ensures that each vision board item is uniquely identified, includes a descriptive name, and has an associated image URL.

A typical app can have multiple models depending on the various type of data objects it requires. Add the given code to **`lib/models/vision_item.dart`** file:

```
// lib/models/vision_item.dart
class VisionItem {
  final String id; // Unique identifier for Firestore document
  final String itemText; // The name of the item
  final String imageUrl; // The URL of the image

  VisionItem({
    required this.id,
    required this.itemText,
    required this.imageUrl,
  });
}
```

Creating board management service

This service is required in the Visionary project to manage the dynamic data of the vision board, ensuring real-time updates and smooth user interaction with the vision items stored in Firestore. The **VisionBoardService** class will be responsible for managing operations related to the vision board, which includes adding, updating, and deleting vision items, as well as fetching and listening to the list of vision items from Firebase Firestore. This service will act as a middle layer between the app and Firestore, making it easier to handle these operations in a structured way. It will contain the following blocks of code:

1. **VisionResult enum**: This **enum** represents the possible results of vision board operations, either success or failure. It is used to indicate whether an operation was successful or encountered an issue.

2. **Firebase Collection Reference**: The **visionCollection** property retrieves the Firestore collection where vision items are stored. It uses a constant from the **Constants** class to reference the correct collection name.

3. **Initial setup**: In the constructor, a listener is set up to listen for changes in the vision items collection in Firestore. Whenever there is a change in the collection, the snapshot is converted into a list of **VisionItem** objects, which are then added to a **stream**. This allows the app to reactively display changes in the vision board in real-time.

4. **Adding a Vision Item**: The **addVisionItem** method adds a new item to the Firestore collection. It takes the item's text and image URL, adds them to the collection, and returns a result indicating whether the operation was successful.

5. **Updating a Vision Item**: The **updateVisionItem** method updates an existing vision item based on its document ID. It allows modification of the item's text and image URL and returns a result indicating whether the update was successful.

6. **Deleting a Vision Item**: The **deleteVisionItem** method deletes an existing vision item by its document ID and returns a result indicating whether the operation was successful.

7. **Fetching Vision Items**: The **visionItemsStream** is a stream of **VisionItem** objects that is updated whenever changes occur in the Firestore collection. This allows the app to reactively fetch and display updated data.

8. **Disposing the Stream**: The dispose method ensures that the **stream controller** is closed when the service is no longer needed, preventing memory leaks.

Add the following code in **lib/services/vision_board_service.dart** to implement vision board operations:

```
// lib/services/vision_board_service.dart
import 'dart:async';

import 'package:cloud_firestore/cloud_firestore.dart';
import 'package:flutter/cupertino.dart';

import 'package:visionary_project/core/constants.dart';
import 'package:visionary_project/models/vision_item.dart';

/// Enum representing the result of a vision operation
enum VisionResult {
  success,
  failure,
}

/// Service class for handling vision board operations
class VisionBoardService {
  final FirebaseFirestore _firestore = FirebaseFirestore.instance;
  // StreamController to manage the stream of vision items
  final StreamController<List<VisionItem>> _visionItemsController =
      StreamController.broadcast();

  /// Gets the collection reference for vision items
  CollectionReference get visionCollection =>
      _firestore.collection(Constants.visionItemsCollection);

  VisionBoardService() {
    // Listen for changes to the vision items collection
    _firestore
        .collection(Constants.visionItemsCollection)
        .snapshots()
        .listen((snapshot) {
      // Convert the snapshot to a list of VisionItem objects
      final visionItems = snapshot.docs.map((doc) {
        // Create a VisionItem object from the document
        return VisionItem(
          id: doc.id,
```

```
          itemText: doc[Constants.itemTextField],
          imageUrl: doc[Constants.imageUrlField],
        );
      }).toList();
      // Add the vision items to the stream
      _visionItemsController.add(visionItems);
    });
  }

  /// Adds a new vision item to the collection
  Future<VisionResult> addVisionItem(String itemText, String imageUrl) async {
    try {
      // Add the vision item to the collection in firebase
      await visionCollection.add({
        Constants.itemTextField: itemText,
        Constants.imageUrlField: imageUrl,
      });
      return VisionResult.success;
    } catch (e) {
      debugPrint("Error adding vision item: $e");
      return VisionResult.failure;
    }
  }

  /// Updates an existing vision item in the collection
  Future<VisionResult> updateVisionItem(
    String documentId,
    String itemText,
    String imageUrl,
  ) async {
    try {
      // Update the vision item in the collection in firebase
      await visionCollection.doc(documentId).update({
        Constants.itemTextField: itemText,
        Constants.imageUrlField: imageUrl,
      });
```

```
      return VisionResult.success;
    } catch (e) {
      debugPrint("Error updating vision item: $e");
      return VisionResult.failure;
    }
  }

  /// Deletes a vision item from the collection
  Future<VisionResult> deleteVisionItem(String documentId) async {
    try {
      // Delete the vision item from the collection in firebase
      await visionCollection.doc(documentId).delete();
      return VisionResult.success;
    } catch (e) {
      debugPrint("Error deleting vision item: $e");
      return VisionResult.failure;
    }
  }

  /// Gets a stream of vision items from the collection
  Stream<List<VisionItem>> get visionItemsStream =>
      _visionItemsController.stream;

  void dispose() {
    _visionItemsController.close();
  }
}
```

By organizing the Firebase logic into dedicated service classes, you implemented the best practices for code maintainability and separation of concerns.

Note: To keep the code clean and easy to understand, the VisionResult enum is used instead of a sealed class. While a sealed class could offer more flexibility in handling different states (such as success, failure, or pending), an enum is a simpler approach that works well for this scenario. It helps maintain readability and ensures that the code remains straightforward without unnecessary complexity.

Integrating Firebase in the main.dart file

o integrate Firebase into the Visionary app and ensure everything is set up correctly, you need to update the **main.dart** file. This step ensures that Firebase is properly initialized when the app starts, and the app is ready to connect to Firebase services, such as authentication and Firestore, without any errors. This is a crucial step to make sure the Firebase features work as expected. Here is the code that should be added to **main.dart**:

```
import 'package:firebase_core/firebase_core.dart';
import 'package:flutter/gestures.dart';
import 'package:flutter/material.dart';
import 'package:flutter_riverpod/flutter_riverpod.dart';
import 'package:visionary_project/core/constants.dart';

import 'firebase_options.dart';

/// The main entry point of the application
Future<void> main() async {
  // Ensures that widget binding is initialized
  WidgetsFlutterBinding.ensureInitialized();
  // Initializes Firebase with the default options for the current platform
  await Firebase.initializeApp(
    options: DefaultFirebaseOptions.currentPlatform,
  );
  // Runs the VisionaryApp wrapped in a ProviderScope
  runApp(ProviderScope(child: const VisionaryApp()));
}

/// The root widget of the Visionary application
class VisionaryApp extends StatelessWidget {
  const VisionaryApp({super.key});

  @override
  Widget build(BuildContext context) {
    return MaterialApp(
      title: Constants.appTitle,
      theme: ThemeData(
        primarySwatch: Colors.blue,
      ),
```

```
        // temporary placeholder widget
        home: Placeholder(),
        debugShowCheckedModeBanner: false,
        // Custom scroll behavior to support touch, mouse, and unknown devices
        scrollBehavior: const MaterialScrollBehavior().copyWith(dragDevices: {
          PointerDeviceKind.touch,
          PointerDeviceKind.mouse,
          PointerDeviceKind.unknown
        }),
      );
    }
  }
```

In the above code, the following tasks have been set up:

- **Firebase Initialization**: The code begins by ensuring that widget binding is initialized using **`WidgetsFlutterBinding.ensureInitialized()`**. This is essential when dealing with asynchronous operations before the app runs. Then, **`Firebase.initializeApp()`** initializes Firebase with platform-specific settings defined in **`firebase_options.dart`**. This ensures that Firebase is properly set up for the current platform (web).
- **State management**: The app is wrapped in a **`ProviderScope`** widget, which is a part of the **`flutter_riverpod`** package. **Riverpod** is a state management solution, and **`ProviderScope`** is used to set up the app's state management for the app's lifecycle.
- **The app**: This is the root widget of the app, where the material design and theme are applied. For now, the home property is set to a **`Placeholder`** widget, which you will replace later with **`routes`** for the pages. The **`scrollBehavior`** ensures that the app is responsive to different input devices like touch, mouse, and other unknown devices.

Once you have added the above code to the **`main.dart`** file, run the app on a browser. If the app runs without issues, the Firebase setup is correct, and you can proceed with adding the authentication UI and logic.

Authentication in app

Authentication is the first and crucial part of any app, as it ensures secure access to user-specific features. In this app, authentication is integrated with Firebase, and the following components work together to manage the user authentication process and UI seamlessly.

Each component plays a vital role in handling various aspects of the authentication flow, from displaying the authentication UI to managing user login states. The following is an overview of the components used in the authentication process:

Component	File	Purpose
Providers	**auth_provider.dart**	Provides instances of **AuthService** and **AuthNotifier**, managing auth logic and state.
Notifiers	**auth_notifier.dart**	Manages the authentication state and provides methods to check login status, sign in, and sign out.
Background image	**vb_image.dart**	Provides a widget to set the background image
UI	**auth_screen.dart**	Manages the authentication UI for Google login.

Table 7.3: Components and their purpose in authentication

These components will be combined to create a robust authentication system in the app, ensuring users can securely log in and access their personalized experience.

Managing authentication state

In this app, the **AuthNotifier** class is responsible for managing the authentication state and providing methods to interact with the authentication system. It uses Riverpod for state management, ensuring that the authentication state is consistent across the app. The **AuthNotifier** works by interacting with the **AuthService** to handle login, sign-in, and sign-out processes. This management is crucial because it ensures that the app can react to changes in authentication, such as showing a login screen when the user is not logged in or displaying personalized content when they are authenticated. Now, add the following code to **lib/notifiers/auth_notifier.dart** to implement authentication state management:

```
// lib/notifiers/auth_notifier.dart

import 'package:flutter_riverpod/flutter_riverpod.dart';
import 'package:visionary_project/services/auth_service.dart';
import 'package:visionary_project/states/auth_state.dart';

/// Manages the authentication state and provides methods to update it
class AuthNotifier extends StateNotifier<AuthState> {
  final AuthService _firebaseService;

  AuthNotifier(this._firebaseService):
```

```
      super(AuthState(isLoggedIn:false));

  /// Checks the login status and updates the state
  Future<void> checkLoginStatus() async =>
      state = AuthState(isLoggedIn:await _firebaseService.isLoggedIn());

  /// Signs in the user using Google authentication and updates the state
  Future<void> signIn() async =>
      state = await _firebaseService.signInWithGoogle();

  /// Signs out the user and updates the state
  Future<void> signOut() async =>
      state = await _firebaseService.signOut();
}
```

The state is updated based on the user's actions and Firebase authentication results. For instance, the **checkLoginStatus** method verifies if the user is logged in and updates the **AuthState** accordingly, while **signIn** and **signOut** handle Google authentication and log the user out respectively.

Setting up authentication providers

Providers are required because they allow the app to access and manage the authentication state efficiently. By using **Riverpod**, the authentication state and logic are decoupled from the UI, ensuring better maintainability and testability. The **auth_provider.dart** file uses Riverpod to set up providers for both **AuthService** and **AuthNotifier**. These providers manage the instances and dependencies related to authentication, ensuring that authentication-related state is easily accessible and can be modified in a consistent and organized manner. The **authServiceProvider** creates an instance of **AuthService**, which is used for handling authentication logic. The **authProvider** provides an instance of **AuthNotifier**, which not only holds the authentication state but also exposes methods to interact with the authentication service. Add the following code to **lib/providers/auth_provider.dart** to set up the authentication provider:

```
// lib/providers/auth_provider.dart

import 'package:flutter_riverpod/flutter_riverpod.dart';
import 'package:visionary_project/notifiers/auth_notifier.dart';
import 'package:visionary_project/services/auth_service.dart';
import 'package:visionary_project/states/auth_state.dart';

```

```
/// Provides an instance of AuthService
final authServiceProvider = Provider<AuthService>((ref) {
  return AuthService();
});

/// Provides an instance of AuthNotifier
final authProvider =
  StateNotifierProvider<AuthNotifier, AuthState>((ref) {
  final authService = ref.watch(authServiceProvider);
  return AuthNotifier(authService);
});
```

This code ensures that both the **AuthService** and **AuthNotifier** are provided globally to the app, making the authentication logic and state management available in any widget that needs it.

Creating a common background widget

The **BackgroundImage** widget takes an optional **localPath** argument, which allows the app to use a custom background image (with a default value of **'assets/images/bg.jpg'**). The image is set to cover the entire screen, repeating as necessary to fill the space, with a **BoxFit.cover** property to ensure the image fills the screen proportionally. This widget is crucial because it simplifies background management. Instead of adding background code to every individual screen, you can use this widget to provide a uniform background wherever required. Now, add the following code to **lib/widgets/background_image.dart** to create the common background widget:

```
// lib/widgets/background_image.dart

import 'package:flutter/material.dart';

class BackgroundImage extends StatelessWidget {
  final String localPath;

  const BackgroundImage({
    super.key,
    this.localPath = 'assets/images/bg.jpg', // default image
  });

  @override
  Widget build(BuildContext context) {
```

```
    return Positioned.fill(
      child: Image.asset(
        localPath,
        fit: BoxFit.cover,
        repeat: ImageRepeat.repeat,
        width: double.infinity,
        height: double.infinity,
      ),
    );
  }
}
```

This approach keeps the UI code clean and manageable while ensuring the app's appearance remains visually consistent.

Designing the authentication UI

Designing the authentication UI is an essential step for creating an engaging user experience. In this app, the **`AuthScreen`** manages the authentication process, displaying a login button and handling user interaction with Firebase. Below is an explanation of the code and how each part contributes to building the authentication UI.

Part 1: Class and State Setup

The **`AuthScreen`** class will extends **`ConsumerStatefulWidget`**, making it a stateful widget that can listen to state changes provided by Riverpod. The **`ConsumerState`** is a subclass that allows the widget to interact with the state managed by Riverpod. Add the following code in the **`lib/pages/auth_screen.dart`** file:

```
class AuthScreen extends ConsumerStatefulWidget {
  const AuthScreen({super.key});

  @override
  ConsumerState<AuthScreen> createState() => _AuthScreenState();
}
```

Part 2: Initialization (initState method)

In this part, **`initState()`** is overridden to ensure that the authentication status is checked right after the widget is built. The **`checkLoginStatus()`** method is called to check whether the user is logged in and updates the state accordingly. Update the following code in the **`auth_screen.dart`** file after the **`AuthScreen`** class:

```
/// State class for AuthScreen
class _AuthScreenState extends ConsumerState<AuthScreen> {
  /// initState() is called after the widget is built for the 1st time
  @override
  void initState() {
    super.initState();
    // this callback is called after the frame is displayed
    WidgetsBinding.instance.addPostFrameCallback((_) {
   // read the authProvider.
notifier and call checkLoginStatus() method
      ref.read(authProvider.notifier).checkLoginStatus();
    });
  }
  @override
  Widget build(BuildContext context) {
    return Placeholder(); // temporary
  }
}
```

Part 3: Sign-In Button Handling

This method is triggered when the sign-in button is pressed. It calls the **`signIn()`** method from the **`AuthNotifier`** (managed by Riverpod) to initiate the Google sign-in process. Update the following code after the **`initState()`** method:

```
void onSignInPressed() {
  ref.read(authProvider.notifier).signIn();
}
```

Part 4: Building the center content

This method builds the center content of the authentication screen. It consists of a title and a sign-in button. The title uses a bold, large font to display the app's name (**`Constants.appTitle`**). Below the title, there is a Google sign-in button styled with **`ElevatedButton.icon`** that displays the Google logo and a text label, "Sign in with Google". When pressed, it calls **`onSignInPressed`** to initiate the sign-in process. Update the following code below the **`onSignInPressed()`** method:

```
Widget buildAuthCenter(BuildContext context) {
  return Center(
    child: Column(
      mainAxisAlignment: MainAxisAlignment.center,
      children: [
```

```
        const Text(
          Constants.appTitle,
          style: TextStyle(
            fontSize: 77,
            fontWeight: FontWeight.bold,
            color: Colors.white,
          ),
        ),
        const SizedBox(height: 20),
        ElevatedButton.icon(
          onPressed: onSignInPressed,
          icon: const Icon(FontAwesomeIcons.google),
          label: const Text(Constants.googleSignInButtonText),
          style: ButtonStyle(
            fixedSize: WidgetStateProperty.all(const Size(350, 60)),
          ),
        ),
      ],
    ),
  );
}
```

Part 5: Listening for AuthState Changes

The **ref.listen<AuthState>()** method will listen to the authentication state. If the user is logged in (**next.isLoggedIn** is true), it navigates to the **VisionBoardScreen**. If there is an error (i.e., **next.errorMessage** is not null), it shows a **Snackbar** with the error message. Update the following code inside the **build()** method before the return statement:

```
@override
Widget build(BuildContext context) {
  ref.listen<AuthState>(authProvider, (previous, next) {
    if (next.isLoggedIn) {
      Navigator.pushReplacementNamed(context, Constants.boardScreen);
    } else if (next.errorMessage != null) {
      ScaffoldMessenger.of(context).showSnackBar(
        SnackBar(
          content: Text(next.errorMessage ?? 'An error occurred'),
          duration: const Duration(seconds: 5),
        ),
```

```
        );
      }
    });
    return Placeholder(); // temporary
  }
```

Part 6: Setting the Page Layout

In the **build()** method, the **Scaffold** widget is used to structure the screen. The background image (**BackgroundImage()**) is positioned at the bottom layer using **Stack**, and the authentication content (**buildAuthCenter()**) is placed above it. The Stack widget allows layering multiple widgets on top of each other. Update the following code inside the **build()** method replacing the **Placeholder()** widget:

```
return Scaffold(
  body: Stack(
    children: [
      BackgroundImage(),
      buildAuthCenter(context),
    ],
  ),
);
```

Updating the main.dart file

Once the **auth_screen.dart** is complete, the next step is to update the **main.dart** file. Update the **main.dart** file, remove the home property and add **initialRoute** and **routes** parameters as shown:

```
class VisionaryApp extends StatelessWidget {
  ...

  @override
  Widget build(BuildContext context) {
    return MaterialApp(
      ...
      initialRoute: Constants.authScreen,
      routes: {
        // Route for the authentication screen
        Constants.authScreen: (context) => const AuthScreen(),
        // Route for the board screen - placeholder for now
        Constants.boardScreen: (context) => const Placeholder(),
```

```
            },
                ...
        );
    }
}
```

Import all the necessary dependencies and run the app to test that the app is working by logging in with your Google accounts, on success the placeholder will be displayed. The following figure shows the completed authentication page in app:

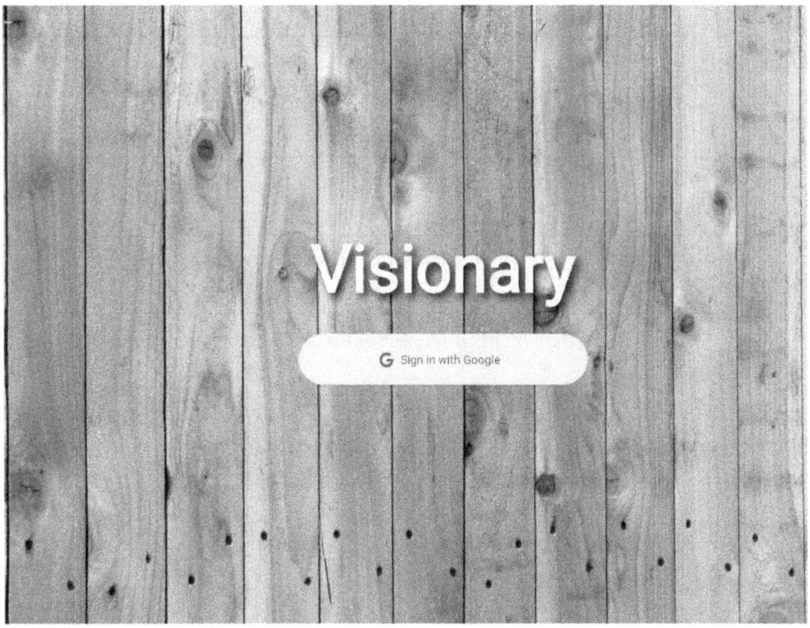

Figure 7.19: *The completed authentication page of visionary app*

Developing vision board

The vision board is the heart of the application, allowing users to organize and visualize their goals. This section focuses on breaking the page into manageable components, each with a specific purpose, to ensure the application remains modular, scalable, and maintainable. The following is a breakdown of the components that will be developed:

Component	File	Purpose
Providers	`vision_provider.dart`	Provides instances to manage the state of the vision board and facilitate communication with notifiers.
Notifiers	`vision_notifier.dart`	Manages the state logic for vision board items, including adding, editing, and removing items.
Widgets	`vb_card.dart`	Displays individual vision board items in a card format.
	`vb_form.dart`	Handles the user input form for adding and editing vision board items.
	`vb_image.dart`	Provides a widget to set the background image
	`vb_sidebar.dart`	Provides navigation and additional options for interacting with the vision board.
	`vb_grid.dart`	Arranges vision board items in a grid layout for easy viewing.
UI	`board_screen.dart`	Combines all components to build the complete vision board user interface.

Table 7.4: Components and their purpose for the vision board

Each of these components contributes to the overall functionality and user experience of the Vision Board. Below, we will explain the purpose of each file in detail and provide code examples to guide the implementation.

Note: This section is very long and detailed. It can feel overwhelming sometimes but as you follow along you will learn the best practices for making modern and scalable apps.

Managing vision board state with notifiers

In the **Authentication** section above, we built the **`AuthNotifier`** to manage user authentication state. Similarly, for the Vision Board, we need a dedicated notifier to manage the state of vision items, enabling real-time updates between the UI and the backend. The **`VisionItemsNotifier`** acts as the central controller for all state-related operations on the vision board. It handles tasks such as fetching vision items, adding or updating items, and deleting them, ensuring a seamless user experience and synchronization with the backend. Below is the implementation of **`VisionItemsNotifier`**, responsible for managing vision board state, write in inside **`lib/notifiers/vision_notifier.dart`** file:

```
// lib/notifiers/vision_notifier.dart

import 'package:flutter_riverpod/flutter_riverpod.dart';
import 'package:visionary_project/models/vision_item.dart';
```

```
import 'package:visionary_project/services/vision_board_service.dart';

class VisionItemsNotifier extends StateNotifier<List<VisionItem>> {
  final VisionBoardService visionBoardService;

  VisionItemsNotifier(this.visionBoardService) : super([]) {
    // Load the vision items when the notifier is created
    _loadVisionItems();
  }

  Future<void> _loadVisionItems() async {
   // Wait for the visionItemsStream to emit the first value
    final visionItems=await visionBoardService.visionItemsStream.first;
    // Update the state with the vision items
    state = visionItems;
  }

  Future<void> addOrUpdateItem(
    String itemText,
    String imageUrl,
    VisionItem? visionItem,
  ) async {
    // If the vision item is null, add a new item; otherwise, update the existing item
    if (visionItem == null) {
      await visionBoardService.addVisionItem(itemText, imageUrl);
    } else {
      await visionBoardService.updateVisionItem(
        visionItem.id,
        itemText,
        imageUrl,
      );
    }
    // reload the vision items
    _loadVisionItems();
  }
```

```
  Future<void> deleteItem(String id) async {
    // Delete the vision item
    await visionBoardService.deleteVisionItem(id);
    // Remove the item from the state
    state = state.where((item) => item.id != id).toList();
  }
}
```

In the preceding code, the following tasks are being done:

- **Loading items**: `_loadVisionItems()` retrieves the list of vision board items from the backend service (`VisionBoardService`) and updates the notifier's state.
- **Adding or updating items**: `addOrUpdateItem()` determines if a new vision item needs to be added or an existing one updated, based on the presence of `visionItem`. After each operation, it reloads the state to reflect the changes.
- **Deleting items**: `deleteItem()` removes an item from the backend and updates the local state to remove it from the current list.

Setting up vision board providers

In this section, we set up the providers necessary to manage and access vision board data. For the vision board, we establish three providers: one for the service, one for the notifier, and one for accessing the stream of vision items. Now, write the following code in the file **`lib/providers/vision_provider.dart`** file to implement the providers:

```
// lib/providers/vision_provider.dart

import 'package:flutter_riverpod/flutter_riverpod.dart';
import 'package:visionary_project/models/vision_item.dart';
import 'package:visionary_project/notifiers/vision_notifier.dart';
import 'package:visionary_project/services/vision_board_service.dart';

/// Provider for the vision board service
final visionBoardServiceProvider = Provider<VisionBoardService>((ref) {
  return VisionBoardService();
});

/// Provides a notifier for vision items
```

```
final visionItemsNotifierProvider =
    StateNotifierProvider<VisionItemsNotifi
er, List<VisionItem>>((ref) {
  // The ref parameter is an instance of Provider-
Ref, which is used to read other providers
  final visionBoardService = ref.watch(visionBoardServiceProvider);
  return VisionItemsNotifier(visionBoardService);
});

/// Provides a stream of vision items
final visionItemsProvider = StreamProvider<List<VisionItem>>((ref) {
  final visionBoardService = ref.watch(visionBoardServiceProvider);
  return visionBoardService.visionItemsStream;
});
```

In the code above, three instances are being created:

- The **visionBoardServiceProvider** creates an instance of the **VisionBoardService**. This service is responsible for backend operations like fetching, adding, and deleting vision items.
- The **visionItemsNotifierProvider** creates an instance of **VisionItemsNotifier** while injecting the **VisionBoardService** instance. This notifier manages the state of the vision board items and provides methods to add, update, delete, and fetch items.
- The **visionItemsProvider** listens to a real-time stream of vision items provided by the **VisionBoardService**. It ensures that any updates from the backend are reflected in the app without manual intervention.

This completes the domain logic of the vision board, the next step is to complete the presentation layers, starting with widgets for the vision board page.

Designing vision board widgets

In this section, we will design the various widgets that are part of the vision board interface. Each widget has a distinct role in displaying the vision items, handling actions like editing and delete, and organizing the layout. The following widgets are to be created before designing the vision board UI as shown in the following figure:

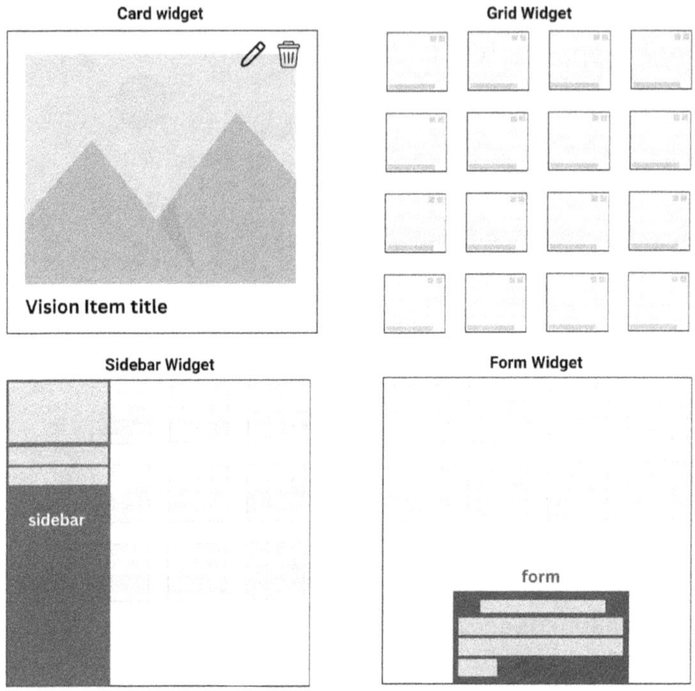

Figure 7.20: *The widgets for the vision board page*

This section is quite detailed, but it provides an in-depth understanding, ensuring you grasp every crucial aspect thoroughly. We will focus on one widget at a time.

Vision board card widget

The **`VisionItemCard`** widget is a core component of the vision board interface. It serves as the visual representation of a single vision item, displaying its associated **image** and **text**, along with action buttons for **editing** and **deleting**. This widget ensures a clean, responsive design while maintaining interactivity for managing vision items. Write the following code in the file **`lib/widgets/vb_card.dart`** file:

```
/// A card widget that displays a vision item
class VisionItemCard extends StatelessWidget {
  /// The vision item to display
  final VisionItem visionItem;

  /// Callback function to handle edit action
  final VoidCallback onEdit;

  /// Callback function to handle delete action
  final VoidCallback onDelete;
```

```

  /// Constructor for VisionItemCard
  const VisionItemCard({
    super.key,
    required this.visionItem,
    required this.onEdit,
    required this.onDelete,
  });

  @override
  Widget build(BuildContext context) {
    return Placeholder(); // temporary placeholder
  }
}
```

In the code above, the **VisionItemCard** constructor initializes the widget with three required parameters; **visionItem** represents the vision item to be displayed. The **onEdit()** is a callback function triggered when the user taps the **Edit** button. The **onDelete()** callback function triggered when the user taps the **Delete** button. The **build()** method contains a temporary placeholder. Next, create the following methods to generate the different sections of the card:

- **The visionImage method:** This method builds the image section of the card. It uses a **FadeInImage.assetNetwork** widget to load the vision item's image from a URL, with a placeholder displayed during loading. If the image fails to load, it falls back to a default placeholder image using the **imageErrorBuilder**. The image is styled to fit the card with appropriate dimensions and scaling. Add it inside the **VisionItemCard** class as shown below:

```
class VisionItemCard extends StatelessWidget {
  ...
  /// Builds the image section of the card
  Widget visionImage(double height) {
    return FadeInImage.assetNetwork(
      placeholder: Constants.placeholderImage,
      image: visionItem.imageUrl,
      fit: BoxFit.cover,
      width: double.infinity,
      height: height,
      imageErrorBuilder: (context, error, stackTrace) {
        return Image.asset(
```

```
          Constants.placeholderImage,
          fit: BoxFit.cover,
          width: double.infinity,
          height: height,
        );
      },
    );
  }
}
```

- **The bottomText method:** This method creates the text section displayed at the bottom of the card. A **`Container`** widget is used to provide padding and a semi-transparent white background, enhancing readability. It displays the vision item's descriptive text using a **`Text`** widget. Add the following code inside the **`VisionItemCard`** class:

```
/// A card widget that displays a vision item
class VisionItemCard extends StatelessWidget {
  ...
  /// Builds the bottom text section of the card
  Widget bottomText(context) {
    return Positioned(
      bottom: 0,
      child: Container(
        width: MediaQuery.of(context).size.width,
        padding: const EdgeInsets.all(10),
        color: Colors.white.withValues(alpha: 0.9), // 90% opacity
        child: Column(
          crossAxisAlignment: CrossAxisAlignment.start,
          mainAxisSize: MainAxisSize.min,
          children: [
            Column(
              crossAxisAlignment: CrossAxisAlignment.start,
              children: [
                Text(visionItem.itemText),
              ],
            ),
          ],
        ),
```

```
          ),
        );
    }
  }
```

- **The actionButton method:** This method builds the action buttons for editing and deleting the vision item. Positioned in the top-right corner, the buttons use **`IconButton`** widgets with distinct colors (blue for edit and red for delete) to improve usability. Each button is linked to its respective callback function (**`onEdit`** and **`onDelete`**), enabling user interaction with the vision item. Add the following code inside the **`VisionItemCard`** class:

```
/// A card widget that displays a vision item
class VisionItemCard extends StatelessWidget {
  ...
  /// Builds the action buttons (edit and delete) for the card
  Widget actionButton() {
    return Positioned(
      width: 100,
      right: 10,
      top: 10,
      child: OverflowBar(
        alignment: MainAxisAlignment.end,
        overflowSpacing: 10,
        children: [
          IconButton(
              icon: const Icon(Icons.edit, color: Colors.blue),
              onPressed: onEdit,
              tooltip: Constants.editVisionItem),
          IconButton(
            onPressed: onDelete,
            icon: const Icon(Icons.delete, color: Colors.red),
            tooltip: Constants.deleteVisionItem,
          ),
        ],
      ),
    );
  }
}
```

- **Update the build method**: The build method constructs the **VisionItemCard** widget's layout. It creates a card with a rectangular shape and uses a **Stack** widget to overlay three key components: the vision image, descriptive text at the bottom, and action buttons at the top-right. This structure ensures the card is visually organized and functional. Replace the **build()** method code in the class:

```
/// A card widget that displays a vision item
class VisionItemCard extends StatelessWidget {
  ...
  @override
  Widget build(BuildContext context) {
    const double height = 600;
    return Card(
      shape: RoundedRectangleBorder(
        borderRadius: BorderRadius.circular(0),
      ),
      child: Stack(
        children: [visionImage(height),
                   bottomText(context),
                   actionButton(),
        ],
      ),
    );
  }
} // End of Card widget
```

This completes the vision board card widget.

Vision board form widget

The Vision board form widget provides a structured way to add or edit a vision item for the Visionary project. This widget includes fields for entering text and an image URL, making it an essential component for user input. It uses the **flutter_form_builder** package to simplify form creation and validation. The form is implemented as a stateless widget called **AddItemForm**, which accepts three primary parameters:

- **initialItemText**: A default text value for the vision item.
- **initialImageUrl**: A default URL for the image associated with the vision.
- **onSubmit**: A callback function triggered upon form submission.

Below the constructor, the **_saveForm()** method extracts and validates the data from the user input fields and then passes the information to the callback method. Write the following code inside the **lib/widgets/vb_form.dart** file:

```
// lib/widgets/vb_form.dart
import 'package:flutter/material.dart';
import 'package:flutter_form_builder/flutter_form_builder.dart';
import 'package:form_builder_validators/form_builder_validators.dart';
import 'package:visionary_project/core/constants.dart';

/// A form widget for adding or editing a vision item
class AddItemForm extends StatelessWidget {
  /// The initial text for the item
  final String initialItemText;

  /// The initial URL for the image
  final String initialImageUrl;

  /// Callback function to handle form submission
  final Function(String, String) onSubmit;

  /// The global form key
  final formKey = GlobalKey<FormBuilderState>();

  /// Constructor for AddItemForm
  AddItemForm({
    super.key,
    this.initialItemText = '',
    this.initialImageUrl = '',
    required this.onSubmit,
  });
  /// handles form submission local and passed data to callback
  void _saveForm() {
    if (formKey.currentState?.saveAndValidate() ?? false) {
      final itemText = formKey.currentState?.fields['itemText']?.value;
      final imageUrl = formKey.currentState?.fields['imageUrl']?.value;
      onSubmit(itemText ?? '', imageUrl ?? '');
    }
  }

```

```
  @override
  Widget build(BuildContext context) {
    return Padding(
      padding: const EdgeInsets.all(16.0),
      child: FormBuilder(
        key: formKey,
        child: Column(
          mainAxisSize: MainAxisSize.min,
          children: [
            buildHeading(),
            buildFormField('itemText', Constants.itemText,
                  Icons.text_fields),
            buildFormField('imageUrl', Constants.imageUrl,
                  Icons.image),
            buildSaveButton(),
          ],
        ),
      ),
    );
  }
} // End of form

```

The Vision board form widget includes three essential helper methods for building its structure: **buildHeading**, **buildFormField**, and **buildSaveButton**. These methods encapsulate specific functionalities, keeping the code modular and readable. Update the **AddItemForm** class with the following code:

```
class AddItemForm extends StatelessWidget {
  ...

  Widget buildHeading() {
    return const Text(
      Constants.addVisionItem,
      style: TextStyle(fontSize: 24),
    );
  }

  Widget buildFormField(String name, String labelText, IconData icon) {
```

```
    return FormBuilderTextField(
      name: name,
      initialValue: name == 'itemText' ? initialItemText : initialImageUrl,
      decoration: InputDecoration(
        labelText: labelText,
        icon: Icon(icon),
      ),
      validator: FormBuilderValidators.required(),
    );
  }

  Widget buildSaveButton() {
    return Align(
      alignment: Alignment.centerRight,
      child: OutlinedButton(
        onPressed: _saveForm,
        child: const Text(Constants.saveVisionItem),
      ),
    );
  }
}
```

In the above code, the following method are defined:

- **buildHeading**: This method creates a heading text widget for the form. It displays a constant title, **`Constants.addVisionItem`**, to provide context for the form.
- **buildFormField**: This method dynamically builds text input fields for the form. It takes the field name, label text, and icon as parameters, making it reusable for multiple input fields.
- **buildSaveButton**: This method creates a button for form submission. It validates the form and triggers the onSubmit callback when clicked.

This completes the form widget for the vision board.

Vision board grid widget

The **`VisionGrid`** widget displays a grid of vision items. It listens to the **`visionItemsProvider`**, which provides the state of vision items. The widget ensures a responsive UI by showing a loading indicator while the data is being fetched, displaying an error message if something goes wrong, and rendering the vision items in a grid once the data is successfully retrieved. the **`VisionGrid`** class is defined, extending **`ConsumerWidget`** from Riverpod, which allows the widget to listen to changes in state. The build method uses the **`visionItemsProvider`** to fetch the vision items. The **visionItemsAsyncValue.when** method is used to handle the different states of the data:

- **Data**: If data is available, the **buildGrid** method is called to display the vision items in a grid.
- **Loading**: If the data is loading, the **buildLoading** method is triggered to show a progress indicator.
- **Error**: If there is an error in fetching the data, the **buildError** method displays an error message.

Add the following code in the **lib/widgets/vb_grid.dart** file:

```
// lib/widgets/vb_grid.dart

import 'package:flutter/material.dart';
import 'package:flutter_riverpod/flutter_riverpod.dart';
import 'package:visionary_project/core/constants.dart';
import 'package:visionary_project/models/vision_item.dart';
import 'package:visionary_project/notifiers/vision_notifier.dart';
import 'package:visionary_project/providers/vision_provider.dart';
import 'package:visionary_project/widgets/vb_card.dart';
import 'package:visionary_project/widgets/vb_form.dart';

class VisionGrid extends ConsumerWidget {
  const VisionGrid({super.key});

  @override
  Widget build(BuildContext context, WidgetRef ref) {
    final visionItemsAsyncValue = ref.watch(visionItemsProvider);
    final visionItemsNotifier = ref.read(
      visionItemsNotifierProvider.notifier);

    return visionItemsAsyncValue.when(
      data: (visionItems) =>
          buildGrid(context, visionItems, visionItemsNotifier),
      loading: () => buildLoading(),
      error: (error, stackTrace) => buildError(error),
    );
  }
}
```

In the above code, the **buildGrid** method is responsible for constructing the grid view of vision items. It will first check if the **visionItems** list is empty: If empty, it will return a message using the **buildEmptyMessage** method to inform the user.

If not empty, it will return a **GridView.builder** that arranges the vision items in a grid layout. The grid is configured with padding, spacing, and a maximum cross-axis extent. For each item in the grid, a **VisionItemCard** is rendered, showing details of the vision item. This card includes options to edit or delete the item, with corresponding actions triggered through modal bottom sheets and asynchronous functions managed by the **visionItemsNotifier**. Update the **VisionGrid** class with the **buildGrid()** method given below:

```
class VisionGrid extends ConsumerWidget {
 ...
  Widget buildGrid(
    BuildContext context,
    List<VisionItem> visionItems,
    VisionItemsNotifier visionItemsNotifier,
  ) {
    if (visionItems.isEmpty) {
      return buildEmptyMessage();
    } else {
      return GridView.builder(
        padding: const EdgeInsets.all(30),
        gridDelegate: const SliverGridDelegateWithMaxCrossAxisExtent(
          maxCrossAxisExtent: 600,
          crossAxisSpacing: 30,
          mainAxisSpacing: 30,
        ),
        itemCount: visionItems.length,
        itemBuilder: (context, index) {
          final visionItem = visionItems[index];
          return VisionItemCard(
            visionItem: visionItem,
            onEdit: () => showModalBottomSheet(
              context: context,
              builder: (context) => AddItemForm(
                initialImageUrl: visionItem.imageUrl,
                initialItemText: visionItem.itemText,
```

```
                onSubmit: (itemText, imageUrl) async {
                  Navigator.pop(context);
                  await visionItemsNotifier.addOrUpdateItem(
                    itemText,
                    imageUrl,
                    visionItem,
                  );
                },
              ),
            ),
            onDelete: () async => await visionItemsNotifier.deleteItem(
              visionItem.id,
            ),
          );
        });
  }}
} // End of grid widget
```

The above code uses small three helper methods to handle different UI states:

- **buildLoading**: Displays a **`CircularProgressIndicator`** in the center of the screen while data is loading.
- **buildError**: Displays an error message in the center of the screen when there is an issue fetching the data.
- **buildEmptyMessage**: Displays a message to the user when no vision items are available. The message is styled with a large, italicized, white font to make it visually prominent.

Add the following code inside the **`VisionGrid`** to complete it:

```
class VisionGrid extends ConsumerWidget {
  ...
  Widget buildLoading() {
    return const Center(child: CircularProgressIndicator());
  }

  Widget buildError(Object error) {
    return Center(child: Text('Error: $error'));
  }

```

```
  Widget buildEmptyMessage() {
    return const Center(
      child: Text(
        Constants.emptyBoardMessage,
        style: TextStyle(
          fontSize: 32,
          color: Colors.white,
          fontStyle: FontStyle.italic,
        ),
      ),
    );
  }
}
```

This completes the vision board grid widget.

Vision board sidebar widget

The **VisionDrawer** class defines a sidebar drawer for the Visionary app, structured as a StatelessWidget. It takes three required parameters: **color** for background customization, **signOut** as a callback for user logout, and **addItem** for adding new items. The build method constructs the drawer using the **Drawer** widget, which has a defined shape, elevation, and background color. Inside, the **Column** widget arranges its elements, including the **buildDrawerHeader()** function for the header and two interactive list tiles. Each list tile is created using **buildListTile()**, displaying an icon and text while triggering the respective callback function when tapped. Write the following code in **lib/widgets/vb_sidebar.dart** file:

```
// lib/widgets/vb_sidebar.dart
import 'package:flutter/material.dart';
import 'package:visionary_project/core/constants.dart';

/// A drawer widget for the Visionary app
class VisionDrawer extends StatelessWidget {
  /// The background color of the drawer
  final Color color;

  /// Callback functions to handle sign out and add item
  final VoidCallback signOut;
  final VoidCallback addItem;

```

```
  /// Constructor for VisionDrawer
  const VisionDrawer({
    super.key,
    required this.color,
    required this.signOut,
    required this.addItem,
  });

  @override
  Widget build(BuildContext context) {
    return Drawer(
      shape: const RoundedRectangleBorder(
        borderRadius: BorderRadius.all(Radius.circular(0)),
      ),
      elevation: 2,
      backgroundColor: color,
      child: Column(
        children: [
          buildDrawerHeader(),
          buildListTile(
            icon: Icons.add_box,
            text: 'A D D  I T E M›,
            onTap: addItem,
          ),
          buildListTile(
            icon: Icons.logout,
            text: ‘L O G O U T’,
            onTap: signOut,
          ),
        ],
      ),
    );
  }
}
```

The **buildDrawerHeader()** method will define the top section of the drawer using **DrawerHeader**, setting its background to white and centering its contents. A **Column** arranges a **FlutterLogo**, serving as a placeholder, and a **Text** widget displaying the sidebar title retrieved from **Constants.sidebarTitle**. The **buildListTile()** function, on the other hand, will generate reusable list items with an icon, text, and **onTap()** function. The **ListTile** widget ensures a consistent structure, with a hover effect set to white for better UI feedback. Update the **VisionDrawer** class by adding the methods as shown below:

```
class VisionDrawer extends StatelessWidget {
  ...
  Widget buildDrawerHeader() {
    return DrawerHeader(
      decoration: const BoxDecoration(
        color: Colors.white,
      ),
      child: Center(
        child: Column(
          children: [
            const FlutterLogo(size: 100),
            Text(Constants.sidebarTitle),
          ],
        ),
      ),
    );
  }

  Widget buildListTile({
    required IconData icon,
    required String text,
    required VoidCallback onTap,
  }) {
    return ListTile(
      hoverColor: Colors.white,
      leading: Icon(icon),
      title: Text(text),
      onTap: onTap,
    );
  }
} // End of Sidebar
```

Now all the widgets are complete, so now you can start building the vision board UI and integrate all the widgets created above.

Building the vision board user interface

In this section, we will walk through the **BoardScreen** widget, which acts as the main user interface for displaying and managing the vision board. The screen adapts its layout for both portrait and landscape orientations, ensuring a seamless experience across different device sizes. The widget leverages **Riverpod** for state management and offers functionalities like adding new items to the board, handling user sign-out, and displaying a grid of vision items. Add the given code to the **lib/pages/board_screen.dart** file:

```
// lib/pages/board_screen.dart

import 'package:flutter/material.dart';
import 'package:flutter_riverpod/flutter_riverpod.dart';
import 'package:visionary_project/core/constants.dart';
import 'package:visionary_project/notifiers/vision_notifier.dart';
import 'package:visionary_project/providers/auth_provider.dart';
import 'package:visionary_project/providers/vision_provider.dart';
import 'package:visionary_project/widgets/vb_form.dart';
import 'package:visionary_project/widgets/vb_grid.dart';
import 'package:visionary_project/widgets/vb_image.dart';
import 'package:visionary_project/widgets/vb_sidebar.dart';

class BoardScreen extends ConsumerStatefulWidget {
  const BoardScreen({super.key});

  @override
  BoardScreenState createState() => BoardScreenState();
}
```

In the above code, the **BoardScreen** class is a widget which extends **ConsumerStatefulWidget** from **Riverpod** to manage state updates for the vision board. This allows the widget to rebuild when the state changes (such as when vision items are added or deleted). The **createState** method returns an instance of the **BoardScreenState**, which contains the logic for building the user interface. Add the **BoardScreenState** class below the **BoardScreen** as show:

```
class BoardScreen extends ConsumerStatefulWidget {
  ...
}

class BoardScreenState extends ConsumerState<BoardScreen> {
  Future<dynamic> buildAddForm(
```

```
      BuildContext context,
      VisionItemsNotifier visionItemsNotifier,
      ) {
    return showFormSheet(context, visionItemsNotifier);
  }

  Future<dynamic> showFormSheet(
      BuildContext context, VisionItemsNotifier visionItemsNotifier) {
    return showModalBottomSheet(
      context: context,
      builder: (context) => AddItemForm(
        onSubmit: (itemText, imageUrl) async {
          Navigator.pop(context);
          await visionItemsNotifier.addOrUpdateItem(itemText,
            imageUrl, null);
        },
      ),
    );
  }

  void handleSignOut(BuildContext context) {
    ref.read(authProvider.notifier).signOut();
    Navigator.pushReplacementNamed(context, Constants.authScreen);
  }

  @override
  Widget build(BuildContext context) {
    final visionItemsNotifier = ref.read(
      visionItemsNotifierProvider.notifier);
    return LayoutBuilder(builder: (context, constraints) {
      if (constraints.maxWidth > 600) {
        return LandscapeScaffold(
          visionItemsNotifier: visionItemsNotifier,
          buildAddForm: buildAddForm,
          handleSignOut: handleSignOut,
        );
      } else {
```

```
          return PortraitScaffold(
            visionItemsNotifier: visionItemsNotifier,
            buildAddForm: buildAddForm,
            handleSignOut: handleSignOut,
          );
        }
      });
    }
  }
```

In the above code, The **BoardScreenState** class holds the core business logic for the board screen. It includes methods for handling various actions like adding items, signing out, and rendering the UI in both portrait and landscape orientations. The **buildAddForm()** method is responsible for showing the form to add a new vision item. It calls the **showFormSheet()** method to display a modal bottom sheet with the **AddItemForm** widget for submitting new items. The **handleSignOut()** method triggers the sign-out process by calling **authProvider.notifier.signOut()** and then navigates to the authentication screen.

The **showFormSheet()** method displays the modal bottom sheet containing the **AddItemForm** widget. When the form is submitted, it calls **visionItemsNotifier.addOrUpdateItem()** to add or update the vision item in the list. Finally, the overridden **build()** method adapts the UI depending on the screen width. If the width is greater than 600 pixels (for larger screens like tablets or desktops), it uses the **LandscapeScaffold** layout; otherwise, it uses the **PortraitScaffold** layout. Add the following code after **BoardScreenState** class:

```
class LandscapeScaffold extends StatelessWidget {
  final VisionItemsNotifier visionItemsNotifier;
  final Future<dynamic> Function(BuildContext, VisionItemsNotifier) buildAddForm;
  final void Function(BuildContext) handleSignOut;

  const LandscapeScaffold({
    super.key,
    required this.visionItemsNotifier,
    required this.buildAddForm,
    required this.handleSignOut,
  });

  @override
  Widget build(BuildContext context) {
```

```
    return Scaffold(
      body: Stack(
        children: [
          const BackgroundImage(),
          Row(
            children: [
              VisionDrawer(
                color: Colors.white.withOpacity(0.9),
                signOut: () => handleSignOut(context),
                addItem: () => buildAddForm(context, visionItemsNotifier),
              ),
              const Expanded(child: VisionGrid())
            ],
          ),
        ],
      ),
    );
  }
}
```

In the code above, The **LandscapeScaffold** widget provides the layout for devices with a screen width greater than 600 pixels, typically tablets or desktops. A **VisionDrawer** on the left side of the screen, which contains a sign-out button and an option to add new items. The **addItem** function calls **buildAddForm**, which triggers the display of the bottom sheet for adding new items. An **Expanded** widget wrapping the **VisionGrid**, which displays the vision items in a grid format. The grid is provided by the **VisionGrid** widget defined earlier. A **Stack** widget is used to layer the **VisionDrawer** and the **VisionGrid** on top of a background image using **BackgroundImage** widget. Finally, write the **PortraitScaffold** widget class below the **LandscapeScaffold** class, as shown below:

```
class PortraitScaffold extends StatelessWidget {
  final VisionItemsNotifier visionItemsNotifier;
  final Future<dynamic> Function(BuildContext, VisionItemsNotifier) buildAddForm;
  final void Function(BuildContext) handleSignOut;

  const PortraitScaffold({
    super.key,
    required this.visionItemsNotifier,
```

```
    required this.buildAddForm,
    required this.handleSignOut,
  });

  @override
  Widget build(BuildContext context) {
    return Scaffold(
      appBar: AppBar(title: const Text("V I S I O N A R Y")),
      drawer: VisionDrawer(
        color: Colors.white.withOpacity(0.9),
        signOut: () => handleSignOut(context),
        addItem: () {
          Navigator.pop(context);
          buildAddForm(context, visionItemsNotifier);
        },
      ),
      body: Stack(
        children: [
          const BackgroundImage(),
          const VisionGrid(),
        ],
      ),
    );
  }
}
```

In the above code, **PortraitScaffold** widget is used for devices with smaller screen widths, typically smartphones. The top displays a simple **AppBar** widget with the title. The **VisionDrawer** is placed in the **drawer** property of the **Scaffold**, which provides a sign-out button and an option to add items. When the user taps **Add Item**, it closes the drawer and shows the bottom sheet to add a new vision item by calling **buildAddForm**. The body contains a **Stack**, which layers the **VisionGrid** on top of a background image similar to the landscape layout. This complete the very long and complex vision board page.

Finalizing the app

To finalize the app, you need to ensure that the **BoardScreen** is correctly added to the routes list in the root widget of the Visionary application. In the **VisionaryApp** class, replace the **Placeholder()** with the **BoardScreen()** widget inside the routes list as shown below:

```
// The root widget of the Visionary application
class VisionaryApp extends StatelessWidget {
  @override
  Widget build(BuildContext context) {
    return MaterialApp(
      // add this in route list
      routes: {
        ...
        Constants.boardScreen: (context) => const BoardScreen(),
      },
    );
  }
}
```

This will link the **BoardScreen** to its corresponding route, allowing it to be navigated to from other parts of the app. Once you have made the changes to include the **BoardScreen** in the routes list, you can now run the app. Ensure that all the necessary dependencies are properly configured, and then start the app to see the Visionary board screen in action. Add vision board item using the form, you will need a image url and a title. The following figure shows the vison board page:

Visionary : Web UI

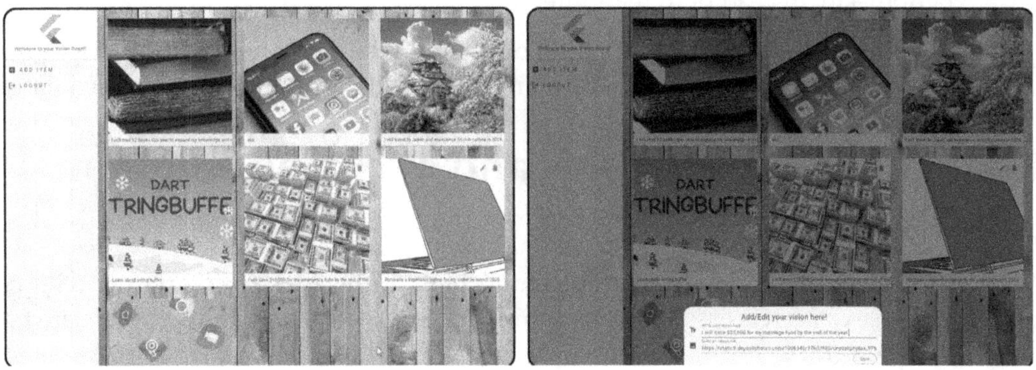

Figure 7.21: The completed visionary app

Optimizing Firebase usage

Efficiently using Firebase is key to ensuring that your Flutter app scales well and remains cost-effective. Firebase offers a wide range of services that can be optimized for performance, data management, and cost control. This section focuses on best practices for structuring Firebase Firestore, managing read/write operations efficiently, and reducing Firebase costs while avoiding common pitfalls.

Best practices for Firebase Firestore structure

Firestore's NoSQL database offers flexibility, but data structure impacts performance and costs. The key considerations include:

- **Use collections and subcollections wisely**: Organize hierarchical data with subcollections instead of deeply nested fields. This reduces document size and improves query efficiency. For example, store user posts in a 'posts' subcollection.
- **Normalize data**: Avoid excessive **denormalization** (duplicating data), as it increases read/write operations and costs. Use references instead of duplicating data. For instance, store user information in a 'users' collection and reference it elsewhere.
- **Efficient query design**: While Firestore indexes data automatically, complex queries may need composite indexes. Create them carefully to minimize latency. Also, optimize data retrieval by fetching only necessary data and using pagination (**`limit()`** and **`startAfter()`**) for large collections.
- **Minimize reads**: Use batch queries to fetch data in bulk instead of multiple small queries. Avoid frequent **`get()`** calls and instead use snapshots() for real-time updates, reducing network requests.
- **Optimize writes**: Use batch writes for multiple document updates in one transaction to reduce overhead. Minimize write frequency to lower costs, updating periodically instead of in real-time.
- **Caching**: Leverage Firestore's offline support to cache data locally, reducing read operations and improving performance, especially for frequently accessed data.

Reducing Firebase costs and avoiding common pitfalls

While Firebase's free tier offers generous limits, high-traffic apps or complex queries can quickly increase costs. It is essential to optimize usage to stay within budget. Here are four things to implement:

- **Monitor usage with Firebase analytics**:
    - **Track Firestore usage**: Use Firebase Analytics and monitoring tools to track your Firestore usage. Keep an eye on the number of reads, writes, and deletes to understand where your app is consuming resources. Identify areas where optimizations can reduce unnecessary operations.
    - **Limit data transfer**: Be mindful of the amount of data your app is transferring. For example, avoid fetching large documents or unnecessary fields when smaller data subsets will suffice.

- **Use Firebase's free tier and budget alerts:**
    - o **Free tier**: Firebase's Spark plan provides generous free limits, including 50,000 Firestore reads, 20,000 writes, and 10,000 deletes per day. Take advantage of these free tiers, especially during development and testing.
    - o **Budget alerts**: Set up budget alerts to avoid unexpectedly high charges. You can configure these in the Firebase Console under the **Billing** section. Alerts help you monitor when you are approaching usage limits.
- **Control Firebase Firestore permissions:**
    - o **Security rules**: Misconfigured Firebase Security Rules can lead to accidental data leakage or unauthorized access, increasing read/write operations and security risks. Write rules that control who can access or modify data, ensuring only authenticated and authorized users have access to certain parts of the database.
- **Optimize images and files in cloud storage:**
    - o **Compress and optimize**: If your app stores images or files in Firebase Cloud Storage, compress files before uploading to reduce data storage costs. Use appropriate image formats (e.g., JPEG for photos, PNG for graphics) and reduce file sizes where possible.
    - o **Delete unnecessary files**: Regularly clean up unused files in Cloud Storage to avoid unnecessary storage costs.

Designing secure applications

Building secure applications is a vital aspect of development, particularly when dealing with sensitive user data. When integrating Firebase into your Flutter app, it is important to ensure that authentication, data storage, and communication between the app and Firebase services are secure. The following figure illustrates how to make a secure Firebase app:

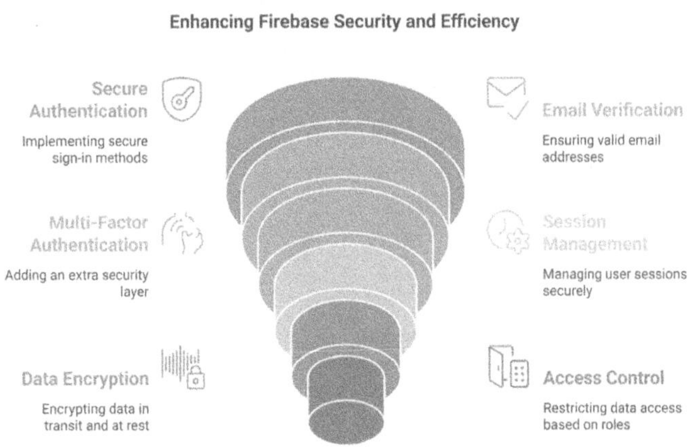

Figure 7.22: *Rules for securing a Firebase-based app*

Note: Something to always keep in mind is that, security is a continuous process. As your app grows, regularly review and update your security practices to stay ahead of potential threats.

Asynchronous programming challenges

In modern app development, handling asynchronous operations effectively is crucial, especially when dealing with data that changes dynamically in real time. Firebase, by nature, operates asynchronously, meaning it performs operations like reading from or writing to a database without blocking the rest of your app's code. This is helpful but can also introduce challenges when managing multiple async tasks. In this section, we will explore the key asynchronous programming challenges using a practical example based on an anime streaming app to help illustrate solutions.

Understanding async/await in Firebase interactions

When you are working with Firebase in Flutter, almost every interaction—whether it is fetching data from Firestore, authenticating users, or writing to the database—is done asynchronously. This means you will typically see the keywords async and await to manage these operations.

Scenario: Fetching anime details

Imagine, you are building an anime streaming app, and users want to view details of a specific anime from your Firebase Firestore database. Since retrieving data from Firestore is an asynchronous task, you would handle this with async and await, the following sample code snippet shows async/await implementation:

```
Future<void> getAnimeDetails(String animeId) async {
  try {
    DocumentSnapshot animeDoc = await FirebaseFirestore.instance
        .collection('animes')
        .doc(animeId)
        .get();

    // Process the anime details
    Map<String, dynamic> animeData = animeDoc.data() as Map<String, dynamic>;
    print('Anime Title: ${animeData['title']}');
  } catch (e) {
```

```
      print('Failed to fetch anime details: $e');
    }
  }
```

In the preceding code snippet, the await keyword ensures that the **get()** method waits for Firestore to return the anime document before continuing with the rest of the code. The app does not block the UI while waiting for the data; other operations can continue while the data is being fetched.

The following are the challenges that are faced:

- **Race conditions**: Asynchronous operations can lead to situations where certain tasks finish in an unexpected order, creating inconsistencies. For example, if a user opens multiple anime details pages quickly, the app might not always display the correct data if the operations return in the wrong order.
- **Error handling**: If Firebase fails to retrieve data (e.g., due to a network error), proper error handling is required to avoid crashing the app.

The following is the solution:

- Use try-catch blocks to handle errors gracefully.
- Be mindful of potential race conditions by either canceling previous requests or using state management solutions like Riverpod or Provider to control the UI state more effectively, as done in the Visionary app of this chapter.

Handling real-time data with Streams in Firebase

Firebase Firestore offers real-time data synchronization using Streams. This is especially useful in scenarios like tracking live updates, such as new episodes being added to an anime series or users leaving comments in a discussion thread.

Scenario: Live updates for new anime episodes

Let us say your anime app displays live updates for new episodes. Whenever a new episode is added to the Firestore collection, you want users to see it immediately without having to refresh the page. The following sample code snippet shows a implementation of **Stream**:

```
Stream<List<Episode>> getLiveAnimeEpisodes(String animeId) {
  return FirebaseFirestore.instance
      .collection('animes')
      .doc(animeId)
      .collection('episodes')
      .snapshots()
      .map((snapshot) => snapshot.docs
```

```
            .map((doc) => Episode.fromFirestore(doc))
            .toList());
}
```

In the preceding snippet, the **snapshots()** method creates a real-time stream that listens for any updates in the episodes collection. The UI will automatically refresh whenever there is a change, displaying new episodes in real time.

The following are the challenges faced:

- **Memory leaks**: Continuous streaming of real-time data can result in memory leaks if the Stream is not properly disposed of when no longer needed.
- **Performance issues**: If your app subscribes to too many Streams at once (e.g., listening to all anime episodes across multiple pages), it could lead to performance degradation due to excessive network requests.

The following is the solution:

- **Dispose of Streams properly**: Always dispose of Streams when they are no longer needed, especially when navigating away from pages. Use Flutter's **dispose()** method to handle this clean-up. An example of disposing Streams is as follows:

```
@override
void dispose() {
  // Cancel stream subscription
  _episodesSubscription.cancel();
  super.dispose();
}
```

- **Stream throttling**: If real-time data is not immediately required, you can throttle the stream or set up a polling interval to limit the number of requests and save resources.

Avoiding pitfalls in asynchronous operations

When dealing with multiple asynchronous tasks, things can get tricky. For example, multiple Firebase calls may be required to load various pieces of anime data, such as episode lists, comments, and user ratings. Managing these operations without proper handling can lead to pitfalls like callback hell, race conditions, and performance bottlenecks.

Scenario: Loading multiple pieces of data for an anime

Your anime app might need to load an anime's details, its episodes, and the latest user reviews simultaneously. Doing these asynchronously would look like this, the code snippet is as follows:

```
Future<void> loadAnimeData(String animeId) async {
  try {
    // Fetch anime details
    var animeDetailsFuture = FirebaseFirestore.instance
        .collection('animes')
        .doc(animeId)
        .get();

    // Fetch episodes list
    var episodesFuture = FirebaseFirestore.instance
        .collection('animes')
        .doc(animeId)
        .collection('episodes')
        .get();

    // Fetch user reviews
    var reviewsFuture = FirebaseFirestore.instance
        .collection('animes')
        .doc(animeId)
        .collection('reviews')
        .get();

    // Wait for all futures to complete using the new syntax
    var results = await (animeDetailsFuture, episodesFuture, reviews
Future).wait();

    // Process the results
    var animeDetails = results[0].data();
    var episodes = results[1].docs;
    var reviews = results[2].docs;

    print('Anime Title: ${animeDetails['title']}');
    print('Total Episodes: ${episodes.length}');
    print('Total Reviews: ${reviews.length}');
  } catch (e) {
    print('Error loading anime data: $e');
  }
}
```

In the preceding code, **`Future.wait()`** is used to handle all Firebase requests concurrently, meaning all data is fetched simultaneously rather than one after the other, optimizing for performance.

The following are the challenges faced:

- **Error handling**: If any one of these requests fails, the entire **`Future.wait()`** will fail, potentially leading to partial data being displayed.
- **Chained asynchronous calls**: If the requests depend on one another (e.g., fetching anime reviews based on user preferences retrieved from Firebase), chaining asynchronous calls can lead to performance bottlenecks.

The following are the solution:

- **Use try-catch for error handling**: Ensure proper error handling for each async call to gracefully manage partial data.
- **Break down dependencies**: If certain async tasks depend on one another, refactor your code to ensure that dependent tasks only start once the required data is available.

Conclusion

In this chapter, you explored the importance of building versatile, scalable, and maintainable architectures for Flutter applications, with a focus on integrating Firebase for authentication, database management, and backend functionality. You learned the key best practices for structuring apps, optimizing Firebase usage, addressing asynchronous programming challenges. These concepts ensure your apps are well-organized, secure, and able to handle future growth.

In the next chapter, Performance Optimization Strategies, you will explore techniques to enhance your app's performance, ensuring it runs efficiently and smoothly, even under heavy loads.

Points to remember

- **Importance of architecture**: A well-structured architecture enhances the scalability and maintainability of Flutter applications, making them easier to develop, test, and update.
- **Key architectural patterns**: Familiarize yourself with various architectural patterns, including MVVM, BLoC, Provider Architecture, to choose the best fit for your project requirements.
- **Firebase integration**: Firebase provides powerful tools for authentication, real-time databases, and cloud storage. Properly integrating these services can significantly enhance your app's functionality.

- **Security practices**: Always prioritize security by using Firebase Authentication for user sign-in, implementing MFA, and defining strict Firestore security rules to control data access.
- **Data management**: Optimize your Firestore structure by fetching only the necessary data, implementing efficient read/write operations, and ensuring that your app adheres to best practices to minimize costs and enhance performance.
- **Asynchronous programming**: Understand the use of async/await to handle asynchronous operations effectively, especially when working with real-time data and network requests.

Multiple choice questions

1. **Which architectural pattern separates the UI from business logic, using a ViewModel as a bridge?**
   a. MVC
   b. BLoC
   c. MVVM
   d. Clean architecture

2. **What is the best practice for ensuring secure user authentication in a Flutter app using Firebase?**
   a. Allow users to log in with any email without verification
   b. Implement multi-factor authentication (MFA)
   c. Use hardcoded passwords for testing
   d. Store user passwords in plain text

3. **What is a common challenge when dealing with asynchronous programming in Flutter apps that use Firebase?**
   a. Managing synchronous data
   b. Handling real-time data updates with Streams
   c. Using only local storage for data
   d. Avoiding UI updates

Answer

1	c
2	b
3	b

Questions

1. Write a Flutter app that implements user registration using Firebase Authentication with email and password. Ensure that the function includes validation for the email format and password strength. After a successful registration, send a verification email to the user.

2. Add Firebase authentication to the Machine learning apps you created in Chapter 5. You can create a new project on Firebase and then add authentication or use the existing Firebase project.

Key terms

- **Model-View-ViewModel (MVVM):** An architectural pattern that separates the UI from business logic, facilitating better organization and testability in Flutter apps.
- **Business Logic Component (BLoC):** A design pattern that uses Streams to manage the flow of data and business logic, keeping the UI reactive and efficient.
- **Firebase Authentication:** A service that provides easy user authentication methods, including email/password, phone number, and social logins for Flutter applications.
- **Firestore:** A NoSQL database provided by Firebase that allows for scalable and flexible data storage and retrieval in real-time.
- **Firestore Security Rules:** Custom rules that dictate access permissions for data in Firestore, ensuring that users can only access data they are authorized to view or modify.
- **Asynchronous Programming:** A programming approach that allows multiple tasks to run concurrently, improving application responsiveness when dealing with data fetching or processing.
- **Optimizing Firebase Usage:** Techniques to enhance the performance and cost-effectiveness of Firebase services, such as minimizing read/write operations and structuring data efficiently.
- **Provider:** A state management solution in Flutter that allows for easy sharing and management of application state across different parts of the app.
- **Modularization:** The practice of breaking down a codebase into smaller, manageable, and independent modules, improving maintainability and scalability.
- **Dependency Injection:** A design pattern that allows for the dynamic provision of dependencies to classes, promoting loose coupling and easier testing of Flutter applications.

Chapter 8
Performance Optimization Strategies

Introduction

In today's digital world, user expectations for responsive and seamless applications have never been higher, making performance optimization a critical focus for developers. This chapter explores essential strategies for enhancing Flutter app performance by understanding, diagnosing, and addressing common bottlenecks. From optimizing memory usage and widget builds to improving load times and utilizing advanced profiling tools, readers will gain the insights and techniques needed to create smooth, efficient, and responsive applications.

Structure

The chapter covers the following topics:

- Profiling Flutter web applications
- Diagnosing performance problems
- Memory management
- Improving load times
- Optimizing widget builds
- Proactive performance optimization strategies
- Practical: Performance tuning laggy gallery app

Objectives

By the end of this chapter, readers will be equipped with practical skills to profile Flutter applications, diagnose and address performance issues, and apply best practices for efficient memory and widget management. They will learn to leverage *Chrome DevTools* for performance analysis and apply proactive optimization strategies to minimize resource usage. Additionally, convert an unoptimized project in an optimized one will reinforce understanding and build mastery over essential performance-enhancing techniques.

Profiling Flutter web applications

To optimize Flutter web applications, developers need tools specifically designed for monitoring performance within a browser environment. Unlike mobile or desktop Flutter apps, where Flutter DevTools provide extensive profiling capabilities, Flutter web applications rely heavily on Chrome DevTools for performance insights. This browser-based tool enables developers to assess rendering speed, network activity, and JavaScript processing, which are crucial for understanding how the app performs in real-world web scenarios. The following figure shows a snapshot of Chrome DevTools window:

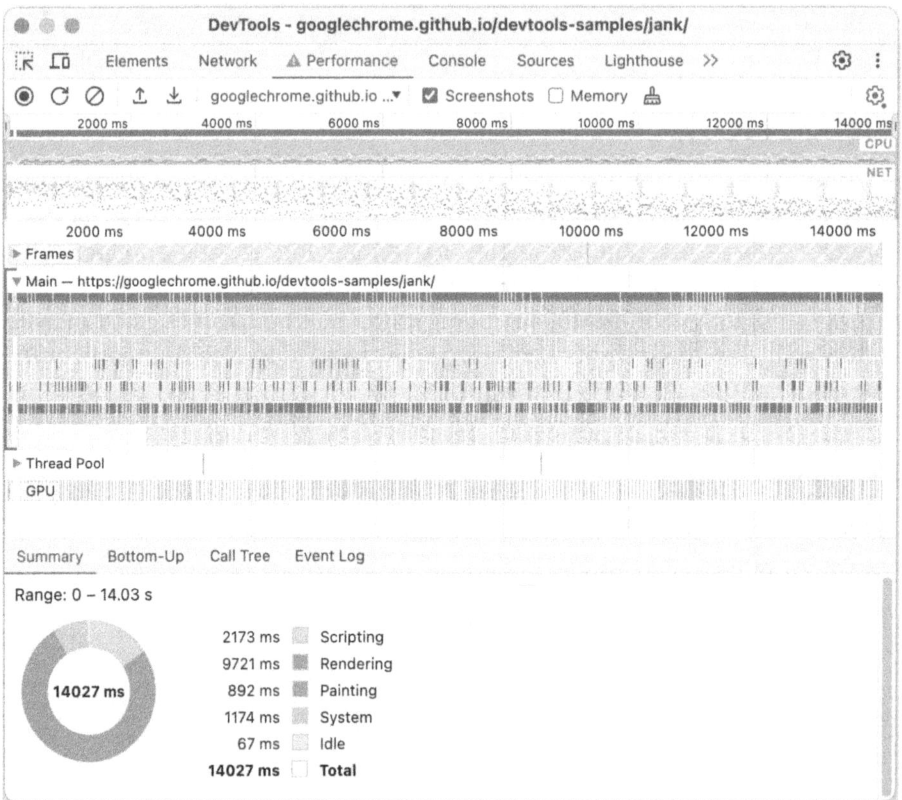

Figure 8.1: *Chrome DevTools UI from (from developers.chrome.com)*

Analyzing key areas

Let us take a look at the important parts to inspect for analyzing Flutter app performance on the web. The following figure helps summarize the key areas to analyze in a Flutter web app:

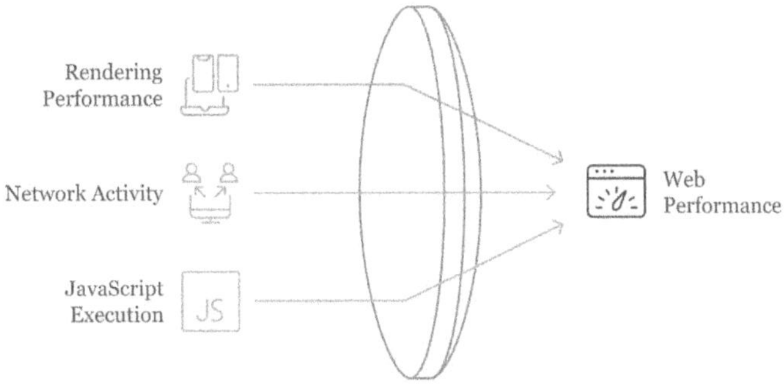

Figure 8.2: *Illustration showing key areas to analyze improving performance*

The key areas for performance optimization are:

- **Rendering performance:** Chrome DevTools provides detailed insights into render time, layout shifts, and paint durations, allowing developers to spot UI components or animations that might be causing lag.
- **Network activity**: By tracking network requests in Chrome DevTools, developers can monitor load times, identify large assets, and optimize requests for faster load times.
- **JavaScript execution**: Since Flutter compiles to JavaScript for web applications, understanding the impact of JavaScript on app performance is essential. Heavy computations or inefficient code can lead to longer execution times and delayed UI responsiveness.

Getting started with Chrome DevTools

Chrome DevTools stands out as an indispensable resource, offering deep insights into various aspects of application performance. Follow these steps to use Chrome DevTools:

1. **Open Chrome DevTools**: Run the Flutter web app in Chrome, right-click on the page, select **Inspect**, and navigate to the **Performance** tab.
2. **Record a session**: Click on the **Record and Reload** button to capture the app performance when the page is loaded, and content is being loaded. Click the **Record** button to capture app activity as you interact with it. This recording generates a detailed report, showing render time, JavaScript execution, and network activity. The following figure shows the **Performance** tab and its important options:

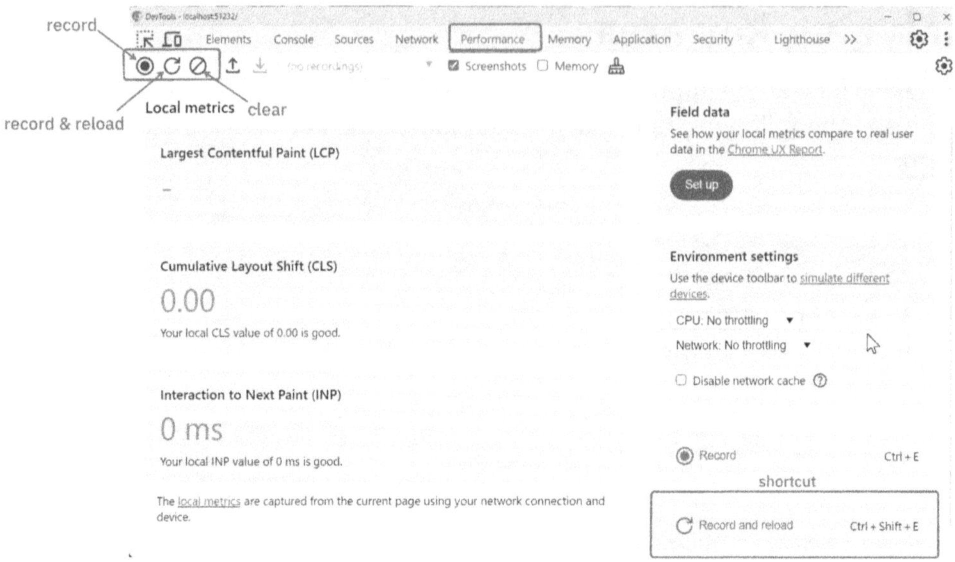

Figure 8.3: Chrome DevTools performance tab and its important options

3. **Interpret results**: Look at the timeline to locate areas of high resource consumption, such as long frames or heavy network requests, and identify opportunities to optimize the UI and backend interactions. The following figure shows the profiling results after its completed:

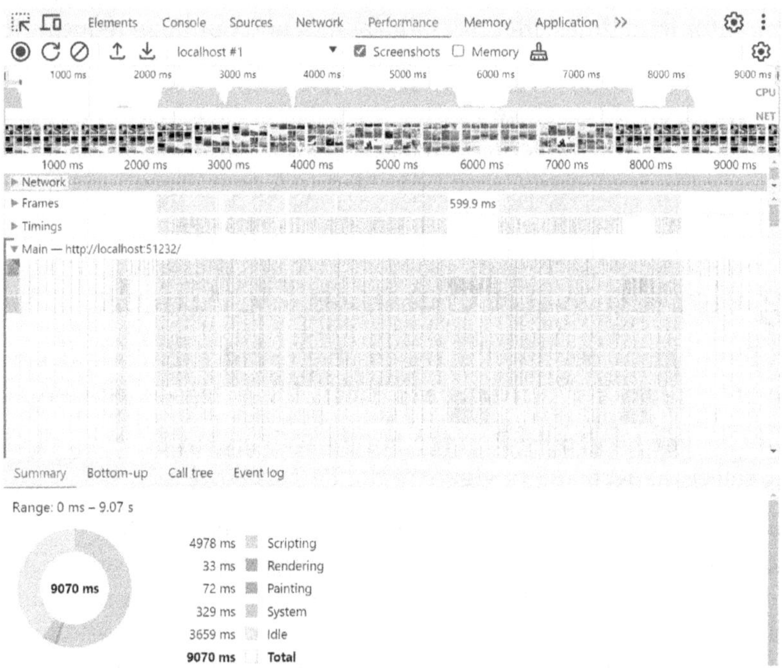

Figure 8.4: Chrome DevTools profiling output showing various details and pie chart summary of various tasks

To summarize, the following figure shows the steps to analyze web app performance in Flutter:

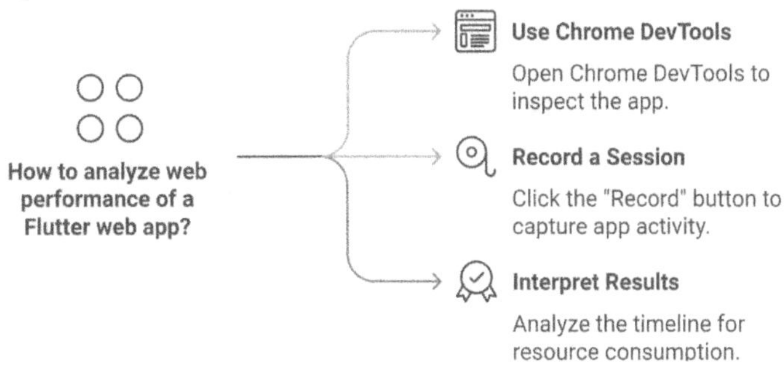

Figure 8.5: *Steps to analyze web performance in flutter app*

Diagnosing performance problems

Effective optimization in Flutter web applications requires identifying bottlenecks that can slow down the user experience. Flutter web applications may experience performance issues due to excessive widget rebuilds, network delays, large assets, or unoptimized layouts. Systematic diagnosis of these bottlenecks enables developers to address problems precisely where they impact performance the most. The most important techniques you can use for identifying bottlenecks in your app are discussed as follows. The following figure shows the Flutter web app performance optimization cycle:

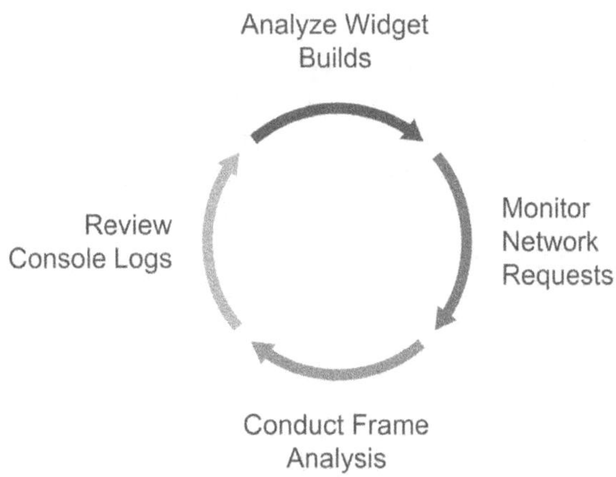

Figure 8.6: *Key technique for identifying bottlenecks in app*

Widget build analysis

Analyzing widget builds helps detect areas where widgets are rebuilding excessively, causing unnecessary workload. Minimizing these rebuilds, using const constructors, and optimizing widget hierarchies can lead to performance gains. A simple implementation of widget with **const** is shown in the following snippet:

```
class MyApp extends StatelessWidget {
  @override
  Widget build(BuildContext context) {
    return const Header(); // Use const to reduce rebuilds
  }
}

class Header extends StatelessWidget {
  @override
  Widget build(BuildContext context) {
    return Text(
      'Welcome to MyApp!',
      style: TextStyle(fontSize: 24),
    );
  }
}
```

Note: IntelliJ IDEA will always show hint whenever a widget is static and that the const keyword should be added to the widget or not, so this makes your work easy.

Network request monitoring

The **Network** tab in Chrome DevTools provides insights into load times and sizes of network requests, enabling developers to identify and optimize large assets or reduce the number of API calls. The following snippet shows an example of caching network data, which can reduce redundant API calls, identified as bottlenecks when network analysis shows repeated requests:

```
class ApiService {
  static final _cache = <String, dynamic>{};

  Future<dynamic> fetchData(String url) async {
    if (_cache.containsKey(url)) {
      return _cache[url]; // Return cached data if available
    }
    final response = await http.get(Uri.parse(url));
    if (response.statusCode == 200) {
      final data = jsonDecode(response.body);
```

```
      _cache[url] = data; // Cache the data for future requests
      return data;
    } else {
      throw Exception('Failed to load data');
    }
  }
}
```

In the preceding code snippet, the **ApiService** class provides a data-fetching method with built-in caching to reduce repeated network requests. It stores fetched data in a static **_cache** map, using the URL as the key. When **fetchData** is called with a URL, it first checks if the data is already cached; if so, it returns this data immediately. If not, it makes an HTTP GET request to retrieve the data. On a successful response (status code 200), it decodes the JSON response, caches it for future calls, and returns the data. If the request fails, it throws an exception to indicate an error.

Frame analysis

Frame analysis is essential for understanding the rendering performance of a Flutter app. Each time something changes in the UI—whether due to user interaction or data updates—Flutter renders a new frame. In general, Flutter aims to render each frame at 60 **frames per second** (**fps**) on mobile and 120 fps on capable devices, which translates to around 16 milliseconds per frame for smooth performance. If rendering a frame takes longer than this time, users experience jank or noticeable lag. The **Performance** tab in Chrome DevTools captures frame rendering times, highlighting areas where frames are taking too long or dropping, which can lead to visual lags in animations.

Flutter divides the UI rendering pipeline into different stages, including:

- **Frame scheduling**: Determines when a frame should start.
- **UI thread**: Processes layout, builds the widget tree, and paints the visuals.
- **Raster thread**: Takes the painted visuals and renders them to the screen.

The following are some common issues that can cause frames to exceed the 16 ms budget, along with strategies to address them:

- **Expensive layout and build operations**: Excessive layout calculations or complex widget builds can cause delays in the UI thread. To reduce this, avoid deeply nested widgets, and try to use widgets like **ListView.builder** instead of **Column** with multiple children.
- **Large or complex paint operations**: Heavy use of custom painters or complex visuals can increase rasterization time. To minimize this, limit the use of custom painting or simplify drawing logic. For example, instead of rendering a complex path, use simpler shapes when possible.

- **Inefficient animations**: Smooth animations are essential for an engaging UI, but they can easily exceed the frame budget if not optimized. Avoid animating heavy layouts or large images and instead animate only small UI components. Use **AnimatedBuilder** to avoid rebuilding the entire widget tree during animations. The following snippet shows an example of animation optimization:

```
AnimatedBuilder(
  animation: controller,
  builder: (context, child) {
    return Transform.translate(
      offset: Offset(controller.value * 100, 0),
      child: child,
    );
  },
  child: Icon(Icons.star),
);
```

Here, **AnimatedBuilder** only rebuilds the necessary widget (in this case, the star icon) during the animation.

Console logs and warnings

The **Console** tab in DevTools logs errors and warnings, such as layout overflow or render-blocking issues, that can impact performance. Using **SingleChildScrollView** or **ListView** for dynamic content can help avoid overflow issues that might otherwise appear in the console logs. Look at the following snippet for the sample implementation:

```
// Example of handling layout overflow issues
Widget build(BuildContext context) {
  return SingleChildScrollView(
    child: Column(
      children: List.generate(100, (index) => Text('Item $index')),
    ),
  );
}
```

By combining Chrome DevTools diagnostics with these optimizations, developers can achieve a smooth, responsive experience for Flutter web applications, addressing bottlenecks in both UI rendering and network efficiency.

Memory management

In web applications, memory management is often the unsung hero of performance optimization. An app that consumes excessive memory can suffer from slowdowns, lagging UI, or even complete crashes on less powerful devices. This section explores the principles and practical approaches that developers can use to manage memory effectively in Flutter web applications, creating experiences that feel lightweight and seamless.

Practical approaches for effective memory management

When a Flutter app runs on the web, it compiles down to JavaScript, which runs within the browser's memory constraints. The browser is responsible for allocating and managing memory for the app, but developers play a critical role in ensuring memory is used efficiently. Good memory management comes down to understanding what resources are being allocated, ensuring those resources are freed when no longer needed, and reducing the overall memory footprint. This section describes the practical approach that you should take for memory management.

Dispose of unused resources

Many widgets in Flutter come with controllers (like **AnimationController**, **TextEditingController**, and **ScrollController**) that consume memory while in use. These resources need to be explicitly disposed of when they are no longer needed; otherwise, they will continue to consume memory, potentially leading to memory leaks. Consider the following example:

```
class ExampleWidget extends StatefulWidget {
  @override
  _ExampleWidgetState createState() => _ExampleWidgetState();
}

class _ExampleWidgetState extends State<ExampleWidget> with SingleTickerProviderStateMixin {
  late AnimationController _controller;

  @override
  void initState() {
    super.initState();
    _controller = AnimationController(
      vsync: this,
```

```
      duration: const Duration(seconds: 2),
    );
  }

  @override
  void dispose() {
    _controller.dispose(); // Ensures memory is released
    super.dispose();
  }

  @override
  Widget build(BuildContext context) {
    return Container(); // Your widget implementation here
  }
}
```

In this example, the **AnimationController** is disposed of within the **dispose** method. This ensures that when the widget is removed from the widget tree, the controller is also removed from memory, preventing any leaks.

Note: The overridden dispose() method should always end with super.dispose() as the last step, similar to how an overridden initState() needs a super.initState() as the first step.

Leverage the const keyword

Flutter encourages the use of **const** in widgets whenever possible. Declaring a widget as **const** means that it will be created once and reused throughout the app, reducing the need for repeated memory allocations. This technique is particularly effective for widgets that do not change after they are first displayed, like static labels, icons, or other UI elements that remain the same across frames.

Optimize lists and large data structures

Lists, maps, or other data structures can grow quickly if not managed carefully. Flutter web applications can suffer memory-related slowdowns when handling a large number of elements in a UI, especially when many of them are visible at once. For example, in cases where you are displaying a long list, consider using **ListView.builder** rather than a regular **ListView** as shown in the following snippet:

```
Widget build(BuildContext context) {
  return ListView.builder(
    itemCount: 1000,
    itemBuilder: (context, index) {
      return ListTile(
        title: Text('Item $index'),
      );
    },
  );
}
```

The **`ListView.builder`** constructor creates only the visible items and disposes of them as the user scrolls out of view, which helps limit memory use in list-heavy applications.

Track and monitor memory usage

To effectively manage memory, it is critical to know where memory is being allocated. Chrome DevTools offers several powerful tools for memory tracking in web applications. The **Memory** tab provides a snapshot of memory allocation, which can reveal areas of high consumption or potential leaks. The following tools help developers analyse and optimize memory usage more effectively:

- **Heap snapshots**: Heap snapshots show all objects currently stored in memory. By comparing snapshots at different points, you can identify retained objects that should have been freed, helping to pinpoint memory leaks.
- **Garbage collection**: Monitoring the garbage collection cycles in DevTools can provide insight into how frequently memory is being reclaimed, which can help assess memory health in the app.

The following figure summarizes best approaches for optimized memory management:

Figure 8.7: *Diagram illustrating strategies for effective memory management*

Combining these memory management practices—disposing of unused resources, leveraging const widgets, optimizing large data structures, and regularly tracking memory allocation—helps ensure a balanced and efficient memory footprint.

Improving load times

Load times play a crucial role in user experience, especially for web applications where users expect quick and seamless access. Slow load times not only frustrate users but can also lead to higher bounce rates. In a Flutter web application, improving load times involves optimizing the initial download size, managing assets efficiently, and reducing any unnecessary network requests.

Techniques for enhancing load times

Unlike traditional mobile apps, web apps are typically downloaded on the first execution and then cached in the browser according to its caching strategies. This caching reduces the need to repeatedly download the entire app, but it is still essential to minimize the data sent to the client to improve loading performance and reduce waiting times. In this section, we will discuss techniques that developers can implement to optimize loading and ensure a smooth user experience. The following chart summarizes the techniques for enhancing load times:

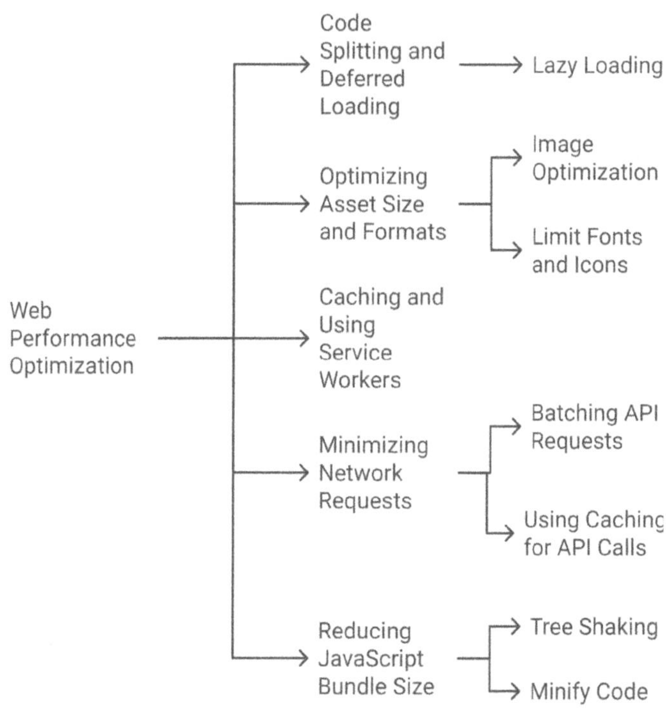

Figure 8.8: Techniques for enhancing load times in flutter web apps

Code splitting and deferred loading

Code splitting breaks the application into smaller chunks, which can be loaded on demand instead of all at once. For example, if a user only needs access to certain parts of an app initially, defer loading other resources until necessary. This can significantly reduce initial load times by allowing only essential features and assets to load first.

Lazy loading

One approach to deferred loading is to use lazy loading for features that are not needed right away. Flutter supports deferred loading for packages and assets, which can be loaded only when required. The following code snippet shows how to implement deferred loading in Flutter using lazy loading for packages:

```
import 'package:my_feature/my_feature.dart' deferred as myFeature;

Future<void> loadFeature() async {
  await myFeature.loadLibrary(); // Load only when needed
  myFeature.MyFeatureWidget();
}
```

Using deferred imports, as shown here, allows the Flutter web app to load only parts of the app on demand, improving the overall loading experience. Let us look at a practical example that combines deferred loading with asset optimization, as shown in the following snippet:

```
// Main widget that includes lazy loading
import 'package:flutter/material.dart';
import 'package:my_feature/my_feature.dart' deferred as myFeature;

class MyApp extends StatelessWidget {
  @override
  Widget build(BuildContext context) {
    return MaterialApp(
      home: Scaffold(
        appBar: AppBar(title: Text("Deferred Loading Example")),
        body: Center(
          child: ElevatedButton(
            onPressed: () async {
              await myFeature.loadLibrary();
              Navigator.of(context).push(
                MaterialPageRoute(builder: (context) => myFeature.MyFeatureWidget()),
```

```
                    );
                  },
                  child: Text("Load Feature"),
                ),
              ),
            ),
          );
      }
    }
```

In this code, the **myFeature** package is only loaded when the button is pressed, which defers the asset loading until it is necessary. This approach reduces initial load time while still making the feature accessible when needed.

Optimizing asset size and formats

Flutter applications often include images, fonts, and other media that can be heavy. Compressing assets, using appropriate file formats, and reducing the number of large assets in the app can all contribute to faster load times.

Image optimization

Convert images to lighter formats like WebP or SVG. For high-quality images that do not require extensive color depth, consider compression methods that reduce file sizes while maintaining acceptable quality.

Fonts and icons

Limit the number of font files and icon libraries included in the project. Custom fonts and icons increase the download size, so stick to essential ones or use a single icon pack if possible. Google Fonts and Flutter's native **Icon** widget both offer lightweight alternatives.

Caching and using service workers

Implementing caching mechanisms allows previously loaded data and resources to be stored on the client side, reducing load times for repeat users. Service workers enable Flutter web apps to cache certain files, improving load speed on subsequent visits and enabling offline functionality.

Setting up service workers

Flutter's web build generates a **flutter_service_worker.js** file that can cache certain assets. By default, assets and the app shell are cached, which can provide immediate load times on subsequent visits. The following code snippet demonstrates how to set up service workers in Flutter to cache essential assets for faster subsequent loads:

```
// flutter_service_worker.js
const CACHE_NAME = 'flutter-app-cache';

self.addEventListener('install', (event) => {
  event.waitUntil(
    caches.open(CACHE_NAME).then((cache) => {
      return cache.addAll([
        // Cache core files
        '/',
        'main.dart.js',
        'index.html',
        'assets/AssetManifest.json',
        'assets/FontManifest.json',
      ]);
    })
  );
});
```

With this setup, cached assets are served without waiting for them to re-download, enhancing load times for users who revisit the app.

Minimizing network requests

Each network request adds to the load time, especially when the requests occur during app initialization. Optimizing and reducing these requests can go a long way toward improving performance.

Batching API requests

For scenarios that require multiple network requests, try batching them into a single call. This can reduce the overhead and time spent waiting for separate responses, as shown in the following snippet:

```
Future<Map<String, dynamic>> fetchInitialData() async {
  final responses = await Future.wait([
    fetchUserProfile(),
    fetchUserSettings(),
    fetchUserNotifications(),
  ]);
  return {
    'profile': responses[0],
    'settings': responses[1],
```

```
        'notifications': responses[2],
      };
    }
```

Using caching for API calls

Cache results from frequently accessed data to avoid repetitive calls. A package like **`dio_http_cache`** can be used to automatically cache and return responses for previously fetched data.

Reducing JavaScript bundle size

Since Flutter web apps compile down to JavaScript, the generated JavaScript bundle size can directly impact load time. Keep the bundle as small as possible by avoiding large libraries and redundant dependencies. To minimize the impact of JavaScript bundle size on load time, consider the following strategies:

- **Tree shaking**: Tree shaking is a process that removes unused code from the compiled JavaScript. Ensure that you are using only the necessary parts of each package to keep your final bundle size minimal.
- **Minify code**: Minifying the JavaScript code reduces the file size by removing unnecessary spaces, comments, and other elements that the code does not require to run. To enable minification in Flutter, ensure the app is built in release mode:

```
flutter build web --release
```

This command generates a minified version of your application, reducing its overall load size.

Enhance performance using WebAssembly

WebAssembly (**Wasm**) is a low-level binary format designed for efficient execution on web browsers. By serving as a compilation target, Wasm offers near-native performance, making it a powerful tool for optimizing Flutter web applications, particularly in scenarios involving computationally intensive tasks. When a Flutter app is compiled for the web, it typically uses JavaScript as the target language. However, with Wasm, developers can compile Dart code into Wasm modules, unlocking several benefits:

- **Performance Gains:** Wasm enables faster execution compared to JavaScript, especially for resource-heavy computations like animations, data processing, or real-time rendering.
- **Optimized Load Times:** Wasm binaries are smaller and more compact than JavaScript bundles, resulting in reduced network latency and faster load times.
- **Browser Compatibility:** Most modern browsers, such as Chrome, Edge, and Firefox, support Wasm. However, developers should verify compatibility with specific browser versions, as some may lack full support for advanced Wasm features.

Starting with recent Flutter versions, developers can compile their apps for Wasm using the following build command:

```
flutter build web --wasm
```

This command generates Wasm binaries alongside JavaScript files, allowing the app to leverage Wasm's advantages without sacrificing compatibility. If a browser does not support Wasm, the app gracefully falls back to JavaScript.

Optimizing widget builds

Efficient widget builds and effective state management are foundational to building responsive Flutter applications. In Flutter, the widget tree is rebuilt whenever there is a change in state, which can quickly become costly if these rebuilds are excessive or unnecessary. By optimizing widget builds and adopting smart state management strategies, developers can improve app responsiveness, reduce resource usage, and enhance the user experience. This section delves into techniques to streamline widget builds and manage state effectively, balancing performance and code maintainability.

Need to optimize widget builds

Each time a widget rebuilds, Flutter recalculates the layout and potentially repaints the UI, which can strain the CPU and memory, particularly for complex UIs or frequent state changes. Minimizing unnecessary rebuilds can significantly enhance app performance, especially on resource-limited devices or when running Flutter on the web. Some common scenarios leading to excessive rebuilds include:

- Directly placing dynamic data in the widget tree without isolating it.
- Using **`setState`** indiscriminately, causing full widget trees to rebuild.
- Not properly managing **`InheritedWidget`** or provider-based listeners.

Practical techniques to optimize widget builds

In this section we will discuss the techniques you can use practically to optimize your widget build for an optimized Flutter web app.

Use const widgets whenever possible

As discussed in previous section, using the **`const`** keyword for widgets that do not change is an effective way to reduce rebuilds. These widgets are created once and reused, saving both processing time and memory.

Minimizing the use of setState

setState triggers the entire widget to rebuild, so it should only be used when necessary. A more efficient approach is to separate dynamic components into smaller widgets, each of which can rebuild independently. The following is the snippet of unoptimized code:

```
class CounterWidget extends StatefulWidget {
  @override
  _CounterWidgetState createState() => _CounterWidgetState();
}

class _CounterWidgetState extends State<CounterWidget> {
  int _count = 0;

  @override
  Widget build(BuildContext context) {
    return Column(
      children: [
        Text('Count: $_count'), // This rebuilds every time.
        ElevatedButton(
          onPressed: () {
            setState(() {
              _count++;
            });
          },
          child: Text('Increment'),
        ),
      ],
    );
  }
}
```

You can optimize this by separating the display of **_count** into a smaller, stateless widget, only the counter widget rebuilds, reducing unnecessary work in the parent. Look at the following optimized snippet:

```
class CounterWidget extends StatefulWidget {
  @override
  _CounterWidgetState createState() => _CounterWidgetState();
}

```

```
class _CounterWidgetState extends State<CounterWidget> {
  int _count = 0;

  @override
  Widget build(BuildContext context) {
    return Column(
      children: [
        CountDisplay(count: _count), // Isolated widget.
        ElevatedButton(
          onPressed: () {
            setState(() {
              _count++;
            });
          },
          child: Text('Increment'),
        ),
      ],
    );
  }
}

class CountDisplay extends StatelessWidget {
  final int count;

  const CountDisplay({required this.count});

  @override
  Widget build(BuildContext context) {
    return Text('Count: $count'); // Only this part rebuilds on change.
  }
}
```

By isolating **CountDisplay**, only this widget rebuilds when **_count** changes, reducing unnecessary processing for the entire tree.

Efficient state management techniques

Selecting an appropriate state management solution is critical in Flutter, especially for complex applications where managing state efficiently can make a significant difference in performance.

Provider and ChangeNotifier

Provider is a popular and efficient state management solution in Flutter. Combined with **ChangeNotifier**, it enables fine-grained control over when widgets should rebuild based on specific state changes, keeping widget rebuilds limited to only those that need updating. Look at the following example snippet code:

```
class Counter extends ChangeNotifier {
  int _count = 0;

  int get count => _count;

  void increment() {
    _count++;
    notifyListeners();
  }
}

// Providing the Counter model at the root level
void main() {
  runApp(
    ChangeNotifierProvider(
      create: (context) => Counter(),
      child: MyApp(),
    ),
  );
}
```

To apply it to the widget, use **Provider.of( )** method to create the object and use it, as shown in the following snippet:

```
class Counter extends ChangeNotifier {
  int _count = 0;
  int get count => _count;

  void increment() {
    _count++;
    notifyListeners();
  }
}

```

```
// Providing the Counter model at the root level
void main() {
  runApp(
    ChangeNotifierProvider(
      create: (context) => Counter(),
      child: MyApp(),
    ),
  );
}
```

With **Provider** and **ChangeNotifier**, only widgets that depend on **Counter** are rebuilt when **notifyListeners()** is called, keeping rebuilds contained and efficient.

Leveraging consumer and selector

To further control rebuilds in provider-based applications, Flutter offers **Consumer** and **Selector**. While **Consumer** is useful for accessing the provider without triggering rebuilds in parent widgets, **Selector** allows fine-grained selection of only the parts of the model that need to trigger rebuilds. Look at the following sample **Consumer** snippet:

```
Consumer<Counter>(
  builder: (context, counter, child) {
    return Text('Count: ${counter.count}');
  },
);
```

Here is the relevant **Selector** snippet:

```
Selector<Counter, int>(
  selector: (_, counter) => counter.count,
  builder: (context, count, child) {
    return Text('Count: $count');
  },
);
```

In this example, **Selector** ensures that only changes to **count** trigger a rebuild, keeping other parts of the widget tree untouched.

Avoid rebuilding widgets in loops and lists

When rendering lists or complex widget trees, avoid using dynamic or **setState** in loops. Instead, as we learnt in memory management section, leverage **ListView.builder** or **GridView.builder** to create widgets on demand as they appear on the screen. Here is a small example of how to use **GridView.builder** to avoid unnecessary widget rebuilds when displaying a list of items:

```
class GridScreen extends StatelessWidget {
  final List<String> items = List.generate(100, (index) => 'Item $index');

  @override
  Widget build(BuildContext context) {
    return GridView.builder(
      gridDelegate: SliverGridDelegateWithFixedCrossAxisCount(
        crossAxisCount: 2, // Display 2 items per row
      ),
      itemCount: items.length,
      itemBuilder: (context, index) {
        return Card(
          margin: EdgeInsets.all(8),
          child: Center(
            child: Text(
              items[index],
              style: TextStyle(fontSize: 16),
            ),
          ),
        );
      },
    );
  }
}
```

This approach avoids loading and building widgets for items that are off-screen, improving performance.

Proactive performance optimization strategies

Proactive performance optimization focuses on anticipating potential bottlenecks or inefficiencies before they become issues in a Flutter application. This approach involves preemptively designing and coding with performance in mind, rather than only addressing problems once they arise. In this section, we will cover some advanced optimization strategies, including pre-caching, deferred loading, and leveraging efficient data handling techniques.

Pre-caching assets and data

One of the simplest ways to improve load times and ensure a seamless experience is by **pre-caching assets**, such as images, icons, or fonts, that the user is likely to need immediately. By pre-loading resources during the app's initialization, you can reduce the chances of stutters or delays when they are first needed. Look at the example code showing pre-caching images:

```
void preloadImages(BuildContext context) {
  final imagePaths = ['assets/image1.png', 'assets/image2.png'];
  for (String path in imagePaths) {
    precacheImage(AssetImage(path), context);
  }
}

@override
void initState() {
  super.initState();
  preloadImages(context); // Load images in advance
}
```

Pre-caching ensures that these images are ready in memory when needed, reducing potential delays or loading indicators during transitions.

Leverage efficient data structures and algorithms

The choice of data structures can make a substantial difference in the responsiveness of your app, especially when working with large datasets or computationally intensive features. For example, using **Map** instead of **List** for lookups, leveraging custom comparators for sorting, or using **Set** for unique collections can save significant time and resources. For example, instead of iterating over a list to check if an item is unique, using a **Set** ensures constant-time complexity for lookups, which is ideal for performance-sensitive operations. Look at the following code showing optimized search with **Map**:

```
Map<String, String> userMap = {
  'user1': 'John',
  'user2': 'Jane',
};

String? getUserById(String id) {
  return userMap[id]; // O(1) complexity for search
}
```

Choosing efficient data structures helps reduce processing times and resource consumption, especially in frequently accessed or updated areas of the app.

Use deferred loading for non-critical code

Deferred loading, or **lazy loading**, is a powerful technique to reduce initial load times and memory usage by only loading parts of the app as needed. Flutter supports deferred loading for widgets and packages, which is particularly useful for large or resource-intensive features that are not needed immediately. For instance, if your app has a section with infrequently used charts or data-heavy visualizations, you can defer loading this functionality until it is requested by the user. This helps keep memory usage low and the initial loading time fast. The following code shows a sample of lazy loading of a feature:

```
late Future<void> _loadHeavyFeature;

@override
void initState() {
  super.initState();
  // simulated delay for demonstration purpose
  _loadHeavyFeature = Future.delayed(Duration(seconds: 5), () {
    // Code to initialize or load the feature
  });
}
```

Deferred loading reduces the app's startup footprint, particularly in apps with large datasets or complex features that are accessed infrequently.

Optimize app lifecycle management

Properly managing app lifecycle events can enhance the app's overall performance and user experience. For example, in Flutter, the **`WidgetsBindingObserver`** allows developers to respond to lifecycle changes and adjust app behavior based on whether the app is in the foreground or background. You can use lifecycle events to pause animations, stop network requests, or save app state when the app moves to the background. This reduces CPU and network usage when the app is not actively being used, thereby optimizing battery and data consumption. The following snippet shows an example of pausing an animation when app goes to background:

```
class MyAppState extends State<MyApp> with WidgetsBindingObserver {
  late AnimationController _controller;

  @override
  void initState() {
```

```
    super.initState();
    WidgetsBinding.instance.addObserver(this);
    _controller = AnimationController(vsync: this);
  }

  @override
  void dispose() {
    WidgetsBinding.instance.removeObserver(this);
    _controller.dispose();
    super.dispose();
  }

  @override
  void didChangeAppLifecycleState(AppLifecycleState state) {
    if (state == AppLifecycleState.paused) {
      _controller.stop();
    } else if (state == AppLifecycleState.resumed) {
      _controller.forward();
    }
  }
}
```

With lifecycle-aware performance optimizations, you ensure efficient resource usage without compromising the user experience.

Implement data pagination

Pagination is an effective way to handle large datasets by loading content incrementally rather than all at once. In scenarios where data is retrieved from a server or displayed in long lists, pagination reduces memory and CPU usage, as it only loads and displays a subset of data at a time. For example, if your app displays a list of thousands of items, use a **`ListView.builder`** to load the items incrementally as the user scrolls, and implement pagination in the backend to fetch data in chunks. This approach minimizes memory usage, keeps the app responsive, and avoids freezing caused by large data loads. An example snippet of paginated list loading in given as follows:

```
List<Item> items = [];
int currentPage = 1;
bool isLoading = false;

Future<void> loadMoreItems() async {
```

```
  if (isLoading) return;

  setState(() {
    isLoading = true;
  });

  List<Item> newItems = await fetchData(page: currentPage);
  setState(() {
    items.addAll(newItems);
    isLoading = false;
    currentPage++;
  });
}
```

By implementing pagination, you improve the app's responsiveness, particularly when handling extensive datasets. The following figure summarizes the strategies for performance optimization:

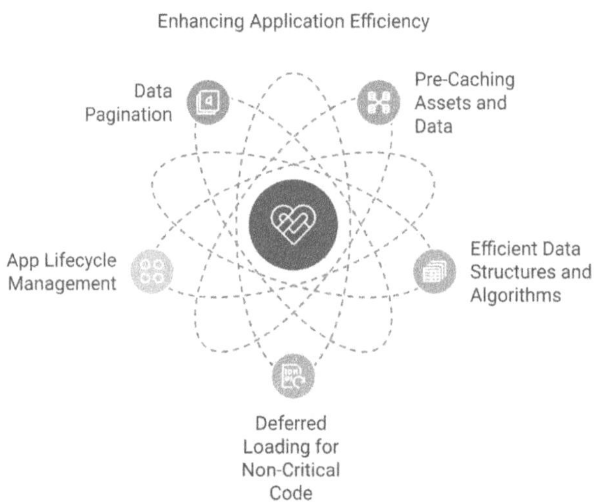

Figure 8.9: *An illustration showing ways to enhance application using optimization strategies*

Practical: Performance tuning laggy gallery app

Let us create a simple app in Flutter that simulates performance issues by avoiding best practices. This app will display a grid of images from the internet, but it will not use const for widgets, will have inefficient code, and avoid optimizations like caching or lazy loading. Then, we will create an optimized version of the same app. Create a new Flutter project call it **Laggy gallery** and the add the following code inside **main.dart** file:

```
import 'package:flutter/material.dart';

void main() => runApp(LaggyGallery());

class LaggyGallery extends StatelessWidget {
  LaggyGallery({super.key});

  @override
  Widget build(BuildContext context) {
    return MaterialApp(
      title: 'Laggy Gallery',
      theme: ThemeData(primarySwatch: Colors.blue),
      home: LgHomePage(),
      debugShowCheckedModeBanner: false,
    );
  }
}

class LgHomePage extends StatefulWidget {
  LgHomePage({super.key});

  @override
  State<LgHomePage> createState() => _LgHomePageState();
}

class _LgHomePageState extends State<LgHomePage> {
  List<String> images =
      List.generate(50, (index) =>
         'https://picsum.photos/id/$index/256/256');

  @override
  Widget build(BuildContext context) {
    return Scaffold(
      appBar: AppBar(
        title: Text('Laggy Gallery'),
      ),
```

```
      body: GridView.builder(
        itemCount: images.length,
        gridDelegate: SliverGridDelegateWithFixedCrossAxisCount(
          crossAxisCount: 4,
        ),
        itemBuilder: (context, index) {
          // Heavy computation in each build
          for (int i = 0; i < 1000000; i++) {
            // Inefficient loop that causes jank
          }
          return Container(
            decoration: BoxDecoration(
              border: Border.all(color: Colors.black12, width: 1),
            ),
            padding: EdgeInsets.all(16),
            child: Column(
              children: [
                // Network image without caching
                Expanded(
                  child: Image.network(
                    images[index],
                    height: 256,
                    width: double.infinity,
                    fit: BoxFit.cover,
                  ),
                ),
                SizedBox(height: 16),
                Text(
                  'Image #${index + 1}',
                  style: TextStyle(fontSize: 16, fontWeight: FontWeight.bold),
                ),
              ],
            ),
          );
        },
      ),
```

```
      );
    }
  }
```

Now, run the unoptimized version of the app in the browser, you will see the app will load images and will have visible jank. This is happening because of the following reasons:

- **`GridView.builder`** that unnecessarily rebuilds every widget.
- Heavy processing within the build method, causing jank.
- Repetitive and avoidable widget rebuilds.
- Images does not use caching.

The following figure shows the output of the unoptimized version of the app:

Figure 8.10: *Laggy gallery app with unoptimized code and UI*

The Chrome DevTools performance profiling shows us that the app needs optimization, as can be seen in the following figure:

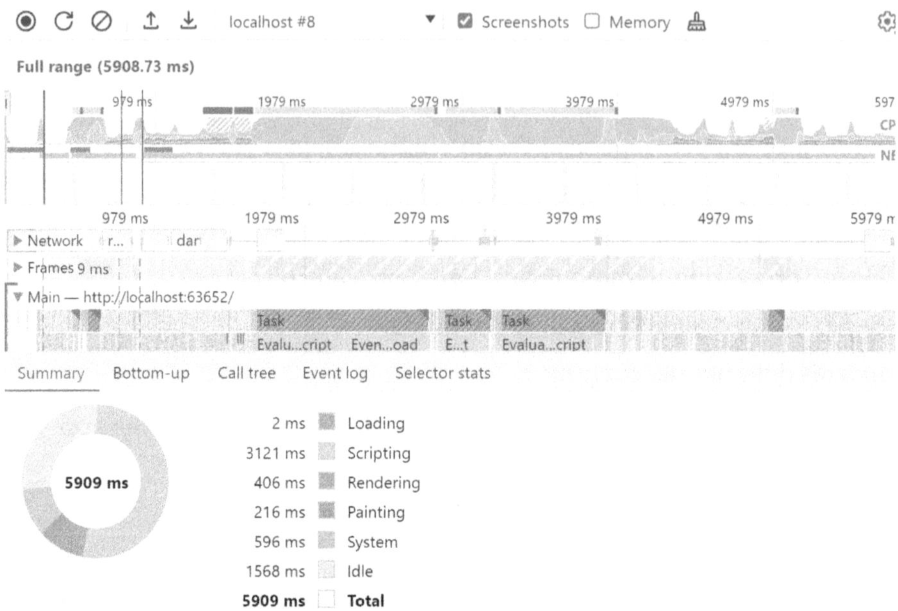

***Figure 8.11:** Result of performance profiling on unoptimized version of Laggy gallery app*

Optimizing the app

To optimize, we will update the code for the app and focus on the following things:

- Use const widgets wherever possible to avoid unnecessary rebuilds.
- Extract static widgets out of the build method.
- Avoid unnecessary **setState** calls to prevent excessive widget rebuilding.

Replace the whole code of **main.dart** file with the following code:

```
import 'package:flutter/material.dart';

void main() {
  WidgetsFlutterBinding.ensureInitialized();
  runApp(const LaggyGallery());
}

class LaggyGallery extends StatelessWidget {
  const LaggyGallery({super.key});

  @override
  Widget build(BuildContext context) {
```

```
    return MaterialApp(
      title: 'Laggy Gallery',
      theme: ThemeData(primarySwatch: Colors.blue),
      home: const LgHomePage(),
      debugShowCheckedModeBanner: false,
    );
  }
}

class LgHomePage extends StatefulWidget {
  const LgHomePage({super.key});

  @override
  State<LgHomePage> createState() => _LgHomePageState();
}

class _LgHomePageState extends State<LgHomePage> {
  // Make images list final and static to prevent rebuilding
  static final List<String> images = List.generate(
    50,
    (index) => 'https://picsum.photos/id/${index + 1}/200/300',
    growable: false,
  );

  @override
  Widget build(BuildContext context) {
    return Scaffold(
      appBar: AppBar(
        title: const Text('Laggy Gallery'),
      ),
      body: GridView.builder(
        itemCount: images.length,
        cacheExtent: 500, // Add cache extent for better scrolling
        physics: const BouncingScrollPhysics(),
        padding: const EdgeInsets.all(8),
        gridDelegate: const SliverGridDelegateWithFixedCrossAxisCount(
```

```
          crossAxisCount: 4,
          childAspectRatio: 0.8,
          crossAxisSpacing: 8,
          mainAxisSpacing: 8,
        ),
        itemBuilder: (context, index) {
          // Removed heavy computation loop
          return _buildImageCard(index);
        },
      ),
    );
  }

  Widget _buildImageCard(int index) {
    return Container(
      decoration: BoxDecoration(
        border: Border.all(color: Colors.black12, width: 1),
        borderRadius: BorderRadius.circular(8),
      ),
      padding: const EdgeInsets.all(8),
      child: Column(
        children: [
          Expanded(
            child: ClipRRect(
              borderRadius: BorderRadius.circular(8),
              child: Image.network(
                images[index],
                height: 256,
                width: double.infinity,
                fit: BoxFit.cover,
                // Add loading placeholder
                frameBuilder: (context, child, frame, wasSynchronouslyLoaded) {
                  if (frame == null) {
                    return const Center(
                      child: CircularProgressIndicator(),
                    );
```

```
                  }
                  return child;
                },
                // Add error handling
                errorBuilder: (context, error, stackTrace) => const Center(
                  child: Icon(
                    Icons.error_outline,
                    color: Colors.red,
                    size: 32,
                  ),
                ),
              ),
            ),
          ),
          const SizedBox(height: 8),
          Text(
            'Image #${index + 1}',
            style: const TextStyle(
              fontSize: 16,
              fontWeight: FontWeight.bold,
            ),
          ),
        ],
      ),
    );
  }
}
```

The optimized code introduces several key improvements aimed at enhancing both performance and organization. To address jank, the heavy computation loop was removed, and the images list was made static and final to avoid unnecessary rebuilds. Additionally, by setting cacheExtent in the GridView, scrolling becomes smoother, while a non-growable list for images improves memory management. The following is the result of profiling on optimized app, which shows considerable improvement in performance of the app:

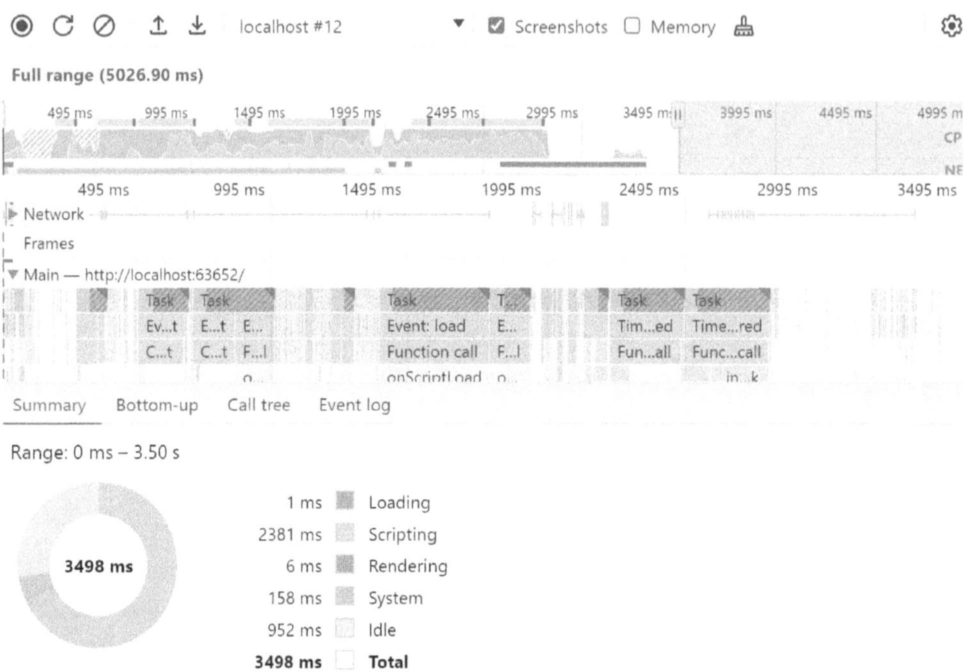

Figure 8.12: Chrome DevTools performance profiling shows improvement after optimizations in app code

The following table shows a comparison of performance in unoptimized and optimized version of Laggy gallery app:

Metric	Unoptimized	Optimized
Total Duration	5909 ms	3498 ms
Scripting	3121 ms	2381 ms
Rendering	406 ms	6 ms
Painting	206 ms	Not tracked
System	596 ms	158 ms
Idle	1568 ms	952 ms

Table 8.1: comparison between optimized and unoptimized versions of Laggy gallery

From the preceding table, you can see that, the optimized version shows a significant increase in scripting and rendering times. This indicates that more computation and updates are being processed, potentially resulting in a more interactive and responsive experience. However, the increased scripting time might also suggest that the optimizations involve additional processing that could be further fine-tuned. Idle time is considerably lower in the optimized version, meaning that more processing is happening within the profiling period. This reduction shows that the application is making better use of its resources and actively managing tasks rather than sitting idle.

These optimizations provide a more seamless, user-friendly app experience. The following figure shows the optimization summary:

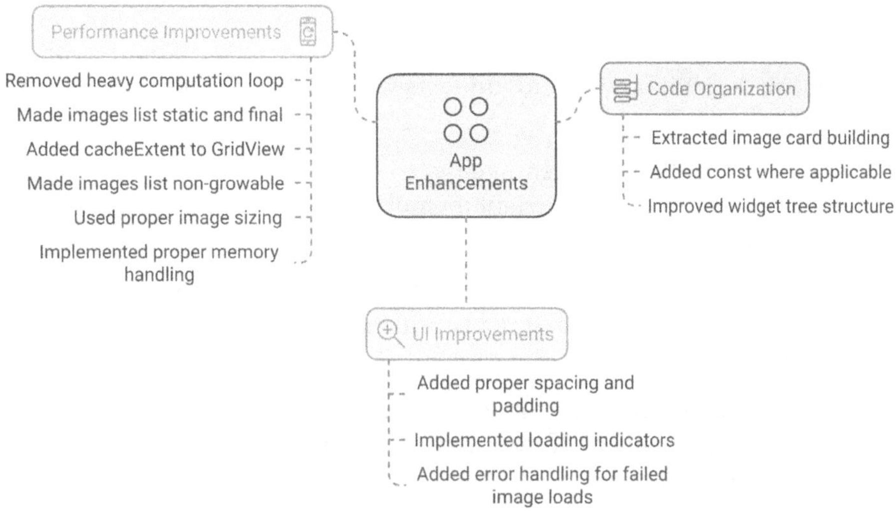

Figure 8.13: *Illustration showing the actions taken to optimize the Laggy gallery app*

Conclusion

This chapter provided a comprehensive approach to optimizing Flutter app performance, guiding developers through essential strategies to enhance responsiveness and user experience. We covered the fundamentals of profiling, showing how tools like Flutter DevTools can be leveraged to identify and resolve performance bottlenecks. By optimizing widget builds, managing memory efficiently, and improving load times, developers can achieve a smoother, faster UI. We also explored the importance of minimizing resource usage in network requests, asynchronous tasks, and list building, which significantly reduces jank and improves frame rates.

Beyond specific techniques, we emphasized the value of a proactive, iterative approach to performance optimization. Regularly profiling, implementing caching, reusing widgets, and reducing redundant tasks ensure that an app remains agile and responsive, even as it scales. Applying these strategies empowers developers to build robust, high-quality Flutter applications that meet modern standards for seamless digital experiences across all platforms.

Points to remember

- Use Flutter DevTools and Chrome DevTools to profile your app regularly, identifying frame drops, CPU usage, and memory allocation to pinpoint performance bottlenecks.

- Avoid rebuilding widgets unnecessarily by using efficient layout practices, caching repeated elements, and leveraging const wherever possible to reduce UI rendering costs.
- Implement proper state management techniques, like Provider or Riverpod, to control rebuilds and avoid unnecessary updates, especially in complex UI structures.
- Dispose of controllers and remove large objects when they are no longer needed to prevent memory leaks. Efficient memory handling is key for smooth, crash-free app performance.
- Avoid placing time-consuming operations in frequently rebuilt functions. Offload heavy tasks to background threads with Flutter's compute function or similar approaches.
- Use **`ListView.builder`** or **`GridView.builder`** to efficiently manage lists and grids with large numbers of items. This minimizes memory usage and improves scroll performance.
- Limit network calls and implement caching strategies to avoid redundant API requests, reducing load times and improving user experience.
- **Reusable widgets**: Reuse and recycle widgets wherever possible to minimize resource usage. Avoid creating new instances of widgets if existing instances can be reused effectively.
- Manage asynchronous operations carefully to prevent UI blocking. Use **`FutureBuilder`** and **`StreamBuilder`** to handle async data efficiently without freezing the interface.
- Regularly profile and optimize your app throughout the development cycle to address potential performance issues early and ensure a responsive user experience.

Multiple choice questions

1. **Which of the following tools can be used to profile a Flutter web app for performance issues?**
   a. Dart DevTools
   b. Flutter DevTools
   c. Android Studio Profiler
   d. Chrome DevTools

2. **What is one of the best practices to avoid rebuilding widgets unnecessarily?**
    a. Rebuild widgets frequently to ensure freshness
    b. Use FutureBuilder in all widgets
    c. Add all widgets to a single screen
    d. Make use of const where possible

3. **What is the purpose of setting cacheExtent in a GridView or ListView?**
    a. To control how many items can be cached off-screen for smoother scrolling
    b. To reduce the number of network requests
    c. To manage memory leaks
    d. To handle asynchronous data loading

4. **What is one of the recommended ways to prevent memory leaks in a Flutter app?**
    a. Avoid using const in widgets
    b. Dispose of controllers and listeners when they are no longer needed
    c. Use Future.delayed to handle memory
    d. Always use a ListView instead of a GridView

Answer

1.	d
2.	d
3.	a
4.	b

Questions

1. Profile, analyze and optimize the Diabetes Classifier from chapter 5.
2. Write an inventory management app and then perform the performance optimization strategies on it.

Key terms

- **Profiling:** The process of analyzing an application to measure its performance, such as identifying bottlenecks in CPU usage, memory, or rendering times.

- **Flutter DevTools:** A suite of performance and debugging tools provided by Flutter to analyze and improve application behavior.
- **Chrome DevTools**: A set of tools within the Chrome browser that developers can use to profile, debug, and optimize web-based Flutter apps.
- **Frame Rendering:** The time taken to draw a single frame on the screen. Maintaining a steady 60 FPS is essential for smooth animations and user interactions.
- **Performance Bottleneck:** A point in the application where resource limitations (e.g., CPU, GPU, or memory) slow down performance.
- **Widget Tree**: The hierarchical structure of widgets in a Flutter application. Optimizing the widget tree helps improve rendering performance.
- **Jank**: A noticeable stutter or lag in the application, often caused by frames taking longer than 16 milliseconds to render.

Additional resources

- **https://docs.flutter.dev/perf/best-practices**
- **https://docs.flutter.dev/perf/web-performance**
- **https://developer.chrome.com/docs/devtools**
- **https://docs.flutter.dev/perf/ui-performance**

Join our book's Discord space

Join the book's Discord Workspace for Latest updates, Offers, Tech happenings around the world, New Release and Sessions with the Authors:

https://discord.bpbonline.com

Index

E

F

G

H

S

T

U

V

W

www.ingramcontent.com/pod-product-compliance
Lightning Source LLC
LaVergne TN
LVHW080802011026
849160LV00015B/1514